DIS-ORIENTING PLANETS

DIS-ORIENTING PLANETS

• • •

Racial Representations of Asia in Science Fiction

Edited by Isiah Lavender III

University Press of Mississippi / Jackson

www.upress.state.ms.us

The University Press of Mississippi is a member
of the Association of American University Presses.

Copyright © 2017 by University Press of Mississippi
All rights reserved

First printing 2017

∞

Library of Congress Cataloging-in-Publication Data

Names: Lavender, Isiah, III editor.
Title: Dis-orienting planets : racial representations of Asia in science
 fiction / edited by Isiah Lavender III.
Description: Jackson : University Press of Mississippi, 2017. | Includes
 bibliographical references and index.
Identifiers: LCCN 2016036167| ISBN 9781496811523 (cloth : alk. paper) | ISBN
 9781496811547 (epub institutional) | ISBN 9781496811554 (pdf single) |
 ISBN 9781496811561 (pdf institutional)
Subjects: LCSH: Science fiction—20th century—History and criticism. |
 Science fiction—21stoth century—History and criticism. | Asians in
 literature. | Race in literature. | Asia—In literature.
Classification: LCC PN3433.6 .D565 2017 | DDC 809.3/8762—dc23
LC record available at https://lccn.loc.gov/2016036167

British Library Cataloging-in-Publication Data available

CONTENTS

ix   Acknowledgments

3   Introduction: Coloring outside Science Fiction's Lines
        Isiah Lavender III

    PART ONE. First Encounters

13   "Great Wall Planet": Estrangements of Chinese Science Fiction
        Veronica Hollinger

26   Race and Black Humor: From a Planetary Perspective
        Takayuki Tatsumi

42   India and Indians in SF by Indians and Others
        Uppinder Mehan

56   "Perpetual War": Korean American Speculative Fiction, Militarized Technogeometries, and Yoon Ha Lee's "Wine"
        Stephen Hong Sohn

    PART TWO. Fear of a Yellow Planet

73   Yellow Perils: M. P. Shiel, Race, and the Far East Menace
        Amy J. Ransom

89   Fictions of Science, American Orientalism, and the Alien/Asian of Percival Lowell
        Timothy J. Yamamura

102 Techno-Orientalism and the End of History in Gary Shteyngart's *Super Sad True Love Story*
     Stephanie Li

117 "Race as Technology" and the Asian Body in *The Bohr Maker* and *Salt Fish Girl*
     Malisa Kurtz

131 Engineering the Techno-Orient: The Hyperrealization of Post-Racial Politics in *Cloud Atlas*
     Haerin Shin

144 Beyond Techno-Orientalism: Virtual Worlds and Identity Tourism in Japanese Cyberpunk
     Baryon Tensor Posadas

160 Many Paths, One Journey: Cixin Liu's Three Body Problem Novels
     Bradford Lyau

175 Crossing the Threshold of B-Mor: Instrumental Commodification and the Model Minority in Chang-rae Lee's *On Such a Full Sea*
     Jeshua Enriquez

PART THREE. Dis-Orienting Planets

189 Bending Culture: Racebending.com's Protests against Media Whitewashing
     Robin Anne Reid

204 The Mako Mori Fan Club
     Cait Coker

218 India, Geopolitics, and Future Wars
     Suparno Banerjee

232 Entanglement and Dis-Entanglement in Vandana Singh's Short Fiction
     Graham J. Murphy

244 Intersubjectivity and Cultural Exchange in Kij Johnson's Novels of Japan
  Joan Gordon

257 Contributors

261 Index

ACKNOWLEDGMENTS

First and most importantly, I must thank God for the fortitude and drive to complete a second edited collection. It can be a hard thing to be a liberal Christian in academia. Second, I am always appreciative of my wife Heather for giving me time and space to do this work. Likewise, I am thankful to my boys, Kingsley and Frazier, for their useful distractions, to my sister Melissa for conversations about my work while walking, and to my recently discovered older brother John for his encouraging words. Family involvement motivates me.

Being able to do a follow-up collection simply amazes me, and I must truly express my gratitude to in-house editor Vijay Shah, and his assistant Lisa McMurtray, for helping me get it done. Similarly, I greatly value the assistance offered by two of my graduate students, Amandine Faucheux and Elizabeth Gilliland, who helped with the initial editing stages, and I hope they learned a great deal from the experience. I am, of course, grateful to my writing exchange partners here at LSU, Sharon Aronofsky Weltman and Sunny Yang, as well as others of my colleagues who listened to my splendiferous miseries with editing, from finding a palatable title to chasing down pesky contributor agreement forms—Brannon Costello, Daren Dean, Bill Demastes, Carl Freedman, Phil Maciak, Patrick McGee, Elsie Mitchie, Daniel Pena, and Pallavi Rastogi.

I would also like to thank my friends and colleagues beyond LSU for the kind wishes and unflagging support—Grace Dillon, Taryne Taylor, Gerry Canavan, David Higgins, Lisa Yaszek, Sherryl Vint, Brooks Landon, Rob Latham, Ritch Calvin, Mark Bould, Nalo Hopkinson, David O'Hara, Dwayne Coleman, Lori Leavell, and Chuck Bane. Old friends and new at ICFA and SFRA, thank you.

I am also thankful to the *Journal of the Fantastic in the Arts*, and its editor Brian Attebery, for giving Takayuki Tatsumi permission to reprint his essay "Race and Black Humor: From a Planetary Perspective," which first appeared in volume 21.3 (2010), pages 439–54. Equally, I would also like to thank Mingwei Song and *The Journal of Comparative Literature in China* for the rights to the original English version of Veronica Hollinger's Chinese language essay "'Great Wall Planet': Estrangements of Chinese Science Fiction," which was translated into Chinese by Chen Guangxing and first appeared in volume 2015.3, pages 27–37.

DIS-ORIENTING PLANETS

INTRODUCTION
Coloring outside Science Fiction's Lines

• • •

ISIAH LAVENDER III

I intended to start this introduction with reminisces on my own childhood experiences of television, film, and books to pursue questions of race and ethnicity in science fiction (SF). I wanted to talk about my love for adaptations of Japanese anime series appearing on American television from the late 1970s to the mid-1980s such as *Star Blazers* (1979–84), *Battle of the Planets* (1978–85), *Astro Boy* (1980–81), *Robotech* (1985), and *Voltron* (1984–85), among others. I also considered discussing my affection for Kung Fu Theater on Saturday afternoons, where I first saw Bruce Lee in *Enter the Dragon* (1973) and watched English-dubbed films like *Five Deadly Venoms* (1978). As a youth, I wanted to kick ass like Bruce Lee did, not Jim Kelly (and I still do!). I thought nothing of wanting to be the Asian lead, Lee, as opposed to the black secondary character, Williams, even if his Afro was ultra-cool.

I have practiced comparative racialization as I understand it long before the idea was codified in *PMLA*'s special topic issue, "Comparative Racialization" (2008). In that volume, Shu-Mei Shih shows how comparative thinking relates to "the worldliness of race" and how affinities between "instances of racialization" hinge on "where the colonial turn has left indelible marks" (1349). Even though my childhood self knew zilch about Western colonialism, I must have somehow recognized that race, negative or positive, structured relations between the so-called yellow, black, and white races when considering *Enter the Dragon*'s evil white henchman O'Hara (Bob Wall). Even as a ten-year-old, I could intuit that white people seemed to be in control of everything that I could see with my own eyes.

As I would later see, there are benefits to the research method of analyzing the specificities of racial difference in novels such as the partly black British writer M. P. Shiel's *The Yellow Danger: or, What Might Happen if the Division of the Chinese Empire Should Estrange all European Countries* (1898) as compared to something like American Thomas Dixon Jr.'s *The Leopard's Spots: A Romance of the White Man's Burden, 1865–1900* (1902). Both novels display white supremacist thinking—Hardy reflects anti-Asian sentiment in England; Gaston reflects anti-black sentiment in America—and project such racism well into the future through white protagonists John Hardy and Charles Gaston, respectively. But I edited out the comparison in my first book *Race in American Science Fiction* (2011).

When thinking about this introduction, I also envisioned talking about when my mother took me to see Ridley Scott's *Blade Runner* (1982). As an eight-year-old, I was captivated by images of a police hover car zipping past an immense advertisement of a pretty Geisha eating candy on the side of a Los Angeles skyscraper turned neon billboard and the scenes from streets where Asian languages and cultures dominate the wet, gritty futurescape. Of course, I was not familiar with the concept of techno-Orientalism then, but I could recognize in the dream of flying cars mixed with commodified Asian images not a sense of anxiety, but instead the norm it was creating for its American audience. With Japan in mind, David Morley and Kevin Robins first formulated "techno-Orientalism" to mean racist images of Asians as "unfeeling aliens . . . cyborgs and replicants" within "the political and cultural unconscious of the West" resulting from "the dystopian image of capitalist progress" (170). I actually prefer Greta Aiyu Niu's revised definition of techno-Orientalism because she does not "limit [her] focus to a specific Asian nation or distance the concept from Asia entirely;" rather, her "version . . . points to the way [techno-Orientalism] ignores the history and construction of relationships between Asian people and technology, particularly those deemed emerging or revolutionary" and suggests how it is "intertwined with capitalism and consumption" (74). Niu's explanation of techno-Orientalism is both broader and deeper, including all of Asia, the Pacific Rim, and the Indian subcontinent in its "practice of ascribing, erasing and/or disavowing relationships between technology and Asian peoples and subjects" (74). I think of techno-Orientalism as an admixture of politics, racism, and technology. This view of techno-Orientalism challenges visions of all Asians as a monolithic group and promotes how scholars practice comparative racialization through genre conventions to interrogate Orientalized futures. Science fiction can generate social change, as such alternative racial futurisms as Afro-futurism, Chicano/a futurism, and Indigenous futurisms attest.

Reorienting Planets

Dis-Orienting Planets: Racial Representations of Asia in Science Fiction continues where *Black and Brown Planets: The Politics of Race in Science Fiction* (2014) left off. This anthology features essays depicting Asia and Asians in science fiction literature, film, and fandom with particular attention paid to China, Japan, India, and Korea. The collection ranges from political representations of Asian identity in science fiction's fearful imagination of the Yellow Peril and its host of stereotypes to techno-Orientalism and the remains of a postcolonial heritage. Clearly, Orientalized futures have been steadily emerging since the late-nineteenth century, though scholars have not always paid attention. And our future visions *must* absolutely include all people of color. To this end, *Dis-Orienting Planets* engages the extremely negative and racist connotations of "Orientalism" that obscure the time, place, and identity perceptions of Asians, so-called yellow and brown peoples, in this historically white genre, provokes debate on pervading imperialistic terminologies, and reconfigures the study of race in science fiction.

This collection brings together theories old and new to further explore and expand the racial politics governing the renewed visibility of the Orient in science fiction. The opening section, "First Encounters," emphasizes the interpretive challenges of science-fictional meetings between the East and West by investigating entwined racial and political tensions. The middle section, "Fear of a Yellow Planet," concentrates on the tropes of Yellow Peril and techno-Orientalism, where fear of and desire for Orientalized futures generate racial anxiety and war. The final section, "Dis-Orienting Planets," explores technologized Asian subjectivities in the eco-critical spaces of mainland China, the Pacific Rim, the Korean peninsula, and the Indian subcontinent. The multidisciplinary approach for this collection offers a wide-ranging critical assessment of Asian representations in science fiction. In various ways all of these chapters push the boundaries of SF race criticism that tiny little bit further.

"Part I: First Encounters" opens with the reflections of long-time *Science Fiction Studies* co-editor Veronica Hollinger on the recent impact of Chinese SF. In "'Great Wall Planet': Estrangements of Chinese Science Fiction," Hollinger offers a few observations about Chinese SF specifically in terms of its potential to defamiliarize what scholars have begun to refer to as "global science fiction." She suggests five ways in which Chinese SF can estrange a taken-for-granted Anglo-American mainstream, ranging from an "alien" cultural product to a different iteration of globalization.

Takayuki Tatsumi, in "Race and Black Humor: From a Planetary Perspective," uses the literary concept of black humor to frame his discussion of race and humanity on a global scale. Starting with a racist joke concerning Hurricane Katrina, Tatsumi traces a conspiracy theory that blames this weather event on the Japanese Yakuza to develop his multi-ethnic literary analysis. From this point, Tatsumi focuses on Brian Aldiss's short story "Another Little Boy" (1966) and how the atomic bombings of Hiroshima and Nagasaki transmute debates on white supremacy, counter-racism, nationalism, technology, and global racial metaphors. In his closing argument, black humor is brought to bear on Japanese-American relations as Tatsumi considers transpacific writers and transpacific imagination.

Uppinder Mehan, in "India and Indians in SF by Indians and Others," examines the representation of India in recent science fiction in the works of contemporary writers outside India, such as Ian McDonald's *River of Gods* (2004) and *Cyberabad Days* (2009). Mehan makes comparisons to the SF of Indian writers such as Anuradha Marwah's *Idol Love* (1999), Manjula Padmanabhan's *Escape* (2008), and Rimi Chatterjee's *Signal Red* (2005) and how they effortlessly explore concerns in their SF that are beyond the received images of India and Indians and surface knowledge available to the casual observer. Mehan interrogates the distorted and truthful reflections of Indian culture in SF.

Rounding out the first part, Stephen Hong Sohn, in "'Perpetual War': Korean American Speculative Fiction, Militarized Technogeometries, and Yoon Ha Lee's 'Wine,'" investigates the look and feel of Korean American SF in its present shape. Sohn identifies how *militarized tehcnogeometries*, defined as the presence of and reference to soldiers, armies, battles, skirmishes, casualties, bombings, and other elements of war, become fundamental to the ways that a science-fictional Korea overlays the historical and social contexts in which South and North Korea actually exist—ever under the peril of territorial dissolution. Sohn then shifts focus by analyzing Yoon Ha Lee's "Wine" (2014) through the lens of militarized technogeometries to demonstrate how Korea materializes through its relationships to perpetual war.

"Part II: Fear of a Yellow Planet" shifts the collection's emphasis to the sense of racial alarm created by Yellow Peril and techno-Orient tropes. Amy J. Ransom, in "Yellow Perils: M. P. Shiel, Race, and the Far East Menace," examines Shiel's three "Yellow Peril" novels—*The Yellow Danger* (1898), *The Yellow Wave* (1905), and *The Dragon* (1913), republished as *The Yellow Peril* (1929)—in relation to their representations of racial others. By situating Shiel's work within the larger framework of Yellow Peril literature and analyzing how its representations of Asians comply with (and depart from) contemporary discourses on race and degeneracy, Ransom reveals Shiel's conflicted attitudes about his own multi-racial background.

In "Fictions of Science, American Orientalism, and the Alien/Asian of Percival Lowell," Timothy J. Yamamura investigates the representation of Asians and "aliens" in American Percival Lowell's writings on the "Far East" and the planet Mars as both within, and against, the grain of Orientalism. In this respect, Lowell's speculations on other worlds functioned as a means to contest the alienating powers of capitalist modernity, however ambivalently, and reveals an important genealogy for contemporary representations of Asia in science fiction.

Stephanie Li, in "Techno-Orientalism and the End of History in Gary Shteyngart's *Super Sad True Love Story*," explores how Shteyngart's 2010 novel imagines troubling visions of abiding racial hierarchies influenced by new technologies and cataclysmic events. By focusing on Lenny Abramov and his doomed love for Korean American Eunice Park, Li assesses the multiple operations of techno-Orientalism as Shteyngart envisions the frightening consequences of America's staggering debt to China.

Malisa Kurtz, in "'Race as Technology' and the Asian Body in *The Bohr Maker* and *Salt Fish Girl*," analyzes the relationships among race, biotechnologies, and genomics in Linda Nagata's *The Bohr Maker* (1995) and Larissa Lai's *Salt Fish Girl* (2002). Asian characters in *The Bohr Maker* and *Salt Fish Girl* are differentiated by their genetics rather than visible physical traits, and both novels question how genomic research might lead to the re-emergence of racist assumptions about biological "destiny." By specifically using techno-Orientalist tropes, both novels reveal the ways in which the bodies of people of color are doubly racialized in science fiction, reduced to instruments of both science and narrative exoticism.

Haerin (Helen) Shin, in "Engineering the Techno-Orient: The Hyperrealization of Post-Racial Politics in *Cloud Atlas*," considers visions of technologized Asia and Asian bodies in the film *Cloud Atlas* (2012), and to a lesser extent the Philips TV commercial *Robotskin* (2007). By focusing on specific scenes that attempt to visualize the motif of crossing but instead deteriorate into problematic instances of conflation, Shin explores the appropriative use of stereotypes in transmedia augmentations related to techno-Orientalism, post-racialist politics, and Baudrillardan simulacra.

In "Beyond Techno-Orientalism: Virtual Worlds and Identity Tourism in Japanese Cyberpunk," Baryon Tensor Posadas demonstrates how the impact of techno-Orientalism on Japanese SF opens up an important space to articulate the larger stakes of how the mechanisms of colonial cognitive estrangement continue to set the terms for the imagination of futurity. It goes beyond the mere cataloging of cultural misrepresentations. He uses Gorō Masaki's *Venus City* (1992) to bring attention to the structural pervasiveness of the gendered and racialized infrastructure that sets the terms of the genre's attempts to imagine other worlds and futurities.

Bradford Lyau, in "Many Paths, One Journey: Cixin Liu's Three Body Problem Novels," carefully places Cixin Liu's Three Body trilogy within both Chinese and Western literary traditions before offering a brief critical analysis of the first two books, where humanity struggles against an impending alien invasion and faces its destiny.

Capping off the second part, Jeshua Enriquez, in "Crossing the Threshold of B-Mor: Instrumental Commodification and the Model Minority in Chang-rae Lee's *On Such a Full Sea*," examines how Lee's 2014 novel presents an acutely globalized and market-driven dystopian vision. In the aftermath of a national collapse, American civilization rearranges itself into stratified sub-societies—Charters, Facilities, and Open Counties—with B-Mor (formerly Baltimore) the ultimate example. Consequently, Enriquez provides a nuanced reading of Asian American commodification as the model minority and the importance of communal story-telling in defeating an oppression generated by racial framing as social control through the novel's key figure—Fan.

Shifting the collection's focus a second time to film fandom, future war, and animal tales, the chapters in "Part III: Dis-Orienting Planets" present new ways of destabilizing and critiquing accepted Asian images. Robin Anne Reid, in "Bending Culture: Racebending.com's Protests Against Media Whitewashing," ruminates on the extent to which the gap between the categories of cultural or fan activism and political activism may be changing, especially with regard to younger people's participation in online activist sites. Reid concentrates her inquiry on one internet community, Racebending.com, which originated in a protest against the casting of white actors in M. Night Shyamalan live-action adaptation *The Last Airbender* (2010). She argues that the group's online activities since the release of the film show the overlap between fan and political activism, thereby demonstrating connections between critical race and intersectional studies.

Through her essay "The Mako Mori Fan Club," Cait Coker examines the subversive nature of Guillermo del Toro's *Pacific Rim* (2013) by utilizing fan works as sources of viable criticism to decenter the white American male action hero with a Japanese heroine. To this end, Coker delves into the major motifs of *Pacific Rim* fandom online and considers its relationship with a film that seemingly "failed" in the American market but exploded internationally, even prompting a sequel slated for 2017. She also reflects on how the depictions of close, but not necessarily romantic, relationships are celebrated in both the film and in fandom as illustrating a cooperative ideal generally not seen in popular, mainstream media.

With "India, Geopolitics, and Future Wars," Suparno Banerjee demonstrates the importance of future-war narratives in the shifting geopolitical posture of India by exploring the genre, origins, and patterns of this SF motif. With particular attention paid to Humphrey Hawksley's *Dragon Fire* (2000) and Ruchir Joshi's *The Last Jet-Engine Laugh* (2001), Banerjee focuses on perceptions of India by Western as well as Indian authors as they speculate about future-wars, highlighting the disillusionment of a postcolonial nation discarding its utopian ideals by involving itself in regional power-struggles. Banerjee effectively illustrates the different patterns that such contemporary future-war narratives create.

In his essay "Entanglement and Dis-Entanglement in Vandana Singh's Short Fiction," Graham J. Murphy investigates Vandana Singh's subtle intersections of utopianism, human-animal affairs, and *biophilia*, defined loosely as a deeply-felt and profound connection with the natural world. For Murphy, stories such as "Entanglement" (2014) and "Are You Sannata 3159?" (2010) stage various issues of globalization and (dis)entanglement experienced by human and nonhuman animals alike who are enmeshed in ever-expanding and all-consuming urban centers, including (but not limited to) the growing metropolises of India that are prevalent in Singh's fictions.

Closing out the collection, "Intersubjectivity and Cultural Exchange in Kij Johnson's Novels of Japan," by long-serving co-editor of *Science Fiction Studies* Joan Gordon, provides an illuminating reading of Kij Johnson's innovative exploration of human and nonhuman animal subjectivities in *The Fox Woman* (2000) and *Fudoki* (2003). Gordon highlights Johnson's use of traditional Japanese autobiographical literary forms to bridge gaps not only between an assumed Western contemporary audience and the medieval Japanese setting of her novels, but also between humans and nonhuman animals. These Japanese forms, using the careful eye of the observer and internal examinations of individual subjects, engage what Gordon calls the "amborg gaze" and collapse the division between subject and object in human/other animal relations and, perhaps, in relations between humans of different cultures.

■ ■ ■

Using black vernacular, I extend my practice of comparative racialization in the title to "dis" culturally inaccurate representations of the eastern hemisphere, first identified by Edward W. Said in *Orientalism* (1978), in my advocacy of a science fiction that causes social revolution. Like many science fictional worlds, Asia functions as "a place of romance, exotic beings, haunting memories and landscapes" (Said 1). In this respect, the fiction of race and its very real effects cast a shadow over the possible futures of this planet we inhabit. The comparative, relational, and global intersections of *Dis-Orienting Planets* help us positively, or at least in a different way, rethink contact among the races. I hope each of these chapters highlights the necessity of speculative fictions, particularly SF, for challenging past and present race paradigms in fashioning Asia as East, as Orient, and as other, and knocks our planet from its regular spin.

Works Cited

Astro Boy. CHCH, Hamilton. 1980–81. Television.
Battle for the Planets. WKBW, Buffalo. 1978–85. Television.
Blade Runner. Dir. Ridley Scott. Warner Brothers, 1982. Film.
Dixon, Thomas, Jr. *The Leopard's Spots: A Romance of the White Man's Burden, 1865–1900*. New York: Doubleday, 1902. Print.
Enter the Dragon. Dir. Robert Clouse. Warner Brothers, 1973. Film.
Five Deadly Venoms. Dir. Chang Cheh. Shaw Brothers, 1978. Film.
Lavender, Isiah, III, ed. *Black and Brown Planets: The Politics of Race in Science Fiction*. Jackson: UP of Mississippi, 2014.
———. *Race in American Science Fiction*. Bloomington: Indiana UP, 2011. Print.
Morley, David, and Kevin Robins. "Techno-Orientalism: Japan Panic." *Spaces of Identity: Global Media, Electronic Landscapes and Cultural Boundaries*. Eds. David Morley and Kevin Robins. London: Routledge, 1995. 147–73. Print.
Niu, Greta A. "Techno-Orientalism, Nanotechnology, Posthumans, and Post-Posthumans in Neal Stephenson's and Linda Nagata's Science Fiction." *MELUS* 33.4 (2008): 73–96. Print.
Robotech. WIVB, Buffalo. 1985. Television.
Said, Edward W. *Orientalism*. New York: Pantheon, 1978. Print.
Shiel, M. P. *The Yellow Danger: or, What Might Happen if the Division of the Chinese Empire Should Estrange all European Countries*. London: Grant Richards, 1898. Kindle Edition.
Shih, Shu-Mei. "Comparative Racialization: An Introduction." *PMLA* 123.5 (2008): 1347–62. Print.
Voltron. WGRZ, Buffalo. 1984–85. Television.

PART ONE

· · ·

First Encounters

"GREAT WALL PLANET"
Estrangements of Chinese Science Fiction

• • •

VERONICA HOLLINGER

> The history of sf reflects the changing positions of different national audiences as they imagine themselves in a developing world-system constructed out of technology's second nature.
> —**Istvan Csicsery-Ronay Jr.**, "Science Fiction and Empire" (236)

In 2013 I co-edited a special issue of the journal *Science Fiction Studies (SFS)* on Chinese science fiction (SF). This project was first proposed by Professor Wu Yan of Beijing Normal University, one of the leading figures in the development and reception of SF in China today. I had the privilege of working with Wu Yan on this special issue, which is one of the most comprehensive English-language critical overviews of Chinese SF published to date. In his guest-editor's introduction, Wu provides a detailed chronology of science fiction's fortunes in China since the beginning of the twentieth century. The issue includes essays by Han Song and Liu Cixin, two of China's most popular contemporary SF authors (I will discuss stories by these authors later in this essay). Other contributions include two studies of early science fiction written in the late Qing period; a discussion of Lao She's 1932 dystopian fiction, *Cat Country*; a study of utopian influences on contemporary science fiction; an analysis of the image of "gloomy China" in Han Song's writing; a detailed history of the crucial function of translation in the development of the genre in China; and an analysis of science fiction tropes in recent films from mainland China, Hong Kong, and Taiwan.

In a happy coincidence, in 2012 the Hong Kong-based journal *Renditions* published a special issue of Chinese science fiction in English translation, "Chinese Science Fiction: Late Qing and the Contemporary." This was edited by Mingwei Song, who also contributed an essay to *SFS*'s special issue. This is the first substantial collection of Chinese science fiction to appear in English since 1989, when Wu Dingbo and Patrick D. Murphy edited *Science Fiction from China*, a collection of eight stories published between 1978 and 1987. The *Renditions* issue opens with four excerpts and stories from the early twentieth century—including an excerpt from Wu Jianren's *New Story of the Stone* (1908)—and then follows these with nine stories, available in English for the first time, representing early twenty-first century science fiction in China. These include Liu Cixin's "The Poetry Cloud" (2003), Wang Jinkang's "The Reincarnated Giant" (2006), and Fei Dao's "The Demon's Head" (2007).

I want to offer a few observations about Chinese science fiction specifically in terms of its potential to defamiliarize—to help us to gain some critical perspective on—what scholars have begun to refer to as "global science fiction."[1] I will suggest five ways in which Chinese SF can estrange a taken-for-granted Anglo-American mainstream: (1) as an "alien" cultural product; (2) as a product of China's "rise" as a global superpower; (3) as the product of an "alternate" cultural history; (4) as representative of something called "global science fiction"; and (5) as a kind of "second-language" version of the discourse of Anglo-American globalization. Needless to say, my own perspective is necessarily very partial. As a long-time co-editor of *Science Fiction Studies*, I am firmly situated at the Anglo-American center of what Andrew Milner, in his recent study *Locating Science Fiction*, refers to as SF's "selective tradition" (3). In Milner's terms, Chinese SF lies on the periphery of this tradition, barely registering as part of "the cultural geography of the genre" (155). But, as Milner also reminds us, the selective tradition remains "essentially and necessarily a site of contestation" (40).

In this regard, the English-language publication by Tor Books in 2014 of the first volume of Liu Cixin's massively popular Three Body trilogy—*The Three-Body Problem* (2008)—is particularly significant. In the December 2014 issue of the influential monthly magazine, *Locus: The Magazine of the Science Fiction and Fantasy Field*, *The Three-Body Problem* was repeatedly cited as one of the best new novels of the year. According to the very positive *Locus* review,

> *The Three-Body Problem* is the first case of a hard SF novel in the modern sense [translated from Chinese into English], informed by genuinely speculative

physics and by a shrewd engagement with some of the major tropes of the genre.... Cixin Liu knows his way around Western SF, apparently, but this isn't quite a Western-style SF novel, and it's no imitation. (Wolfe 14)

The reviewer concludes: "If Tor (or someone) doesn't follow up with the next two volumes in this series, it will be a crime against trilogies (a line I never thought I would write)" (Wolfe 15).[2] *The Three-Body Problem* went on to win the Hugo Award for Best Novel in 2014, the first time this SF award, established over sixty years ago, has been won by an Asian writer.[3]

Liu's Hugo Award makes it all the more likely that some of his fiction will be adapted for film. China Film Group Corporation is already considering some stories from *The Wandering Earth* (2013), and there are at least rumors of plans to film the Three Body novels (Anders). All of this has the potential vastly to increase Liu's profile in the Anglo-American market, and thus the profile of Chinese science fiction as a whole, supporting Milner's suggestion that SF's selective tradition is "a site of contestation."

First Estrangement: "Great Wall Planet"

In his introduction to the special issue of *Science Fiction Studies*, Wu Yan refers to China as "Great Wall Planet," a phrase he borrows from British writer Brian Aldiss. Expanding on this image, Wu concludes by observing that "Every nation with a distinctive culture and history is like an alien planet, and visitors can stand on this planet and look up at its sky. What will visitors from the west discover in the unfamiliar sky of Planet China?" (7). Deliberately invoking the image of China as ineluctably "foreign" in the West's collective imaginary, Wu claims the iconic image of the alien planet in a self-conscious statement of difference and alterity, acknowledging that, for the Western reader, Chinese SF is always already an estrangement, an "other" to the Anglo-American selective tradition. The Great Wall simultaneously maintains the boundary between East and West and challenges Western visitors to explore what lies behind it. Chinese SF is at once foreign to the traditions and conventions of Anglo-American SF and familiar—it is, after all, science fiction. Arguably, this dialectical play of difference and sameness also marks the intersections between Chinese culture in particular and the increasingly globalized culture of technoscientific modernization with which it must now contend.

According to Wu Yan, several features have served to distinguish Chinese SF from its Western "other." First is its focus on "themes of liberation and release from old cultural, political, and institutional systems" (Wu 5). Second is "the reactions of Chinese writers to Western science and culture in their pursuit of themes of liberation" (Wu 5–6). As Wu notes, "This raises a series of key questions: what is science? is science specifically Western or is it a universal human pursuit? how can writers integrate scientific and local cultural traditions into new and vital forms?" (6). A third feature is "its concern for the future of China and of Chinese culture, which is among the oldest surviving human cultures.... Whereas Western SF is focused on the opportunities and losses of technoscientific development, Chinese SF, although it examines similar ideas, is more focused on anxieties about cultural decline and the potential for revitalization" (Wu 4–5).

As Wu's description suggests, Chinese writers find themselves in a contradictory relationship with the discourses of Western technoculture. Writer Han Song, for instance, insists that "Science, technology, and modernization are not characteristic of Chinese culture. They are like alien entities. If we buy into them, we turn ourselves into monsters, and that is the only way we can get along with Western notions of progress" ("Chinese Science Fiction" 20). In ironic appropriation, both Wu Yan and Han Song invoke metaphors of the alien to represent Chinese science fiction's self-conscious sense of difference from the Anglo-American tradition.

Second Estrangement: The "Rise" of Global China

I want to look briefly at two twenty-first-century stories that evoke for me a sense of China's complicated position in this period of rapid globalization. The first is Liu Cixin's "The Village Schoolteacher" (2001) and the second is Han Song's "The Passengers and the Creator" (2005), both of which are included in the recent *Renditions* collection.

In "The Village Schoolteacher," Liu Cixin juxtaposes the moving story of a dying teacher in an impoverished rural village and the events of a galactic war between unimaginably powerful alien civilizations: "Fifty thousand light years from Earth, near the centre of the Milky Way, an intergalactic war that had raged for 20,000 years was near its conclusion" (121). Meanwhile, the teacher looks back on a wasted life, his ambitions for his students all but overcome by the twin spectres of poverty and ignorance: "He had spent his entire life lighting the fires of science and civilization in their hearts but he knew that in a remote mountain village shrouded in ignorance, the fires he lit were small in comparison to the fires of superstition . ." (117). Tellingly, the teacher remembers the great writer Lu Xun's well-known early-twentieth-century image of China as an "iron room":

It has no windows and is nearly impossible to destroy. Inside there are a great number of people, all of them sound asleep. They will soon suffocate and die. But they will die in their sleep, feeling no pain or sorrow. Suppose you were to shout, waking a number of them who are a bit more clear-headed, thereby bringing this unfortunate minority to an awareness of their irremediable predicament. Wouldn't you owe them an apology? (qtd. in Liu, "The Village Schoolteacher" 127)

In a last futile effort before his death, the teacher insists that his uncomprehending students memorize Newton's three laws of physics. The victors of the galactic war, meanwhile, are in the process of destroying vast areas of the galaxy to create "a 500-light-year-wide quarantine zone" (124) that will effectively immobilize their erstwhile enemies. Earth is spared destruction, however, because these same students, able to recite Newton's physical laws, are a convincing proof to the aliens of humanity's status as an intelligent "carbon-based civilization" (140).

"The Village Schoolteacher" is at once deeply sympathetic to and deeply ironic about the value of human endeavor in a universe of overwhelming contingency. The narration moves between the dismal insignificance of village life in China and an intergalactic history of unimaginable scale that evokes sublime vistas and vast distances. China's children are responsible for saving the Earth, but this is an accidental salvation in the face of incomprehensible cosmic events. The teacher is buried by his students in an unmarked grave, while "a whole universe of dazzling stars look[s] silently at them" (140).

Mingwei Song suggests that Liu Cixin's "master plot" is humanity's "encounter with the unknown dimensions of the universe, a place that remains largely alien to human understanding" ("Preface" 11). The immensity of scale in stories such as "The Village Schoolteacher" radically reduces the significance of human action in the world even as it encourages the reader's science-fictional sense of wonder. At the same time, Liu's story remains firmly embedded in the everyday, dramatizing in "The Village Schoolteacher" his frustration at the impoverished lives of so many people in rural China. Driven by his own sense of wonder at the beauty of the physical universe, as he writes in his Afterword to *The Three-Body Problem*,

> I've always felt that the greatest and most beautiful stories in the history of humanity were ... told by science. The stories of science are more magnificent, grand, involved, profound, thrilling, strange, terrifying, mysterious, and even emotional.... Only, these wonderful stories are locked in cold equations that most do not know how to read.

> The creation myths of the various peoples and religions of the world pale when compared to the glory of the big bang. (Liu, *Three-Body Problem*)

In contrast to Liu Cixin's wide-angle science fiction, Han Song's "The Passengers and the Creator" is a bizarre tale of China's future told in stifling close-up, strangely reminiscent of Western generation-starship stories in which all memory of the original purpose of the voyage has been lost. In Han's story, which includes incidents of cannibalism and "perverse" sexuality, the Chinese people are confined to airplanes that endlessly circle the earth—thousands upon thousands of planes—and the people themselves have been reduced to programmed zombies, indoctrinated with false memories and "specialized education" (147) so that they have forgotten who they are: "We spend most of our time sitting still like potted plants, our countenances facing the same direction, expressionless as if carved from wood" (148). This is eerily like a technologically updated version of Lu Xun's image of the Chinese people trapped and sleeping in an iron room: "in this World nothing matters" (Han 146).

The passengers on one of the planes begin to question their situation and eventually realize that the machine "has a limited lifespan.... The end will be upon us any day now" (166). In desperation, the narrator and protagonist causes the plane to crash. He is the only survivor. And, finally, both narrator and reader discover the truth of this strange dystopian existence:

> I spy a group of black metal carapaces like cockroaches riding on four spinning wheels speeding toward me. They stop and surround me.... From inside the metal carapaces, a number of golden-haired, tin-white-skinned men leap out, speaking in a garbled tongue I cannot understand.... They raise some sort of metal sticks, aiming the ends at me. (172)

This is the story's disorienting finale, this image of "white-skinned" soldiers, members of the nation, we are to assume, that has imprisoned the Chinese people and destroyed their history. The truth of the future is here the destruction of China by its Western "others." The shock is double for Western readers who find themselves identified with the profoundly alien villains responsible for China's ironically destructive "rise" in this future world.

"The rise of China" is commonly identified as a particular focus of contemporary Chinese science fiction. The entry on Han Song in the *Encyclopedia of Science Fiction*, for example, points out that his "recurring theme is the rise and possible supremacy of China in contention with the West, which Han often treats with an ambiguity of tone sure to confuse the authorities"

(Clements). More broadly, in a recent overview published in the *Global Times*, Xuyang Jingjing notes that "The rise of China and the problems caused by its rapid development provide ample materials for science fiction writers to feed their imaginations." Song's "The Passengers and the Creators" presents readers with a particularly ironic and enigmatic story of China's "rise." Radically different from the sublime perspectives of Liu's "The Village Schoolteacher," Song firmly situates his aesthetic in the grotesque. Nevertheless, like Liu's fiction it powerfully evokes the sense of wonder that is at the heart of science fiction as a narrative genre.

Third Estrangement: Chinese SF as Alternate History

In his essay for *Science Fiction Studies* on contemporary Chinese science fiction, Mingwei Song concludes that SF in China has found itself both speaking for and being silenced by "China's century-long program of national development, social revolution, and cultural reform" (98–99). Since the beginning of the twentieth century, the history of Chinese SF has been a history of "breaks and ruptures" (98). This "alternate history" of Chinese SF in all its "otherness" suggests the historical and cultural contingencies of what we tend to think of simply as "science fiction," that is, Anglo-American science fiction as the unmarked centre of Milner's selective tradition. In contrast to the relatively smooth development of Anglo-American SF, Chinese SF is a radically fragmented genre constituted by the products of several quite different historical periods separated by years of non-production. Song points out that "each time the genre was revived in a later age, the new generation of science fiction writers had to invent their own tradition, giving Chinese science fiction multiple points of origin" ("Preface" 8). For this reason, the history of Chinese science fiction is both very long and very brief. There has been no sustained archive accumulating since the early twentieth century, and so each generation has virtually had to invent its own traditions and discourses.

In its earlier iterations Chinese SF owed much to the influence of foreign writers—European, British, Russian, and American—whose works have been made available in translation, in a constant process of virtually one-way transculturation. In its first iteration, and influenced by works such as those by Jules Verne and H.G. Wells, this SF appeared at the end of China's last imperial dynasty in the very early years of the twentieth century. SF translations and original works were produced by the intellectual élites as one response to the perceived political hegemony and advanced technoscientific development of Western nations. This period came to an end with the May Fourth

Movement (roughly 1915–21) and its consequent devaluation of non-realist literature.

Except for a brief re-appearance in the 1950s as Soviet-influenced literature for young people, Chinese SF did not flourish again until about 1978, with Deng Xiaoping's ascension as leader of the People's Republic of China and its new "Open Door Policy." During this brief period, which was over by the mid-1980s, "use value" once again justified the production of science fiction. SF stories were expected to be optimistic about China's future technoscientific development and to represent the patriotism and utopian aspirations of the scientific community. As SF writer Zheng Wenguang stated in 1979:

> We eulogize science. We eulogize the glorious future which a highly developed science will give to human life. We ... eulogize millions of people who heroically strive for the materialization of the four modernizations [agriculture, industry, national defense, and science and technology]. (qtd. in Wu Dingbo xxv)

This late-1970s resurgence of the genre came to an abrupt halt when the conservative "Campaign Against Spiritual Pollution" tarred SF with the brush of pseudo-scientific corruption (see Huss 94).

Government approval of science fiction in its familiar role as support for technoscientific development and innovation was renewed in the early 1990s and, since the turn of the new century, SF in China has once again flourished in a thriving community of writers, fans, conferences, publications, and awards.[4] But its fortunes in China remain uncertain, given its troubled past and its still tenuous position within China's current authoritarian cultural regime. Lavie Tidhar points out, for instance, that, while Chinese SF may well enlighten its readers about science, it has conventionally had little to say about issues that the genre is so well designed to address in all their potential differences: sexuality, religion, the environment, alternatives to current social and political systems, and so on (96).

It is my understanding that time-travel and counterfactual alternate-history stories have not always been popular with the Chinese cultural authorities (see, for instance, Sebag-Montefiore). Given how alternate history "stress[es] the role of contingency in history, and ... the open-endedness of historical change, alternate history is inherently anti-deterministic" (qtd. in Gomel 97). In contrast, to affirm the stable and fixed character of past history is to suggest a fixed future as its inevitable outcome, thus safeguarding the official historical record while maintaining control of its unfolding into the future.

Wu Yan is by no means alone in criticizing the limitations these authoritarian constraints have placed on the development of SF in China. In the late 1990s, he wrote that such a "utilitarian" approach, encouraging as it does a strictly didactic view of the genre, "has created a great crisis for Chinese SF, [has] restricted its scope and directly influenced the writer's creative work, and [has] even limited the layman's understanding of this literary form" (qtd. in Huss 99).

Fourth Estrangement: Chinese SF as Global SF

At the same time as China is the alien Great Wall Planet, it has also been taken as proof that something called "global science fiction" really does exist. More than one commentary has directly linked the resurgence of Chinese SF in the past couple of decades to the processes of globalization. In 2003, for instance, Lavie Tidhar published an article in the British journal *Foundation* titled "Science Fiction, Globalisation, and the People's Republic of China," in which he suggests that "to understand the emergence of SF as a global social movement ... and the interplay between the world of science fiction and globalisation, we may do well to study China as a case in point" (93).

A version of "SF as a global social movement" re-appears in an article published in 2012 in *The Guardian*, "Is science fiction literature's first international language?" In it Damien Walter makes the by-now familiar claim that "as the technological revolution has spread outward from the western world, so the symbols and archetypes of science fiction have become a shared language for understanding the new world we are entering." Like Tidhar, Walter points to Chinese SF as a leading exhibit. Noting the popularity of Liu Cixin's work in China and its increasing availability in translation, Walter sees Liu's writing as "characteristic of an SF genre which has been embraced by Chinese culture because it is seen as representing the values of technological innovation and creativity so highly prized in a country developing more quickly than any other in the world today."

That science fiction is now the international discourse of the globalized world is attested to by the fact that *even China* is producing science fiction, that world power, nation, or empire whose history, politics, and culture continue to appear so foreign to the West. And the fact that China is speaking science fiction—even if it may be only as a kind of "second language" at present—is proof that *even China* is going global.

Fifth Estrangement: The Future of the Same

Recalling the image of Lu Xun's "iron room," it is thought-provoking to come across a reference to globalization as an "iron cage" in Elana Gomel's study of temporality in postmodern science fiction. Gomel returns readers to Fredric Jameson's well-known argument about the (perceived) failure of the contemporary utopian imagination resulting from "the systemic, cultural and ideological closure of which we are all in one way or another prisoners" (qtd. in Gomel 147). This "closure" also goes by the name of globalization.

If *The Guardian*'s Damien Walter celebrates science fiction as "a shared language for understanding the new world we are entering," Jutta Weldes, in her essay "Globalisation is Science Fiction," approaches SF from a significantly different perspective. Instead, she identifies it as one of the influential discourses currently *determining* the outlines of that "new world." She argues that "as a discursively constructed *fait accompli*," globalization is a fantasy, "the millennial dream of capital [that] partakes . . . of Enlightenment notions of progress and the inevitability of technological development" (648).

Science fiction is certainly a powerful "shared language" through which to participate in this millennial space-time. We hear this sharing in writer Han Song's conviction that "Science fiction is now the label for China's economic miracle, as well as for its achievements in modern technologies such as Chinese-made spaceships, high-speed computers, and gene-modified crops" (16). And we can recognize the familiar attitude of science-fictionality—to borrow a term from Istvan Csicsery-Ronay Jr.—in Han's vision of China's future-present:

> While most mainstream literature today focuses on China's past, science fiction looks to the future. And in China the future is now. A writer in present-day China does not even have to make an effort to imagine the future, as any day-to-day record of urban China's dramatic transformations is futuristic in itself" ("Chinese Science Fiction" 18).

But might not science fiction, as "the language of globalization," contribute to the reification of the future? Might it not risk imprisoning us in some postmodern version of Lu Xun's "iron room"? What is to be done once globalization has been completed—once late capitalism's technoscientific future has become, as William Gibson might put it, more evenly distributed?[5] At that point, the outcome—for good or ill—would seem to be that we all end up inhabiting the same worldwide networks: we will all have arrived at some version of capital's future. Whether neo-liberal or authoritarian, it will be the same.[6] In Jameson's gloomy view, "This is the future prepared by the elimination of historicity, its neutralization by way of progress and technological evolution: it is the future of globalization" (228).

But the future, for all the claims of its inevitable unfolding, is by no means determined. The challenge for the contemporary science fiction imagination, including for China's second-language contestations of SF's selective tradition, is to remain open to what Jameson describes as "the future as *disruption* . . . of the present, and as a radical and systemic break with . . . that predicted and colonized future which is simply a prolongation of our . . . present" (228). After all, even Lu Xun's vision of China as an "iron room" is not utterly devoid of possibility. The passage quoted by Liu's village schoolteacher concludes, "But now that several people are awake, you [can] no longer say that there is absolutely no hope of destroying the room" (qtd. in Liu, "The Village Schoolteacher" 127).

If Milner is right that SF's selective tradition is "a site of contestation" (40), then Liu Cixin's Hugo Award might promise a meaningful disruption (to use Jameson's term) in the space-time of that tradition, as relations shift between periphery and center. On the other hand, given globalization's dream of a perfect unity in which all differences are collapsed, it may also be a demonstration of globalization's powerful drive toward predictability and sameness. The one does not preclude the other. This tension between an inevitable future that is simply more of the same and a future open to radical transformation marks the contemporary SF imagination as surely as it marks the cultural and political relations of nations in the global field.

Acknowledgments

This essay was originally published in Chinese translation in *Comparative Literature in China* 100.3 (2015). I am grateful to the editors for their permission to reprint it here.

Notes

1. In 2012, *Science Fiction Studies* published a special issue on "Science Fiction and Globalization." Guest editor David M. Higgins describes globalization as "the imperial expansion of planetary capitalism because this approach reflects how our object of study, science fiction, historically relates to the phenomenon of accelerated global interconnection" (370).

2. Tor published a translation of the second volume of Liu's trilogy, *The Dark Forest* (2008), in August 2015; the third volume, *Death's End* (2010), is scheduled to appear in 2016.

3. As SF writer Jia Liyuan (a.k.a. Fei Dao) wrote to me at the time, "Chinese fans are so happy now since Liu Cixin's *Three-Body Problem* won the Hugo Award. As a result, SF has

been getting more attention in China. Liu even received an interview with the vice president of the PRC" (Liyuan).

4. According to one of the editors of China's *Science Fiction World* magazine, "Sf writing is now supported by the Chinese government, as it is considered to be a genre that can inspire the whole nation's ability to think imaginatively and popularizes science nationwide" (qtd. in Han Song, "Chinese Science Fiction" 17).

5. This is a reference to cyberpunk author William Gibson's often quoted observation that "the future is already here. It's just not evenly distributed." While there is no agreement as to the provenance of this aphorism, Gibson's Wikipedia entry notes that "he is reported to have first said this in an interview on *Fresh Air*, NPR (31 August 1993)."

6. See, for instance, David Harvey's analysis of China's position in the global economy, "Neoliberalism 'with Chinese Characteristics'" (120–51).

Works Cited

Anders, Charlie Jane. "*Three-Body Problem* Author Liu Cixin is Getting 5 Movie Deals." *io9*. 26 Nov. 2014. Web. 8 Mar. 2015.

Clements, Jonathan. "Han Song." *The Encyclopedia of Science Fiction*. 13 Sept. 2012. Web. 20 Mar. 2015.

Csicsery-Ronay, Istvan, Jr. "Science Fiction and Empire." *Science Fiction Studies* 30.2 (2003): 231–45. Print.

Gomel, Elana. *Postmodern Science Fiction and Temporal Imagination*. New York: Continuum, 2010. Print.

Han Song. "Chinese Science Fiction: A Response to Modernization." *Science Fiction Studies* 40.1 (2013): 15–21. Print.

———. "The Passengers and the Creator." 2005. Trans. Nathaniel Isaacson. Ed. Mingwei Song. *Renditions: A Chinese-English Translation Magazine* 77/78 (2012): 144–72. Print.

Harvey, David. *A Brief History of Neoliberalism*. Oxford: Oxford UP, 2005. Print.

Higgins, David M. "Introduction: Science Fiction and Globalization." *Science Fiction Studies* 39.3 (2012): 369–73. Print.

Huss, Mikael. "Hesitant Journey to the West: SF's Changing Fortunes in Mainland China." *Science Fiction Studies* 27.1 (2000): 92–104. Print.

Jameson, Fredric. "The Future as Disruption." *Archaeologies of the Future: The Desire Called Utopia and Other Science Fictions*. New York: Verso, 2005. 211–33. Print.

Liu Cixin. "Author's Postscript for the American Edition." *The Three-Body Problem*. 2006. Trans. Ken Liu. New York: Tor, 2014. E-book.

———. *The Three-Body Problem*. 2006. Trans. Ken Liu. New York: Tor, 2014. E-book.

———. "The Village Schoolteacher." 2001. Trans. Christopher Elford and Jiang Chenxin. Ed. Mingwei Song. *Renditions: A Chinese-English Translation Magazine* 77/78 (2012): 114–43. Print.

Liyuan Jia. Personal correspondence. 17 Sep. 2015.

Sebag-Montefiore, Clarissa. "Cultural Exchange: Chinese science fiction's subversive politics." *Los Angeles Times*. 25 Mar. 2012. Web. 8 Mar. 2014.

Song, Mingwei. "Preface: Chinese Science Fiction: Late Qing and the Contemporary." *Renditions: A Chinese-English Translation Magazine* 77/78 (2012): 7–14. Print.

———. "Variations on Utopia in Contemporary Chinese Science Fiction." *Science Fiction Studies* 40.1 (2013): 86–102. Print.

Tidhar, Lavie. "Science Fiction, Globalisation, and the People's Republic of China." *Foundation: The International Review of Science Fiction* 89 (2003): 93–99. Print.

Walter, Damien. "Is science fiction literature's first international language?" *The Guardian* 27 April 2012. Web. 8 Mar. 2015.

Weldes, Jutta. "Globalisation is Science Fiction." *Millennium: Journal of International Studies* 30.3 (2001): 647–67. Print.

Wolfe, Gary K. Review of *The Three-Body Problem*. *Locus* 73.6 (2014): 14–15. Print.

Wu Dingbo. "Looking Backward: An Introduction to Chinese Science Fiction." *Science Fiction from China*. Eds. Dingbo Wu and Patrick D. Murphy. New York: Praeger, 1989. xi–xli. Print.

Wu Yan. "'Great Wall Planet': Introducing Chinese Science Fiction." *Science Fiction Studies* 40.1 (2013): 1–14. Print.

Xuyang Jingjing. "Sci-fi made in China." *Global Times* 7 Jan. 2013. Web. 20 Mar. 2015.

RACE AND BLACK HUMOR
From a Planetary Perspective

■ ■ ■

TAKAYUKI TATSUMI

A Racist Joke Storming Katrina

Black humor is a literary concept that is undoubtedly very useful for rethinking the fantastic in the arts. However, before reexamining this concept seriously in the context of multi-ethnic literary history, let me start by identifying our own allegedly postcolonialist and globalist reality as full of black humor. Let me illustrate the point with an episode that came in the wake of the apocalyptic disaster that stormed the Deep South half a decade ago. When Hurricane Katrina ravaged New Orleans on August 29, 2005, Scott Stevens, a thirty-nine-year-old Idaho weatherman and nine-year veteran at KPVI-TV News Channel 6, blamed the Japanese Mafia for the hurricane. Since Katrina, Stevens has been in newspapers across the country where he has been quoted as saying the Yakuza Mafia used a Russian-made Cold War device—an "electromagnetic generator"—to cause Katrina, in a bid to avenge the atomic bomb attack on Hiroshima ("Weatherman"). This kind of ridiculously funny idea reminds us of those outrageous or preposterous books, what are called "Tondemo-bon" in Japanese, that are obsessed with conspiracy theories, pseudo-science, or historical revisionism. These books detail, for example, the theory that the Japanese and the Jews have a common ancestry, or the theory that locates the ethnic origins of the Native Americans in the Japanese, or the theory of what one book calls "A Final Warning from Mother Earth, a guide to the future based on the knowledge of the ancients of Atlantis and other civilizations." One might compare this with Thomas Pynchon's latest novel *Inherent Vice* (2009) which is full of outrageously paranoiac ideas such as the notion that President Richard Nixon is "a descendant of Atlantis" and Ho Chi Minh is "of Lemuria" (109). However, it is also true that these outrageous and preposterous books are all "amusing from a perspective that differs from what the author intends" ("Tondemo-bon"). And as the works of Jack Womack demonstrate, without this outrageous and preposterous imagination, science fiction (SF) and fantasy could not have thrived.

Therefore, although hard scientists discount as ludicrous Scott Stevens's claims about Hurricane Katrina, his paranoid conspiracy theory still seems to make sense to some US citizens wrapped in Cold War pride and prejudice, even if they don't have a taste for the fantastic. Yes, conspiracy theory has long remained the one and only tool for enjoying disasters, whether natural or artificial. To put it another way, it deconstructs the boundary between the natural disaster and the artificial disaster. Thus, whoever loves and consumes these theories deserves Mark Svenvold's designation "catastrophilia." At this point, we find Scott Stevens's racist responses to Hurricane Katrina a second-rate parody of black humor fiction. What makes this episode most blackly humorous is that given the danger of this techno-racist statement, a statement that cost Stevens his job, he felt forced to explain his paranoid conspiracy theory in detail. Sometimes people cannot help but repeat saying or doing what is contrary to their own interests. This mental history testifies to the effect of what the guru of the fantastic, Edgar Allan Poe, called "the Imp of the Perverse." In her 1984 book *The March of Folly*, the noted historian Barbara Tuchman illustrated our inherent folly with the examples of Troy, the Renaissance Popes provocation of Protestants, the British loss of the American colonies, and the United States' war in Vietnam. What she proved in that book is that human history is not only a series of unreformed follies but also a sequence of black humor narratives.

There is another reason why I began with the black humor episode from the wake of Katrina. For, much as Scott Stevens embedded racist discourse within his conspiracy theory about the natural disaster, the period of artificial disasters that included the Sino-Japanese War and the Russo-Japanese War saw the rise of the *gelbe Gefahr* or "Yellow Peril" discourse invented in 1895 by Kaiser Wilhelm II. What is more, the "Russian-made Cold War device" Scott Stevens describes undoubtedly refers to a high-tech weapon allegedly designed by the magician-like Serbo-Croatian inventor Nikola Tesla (1856–1943), a notorious competitor of Thomas Alva Edison, and a close friend and admirer of the all-American black humorist Mark Twain—especially in the 1890s and 1900s, the heyday of the Sino-Japanese War and the Russo-Japanese War.[1] And there are more recent examples as well. In January 1995 the Kobe earthquake, which measured 7.2 on the Richter scale, transformed the southern part of Hyogo prefecture in the western center of Japan into a wasteland. In the wake of that disaster, the high-tech terrorist cult AUM Shinrikyo, which was responsible for the Tokyo subway gas attack in March 1995, accused a great power, supposedly the United States, of having caused this disaster by means of an electromagnetic Doom Weapon supposedly designed by Nikola Tesla, a weapon whose blueprint AUM Shinrikyo itself was dying to discover. Whether this sinister cult was also responsible for this apocalyptic earthquake remains unknown. Nevertheless, it is plausible that the more apocalyptic a natural disaster gets, the more racist or xenophobic or conspiracy-minded one becomes; one is tempted to relate the ethnic other with high technology as a kind of uncanny magic.

Witnessing the side-effects of the Sino-Japanese War and Russo-Japanese War more than a century ago, Mark Twain already delineated this technoracist discourse in his minor black humor pieces "Flies and Russians" (1904 or 1905) and "The Fable of the Yellow Terror" (1904–5). In the former, the author proposes that if we combine the rabbit and the mollusk and the idiot and the bee, then we get a Russian. In the latter, he contrasts the Butterflies, who hold a vast territory like the United States, with the Bees as a Yellow Peril ignorant of civilization. Thus, a grave gray Grasshopper says to a prominent Butterfly: "You have taught one tribe of Bees how to use its sting, it will teach its brother tribe. The two together will be able to banish all the Butterflies some day, and keep them out; for they are uncountable in numbers and will be unconquerable when educated" (429). The most ironic black humor imprinted within the text is that Twain's techno-racist logic turns out to be a pastiche of the logic of slavery, an institution with whose victims the writer must have felt deep sympathy in *Adventures of Huckleberry Finn* (1885). Mocking the same logic as stated in Twain's black humor works, the fugitive slave Frederick Douglass states, "in teaching me the alphabet, in the days of her simplicity and kindness, my mistress had given me the '*inch*,' and no precaution could prevent me from taking the '*ell*'" (154–55; italics in the original). Thus, Twain's tiny black humor pieces will make it easy for us to grasp not only the discourse of the Yellow Peril, but also the general xenophobia pervading *fin de siècle* America. According to the xenophobic logic Twain transcribes very clearly from the political unconscious of his country, if we provide the ethnic other with the chance of technological education, then we will get a disaster menacing the Caucasian countries.

"Another Little Boy" in the Tradition of Black Humor

Insofar as my field of American Studies is concerned, it seems self-evident that since the nineteenth century, black humor has consistently expanded the potential of literature, ending up with postmodern avant-garde narratives such as metafiction, surfiction, slipstream, avant-pop, and magical realism. It started with Hugh Henry Brackenridge's American recreation of Don Quixote and Sancho Panza in *Modern Chivalry* (1846); Edgar Allan Poe's ferocious take on fairy tales, "Hop-Frog" (1849); Mark Twain's cynical attack on Christianity, "The War-Prayer" (1904–5); Ambrose Bierce's sardonic parody of a reference book, *The Devil's Dictionary* (1911); Joseph Heller's absurd novel, *Catch-22* (1961); Kurt Vonnegut's comic apocalypse, *Cat's Cradle* (1963); and Thomas Pynchon's conspiracy fiction, *The Crying of Lot 49* (1966), to name just a few. Nonetheless, major literary critics have tried to locate the heyday of black humor in 1960s Euro-American novels including Vladimir Nabokov, Günter Grass, Louis-Ferdinand Céline, and Jorge Louis Borges, neglecting its transpacific interaction with race and ethnicity.

Why are the 1960s privileged in historical accounts of black humor? For example, Robert Scholes identified black humor with the recurrent intellectual reaction of artists to the limitations of realism, defining its writers as master fabulators in the tradition of the Romance and its baroque configurations, writers who are all absorbed by the possibilities of playful and artful construction (35–46). Conrad Knickerbocker, one of the great theoreticians of black humor, diminishes the black humorist to "*poète maudit*, a scorpion to the status quo, so full of the poison of self-loathing for the 'specially tailored, ready-to-wear identities' given to us by TV, movies, the press, universities, the government, the military, medicine, and business, that he mortally stings himself, pricking the surrogate skin of society" (qtd. in Schulz 5). Furthermore, in his remarkably comprehensive work *Black Humor Fiction of the Sixties: A Pluralistic Definition of Man and His World*, Max Schulz considers black humor as "a phenomenon of the 1960s, comprising a group of writers who share a viewpoint and an aesthetics for pacing off the boundaries of a nuclear-technological world intrinsically without confinement" (5). These definitions are all inspiring, but they all take for granted the Western heritage of modern literature. They lack any sense of race and ethnicity. What I would like to attempt here is to renovate and expand the concept of black humor in the fantastic arts from a planetary perspective, in the context of transpacific narratology.

There is no doubt that the 1960s saw the rise of nuclear fiction intertwined with literary avant-gardism. Its origin might be located in J. D. Salinger's longtime bestseller *The Catcher in the Rye* (1951), whose sixteen-year-old Holden Caulfield challenges his "phony" society at every turn. Despite his adolescent and innocent outlook, however, Holden sometimes performs just like a typical suicide terrorist. Let us listen to him at the end of chapter 18: "Anyway, I'm sort of glad they've got the atomic bomb invented. If there's ever another war, I'm going to sit right the hell on top of it. I'll volunteer for it, I swear to God I will" (141). Whether Holden Caulfield is serious or not, it is certain that he not only approves of the disasters in Hiroshima and Nagasaki but also looks forward to participating in the next World War—that is, World War III. Yes, *The Catcher in the Rye* is not so much an adolescent novel as a work of crypto-nuclear fiction filled with black humor. We might even assume that it is Salinger's post-apocalyptic imagination in 1951 as well as the Cuban Missile Crisis in 1962 that inspired Peter George and Stanley Kubrick to produce the greatest black humor film, *Dr. Strangelove Or: How I Learned to Stop Worrying and Love the Bomb* (1964), which coincided with Kurt Vonnegut's *Cat's Cradle* (1963) and Sakyo Komatsu's *The Day of Resurrection* (1964), the original story for the film *Virus* (1980). Salinger's novel also prefigures Thomas Pynchon's *Gravity's Rainbow*, whose alternate history of World War II incorporates the possibility of nuclear attack on Nixonian America in the early 1970s.

And yet, today I would like to single out another black humor masterpiece, written by Brian Aldiss, "Another Little Boy," published in *New Worlds* in 1966. This story is set in the year 2044, when humans have entered the "CM age," in which the newly discovered energy source "Coherent Matter" has revolutionized life. Humans have reached and colonized Mars, Venus, Mercury, and Jupiter, with discoveries in space distracting them from their own past. Meanwhile, an increasing number of conflicts keep murdering millions of people, making them dismiss the wars of a hundred years ago as trifles. Against this backdrop, the head of Zadar Smith World, the largest advertising agency in existence, agrees with J. J. Spillaine, President of the United States of Both Americas to produce on August 6, 2045, the most impressive festival ever held on Earth in order to commemorate the centenary of the birth of the modern age, that is, the age of nucleonics or Nuclear Power. However, Zadar's international executives have no idea how to produce the event, for they are all unfamiliar with what happened on that day in history one hundred years ago, August 6, 1945. Some mistake that date for the bicentenary of Abraham Lincoln, others misconceive it to be the centenary of the discovery of radio, the first moon landing, the birth of Arthur C. Clarke, the foundation of the Scandinavian Republic, or the birthdays of Grace Metalious, Ho Chi Min, Picasso, or even Walt Disney (249–50). At a loss about what to do, Thora Peabright from Bonn, the German member of the company's executive board and the heroine of the story, begins conducting research on the date by means of the satellibrary's encyclopedia. The entry on "the Cold War" initially reminds her only of the Contained Conflict between Australia and Antarctica. But it is this entry that finally explains what happened on August 6, 1945. Aldiss writes:

> More references met her eye. She chased them down with increased éclat, and was finally confronted with the history of the Second World War, of which she had never even heard—but then it had been a smaller world in those days, and no one had even set foot on Mars and Venus and Mercury, not to mention the New Planets. After a few moments, she began skimming, bored by accounts of national groups of which she had never even heard, Estonians, Belgians, Croats. She tumbled on to Japan. That was more interesting. United Germany had a lot of trade with Japan; indeed, since the Japanese-Korean debacle of '39, the Japs were competing rather unpleasantly in world markets. In spaceware particularly, Jap ablation shields, LORs, stargaffies, glitch baffles, space suits, and even Molabs were sweeping the market, and particularly squeezing Mei [one of the world's largest microelectronic firms] whose spaceware department had emitted down-falling graphs every one of the last five accountancy years.
>   Finally Thora caught up with the date again. August 6, 1945. First nuclear device, a small atomic bomb, delivered by plane from an American airstrip on Tinian Island and dropped over the Japanese city of Hiroshima. As a result of this, and a second bomb dropped later on Nagasaki, the Japanese emperor capitulated. (253–54)

Even further research using pre-electronic hard copies of old historical books at the Museum of Pre-CM History does not lead her to feel empathy with the defeated nation, but only to expand her detachment from the people of the past: "the denizens of the mid-twentieth century were a poor lot, reeking of a million guilts and repressions" (257). Reading the biography of Major Eatherly, who dropped Little Boy on Hiroshima, and who became mentally deranged in the postwar years, Thora finds him "an unmitigated idiot" (257). At this point, she feels convinced by the reasoning of the Museum librarian who discourages her from reading past books: "Our immediate ancestors were bores, don't you think—crippled with guilt about sex and war and food and drugs and all the things we most enjoy" (256). Thus, the point of the story turns out to be the transformation of common sense.

From this perspective, the seemingly shocking but final and definitive proposal for the Centenary of Nuclear Power makes sense. While other senior executives propose funny but modest ideas like "Auroral display in ionosphere visible everywhere spelling BLESS OUR EARTH," "Rebuilding Stonehenge and placing enlarged plastic reproduction of same on Moon," "Setting fire to Jupiter with super-CM-bomb to provide new mini-sun," and "Great Orbital Electronic World's Fair" (257), Thora makes up her mind to persuade the head of the company to attempt a far more radical but spectacular project:

> The bomb stopped the war ... and paved the way for all the better bombs, like the Coherent Matter bomb, and the quickly contained conflicts with which we are now familiar. It certainly was progress. Yet our queer old ancestors went crazy with guilt about it, wanted to ban it, made a martyr out of Eatherly, wrote books and sick novels and dislocated prose and gonnows—what about it. ... We get a replica of the *Enola Gay* and find if one of the minor nations don't still have an atom bomb, and we fly it over with a blaze of publicity and we drop it on Hiroshima again smack on 8.16 in the morning! How do you like it, Morgan?! (258–59)

Her radical idea is approved not only by Morgan Zadar but also by the Universal Board, which might be the twenty-first-century version of the United Nations, over the objections of the Japanese delegate, who is shouted down. The reason is economic: "most of the nations present had suffered too much unfair trade competition to listen to him" (259). Thus, the project ends up with a shaky old Tunisian Dakota dropping a rusty old British H-Bomb over Hiroshima and Nagasaki, which excites everyone but the Japanese. For them this is nothing more than a gigantic fire-ball like fireworks "brighter than a thousand suns" (260).

It is very natural that in 1969 when this story was translated into Japanese and published in *Hayakawa's SF Magazine* (Feb. 1970), "Another Little Boy" caused a heated controversy in the Japanese SF community. For example, one of the founding fathers of Japanese SF, Mr. Tetsu Yano, who is very well known for being the translator of R. A. Heinlein and the author of a highly admired story, "The Legend of the Paper Spaceship," attacked the story as a type of white supremacy (2).

Moreover, only a couple of months later, author Aritsune Toyota published a counterwork entitled "Another Prince of Wales" in the April 1970 issue of *Hayakawa's SF Magazine*, which describes a twenty-first-century media-saturated reality providing people with wars to satisfy their desires. Thus, the year 2041 sees the simulation of the Pacific War, featuring a replica of the battleship *Prince of Wales* and its nine escorts totally devastated by Japanese planes, repeating their fate in the battle of the Malay Straits a hundred years before. In the wake of the war, Pakistan, India, Australia, China, Egypt, and Russia all come to declare war on England. Furthermore, Malaysia, Korea, and Both Americas, as well as Scotland, Ireland, and Wales declare war against England. The reason is very simple. In the new century, England is reconsidered as a poor old country and "the world's scapegoat, just as the Jews, the blacks and, at one time, the Japanese, had been in the twentieth century" (141). Toyota's story not only mocks the consumerist ideology Aldiss foregrounded, but also subverts the logic of white supremacy Yano felt so uncomfortable with.

Yano's and Toyota's responses to "Another Little Boy" could themselves be considered highly nationalistic.[2] However, I would like to emphasize that these kinds of counter-racist attacks are not necessarily typical. For instance, Takumi Shibano, Yano's close friend and another founding father of Japanese SF, admires "Another Little Boy" by noting in it a type of hardcore science-fictional imagination that relativizes everything, rendering the most serious things today the most trifling in the next age (61). What is more, "Another Little Boy" was championed by no less than a member of the Japanese imperial family: Princess Asaka Fukuko, who made her semi-professional debut as an SF writer in the early 1960s under the pseudonym Bien Fu, and who criticized Yano and reconfirmed the science-fictional privilege to mock everything.

Furthermore, in mentioning Toyota's own alternate historical novel *Pax Mongolica* (1967), which proposes a huge Chinese empire of yellow supremacy that oppresses two million white slaves, this female writer Bien Fu assumed that even some of Japanese SF is incomprehensible from the Western perspective (65). It is very interesting that a member of the Japanese imperial family kept writing SF featuring cyborgs and Native Americans, fully understanding the essence of SF as embodied by the black humor of Brian Aldiss. Deeply identifying herself with the vanishing Americans described in Hollywood films of the postwar era, she apparently found it necessary to reconstruct her imperial subjectivity as a transnationalist cyborg, the phantasmagoric chimera of the emperor system and American democracy. This is why she could so easily comprehend the black humor aspect of SF.

To me, "Another Little Boy" seems to gain even more significance today. What has happened in the past fifty years is a huge paradigm shift ranging from ideology to representation, a shift whose seeds could be rediscovered in 1960s speculative fiction. Now let me give several reasons for this shift.

First, on the topic of nationalism, when R. A. Heinlein's 1959 novel *Starship Troopers*, which is now well known for introducing the concept of the "powered suit," was translated by the aforementioned Yano in 1967, the novel spawned a stormy ideological debate about whether Heinlein's ideas were fascist, especially between Yano, who supported the novel by transfiguring Heinlein's fascism into a Japanese patriotism cultivated through his own experience of military service, and the critic Takashi Ishikawa, who completely repudiated the novel from the viewpoint of postwar democracy. It is very ironic that while Yano felt sympathy with the fascist aspect of *Starship Troopers*, he attacked the black humor aspect of "Another Little Boy." Nonetheless, what matters most is that when Hayakawa Publishers issued a new paperback edition of *Starship Troopers* in 1977 with a cover illustration of the powered suit beautifully drawn by Naoyuki Kato of Studio Nue, this image had a profound impact on the design of "mobile suits" in Japanese robot anime, starting with "Gundam," whose global influence is widely known. This is the way design philosophy gradually replaced political ideology in the transition between the High Growth period and the Advanced Capitalist period. Tired of 1960s agonizing over abstract problems such as nationalism, patriotism, and racism, problems with no solution or conclusion, people became entranced by the aesthetics of a technology that symbolized such stylish agility—the mobility to outflank any opponent.

Likewise, as Akira Mizuta Lippit's insightful book *Atomic Light (Shadow Optics)* points out, we can easily trace the paradoxical way visual technology came to express the atomic bombings of Hiroshima and Nagasaki and transfigure their impact into the aesthetic tropes of invisibility or transparency. In chapter 4 of the book, "An Atomic Trace," Lippit reconstructs Paul Virilio's theory about the photographic legacy of the atomic bombing and reinterprets Hiroshima and Nagasaki as the photographic moments where "a blinding flash vaporized entire bodies, leaving behind only shadow traces" (86). Furthermore, Lippit asserts, "There can be no authentic photography of atomic war because the bombings were themselves a form of total photography that exceeded the economies of representation, testing the very visibility of the visual" (95). This paradigm shift enables us to develop new ways of reading the fantastic. As hardcore SF writer Hiroshi Yamamoto attempted to describe in his 2009 story "Another Little Girl" (itself a homage to "Another Little Boy"), which dramatizes Japan as another nuclear-armed state in the year 2109, what we believe to be self-evident now is very likely to be displaced with some brand new absurdity, which will be naturalized in the near future. Today's common sense is nothing but tomorrow's uncommon sense.[3]

Second, reading Arthur C. Clarke and Frederik Pohl's first and last collaboration, *The Last Theorem*, I feel fascinated with the novel as well as Pohl's preface recollecting the International Science Fiction Symposium held in Japan in 1970. According to him, in the summer of that year, Judith Merril had earlier come to Japan and told the other guests about what she had already seen in Hiroshima, especially the Atomic Bomb Memorial Dome, whose "twisted ironwork the Japanese preserved as a memorial when every other part of that building had been blown away by that first-ever-deployed-in-anger nuclear bomb" (xi). As if endorsing Akira Lippit's theory mentioned earlier, now Pohl recalls the picture everyone knows—that is, the picture of "the shadow of a man that had been permanently etched, onto the stone stairs where he had been sitting, by the intolerably brilliant nuclear blast from the overhead sky" (xi). Inspired by this topic, the Anglo-American Science Fiction masters started a casual discussion:

> "That must have been bright," someone said—I think Brian [Aldiss].
> Arthur [C. Clarke] said, "Bright enough that it could have been seen by a dozen nearby stars by now."
> "If anyone lives there to be looking," someone else said—I think it was me.
> And, we agreed, maybe someone might indeed be looking . . . or at least it was pretty to think so. (xii)

It is important that here Aldiss allegedly said, "That must have been bright," conjuring up his own story "Another Little Boy." His comment also relates to *The Last Theorem*, a story of overlord-like super-intelligent aliens called the Grand Galactics who feel so disturbed by microwave emanations and far brighter fire bursts from Earth that they begin to wonder whether to invade and exterminate the planet. In this near future, the United States invents a super weapon called "Silent Thunder," which is to deprive North Korea, Venezuela, and Colombia of electrical power and defeat these whole nations totally and irrevocably "without anyone hurt" (233). It is this super weapon that the aliens assumed could "endanger parts of the Grand Galactics' own armorarium" (235). Since the aliens "had encountered some 254 similarly dangerous races, and terminated some 251 of them" (237), they feel no hesitation about exterminating the occupants of Earth. Just the way "Another Little Boy" depicted how the Universal Board took economic sanctions against Japan by repeating Hiroshima and Nagasaki as a comically apocalyptic show, *The Last Theorem* also seems to suggest the possible extermination of problematic nations and even the very race of Earthlings with post-nuclear weapons, as if renovating the narrative of Clarke's apocalyptic novel *Childhood's End* (1953). Mocking Karl Marx's formulation that history repeats itself first as tragedy and second as farce, this time I feel like replacing the term "farce" with "black humor."

Third, to tell the truth, I started rereading "Another Little Boy" in the wake of the 9/11 terrorist attacks in 2001. After a lapse of ten years, it seems to me that this short story and this fearful event have become intertwined with each other more closely, not because 9/11 cannot help but recall Hiroshima and Nagasaki, but because the term "Ground Zero," now tightly attached to the site of the demolished World Trade Center, is nothing other than a kind of abuse of metaphor, that is, a catachresis for Hiroshima and Nagasaki, which will undoubtedly accelerate the forgetting of these origins. Back in the 1980s, Jacques Derrida's influential essay on nuclear criticism "No Apocalypse, Not Now" (1984) presupposes that total nuclear war has never taken place, trivializing Hiroshima and Nagasaki from the typically Western rhetorical perspective (see Nagano 134), whereas the current site internationally known as "Ground Zero" helps further erase the memory of Hiroshima and Nagasaki and promotes global amnesia, by associating that term exclusively with the 9/11 terrorist attacks. This rhetorical reading invites us to rediscover "Another Little Boy" as a story of amnesia caused by too many wars, which could have included the 9/11 terrorist attacks and the subsequent Iraq War—an amnesia which has helped trivialize what took place on August 6th, 1945 in Japan. Yes, it is this catachrestic term "Ground Zero" that positioned the 9/11 terrorist attacks as pseudo-nuclear attacks, providing the United States with a cause for waging a small scale nuclear war; the Bush Administration rationalized the declaration of the Iraq War by cunningly supposing that Iraq possessed weapons of mass destruction, and employed its own depleted uranium ammunition in the Iraq War. In this sense, rereading "Another Little Boy" will lead us to recall how we have lived the postwar history of amnesia, and how we have been forced to naturalize the fictional history of faked nuclear war.

Transpacific Writers, Transpacific Imagination

Although I'm neither nationalistic nor patriotic, I find the diaspora of the Japanese nation peculiar to postwar Japanese SF. Just as William Faulkner appealed to the Japanese audience in 1955 by identifying himself as a descendant of another defeated nation, postwar Japanese writers endowed with a talent for the fantastic came to expand the sensibility of what I have designated "Creative Masochism," as detailed in my own book *Full Metal Apache*. In fact, the Japanese boom in SF in Japan was triggered by Sakyo Komatsu's best-selling novel *Nippon Chinbotsu* (*Japan Sinks*) in 1973. More than thirty years later, the year 2006 saw a stimulating revival of Komatsu's *Japan Sinks*, which involved not only Koshu Tani's publication of the sequel to the novel but also Shinji Higuchi's ambitious remake of the film version, and Minoru Kawasaki's film version of Yasutaka Tsutsui's black humor short story "Nippon Igai Zenbu Chinbotsu" ("Everyone Other Than Japan Sinks") published in 1973 as a parody of *Japan Sinks*. Tsutsui's parody ironically narrates the diaspora of all non-Japanese people on Earth and the fate of their immigration into the Japanese Archipelago.

Here let me note that back in the 1960s Tsutsui had already published a typical black humor SF story entitled "Vietnam Travel Bureau" (1967), in which the hero selects for his own honeymoon not Mars or Saturn but Vietnam, where the Vietnam War is kept going on to entertain visitors, without any connection whatsoever to its original causes. Tsutsui's "Vietnam Travel Bureau" redefines war as a spectacular commodity and precedes *Sarajevo Survival Guide* (1993) by twenty-five years. "Another Little Boy" and "Vietnam Travel Bureau" were roughly contemporaneous. While the former excited Japanese nationalist and patriotic readers, Tsutsui's seemingly anti-white supremacy black humor would have infuriated their North American counterparts. Starting from Tsutsui's sense of black humor as represented in "Everyone Other Than Japan Sinks," Kawasaki visualizes the way it becomes more and more difficult for non-Japanese people to survive the diaspora unless they decide to go native in Japan. Despite its counter-racist taste, this is one of the black humor critiques of Western SF from a planetary perspective. I am not sure if this kind of radically subversive literary experiment was considered nationalistic or patriotic by serious readers. However, it is true that this black humor writer Tsutsui received the Medal with Purple Ribbon for academic or artistic excellence from the Japanese government in 2004.

Now that black humor has been naturalized in contemporary literature, how can we recuperate the original power of the subversive imagination? Let me conclude this chapter with a few transpacific examples.

First, the Yasusada Araki hoax that stormed American poetry. The mid-1990s saw a variety of splendid poems published in poetry journals by a Japanese poet and Hiroshima survivor named Yasusada Araki. However, in 1997 this poet was revealed to be a complete fake. Kent Johnson, who submitted the poems to the journals, disclosed that Araki's poems were actually written by one of his translators "Tosa Motokiyu," itself a pseudonym of a person whose national or ethnic identity still remains unknown. Although American literary history has cultivated a heritage of passing narratives, this Araki hoax, what Brian McHale designated a typical "mock hoax," is exceptional, for the author tried to pass not only for Yellow but also for an atomic bomb survivor. Of course, this kind of passing must have disgusted Japanese survivors of Hiroshima. Whether the real author is racially Mongoloid or not, however, the black humor of the Araki hoax, as Yunte Huang pointed out, leads us less into the problem of empathy than into the problem of "nuclear universalism," which I would like to rephrase as "nuclear planetarity," through which

Hiroshima and Nagasaki should be "remembered from the transcendent and anonymous position of humanity" (149).

My second example is from the Asian American feminist black humor author Karen Tei Yamashita's metafictional piece "Siamese Twins and Mongoloids: Cultural Appropriation and the Deconstruction of Stereotype via the Absurdity of Metaphor." Yamashita's story is based upon the famous Siamese twins Chang and Eng Bunker, who were born in 1811 in Meklong in the country then known as Siam, and who were brought to America and Europe as a circus attraction and briefly hired by P. T. Barnum, one of the greatest entrepreneurs in Victorian America. Yamashita recreates Mark Twain's story of extraordinary twins with a story of Asian American Siamese twins named "Heco" and "Okada"—after Hikozo Hamada, the first Japanese to become an American citizen, and John Okada, author of the great Asian American novel *No-No Boy*. Although these kinds of ethnic freaks have recently been considered post-nuclear monsters or mutants, Yamashita deconstructs the black humor stereotypes of the freaks and depicts them as perfect boys endowed with exceptional talents. Very successful in the field of business, Heco and Okada wind up marrying two sisters: "Heco married a strangely beautiful Eurasian with green eyes and perfect hair," while "Okada's sister was one-quarter Cherokee, one-quarter African, and one-eighth Palestinian and three-eighths Micronesian" (134). Just as the original Siamese twins used to signify the close bond between the North and the South, these Asian American twins disclose the catachrestic limit of "Siamese Twins" and represent the multiethnic unity of the whole planet. Hence, Yamashita's twins succeed in transcending the boundary of conventional racism.

Finally, there is Shelley Jackson's *Half Life*, which intrigued me so much that I nominated it for the Tiptree Award in 2007. This highly intricate and superbly hypertextual novel provided us with an incredibly intertextual space inhabited by a number of literary and cultural figures such as Edgar Allan Poe, P. T. Barnum, Mark Twain, Virginia Woolf, Samuel Beckett, Vladimir Nabokov, Leslie Fiedler, Katherine Dunn, and Allen Kurzweil. The author contrasts the "twofers" in the story—that is, the Siamese twins naturalized in the post-apocalyptic age—and their contemporary "singletons" who are dying to have a couple of heads just like the twofers. It sounds strange enough to recall the grotesque garden of freaks represented in *The Obscene Bird of Night*, a magnum opus by the major Latin American magic realist José Donoso. Reappropriating post-Twain and post-Vonnegut black humor in her own nuclear fiction, Jackson skillfully compares the rise of twofers to the rise of ethnic or sexual minority groups involved with the civil rights movement. And yet, what attracted me most is not only the idea but also the narrative, in which the heroine Nora Olney, who succeeded in erasing her twin sister Blanche, becomes unable to distinguish between her waking world and Blanche's dream one. Moreover, just as the title of the novel refers to both the double life of the Siamese twins and the amount of time that a radioactive substance takes to lose half its radioactivity, so the name of the heroine's sister metafictionally connotes the "carte blanche" Nora abuses and the "blank pages" she fills up by scribbling away at her autobiography. The author's speculation on Hiroshima and Nagasaki makes the novel more philosophical, inviting us to consider what will happen to sexuality and ethnicity in the post-nuclear future.

> In 1951, saddened by Hiroshima and Nagasaki, and recognizing the need for a national activity of penance, a despondent American government commenced organized hostilities against itself. For three years, they hammered a sparsely populated part of the Nevada desert with the most powerful bombs in existence. The cratered sand turned to glass. In it Uncle Sam could see his own, still grief-stricken face. Stronger measures were called for. (225)

Yes, featuring the double life of the twofers, this seemingly sororophobic novel also grapples with the future of race, class, and gender in general. Just the way James Tiptree Jr. was a writer who enjoyed his/her "double life," this post-apocalyptic black humor fiction about brand-new Siamese twins gives us a wonderful way to reinvestigate—now from a planetary viewpoint—the afterlife of the human race and the double life of post-humans.

Notes

1. Without the help of Nikola Tesla, Hugo Gernsback could not have envisioned the new literary genre of SF. For the impact of Tesla's imagination, see also Christopher Priest's 1995 novel *The Prestige*, which was made into a 2006 movie featuring David Bowie as this mad scientist.

2. At the 1970 International SF Symposium held in Japan, Takashi Ishikawa, a leading SF critic who once repudiated Heinlein's fascist vision in *Starship Troopers*, had a chance to argue with Aldiss himself about "Another Little Boy." Ishikawa recollects: "Under the influence of liquor I started accosting Brian for having written 'Another Little Boy.' Admitting his literary guilt, he said 'sorry,' and dove into the Biwako Lake with his clothes on" ("Bungaku" 129–30).

3. In coming up with the figure of "Little Girl," Yamamoto is undoubtedly aware of the disfiguring effect of the term "Little Boy." Here Fumika Nagano's analysis of Kurt Vonnegut's *Cat's Cradle* (1963) is very helpful:

As the playful naming suggests, the midget Newton is intimately connected with this scientific disaster, for his father, like Stanley Kubrick's Dr. Strangelove, was an influential scientist who worked for the American military machine, inventing both the A-bomb and ice nine.... The science fiction of the same period saw the birth of boy-robots depicted as freakish and therefore alienated even from their producers. However, unlike Brian Aldiss's "Supertoys Last All Summer Long" (1969) and Osamu Tezuka's *Tetsuwan Atomu* (*Mighty Atom* 1951–68), Vonnegut's Newton is a human character who is transformed into the equivalent of a scientific invention through the writer's narratology.... In comparison with the human nickname "Little Boy," this little boy is transformed into something like a scientific invention, a disfiguration of the bomb: he certainly serves Jonah's purpose since he embodies the "human" side of the superweapon. (127–28, 132)

Works Cited

Aldiss, Brian. "Another Little Boy." 1966. *Best Science Fiction Stories of Brian W. Aldiss*. Rev. ed. London: Faber, 1970. 248–60. Print.
Bien Fu. "Letter." *Uchûjin* (May 1970): 65. Print.
Clarke, Arthur C., and Frederik Pohl. *The Last Theorem*. 2008. London: Harper, 2009. Print.
Derrida, Jacques. "No Apocalypse, Not Now (Full Speed Ahead, Seven Missiles, Seven Missives)." Trans. Catherine Porter and Philip Lewis. *Diacritics* 14.2 (1984): 20–31. Print.
Douglass, Frederick. *My Bondage and Freedom*. 1855. Salem: Ayer, 1984. Print.
Huang, Yunte. *Transpacific Imaginations: History, Literature, Counterpoetics*. Cambridge: Harvard UP, 2008. Print.
Ishikawa, Takashi. "Bungaku to Jikan" ["Literature and Time"]. *Jikan to Ningen* [*Time and Man*]. Ed. Yoichiro Murakami. Tokyo: U of Tokyo P, 1981. 127–58. Print.
———. *SF no Jidai* [*The Age of Science Fiction*]. Tokyo: Kiso-Tengaisha, 1977. Print.
Jackson, Shelley. *Half Life*. New York: Harper, 2006. Print.
Knickerbocker, Conrad. "Humor with a Mortal Sting." *New York Times Book Review* 27 Sept. 1964, sec. 7:3. Print.
Komatsu, Sakyo. *Nippon Chinbotsu* [*Japan Sinks*]. 1973. Trans. Michael Gallagher. London: New English, 1977. Print.
Lippit, Akira Mizuta. *Atomic Light (Shadow Optics)*. Minneapolis: U of Minnesota P, 2005. Print.
McHale, Brian. "'A Poet May Not Exist': Mock-Hoaxes and the Construction of National Identity." *The Faces of Anonymity: Anonymous and Pseudonymous Publication from the Sixteenth to the Twentieth Century*. Ed. Robert J. Griffin. New York: Palgrave, 2003. 233–52. Print.
Nagano, Fumika. "Surviving the Perpetual Winter: The Role of Little Boy in Vonnegut's *Cat's Cradle*." *Kurt Vonnegut*. Ed. Harold Bloom. New York: Chelsea, 2009. 127–41. Print.
Priest, Christopher. *The Prestige*. 1995. New York: Tor, 2006. Print.
Pynchon, Thomas. *Gravity's Rainbow*. New York: Viking, 1973. Print.
———. *Inherent Vice*. New York: Penguin, 2009. Print.

Salinger, J. D. *The Catcher in the Rye*. 1951. New York: Little, 1991. Print.
Scholes, Robert. *The Fabulators*. New York: Oxford UP, 1967. Print.
Schulz, Max. *Black Humor Fiction of the Sixties: A Pluralistic Definition of Man and His World*. Athens: Ohio State UP, 1973. Print.
Shibano, Takumi. "Atogaki" ["Editor's Note"]. *Uchûjin* (Mar. 1970): 61. Print.
Svenvold, Mark. *Big Weather: Chasing Tornadoes in the Heart of America*. New York: Henry Holt, 2005. Print.
Tatsumi, Takayuki. *Full Metal Apache: Transactions between Cyberpunk Japan and Avant-Pop America*. Durham: Duke UP, 2006. Print.
"Tondemo-bon." Wikipedia, 2010. Web.
Toyota, Aritsune. "Prince of Wales Futatabi" ["Another Prince of Wales"]. 1970. Trans. David Aylward. *Speculative Japan: Outstanding Tales of Japanese Science Fiction and Fantasy*. Ed. Gene van Troyer and Grania Davis. Fukuoka: Kurodahan, 2007. 125–42. Print.
Tsutsui, Yasutaka. "Nippon Igai Zenbu Chinbotsu" ["Everyone Other Than Japan Sinks"]. 1973. *Everyone Other Than Japan Sinks and Other Panic Stories*. [In Japanese.] Tokyo: Kadokawa, 2006. Print.
———. "Vietnam Kanko Kosha" ["Vietnam Travel Bureau"]. 1967. *Vietnam Travel Bureau*. Tokyo: Hayakawa, 1967. 255–79. Print.
Tuchman, Barbara. *The March of Folly: From Troy to Vietnam*. New York: Ballantine, 1985. Print.
Twain, Mark, and John S. Tuckey. *Mark Twain's "Which Was the Dream?" and Other Symbolic Writings of the Later Years*. Berkeley: U of California P, 1967. Print.
"Weatherman Claims Japanese Mafia behind Hurricane Katrina." 8 Sept. 2005. *Flashnews.com*. Wireless Flash News, 2005. Web. 11 Sept. 2005.
Yamamoto, Hiroshi. "Little Girl Futatabi" ["Another Little Girl"]. *Shosetsu Gendai*. (Aug. 2009): 219–37. Print.
Yamashita, Karen Tei. "Siamese Twins and Mongoloids: Cultural Appropriation and the Deconstruction of Stereotype via the Absurdity of Metaphor." *Yellow Light: The Flowering of Asian American Arts*. Ed. Amy Ling. Philadelphia: Temple UP, 1999. 126–35. Print.
Yano, Tetsu. "SF at Random: 42." *Uchûjin* (Mar. 1970): 2–3. Print.

INDIA AND INDIANS IN SF BY INDIANS AND OTHERS
■ ■ ■

UPPINDER MEHAN

Science fiction (SF) is perhaps more prone to anthropological and ethnographic writing than other genres, in part, because of one of its defining conventions: extrapolation. Projecting current demographic patterns, scientific knowledge, technological praxis, etc., requires a good measure of objectivity. Having created that extrapolated world, writing back from it to the current world results in the depiction of the unknown described in the terms of the known—a temporal ethnographic writing. Such a conception of SF writing places it comfortably in the same generic neighborhood as anthropological and travel writing. While ethnographers and travel writers have worked diligently to describe and analyze cultures different from their own as objectively as possible, they are still constrained to writing about difference in terms of similarity. The necessity of writing the unknown in terms of the known is especially difficult when the known itself is not particularly well understood, as is the case in SF writing that extrapolates from a culture other than one's own. SF writing that incorporates India or Indians (and I use both terms broadly) is open to greater errors of stereotyping and cultural misunderstandings when the author lacks the lived experience to understand a culture well enough to extrapolate. Writing about other cultures far away is tantamount to writing about cultures in extrapolated worlds.

Much work has been done on the Orientalist depiction of the racial other as an exotic who is both feared and desired, but I will move the focus somewhat to the representation of the Indian as an anthropological exotic in recent science fiction. Graham Huggan (from whom I borrow the term) defines it as "a particular mode of aesthetic perception—one which renders people, objects and places strange even as it domesticates them" (13). The pleasure of the SF text, however, seems to hover between the familiar and unfamiliar. The appeal of the other lies in its otherness, "but insofar as it retains its ontological difference the encounter with it is liable to be marked by frustration, failure, lack" (Basu). The SF text in this regard doubles the romantic, exoticizing text in seeking to provide a frisson of the foreign in the safety of the familiar.

The anthropological exotic produces its sense of familiarity through a construction of the other with the knowledge provided and guaranteed by science; "it invokes the familiar aura of other, incommensurably 'foreign' cultures while appearing to provide a modicum of information that gives the uninitiated reader access to the text and, by extension, the 'foreign culture' itself" (Huggan 55). The anthropological exotic represents the native as an embodiment of the culture's mythic worldview at one extreme and as an everyman constructed from the findings of research in cultural anthropology at the other. In the case of Indians in SF, characters are most often symbolic reconstructions of the authoritative statements by researchers about caste structures and hierarchies, extended families, rituals and myths about various gods and goddesses, karmic retribution, and reincarnation. Indians become markers of Indian-ness which in turn is not only the India of ancient wonders but also of present-day grinding poverty and pollution. SF is already at risk for characters being little more than ideas given flesh. Writing about a culture through the lens of travelers, anthropologists, and ethnographers compounded by the process of extrapolation doubles the chances of a cavalier treatment of the other.

India and Indian characters have rarely appeared in SF, as I chart in the first section of this essay through a recounting of my early reading. In Ian McDonald's Indian SF, including *River of Gods* (2004) and *Cyberabad Days* (2009), he treats the setting and characters of the novel and short stories with a consideration rarely found in fiction by cultural outsiders. McDonald is a strong writer with a firm grasp of style and structure and an inventive imagination, but his lack of cultural immersion becomes apparent in comparison to SF works by writers from India. Anuradha Marwah's *Idol Love* (1999), Manjula Padmanabhan's *Escape* (2008), and Rimi Chatterjee's *Signal Red* (2005), to name three, are able to effortlessly explore issues and concerns in their SF that are beyond the received images of India and Indians and surface knowledge available to the casual observer. While the first section of the essay is an autobiographical recounting of my early reading life, it is also an attempt at a kind of travel and ethnographic writing. Perhaps it might be better described as the diary of someone seeing a distorted reflection of one's own self and culture in another culture's imagination.

The Early Years

As a teenager growing up in a small town in Ontario, Canada, where my family was not only the only Indian family but also the only non-white family, I was tremendously attracted to science fiction. I am sure I shared with many a bookish teen the feeling of being a stranger in a strange land to begin with, but add to it the cultural dislocation of not only moving from India to Canada but also from a big city to a small town (Mumbai—or Bombay, as it was known when we moved—to Lucknow; several million to several hundred people). There were enough similarities between the two places that beyond the initial very visible difference, there existed a couple of uncanny elements. Since my parents sent my brothers and me to a Catholic school, the English I spoke and wrote and read was more English than that of my schoolmates. Both Canada and India are former British colonies and that meant we shared some strong elements but also diverged quite remarkably. The town in which I found myself was settled by Scots who had been part of the regiment that had fought against the natives in the 1857 Indian "Rebellion" in Lucknow, India.

Thus, reading science fiction became for me an act of complicated identification. I had been drawn to science fiction as a young boy for much the same reasons given by others (a fascination with the alien, a love of technology and science, an eagerness to engage in ideas) and since it formed the bulk of my reading experience, I looked to it for many of the same rewards and consolations that others would find in other kinds of literature. Perhaps unlike other SF readers, I found it much easier to identify with the aliens than the humans. The humans were always white guys, mostly Americans and Englishmen with an occasional Frenchman or Russian, and, to paraphrase Chinua Achebe, the texts were structured to make me sympathize with Marlow.[1] When the novels did not include aliens but were dystopias or future romances (to use Northrop Frye's terminology[2]), there were no brown people to be seen anywhere. I was left to imagine that only white people had a future.

The first character from India in a science fiction work that I rememder encountering was in Roger Zelazny's novel *Lord of Light* (1967). The first page of the novel mixes signs of Indian-ness with something else, along with a touch of the West. Zelazny's language throughout makes use of the indirect and metaphorical speech preferred by religious texts, and he cites an actual Buddhist text on the first page. But beginning on the first page, and sprinkled throughout, Zelazny signals the playfulness of the entire project by dropping a few lines of demotic into the religious language: "His followers called him Mahasamatman and said he was a god. He preferred to drop the Maha- and the -atman, however, and called himself Sam. He never claimed to be a god. But then, he never claimed not to be a god" (1). The reader learns that humans came to this unnamed planet ages ago, took the land from the beings that had "evolved" out of the need for a body, and then some of these humans set themselves up as gods out of the Hindu pantheon. The picture I grasped, eventually, was that the Indian part of the work could as easily have been Greek. The Indian names and mythology were emptied of meaning and left me feeling empty as well.

I had a similar response to Arthur C. Clarke's Rama series of novels. The first novel of the series, *Rendezvous with Rama* (1972), introduces the reader and the inhabitants of a future Earth to a multi-generational alien spaceship in the shape of a long cylinder. The ship, first mistakenly identified as an asteroid and given a number, is named Rama only because the astronomers had run out of names from the Greek and Roman pantheons. Clarke's empty usage seems to be benign in that the "India" signaled by "Rama" is afforded the same status as naming a planet "Mars" signals Rome and naming one of its satellites "Phobos" signals Greece. It could be argued that the Indian pantheon is given some social capital in a system of scientific research that has been dominated by an English tradition that traces its lineage back to ancient European roots; India is invited into the discourse. There is a crucial difference, however, in that the Indian pantheon is part of a live tradition, whereas the ancient Roman and Greek pantheons have been superseded by Christian beliefs and practices for more than two millennia (*Rendezvous with Rama* is set less than two hundred years after its publication date).

The nominal use of Rama by Clarke is a variety of the imperialist strategy of negation whereby "colonized peoples are systematically represented in terms of negation and absence—absence of order, of limits, of light, of spirit" (Spurr 96). The discourse of negation by which a people are denied a history is most often used to describe Africa rather than India, but to equate a people's living religion to a dead set of beliefs and practices as Clarke's narrator does in the novel is akin to an erasure. Clarke's negation pales, though, compared to Zelazny's greater deployment of Indian cultural and religious elements. Zelazny's *Lord of Light* engages more actively with the Indian pantheon than does Clarke's *Rendezvous with Rama* and, ultimately, is a greater betrayal. The Indian-ness of the protagonist is built up only to be discarded in favor of an American-ness. That Mahasamatman would rather go by Sam is played to good comic effect, but it also indicates a preference for American individualist and democratic ideals rather than Indian ideals of spirituality and mysticism (even though both are stereotypes). Contrasted to the Westernized protagonist Sam are characters such as Yama, the god of death, who is represented as scheming and devious. None of the other characters evince any desire to take on popular American names.

I have focused on the two works above partly because those were the novels that I happened to come across, but also because Indian characters rarely appear in science fiction, and when they do, they do so as part of the undifferentiated masses. The advent of cyberpunk with its focus on the complete domination of the economics and politics of first world nations by wealthy multi-national corporations, combined with a shift of power toward the third world, may have raised hopes of a more sophisticated representation of India and Indians. The move eastward, however, skipped Africa, the Middle East, and India altogether. It might be more accurate to say that the attention of cyberpunk writers moved West across the Pacific and came to rest on the shores of Japan. The rise of Japan and the Far East is hardly surprising given the prominence of Japanese economics, interest in computers and artificial intelligence, and a tradition of anime that offers both aesthetic and thematic appeal. Japan appears as a dynamo in comparison to the U.S. during the 1980s and into the 1990s, when cyberpunk writers such as William Gibson, Neal Stephenson, and Bruce Sterling give birth to the new genre.

Of course, many of the Orientalist and imperialist tropes that had structured the representation of other peoples and other lands come into play in the cyberpunk Far East. The western characters have their adventures in the exotic playground and the natives are a faceless mass in William Gibson's *Neuromancer* (1984). Neal Stephenson's often wonderfully inventive, comic and satiric *Snow Crash* (1992) has a number of Asian characters. The story's main protagonist is a young hacker and sometime pizza delivery boy named Hiro Protagonist who is of mixed descent (African American father and Korean mother) and favors a katana. Ng is a Vietnamese weapons designer whose body has been so damaged during the helicopter evacuation from Saigon that he has built a large armored truck as an extension of his body. One of the more successful sovereign franchises in the decrepit U.S. is named Mr. Lee's of Greater Hong Kong. Despite the presence of these characters, the action turns around the refugee masses that are coagulating around the aircraft carrier "raft" of L. Bob Rife. In addition to Hiro running around with a sword, Mr. Lee speaks broken English, the refugees are mindless subjects of Rife's manipulations with pockets of anarchic piraticism, and Mr. Ng can only function as a cyborg.

Greta Aiyu Niu's insightful article, "Techno-Orientalism, Nantechnology, Posthumans, and Post-Posthumans in Neal Stephenson's and Linda Nagata's Science Fiction," extends postcolonial and anti-Orientalist discussions of the stereotyping at work to an element crucial to science fiction: the relationship between technology and its producers and users. She defines techno-Orientalism broadly as a "practice of ascribing, erasing, and/or disavowing relationships between technology and Asian peoples and subjects" (74). While the hyphenated word serves as a useful marker to designate a new arena of postcolonial concern, her usage suggests a dimension unseen by conventional postcolonial criticism. In her analysis of the cyberpunk fiction of Stephenson and Nagata, techno-Orientalism "ignores the history and constructions of relationships between Asian people and technology, particularly those deemed emerging or revolutionary" (74). Techno-Orientalism could be seen as a particular kind of negation—a negation of modernity.

India, along with the non-West in general, has a bit of an issue with modernity. Depicted by Orientalist notions of Indian mysticism as other-worldly and spiritual, Indians have had a difficult time being perceived and thus represented by others as having any competence or interest in the material, technological, or scientific. Indians are seen to be especially lacking in any technical graces when compared with the Japanese. As we know, these cultural biases change over time. It was not too long ago, for example, that Westerners thought of the Japanese as lazy. Ha-Joon Chang sums up nicely the change in perception of a nation's people and culture as an outcome of their technical and economic capability: "a century ago, the Japanese were lazy rather than hardworking; excessively independent-minded rather than loyal 'worker ants'; emotional rather than inscrutable; light-hearted rather than serious; living for today instead of considering the future" (170). Chang illustrates his point more strongly by citing an example from within the West of a cultural disappointment in the expectation of a modernized sensibility (and, it is not the Irish). Some time before the Japanese, "a century ago, the Germans were [considered] indolent rather than efficient; individualistic rather than co-operative; emotional rather than rational; stupid rather than clever; dishonest and thieving rather than law-abiding; easy-going rather than disciplined" (170).

The example of Germany as a nation and culture ill-suited to be a modernized country is particularly jarring because of the conflation of modernity and the West. The West considers itself modern because its countries sport a rationalized and industrial economy with a sober and democratic polity invested in technological innovation and scientific research. Still, the stereotypical understanding operates at various levels that the set of economic policies needed to create particular opportunities and industrial capacities which then generate particular conditions of work and industry are causally connected to the cultural superiority of the West. The postcolonial response to this confusion has been to tease it into two strands: "modernity [as] a feature of the Enlightenment and its aftermath, and therefore a specific event in world history," and modernity as a "set of values and attributes (public reasoning, democratic debates, religious heterodoxy, and so on) engendered by historical events not necessarily limited to the Enlightenment" (Mishra 316). To be sure, the second strand has the greater explanatory power in clarifying the reactions and counterreactions to Enlightenment values in post-Independence India.

Since its independence from the British in 1947, India has had two broad phases: secular and fundamentalist. Mapped onto and overlapping the secular phase is a period of protectionist economic policies combined with a top-down management directed by the government, and overlaying the fundamentalist phase is a period of neo-liberal economic policies with a government less interested in promoting workers' rights and more interested in the rights of corporations. Many regard the election of the conservative fundamentalist Bharatiya Janata Party (BJP) government as the watershed moment between the two phases.

It seems to me that postcolonial stances toward technology and science are built on a few arguments: that technology belongs to the West and is therefore an imposition of imperialist thought and practice, so the recuperation of native technology necessitates a true decolonization; that native values can transform alien technology; that native values give rise to native technology; and finally, that technology goes beyond cultural identity in its universality. Meera Nanda, one of the very few critics who assumes that technology and science are not matters of culture-specific understandings, argues that a confluence of postmodern and postcolonial critiques of science and modernity along with Hindu nationalism makes it possible for fundamentalist Hindus to turn to "scientific" support for their patriarchal and chauvinist attitudes. The defining spirit of independent postcolonial India has not been a critical Enlightenment but cultural nationalism. As Nanda writes,

> Anti-colonial nationalist fervor saw to it that rational critique of Hindu metaphysics, inspired by the introduction of modern scientific discourse by the British colonists and missionaries, quickly gave way to reinterpreting scientific reason itself into Hindu metaphysical terms.... The naturalism and skepticism of modern science was declared to be either already contained in the Vedic literature, or

declared to be of secondary status as compared to the ultimate spiritual truths of Vedanta. (*Breaking* xiv)

Science-fictional treatments of India should be aware of this general trajectory of contemporary history if they are not to repeat the Orientalist discourses of the past. The SF under consideration by an outsider, Ian McDonald, manages for the most part to envision how an India some years from now might look, but only if much of its particular relationship to technology and of technology's cultural embeddedness is set aside. The SF by those writing from within India, Anuradha Marwah, Manjula Padmanabhan, and Rimi Chatterjee trace a much more direct line between India's particular present and potential future.

The Novels

Ian McDonald's *River of Gods* (2004) and *Cyberabad Days* (2009) are SF works set in a future India with primarily Indian characters. *River of Gods* won the 2004 British Science Fiction Award and the collection *Cyberabad Days* contains one story that was a Hugo nominee ("The Little Goddess," 2006) and another that won a Hugo ("The Djinn's Wife," 2007). *River of Gods* is an exploration of India one hundred years after its independence from Britain. Set in 2047, the India of McDonald's novel is a tumultuous mix of all the usual markers of Indian-ness with the added dimension of AIs, robots, and bioengineering. I have been a fan of McDonald's fiction for years and was excited by his turning toward India; I was also filled with trepidation. On the one hand, I did not want to find stereotypes of either India or Indians; on the other hand, I did not want to find stereotypical SF stories with the white characters or alien characters swapped out for brown characters.

What I found at first was promising; his Indian characters refer to the Ganga River not by its anglicized name, the Ganges, but as Ganga. A small thing perhaps, but many get it wrong. McDonald also gets right the combination of religiosity and commerce that marks the Ganga and will most likely be only exacerbated in the future. The river hosts naked sadhus, street kids, and pious pilgrims on the shore and incessant traffic on the bridge, with power plants not far from shore.

A small information dump tells the reader that this version of the city of Varanasi on the banks of the river Ganga is about to be rebuilt into New Sarnath, the capital of the newly formed nation of Bharat. India has not survived its first hundred years of Independence intact. To make matters worse, a dam upstream, combined with a three-year-old drought, has reduced the Ganga to a trickle in places, and the population mobilizes to do something against the Bangladeshis who will not share the water from the iceberg they have captured to solve their drinking water shortages. McDonald convincingly extends into the future the various resource pressures India faces now. A wide variety of characters and stories fill the novel. An Indian family conducts research into alternative energy that promises a limitless, nearly free, and non-polluting power source. Another major storyline involves a couple of Americans on the trail of sentient AIs they may have helped to develop and an Indian civil servant determined to make sure AIs on the verge of self-awareness are terminated. Most of the characters seem to escape the anthropological urge, and I find much to admire and enjoy in McDonald's novel. Unfortunately, the narrative voice too frequently sounds like a tourist.

The burning building in which Indian computer programmers are caught in a crossfire between the AI cop and the rogue AIs smells of vindaloo, the Indian meat dish that is perhaps the most stereotypical of Indian food in England after curry. The rich businessman, researcher, and father decides, contrary to any signs given to his family, to take on the orthodox Hindu life-path of renouncing all worldly attachments and going in search of peace and wisdom at the last stage of his life. His King Lear-like act forces his ne'er-do-well son to set aside his stand-up comic aspirations and come home to look after the business. In imitation of cyberpunk tropes, the AIs reach sentience and take on avatars. McDonald proves himself better than less aware writers by having the avatars become Bollywood media stars, but the pull of the stereotype is too strong and Indian mythology is not to be denied: the Indian civil servant, colloquially called a Krishna Cop, and the software countermeasures he uses against the AIs, appear to him as appropriate gods and goddesses.

The Krishna Cop, Mr. Nandha, is one of the more complex characters. He yearns to give his wife everything she wants but sees her as an innocent and wants to protect her from the viciousness of middle-class social climbing and grasping all around them and ends up alienating her. His strident mother-in-law diagnoses Mr. Nandha's preference for Western music and bland food as a symptom of his desire to be a hybrid, an Indian-gora (an Indian white man). Even though the reader is meant to be sympathetic to Mr. Nandha, there is some truth to the characterization as he ends up bereft of any family and is left alone at the end of the novel: an Indian equivalent of the tragic mulatto.

The constant pull of the exoticizing gaze ends up being too strong for McDonald's understanding of the intersection of science and religion in India. In both *River of Gods* and *Cyberabad Days*, science and technology remain tangential rather than transformative with the exception of two groups: the nutes and the Brahmins. The nutes seek through surgical means, neural realignments, and hormonal therapy to recreate themselves as a third sex, completely androgynous neuters. The second group are the genetically modified results of those who seek to confer the advantages of a superior intellect and long lives to their progeny. Satirically, McDonald refers to these sexually perverse and morally bankrupt children as Brahmins. Mr. Nandha calls both the AIs and the Brahmins monsters partially because he sees both as life threatening. The cultural stereotype of the Brahmin as a patriarchal elite ascetic more concerned with esoteric religious matters masking a hypocritical and venal, grasping manipulator exaggerates the SF pop culture stereotype of the stunted child genius/monster.

Patriarchal and fundamentalist expectations feature strongly in Anuradha Marwah's *Idol Love* (1999) and Manjula Padmanabhan's *Escape* (2008). Both works put science and technology at the service of an elite male ruling class, with *Escape* set in an apocalyptic landscape and *Idol Love* in a future India less radically transformed and isolated. The powerful in both novels are patriarchal elites. Those who would promote a patriarchal orthodoxy "use the vocabulary of science" in order, according to Nanda,

> to claim that the most sacred texts of Hinduism—the Vedas, the Upanishads which contain the essence of Vedic teachings (also called the Vedanta), and Advaita Vedanta—are, in fact, scientific treatises, expressing in a uniquely holistic and uniquely Hindu idiom, the findings of modern physics, biology, mathematics, and nearly all other branches of modern natural science. (*Prophets* 65)

Under the nationalist and egoistic desire not only to have the answers to all spiritual concerns but also to have and have had all the answers to all scientific concerns, sexist and patriarchal practices are recast as a rational and scientific ordering of the world.

Marwah's *Idol Love* mostly occurs in the present with the last third extending its themes into the future. Hindutva ideology, the perspective of "India for Hindus" fundamentalists, has refined the many layers of caste and class in Indian society into three, with the Brahmins at the top (the novel's Ramins), the Untouchables occupying the second position, and the spot at the bottom reserved for "traitors" (read "Muslims" and other ethnicities). A large part of the attempt at naturalizing the order is carried out through the mapping of color and stereotyped Western notions of beauty made possible by scientific advances. Women feel pressure to embody the ideals of light skin and an elongated frame through surgery and hormonal therapies. The preference for light skin comes from both a historical structuring of social worth and a more contemporary orientation toward the West. Wealth still looks outward in *Idol Love*. There is no mythological play of gods and goddesses, no *mise-en-scène* of a horrified spectator looking at the casual brutalities of poverty and pollution, no tragic in-between or hybrid figure in this future India. An ideology that puts science and technology at the service of repression rather than liberation or convenience traps the characters.

Padmanabhan's dystopian *Escape* places its characters in an India isolated from the world and controlled by a group of cloned megalomaniacs calling themselves the Generals. Women have been demonized and forcibly removed from the country. Docile subhumans grown in animal wombs provide labor needs. Padmanabhan creates characters named the Generals in rather broad strokes; they are caricatures of the misogynistic chauvinists seen in *Idol Love*. She excels in the coming to awareness of the lone young girl, Meiji, who is secretly being raised by her three "uncles" as she begins to realize that her world sees her as a sport of nature. The plot of the novel concerns an attempt by her youngest uncle, named Youngest, to get her to a free-zone where the Generals' reach is limited, and this journey chronicles both Meiji's growing awareness of her difference and the Generals' brutally effective rule. Although a number of Generals exist, only one General makes himself visible to the populace at any given time.

The General has taken the linear progression of science and technology and broken it to fit his needs. In the wasteland, roving gangs of Boy Warriors created by the General's technological resources serve to keep any adventurers in check. An old man informs Youngest and Meiji that these warriors are "mass produced like peas in a pod ... given special drinks and forced to grow overnight. Twenty years for us is five years for them. But they have only brains and muscles, bones and teeth—no experience.... Their leaders don't last more than a handful of days if their General isn't watching over them.... They blow each other up at the slightest excuse" (148). The infrastructure that existed previously has been neglected or destroyed and replaced at a preindustrial level. No necessary link exists between technological development and the future. Padmanabhan's technoscape radically differs from the one offered by an extrapolation that focuses only on the recent outsourcing of computing and call-center jobs from First World countries to Third World countries. India has gone through a technological interruption before, under colonial rule, and it may be easier for an Indian to imagine such an interruption again.

The final novel under consideration in this chapter is Rimi Chatterjee's *Signal Red* (2005). She also focuses on the patriarchal control of women and society through an appeal to science. An early dialogue in the novel between Anu and the Sanskrit scholar, who has been pressed into service to decipher ancient texts in terms of scientific secrets, reveals the scholar's conservative bent. As far as the scholar is concerned, and he has the support of a highly placed government official, ancient India had discovered all the important scientific and moral truths and had written these down in code so as not to trouble the minds of the less educated. Over the years, India's glory dims. "There is much corruption," says the scholar, "that has entered our mindset because of the unfortunate degeneration of our society in recent centuries and the entry of foreign ideas" (22). He is the very picture of the Hindu nationalist that Meera Nanda warns against. She especially faults Indian intellectuals for not having criticized such mysticisms: "This betrayal has made it easier for the religious right to present itself as the defender of the tradition, dressed up as 'alternative science,' which it claims has been unfairly rejected and willfully suppressed by the secular elite" ("Response" 148). Chatterjee's novel movingly shows the price paid by the male researchers, their wives, and the poor in the village that has been selected as a testing ground for weapons research and manufacture by a government in the thrall of patriarchal and chauvinist ideas and practices.

Spiritual Natives in a Material World

Much of what Wendy Faris says about magical realism in *Ordinary Enchantments* (2004) can be applied to SF writing, indeed the categories seem to get rather porous in most discussions. For Faris, magical realism "undermines the right to represent the world, with which Western readers and their communities have typically invested realism and which constitutes a kind of narrative authority" (133). According to Faris, magical realism disrupts realism's replication of a Western understanding of the world and itself becomes a guide to the native culture. Viewing magical realism as the representation of native worldviews continuing into the present alongside scientific worldviews not only sets up the native as the one who is both prescientific and scientific but also sets up only the European as scientific. To say that such a categorization of the native and the European is simplistic is almost unnecessary.

Faris adds that "a component of spirit in magical realism undermines many colonial paradigms, since it often operates toward the past and belief rather than toward the future and material progress" (135). Unfortunately, this exact dynamic created by the colonizer perpetuates the schizoid and repressive culture of the colony. The colonizer convinces the native that the material world is much too complicated and difficult for his or her primitive worldview, so perhaps it is for the best that the colonizer take up the burden. Decades and centuries of work have contributed to the separation of a religious East from a secular West. In *Culture and Imperialism* (1993), Edward Said finds that as the mix of the humanist tradition, Enlightenment insights, and secular anthropology spread through the West, it seems apparent that "when most European thinkers celebrated humanity or culture they were principally celebrating ideas and values they ascribed to their own national culture, or to Europe as distinct from the Orient, Africa, and even the Americas" (44). The native is enjoined to dwell on the spiritual while his or her religion also comes under attack. The native's religion becomes the sole locus of agential identity. So it may not be surprising that religion looms so large in postcolonial societies.

Magical realism helps to perpetuate the colonial schism by validating the separation of the spiritual and the mundane. And so does SF that presents India and Indians through the lens of Orientalism and exoticism. SF writing of India and Indians by outsiders, even well intentioned ones such as Ian McDonald, ultimately understands technology as a universal construct that ignores local cultural histories and praxis. The concessions made to the local culture are primarily through the most obvious of stereotypical markers such as food and religious or mythological character names. Religion is treated in India by writers such as Ian McDonald as a private spiritual practice rather than as an intricate part of daily public life that shapes technology and material life, as it is treated by writers such as Padmanabhan, Marwah, and Chatterjee.

Notes

1. Achebe's comment appears in his essay "An Image of Africa: Racism in Conrad's 'Heart of Darkness'" (1977).

2. See Northrop Frye's influential text *The Critical Path: An Essay on the Social Context of Literary Criticism* (1971), where he discusses "Marxist progressive myths" in dystopian terms (88).

Works Cited

Achebe, Chinua. "An Image of Africa: Racism in Conrad's *Heart of Darkness*." 1977. *Heart of Darkness*. 4th ed. Ed. Paul B. Armstrong. New York: Norton, 2006. 336–49. Print.

Basu, Sriparna. "Passionate Fictions: Horizons of the Exotic and Colonial Self-Fashioning in Mircea Eliade's *Bengal Nights* and Maitreyi Devi's *Na Hanyate*." *Genders* 34 (2001): n. pag. Web. 9 July 2012.

Chang, Ha-Joon. *Bad Samaritans: The Myth of Free Trade and the Secret History of Capitalism*. New York: Bloomsbury, 2007. Print.

Chatterjee, Rimi. *Signal Red*. New Delhi: Penguin, 2005. Print.
Clarke, Arthur C. *Rendezvous with Rama*. 1972. New York: Bantam, 1990. Print.
Faris, Wendy B. *Ordinary Enchantments: Magical Realism and the Remystification of Narrative*. Nashville: Vanderbilt UP, 2004. Print.
Frye, Northrop. *The Critical Path: An Essay on the Social Context of Literary Criticism*. Bloomington: Indiana UP, 1971. Print.
Huggan, Graham. *The Postcolonial Exotic: Marketing the Margins*. London: Routledge, 2001. Print.
Marwah, Anuradha. *Idol Love*. New Delhi: Ravi Dayal, 1999. Print.
McDonald, Ian. *Cyberabad Days*. London: Gollancz, 2009. Print.
———. *River of Gods*. New York: Simon & Schuster, 2004. Print.
Menon, Anil. *The Beast with Nine Billion Feet*. New Delhi: Young Zubaan, 2009. Print.
Mishra, Sudesh. "News from the Crypt: India, Modernity, and the West." *New Literary History* 40.2 (2009): 315–344. Print.
Nanda, Meera. *Breaking the Spell of Dharma and other essays*. New Delhi: Three Essays, 2002. Print.
———. *Prophets Facing Backward: Postmodern Critiques of Science and Hindu Nationalism in India*. New Brunswick: Rutgers UP, 2003. Print.
———. "Response to my Critics." *Social Epistemology* 19.1 (2005): 147–191. Print.
Niu, Greta Aiyu. "Techno-Orientalism, Nanotechonolgy, Posthumans, and Post-Posthumans in Neal Stephenson's and Linda Nagata's Science Fiction." *MELUS* 33.4 (2008): 73–96. Print.
Padmanabhan, Manjula. *Escape*. London: Picador India, 2008. Print.
Said, Edward. *Culture and Imperialism*. New York: Random House, 1993. Print.
Spurr, David. *The Rhetoric of Empire: Colonial Discourse in Journalism, Travel Writing, and Imperial Administration*. Durham: Duke UP, 1993. Print.
Zelazny, Roger. *Lord of Light*. Garden City: Doubleday, 1967. Print.

"PERPETUAL WAR"
Korean American Speculative Fiction, Militarized Technogeometries, and Yoon Ha Lee's "Wine"

■ ■ ■

STEPHEN HONG SOHN

A question I was posed recently got me thinking: what exactly is *Korean* about Korean American speculative fictions and associated cultural productions? To construct some answers, I began by examining what the terrain of Korean American SF looks like in its current form.[1] A natural starting point is Chang-rae Lee's *On Such a Full Sea* (2014), which stands arguably as the best-known example of a Korean American SF text. But even in that novel's case, the most prominent character is of Chinese descent. Certainly, Lee's work dovetails with a longer genealogy of techno-Orientalist depictions in which China looms as a fierce global economic competitor, one that threatens the primacy of the United States as world leader. Not surprisingly, China also appears as a crucial national nexus for other Korean American SF writers, as evidenced by works such as Cathy Park Hong's *Engine Empire* (2012) and Heinz Insu Fenkl's *Cathay* (2007).[2] Hong's *Engine Empire* incorporates China as a pivotal example of rapid modernization and the colonial impulses that are necessarily intertwined with industrialization and expansion. Fenkl's *Cathay*, a mixed-genre work, explores Orientalism from a variety of contexts, discussing, for example, *The Cantos of Ezra Pound* (1970), classic Chinese poetry, and Western fairytales as seen through the lens of Eastern cultural elements and signifiers.

On Such a Full Sea, *Engine Empire*, and *Cathay* are oriented toward an adult reading audience, but Korean American SF writers have made their biggest publication milestones in the young adult (YA) paranormal genres. As noted above, most of these writers do not include Korean or Korean American contexts in any explicit or sustained ways in their fictional worlds. Renée Ahdieh's Rose and Dagger series, for instance, reimagines *One Thousand and One Nights* with its requisite Near Eastern contexts. Lydia Kang's *Control* (2013) and its sequel *Catalyst* (2015) involve a group of humans who possess superpowers but who are targeted for their genetic abnormalities and their fantastic abilities. Gabrielle Zevin's Birthright trilogy is set in an alternate reality version of New York City.[3] And Kendare Blake's *Anna Dressed in Blood* (2011) and its sequel *Girl of Nightmares* (2012) are both told from the first person perspective of Cas Lowood, a ghost hunter, who must vanquish a specter who seems to operate with a different set of ethics than the other more dangerous spirits he's encountered in the past.

Of the YA writers, Linda Sue Park, E. C. Myers, and Ellen Oh engage the most direct Korean depictions in their paranormal-oriented speculative fictions. Though Park is best known for her realist conventions in children's fictions,[4] *Archer's Quest* (2006) and *Forest of Wonders* (2016) illustrate her command of fantasy tropes. *Forest of Wonders* offers little in the way of Korean contexts or cultural signifiers, but in *Archer's Quest* a legendary figure from premodern Korea finds himself stuck in the fictional world's present day. The protagonist, a young Korean American, must help the titular archer return to the correct temporality. E. C. Myers's *Fair Coin* (2012) and sequel *Quantum Coin* (2012) boast a significant character of half-Korean descent and stand as prominent deviations from these other examples, but the ethnicity of this character is more incidental to the plot, which focuses squarely on alternate realities.

The most sustained focus on Korea in YA fictions appears in Ellen Oh's Dragon King Chronicles trilogy. Her work is perhaps the best route of entry into finally answering the pesky question about how Korea comes to be instituted, imagined, and depicted in SF. In a work like *Prophecy* (2013), the first of the series, Korea stands a little bit out of focus. Oh explains that the vagueness of the work is related in part to the problem of historical record, which is especially spotty in its documentation of premodern Korea.[5] Even with some detailed research and embedding of ethnic place names and cultures (e.g., the kingdom of Hansong), Oh complicates the realist equation by including otherworldly creatures hailing from a genealogy linked more closely to fantasy fiction. But what is most crucial about Oh's novel and how it contributes to a larger understanding of Korean American SF is its devotion to a militarized fictional world. Kira, the protagonist of the trilogy, is tasked with a rather large burden: to fulfill a prophecy, while repelling endless hordes of demons, and to finally unite the fragmented kingdom. Oh's work is catalyzed by large action sequences in all three novels, as Kira must use her combat skills to survive and to complete her epic quest.

Oh's trilogy and other allied Korean American SF works—including Yoon Ha Lee's short story "Wine" (2014), which is the focus of this chapter—depict Korea as a geographical location, setting, and cultural landscape defined by territorial incursions, military violence, and outright war. In Cathy Park Hong's *Dance Dance Revolution* (2007), for example, Korea is referenced directly through a lyric figure's association with the Kwangju uprising, a democratic movement that was violently suppressed by internal military forces. Minsoo Kang's *Of Tales and Enigmas* (2006) incorporates Korea into its fictional worlds both directly and circuitously. For instance, the story "Hwansang of Munmyeong" primarily uses places (e.g., "the district of Junggu" (49)) and ethnic names (e.g., the story's title) to suggest the fictional world's correlation with Korean geographies and cultures; the stories in the book's final section, "Stories from an Imaginary Homeland," involve ghosts and are set in Korea. Most important for our purpose here, however, is that the majority of pieces in Kang's collection cohere around military cultures and contexts, with kingdoms in peril, sentries guarding a border point, or empires in conflict. Similarly, "Ghostweight" from Yoon Ha Lee's *Conservation of Shadows* (2013) is described by the author as a story influenced by "Japanese colonialism and Korean history."[6] Similar to Oh's trilogy and the earlier stories in Kang's collection (primarily from the first section), Lee relies on vaguely ethnic place and character names to imply a potential East Asian or Korean geography. But the story's plot ultimately revolves around the main character's quest of vengeance against the military forces that devastated her home world of Rhaion.

Thus are we getting closer to one answer to our question of what is *Korean* about Korean American SF: some key publications in Korean American SF operate with a common defining feature I denote as *militarized technogeometries*. In such speculative fictions, the presence of and references to soldiers, armies, battles, skirmishes, casualties, bombings, and associated entities, events, and structural forces become crucial to the ways that Korea comes into more sustained focus within the narrative, even if such a focus is more elliptical in its construct. These cultural productions embed the technologies of warfare as a key component to the formation and the development of territorial disputes and conflicts that necessarily involve tactical decisions, mathematical calculations, and biopolitical discourses. At the same time, these Korean American writers embed contexts and elements that exceed the bounds of realism, employing common tropes of SF as the term is most broadly defined. Consequently, to engage and to read militarized technogeometries, we must attend to (1) the ways that Korea remains ever under the peril of territorial dissolution; (2) the nature of biopolitics in the context of battle and invasion, especially with respect to efficiency in the production of violence, death, and conquest; and (3) how such themes work their direct or elliptical routes into Korean American SF.

But why would Korean American writers of SF be so invested in the link between Korea, SF, and such militarized technogeometries? We can look to the work of scholars and academics of Korean history and culture to hazard our answer.

> Strategically located at a peninsular tip of the East Asian continent, Korea has long been a pawn of contention between its two powerful neighbors, China and Japan. From the earliest recorded history, the Korean people have fought fiercely to maintain their independence in the face of multiple invasions by Mongols, Manchurians, Han Chinese and Japanese pirates and samurais. The sum total of these invasions may qualify Korea as the most oft-invaded territory in the world. (G. Lee 108)

Lee's use of the phrase "strategically located" is essential to Korea's history of many inter-empire, inter-kingdom, and international conflicts precisely because its rough boundary points and geographical layout make it a crucial "intersection of land and sea with significant military potential" (S. Lee 4). To possess any influence or power over Korean land, then, becomes a potential matter of territorial conquest in East Asia as a region. Of course, in terms of American culture, Korea is often invoked through the ambivalent framing of the so-called forgotten war, which ended in an infamous stalemate and resulted in the construction of the Korean peninsula's Demilitarized Zone (DMZ).

My admittedly unwieldy phrase *militarized technogeometries* also riffs on Seungsook Moon's scholarship (2005), as her work explores a period in South Korean history following the 1953 armistice (17–43). Though the level of militarization that the nation-state at first demanded has waned amid the shift to a more democratized form of governance, the country nevertheless stands committed to the presence of robust internal defense forces and organizations, while sustaining and cultivating international alliances no doubt desired for the perceived support they might provide to maintaining territorial integrity and sovereignty. The border between North and South Korea has been described as "among the most heavily fortified borders in the world, with both sides ready to launch into full-scale war at a moment's notice" (S. Kim 382). Christine Hong further notes that "although China recalled all its forces from North Korea within half a decade, the United States to this day still stations 28,500 troops and operates roughly 100 military installations south of the demilitarized zone (DMZ)" (597). Ever vigilant, South Korea stands at the ready in a state of "perpetual war" (Christine Hong 598), especially as international discourse continues to frame North Korea as a rogue state intent on inciting World War III. And of course, military service remains mandatory for both North Korean and South Korean men. As of 2015, North Korean policy now requires mandatory military service for its women.

Thus, we can understand Korean American SF through its militarized technogeometries precisely because of these historical and social contexts in which Korea materializes through its relationships to perpetual war. Works such as Oh's Dragon King Chronicles and Kang's *Of Tales and Enigmas* follow more closely the conventions of fantasy fictions, especially in the emphasis on magic and feudal terminology. Lee's *Conservation of Shadows* and stories within it like "Ghostweight" and "The Battle of Candle Arc" might more aptly be described as space operas, with the requisite galaxy-trotting and battle sequences set among the stars. From far back in the premodern era in Oh's and Kang's publications to well into the future in Lee's brutalizing tomorrows, ones still filled with battles and imperial edicts, Korean history and time as evoked by SF is haunted by this specter of "perpetual war."

But now I shift my focus to an extended analysis of Yoon Ha Lee's "Wine." Even among the militarized technogeometries of what we can now tentatively call Korean American SF, this short story stands out for how it incorporates its central protagonist, General Loi Ruharn, who we might be able to label both as transgender (hereafter, *trans*) and as queer.[7] I use the word *might* because the fictional world does not incorporate *trans* or *queer* in its internal lexicon. Instead, Lee describes the protagonist as a "womanform soldier who lived as a man," gesturing to her status as an FTM (female-to-male) character. The other unique gendered term used in the story is *girlform*, with which Lee describes children born female. Complicating matters further is that Ruharn, who comes from lower classes, ends up the lover of a cisgender woman named the Falcon Councilor, who is part of the Council of Five, the ruling oligarchy of an isolationist world known as Nasteng. (Due to Lee's choice to identify Ruharn through a specific gender, I hereafter refer to the character using masculine pronouns.)

The gendering and class ascension of this character is especially intriguing given the dynamics of the larger corpus of Korean American SF, which has generally avoided such intersectionalities of identities and social differences. Even in a genre as flexible and expansive as SF, Lee's "Wine" surfaces as particularly anomalous in the narrative space it provides for the trans/queer protagonist, whose social difference as this "womanform soldier who lived as a man" exerts incredible pressure on how to read the narrative's critique of militarized technogeometries. Through my textual analysis, I argue that the short story ultimately renders the trans/queer subject as a figure charged with a treasonous, unpatriotic quest to mitigate the destructive biopower of military techogeometries.

Inspired, then, by diffuse connections to Korean sociohistorical circumstances related both to militarism and to trans/queer discourses, I show how the trans/queer subject must engage the militarized technogeometries undergirding Nasteng's response to invasion in order to uphold a different loyalty: to increase the odds of mass survival in the face of war. "Wine" is thus intent on describing an admittedly ambivalent but no less intriguing depiction of the trans/queer hero who must work within the confines of militarized technogeometries to enact a limited, though still revolutionary form of change. This decision is costly: the trans/queer disappears from the narrative, thus in some sense ultimately upholding the ghostliness accorded to the social deviant, the reproductively barren figure who cannot register in the imaginative terrain of Korean American SF and who certainly reminds us of his perilous state in actual Korean social contexts.

"Wine," much like Oh's Dragon King Chronicles and other previously mentioned works, never directly references Korea, but Lee's tactical use of particular vocabulary and vague historical and sociocultural details invites the reader to make a hazy connection. The fictional world of Nasteng is known for its isolationist tendencies, a characteristic that has long been associated with Korea, especially given its nickname: the Hermit Kingdom. Lee also tellingly employs colonial terminology in the description of the initial invasion sequence: "Worse than the fire was the metal: creatures of variable form and singing cilia, joining together into colonial masses that floated high above the moon's surface and dripped synthetic insects that ate geometer's traps into its substance." Later, Lee describes the brutality of these colonial masses as collectives that "did not think in words, did not recognize *negotiation* or *compromise*. They understood only heuristic target recognition and ballistic calculations" (emphasis in original). As with Lee's aforementioned "Ghostweight," then, we can see the possible influence of Japanese colonialism, especially in its necroproductive—death generative—use of biopower.[8] In other words, the "colonial masses" and their desire to find the most efficient ways to terminate Nasteng inhabitants is analogous to Japan's slaughterous imperial enterprise. Central to the story is the more generalized deployment of militarized technogeometries. Nasteng, in a manner similar to Korea, is a valuable economic, geographical, and geopolitical location tied to many invasions, armed forces occupations (both foreign and domestic), bloody battles, and problems over territorial sovereignty.

To combat invading forces, the Council of Five relies on a beacon possessed by the Falcon Councilor. This beacon calls forth two powerful beings (Ah-rep Na and an unnamed figure who accompanies her, but who seems to be her subordinate). The Council of Five brokers a deal to save Nasteng, even though it comes at a great price. These so-called saviors make two gargantuan requests: a full year's harvest of Nasteng's most precious resource, its titular wine, and trained mercenaries who will repel the colonial forces. The wine, readers eventually discover, is the commodity that the invaders are seeking. It is made through the biological properties of Nasteng's lower-class children, who are occasionally taken from their homes by figures known as the Gardeners and then hooked up to specialized plants and botanicals. The wine is so sought after because of its life-giving properties: drinkers retain their youth and, if imbibed in large-enough quantities, may reverse the aging process completely. What happens to the children in the process of harvesting remains unclear. They seem to exist in some sort of suspended animation, but more important to the story is that the conflict between Nasteng and the foreign forces is directly tied to the value of this wine.

The story moves toward its concluding arc when General Ruharn disobeys the Falcon Councilor in his attempt to mitigate the loss of what he considers to be lives of the powerless. Indeed, he breaks the Falcon Councilor's arm in a pivotal scene during which he learns about the deal the Council of Five has brokered: Nasteng's children have been given to Ah-rep Na and the unnamed being so that they can be trained as mercenaries who are then sent to battle the colonial masses. Ruharn decides he must take action to save as many lives as possible. He understands that the intermediaries are using the child mercenaries in the most rudimentary way: that the children will repel the invading forces due to sheer numbers, even if they are dying at astronomical rates because they do not know how to organize in battle. Thus, Ruharn uses some of the wine still available to reverse his aging so that he will look youthful, be taken by the intermediaries, and trained alongside the other children. He then plans to use his position to infiltrate and provide guidance to the children, thereby reducing Nasteng's casualties. It would seem his ruse is successful, as the story ends with the colonial masses being repelled, though we have no word whether Ruharn actually survives.

Lee creates an intriguing fictional world in that it shows signs of a trans/queer-positive culture. The Falcon Councilor does not mind, for instance, that Ruharn is biologically female. Indeed, she seems to take much pleasure in Ruharn's trans identity, a "minor novelty" since the Falcon Councilor had "never taken such a lover before." Others are well aware of her indiscretion with a mere commoner, but they do not act to curtail her sexual affairs. If they feel any discomfort around Ruharn's place by the Falcon Councilor's side, they do so primarily based on his class background, not his gender identification. At other instances, characters who have knowledge of his gender transition harbor no ill will against him for this fact. If we consider contemporary Korean policies concerning trans/queer individuals and their service in the military, this story already violates policies that forbid FTM soldiers from serving in any active duty post (Na 366). Rampant anti-queer sentiment within the Korean military makes it a hostile environment for anyone who reveals a trans/queer identity. In this sense, Ruharn's trajectory into the military and his eventual affair with a top governing official seems rather idyllic when compared to actual Korean social contexts.

But, at the same time, I contend that we should understand the story through its connection to contemporary discourses of trans/queer identity precisely because of the way the narrative eventually plays out. As Tari Youngjung Na notes, those who identify as trans/queer in Korea suffer multiple modes of marginalization, but one of the primary reasons for this kind of social ostracization is tied to *kungmin*, which translates roughly as "duty to the nation." *Kungmin* is defined in part by what Na identifies as compulsory reproductive heterosexuality: "To marry someone of another gender and produce an offspring is considered to be the fulfillment of one's duty as a *kungmin* in service of the nation" (360). This reproductive heterosexuality directly enforces Korean militarism because the state of perpetual war requires all citizens to be ready to defend the country in case of possible attack. Any child therefore represents a potential figure who will contribute to, participate in, or support military cultures, communities, and forces. Here, the trans/queer cannot fulfill the *kungmin* and thus stands as a figure deemed ultimately to be unpatriotic. As the trans/queer is assumed to fail in the duty of compulsory reproductive heterosexuality, he is also targeted and regulated by military policies that deny equal opportunity and protection.[9]

If the trans/queer subject is imbued with this form of treasonous subjectivity in Korean social contexts, then it becomes a productive way to reconsider "Wine" and to analyze Ruharn's self-destructive actions. Indeed, why would Ruharn, living in the lap of luxury in a cushy military position, put himself in harm's way for the lower-class children of Nasteng? To answer this question, we must return first to Ruharn's eventual ascension into the ranks of the elite. He maintains his position in large part become others assume he is the Falcon Councilor's military consort, a profession that implies a kind of prostitution: the Falcon Councilor "offered riches; she offered to buy Ruharn a commission in the Council's own army, and an adoption into a noble family; and most of all she offered a place in her bed. Ruharn wasn't sentimental about the honor of his chosen profession, although he knew what people would be saying about him." Ruharn's choice is certainly tactical because so many soldiers "died young anyway," a fate that Ruharn escapes not only because of top-notch military skills but also because he comes to the attention of the Falcon Councilor due to his gender identity. In this sense, without his trans/queerness, he would not have been noticed by this government official at all and might not even have lived to the point at which the invasion by the colonial masses begins.

His description as a "minor novelty" betrays a kind of superficial consumption practice engaged by the Falcon Councilor that necessarily marks Ruharn as a gendered or sexualized commodity, nothing more than a plaything for those in positions of power. In some sense, this depiction is not unlike actual Korean contexts in which trans/queer discourses, figures, and identities are only superficially embraced in popular culture. The androgynous aesthetic of male pop stars (Maliangkay 6–7) and the rise of Harisu, a transgender singer, model, actress, and activist (Ahn 249), do reveal a tentative opening to some dimensions of trans/queer discourses and lives. Yet these changes remain small ripples on the surface of Korean society, especially as trans/queer subjects still live in an atmosphere in which they are "harshly stigmatized" (Kim and Kim 10). In this sense, Lee's fictional world again departs from actual social contexts due to the rather commonplace acceptance of Ruharn's gender transition, but Ruharn's objectification as a trans/queer commodity is also part of the intricate web of the militarized technogeometries of the short story: the Falcon Councilor's position enables Ruharn's pivotal place in Nasteng's defense forces, however limited in their capabilities, but at the price of his gendered or sexualized conscription. He must play his part as the "minor novelty" as the Falcon Councilor's grotesque lover to come into any sustained form of social recognition. But Ruharn's participation in the militarized technogeometries of "Wine" is tied primarily to his individual choice: he sees that his position as an elite general and as the Falcon Councilor's sexual partner must be placed in comparison to the fates of the Nasteng children, whose transitions from family members to mercenaries are not so agential.

Ruharn is not meant to be depicted as an unadulterated hero. Indeed, the Falcon Councilor questions his motives for helping the children being trained as mercenaries because he never did anything when their bodies were being harvested for the wine. Only when their military service makes the children potential targets does Ruharn find their exploitation intolerable. Ruharn then deploys the military skills he possesses to train the child mercenaries. Thus, the story accrues a kind of biopolitical rhetoric in its stance that Ruharn, though flawed and certainly complicit in some ways to the systemic social inequalities undergirding Nasteng's culture, can still potentially act to reduce the casualties catalyzed by his world's militarized technogeometries. If Ruharn cannot prevent the war, he will work within its confines to effect some sort of productive change: for him, it is making sure that as many of Nasteng's children as possible will endure the battles. Tellingly, the surviving mercenary defense forces eventually turn their necroproductive power to destroy the Garden, the location where children are harvested on Nasteng to make the wine.

But the cost of Ruharn's betrayal of the Falcon Councilor is his termination from narrative materiality: as one trans/queer character stands against the biopower of an entire world's militarized technogeometries, his own survival unsurprisingly is destabilized. Though his disappearance by the story's end might be seen as a problematic reinscription of the actual social contexts that promote the ostracization of the Korean trans/queer, Lee's "Wine" reminds us to consider an individual life alongside systemic social forces that entrap and endanger multitudes in the context of militarism.

The logic of Ruharn's sacrifice, both in terms of his social positioning and narrative centrality, accrues more texture when we reconsider his final actions alongside actual Korean historical circumstances and militarisms. For instance, we can consider the conscription of the Nasteng children as a convenient analogue to what Jin-kyung Lee calls military "surrogate labor" (657) in the context of Korean history. Lee specifically references the time period in which South Korea deployed troops to Vietnam in support of the United States. Notably, these support forces were comprised of volunteers who hailed from "the rural peasant background, drawn to the economic advantages of the service, which was financed by the United States" (663). But such surrogacy and biopolitical harnessing of bodies has occurred many times, including the infamous use of Korean units in the Japanese military during the imperial period (Fujitani 17). Korean women have also historically been understood as crucial to the Japanese war effort, as they were targeted for their fertility, especially as the imperial project extended in scope and size and required more men to serve (Jin-kyung Park 215). In this case, Japanese imperial biopower draws from a pool of bodies it needs even as it marks them as inferior due to racialized, colonial differences. These various forms of military surrogacy find an elliptical relationality to Lee's fictional world, as a foreign force's presence requires tribute in the form of reproductive labor and associated battle units.[10]

If heterosexual reproductive labor has been couched in terms of duty to the nation, the *kungmin*, then how does this kind of patriotism function in the context of foreign dependence as it appears in Korean American SF? In relation to "Wine," we see that the burden of reproductive patriotism as it is funneled into the militarized technogeometries appears shouldered by the lower classes of Nasteng. Indeed, the children taken by the intermediaries come only from families of impoverished backgrounds. In this sense, biopower's bias in the context of militarized technogeometries specifically targets reproductive labor (and its associated "infant" fruits) offered by those individuals considered to be Nasteng's social detritus. Though Ruharn might be said to escape this fate when he becomes the Falcon Councilor's lover, his birth as the "girlform" child from the lower classes of the Nasteng inhabitants already marks him as someone tied to the potential of heterosexual reproductive labor, which he avoids having to perform due to his class ascension and by virtue of the gender/sexual identity of his romantic partner. Hence, Ruharn fails to uphold what we might call *Nastengian kungmin* in terms of his biological capacity to reproduce more units for his world in the time of conflict. Ruharn's awareness of his avoidance of reproductive labor becomes apparent when he visits his younger sister, whose grandchildren have been sent off to the battlefield as child mercenaries. In this sense, Ruharn reclaims his class background and his link to a biological ancestry that could have placed him at risk for heterosexual reproductive conscription.

Though Ruharn's choice to defend Nasteng by trying to train the child mercenaries suggests his loyalty to the militarized technogeometries promoted by the Council of Five, we must be reminded that the child mercenaries turn their necroproductive powers against the Council by destroying the Garden. The endgame for Ruharn is the advocacy of the lower classes of Nasteng who would have had to continue to produce children for the wine in the case that they defeated the colonial masses. To destroy the Garden means that the heterosexual reproductive labor of the lower classes might be curtailed or perhaps even terminated entirely.

In this sense, Ruharn's decision to drink the wine and reverse his aging process reveals his desire to challenge the asymmetrical nature of biopower as it marks certain bodies and lives for more perilous trajectories in the militarized technogeometries of the fictional world. In "Wine" the locus of social inequality appears related to class dynamics, associated reproductive labor, and the meaninglessness of the children's lives in the context of war. And we must remind ourselves here that though Ruharn does not find himself reproductively exploited in the context of childbearing, he nevertheless must uphold his trans/queer identity through a form of sexual conscription—borne through his romantic relationship with the Falcon Councilor—that maintains both his military and social positioning. In other words, gendered and sexual exploitation for Ruharn take on a different form, though no less tied to militarized technogeometries. Both Ruharn and the lower classes of Nasteng only achieve social recognition in the guise of war through the particular ways in which they can be exploited for gendered or sexualized properties.

As we see, "Wine's" fictional world never directly references Korean history, culture, and contexts, which places the story in good company among the other Korean American SF works briefly discussed in this chapter. Yet the story finds rhetorical traction through its diffuse connection to actual discourses concerning militarism and trans/queer identity. The story reveals the need to consider powerlessness through a multidimensional engagement of situational privilege and structural oppressions: in Nasteng, Ruharn finds some social mobility in part due to his trans/queer identity, but his ascension does not erase his connection to other figures who demand care and the right to life. If anything, his trans/queer identity charges him with a different *Nastengian kungmin*: advocacy for those whose lives as gendered or sexualized others are put at risk due to their entrapment in the militarized technogeometries of the fictional world. But the short story's conclusion is far from triumphant. Ruharn saves many lives of those forced to fight, but he may not have survived himself, thus leaving the trans/queer as a ghostly presence in the narrative space. Finally, the conflicts for Nasteng may continue, especially since its government is left in shambles and outsiders now know that its children possess unusual biological properties that can be transformed into age-defying products.

By way of this sobering ending to "Wine," we can return to the original question: what exactly is *Korean* about Korean American SF? In the fragile space of possible invasion, Korea materializes in fraught SF worlds in which war is always over the horizon, militaries ever ready to cross the border, and innovative technologies primed for maximum destruction. Perpetual war indeed.

Acknowledgments

To maintain standardization in the use of Korean names, I follow the Western practice of using the family name as the bibliographic entry point. I also standardize "first" names by leaving any second portion of a hyphenated name in the lowercase. I want to thank Cole Jack Pittman, Crystal Mun-Hye Baik, and Isiah Lavender for crucial feedback during the chaotic revision stages.

Notes

1. I use *SF* to abbreviate the catchall term *speculative fiction*. My piece is not the first to consider speculative fiction in relation to Korean American literature; one of the best explorations appears in Seo-young Chu's "Science Fiction and Postmemory Han in Contemporary Korean American Literature" (2008).

2. Hong's *Engine Empire* is a poetry collection that engages some obvious SF tropes through techno-Orientalism.

3. These represent only a sampling of YA SF works by Korean American authors. Zevin's Birthright trilogy includes *All These Things I've Done* (2011), *Because It Is My Blood* (2012), and *In the Age of Love and Chocolate* (2012).

4. Park is probably best known for her children's novel set in premodern Korean, *A Single Shard* (2001), which won the Newberry Medal.

5. For more information on the Korean contexts embedded in the Dragon King Chronicles, a series comprised of three novels including *Prophecy* (2013), *Warrior* (2013), and *King* (2015), see http://ellenoh.com/books/map-of-the-seven-kingdoms/.

6. For the full interview, see Lara and Odo.

7. "Wine," first published in *Clarkesworld* (January 2014), appears in *The Year's Best Speculative Fiction and Fantasy 2015*, ed. Rich Horton (Germantown: Prime, 2015).

8. Here, I am indebted to both Michel Foucault and Achille Mbembe in their considerations of entities (such as governing councils) that oversee the regulation of living bodies and how they can be functionalized to kill others. See Foucault 247; Mbembe 12.

9. Though some work has been completed in relation to queer and homosexual identities, lives, and practices, specific attention paid to transgender issues and genderqueer issues are scant (Koh). For more on homosexuality in Korea, see Youngshik D. Bong.

10. Even in the context of intranational military policy, specific bodies are targeted for conscription over others. Seungsook Moon notes that the mass media cast a negative light on mandatory military service in South Korea due to reported instances of "evasion and irregularities among the wealthy and the powerful" (16).

Works Cited

Ahdieh, Renée. *The Rose and the Dagger*. New York: Putnam's, 2015. Print.

———. *The Wrath and the Dawn*. New York: Putnam's, 2015. Print.

Ahn, Patty Jeehyun. "Harisu: South Korean Cosmetic Media and the Paradox of Transgendered Neoliberal Embodiment." *Discourse* 31.3 (2009): 248–72. Print.

Blake, Kendare. *Anna Dressed in Blood*. New York: TorTeen, 2011. Print.

———. *Girl of Nightmares*. New York: TorTeen, 2012. Print.

Bong, Youngshik D. "The Gay Rights Movement in Democratizing Korea." *Korean Studies* 32 (2008): 86–103. Print.

Chu, Seo-young. "Science Fiction and Postmemory Han in Contemporary Korean American Literature." *MELUS* 33.4 (2008): 97–121. Print.

Hong, Cathy Park. *Dance Dance Revolution*. New York: Norton, 2007. Print.
———. *Engine Empire*. New York: Norton, 2012. Print.
Hong, Christine. "The Unending Korean War." *positions: east asia cultures critique* 23.4 (2015): 597–617. Print.
Fenkl, Heinz Insu. *Cathay*. New Paltz: Codhill, 2007. Print.
Foucault, Michel. *Society Must Be Defended*. New York: Picador, 1997. Print.
Fujitani, Takashi. "Right to Kill, Right to Make Live: Koreans as Japanese and Japanese as Americans During WWII." *Representations* 99.1 (2007): 13–39. Print.
Kang, Lydia. *Catalyst*. New York: Dial, 2015. Print.
———. *Control*. New York: Dial, 2013. Print.
Kang, Minsoo. *Of Tales and Enigmas*. Germantown: Prime, 2006. Print.
Kim, Suk-young. "Staging the 'Cartography of Paradox': The DMZ Special Exhibition at the Korean War Memorial, Seoul." *Theatre Journal* 63.3 (2011) 381–402. Print.
Kim, Young-jin, and Tong-hyung Kim. "Gradually Accepted, Politically Invisible." *Korea Times* 21 June 2013: 10–12. Print.
Koh, Dong-yeon. "Globalizing Korean Queers? Project L(esbian), the First Exhibition of Lesbian Arts in South Korea." *Inter-Asia Cultural Studies* 14.3 (2013): 378–400. Print.
Lara, Leticia, and Odo. Interview with Yoon Ha Lee. *Sense of Wonder*, 22 April 2014. Web. 19 March 2016. <http://sentidodelamaravilla.blogspot.com/2014/04/interview-with-yoon-ha-lee.html>.
Lee, Chang-rae. *On Such a Full Sea*. New York: Riverhead, 2014. Print.
Lee, Grace. "The Political Philosophy of Juche." *Stanford Journal of East Asian Affairs* 3.1 (2003): 105–12. Print.
Lee, Jin-kyung. "Surrogate Military, Subimperialism, and Masculinity: South Korea in the Vietnam War, 1965–73." *positions: east asia cultures critique* 17.3 (2009): 655–82. Print.
Lee, Sung-chool. *The ROK-U.S. Joint Political and Military Response to North Korean Armed Provocations*. Washington: Center for Strategic and International Studies, 2011. Print.
Lee, Yoon Ha. *Conservation of Shadows*. Germantown: Prime, 2013. Print.
———. "Wine." *Clarkesworld*, January 2014. N. pag. Web. 19 March 2016.
Maliangkay, Roald Maliangkay. "The Effeminacy of Male Beauty in Korea." *Newsletter* 55 (Autumn/Winter 2010): 6–7. Print.
Mbembe, Achille. "Necropolitics." *Public Culture* 15.1 (2003): 11–40. Print.
Moon, Seungsook. "Gender, Conscription, and Popular Culture in Contemporary Korea." *The Military and South Korean Society*. Eds. Young-key Kim-Renaud, R. Richard Grinker, and Kirk W. Larsen. The Sigur Center Asia Papers no. 26. The Elliott School of International Affairs, George Washington University (2006): 15–27. Print.
———. *Militarized Modernity and Gendered Citizenship in South Korea*. 2nd Ed. Durham: Duke UP, 2005. Print.
Myers, E. C. *Fair Coin*. Amherst: Pyr, 2012. Print.
———. *Quantum Coin*. Amherst: Pyr, 2012. Print.
Na, Tari Young-jung. "The South Korean Gender System: LGBTI in the Contexts of Family, Legal Identity, and the Military." Trans. Ju Hui Judy Han and Se-Woong Koo. *Journal of Korean Studies* 19.2 (2014): 357–77. Print.

Oh, Ellen. *King*. New York: HarperTeen, 2015. Print.

———. "Map of the Seven Kingdoms." Ellen Oh, n.d. Web. 19 March 2016. <http://ellenoh.com/books/map-of-the-seven-kingdoms/>.

———. *Prophecy*. New York: HarperTeen, 2013. Print.

———. *Warrior*. New York: HarperTeen, 2013. Print.

Park, Jin-kyung. "Bodies for Empire: Biopolitics, Reproduction, and Sexual Knowledge in Late Colonial Korea." *Korean Journal of Medical History* 23 (August 2014): 203–38. Print.

Park, Linda Sue. *Archer's Quest*. New York: Houghton, 2006. Print.

———. *Forest of Wonders*. New York: HarperCollins, 2016. Print.

———. *A Single Shard*. New York: Clarion, 2001. Print.

Pound, Ezra. *The Cantos of Ezra Pound*. New York: New Directions, 1970. Print.

Zevin, Gabrielle. *All These Things I've Done*. New York: Farrar, 2011. Print.

———. *Because It Is My Blood*. New York: Farrar, 2012. Print.

———. *In the Age of Love and Chocolate*. New York: Farrar, 2012. Print.

PART TWO

Fear of a Yellow Planet

YELLOW PERILS
M. P. Shiel, Race, and the Far East Menace

■ ■ ■

AMY J. RANSOM

Born in the West Indies, but emigrating to England in 1885 where he pursued a literary career, M. P. Shiel (1865–1947) masked his own mixed racial heritage, identifying as white and English. The result of Shiel's problematic relationship with race is a body of fiction offering a "tangle of contradictions . . . in which racial denigration shades into dread of evolutionarily superior rivals and visions of progress are shaped by fears of decline" (Svitavsky 1). In particular, Shiel's three "Yellow Peril" novels—*The Yellow Danger* (1898), *The Yellow Wave* (1905), and *The Dragon* (1913), republished as *The Yellow Peril* (1929)—represent his most problematic works in relation to their representations of racial others. At the same time, however, these works tantalizingly undermine the dominant ideology of white supremacy. On the one hand, Shiel exploited developing fears in the West about the rising powers of Japan and China, depicting "Orientals" as racially inferior; on the other, as biographer Harold Billings asserts, "he saw evolution leading all races towards a human physiological blend just as he had observed in the West Indies—'a flushed brown' harmony" (*Early Years* 42).

According to Gina Marchetti, "the yellow peril [narrative] combines racist terrors of alien cultures, sexual anxieties, and the belief that the West will be overpowered and enveloped by the irresistible, dark, occult forces of the East" (2). Although he did not coin the term *Yellow Peril*, Shiel's work exploits a perception in the Anglo-American world of an impending threat from the East which fuelled this new literary sub-genre. Largely adhering to the conventions of the future war subgenre,[1] Shiel's Yellow Peril novels—like much of his work—draw on contemporary headlines (Billings, *Middle Years* 56; Wei Tchen 487), referencing directly or indirectly the opening of Japan to the West in the Meiji period (1868–1945), the Boxer Rebellion (1898–1900), the Anglo-Japanese Alliance (1902; 1905; 1911), and the Russo-Japanese war (1904–5), events at the source of Western fears of the Far East. At the same time, engaging in near future extrapolation he exploits proto-science-fictional elements in these works, speculating about the role of technology in potential East-West conflicts. After outlining Shiel's mixed-race heritage and its role in his writing career, I introduce what Ruth Mayer calls Shiel's "yellow trilogy" for readers unfamiliar with their plotlines. The body of the chapter offers the closest readings to date of these novels' engagement with race. My analysis reveals the subversive potential underlying their depictions of a sub-human and threatening Asian horde coupled with an apparent acceptance of a hierarchy of white supremacy with the English at its apex. I conclude that Shiel's conflicted attitudes about his own multi-racial background inform these works' contradictory discourses about race, including the surprising extrapolation of humanity's future *métissage* into a single brown race.

Shiel's Mixed-Race Heritage and the Yellow Peril Novels

Matthew Phipps Shiell [*sic*] was born on July 21, 1865, on Montserrat, a tiny island in the West Indies. His father, Matthew Dowdy Shiell (1824–88) was an Anglo-Irish "shop-owner, trader, shopkeeper, and lay Methodist minister" and his mother, Priscilla Ann Blake (1828–1910), was "identified as 'free' on her birth record, indicating that she was, at least to some degree, a descendent of slaves" (Billings, *Early Years* 12). Phipps's—as he preferred to be called—sister Harriet, who married a prominent black merchant on St. Kitts (Billings, *Middle Years* 102), wrote that Priscilla's mother, "Granny Blake, was I think what you call an octoroon" (Billings, *Early Years* 12). Growing up the son of a local leader, however, the light-skinned Phipps identified as white (Billings, *Early Years* 41). The ambitious young man soon moved to London and published his first stories in the periodical press in the late 1880s and 1890s (Billings, *Early Years* 31, 125). While he admitted his tropical origins, he attributed his dark eyes and wavy hair to "a dash of Spanish blood" in later interviews (Billings, *Middle Years* 143–44).

At the turn of the twentieth century, he was at the height of his popularity, with "*The Yellow Wave* . . . on best-seller lists in August and September of 1898" and ten reprints over the next few years (Billings, *Middle Years* 80).

Published a little more than a decade after Kaiser Wilhelm II purportedly coined the term in 1885 (Métraux 29), Shiel's first Yellow Peril novel, *The Yellow Danger: or, What might happen if the division of the Chinese empire should estrange all European countries* (1898), was a catalysing work in the developing perception of an Asian threat in Great Britain (Hashimoto 52–53). Yorimitsu Hashimoto describes it as "the archetypal yellow peril novel in Britain" (64). The second novel in the cycle, *The Yellow Wave* (1905), directly referenced the recent Russo-Japanese War (1904–5), which itself inspired Jack London's essay "The Yellow Peril" (1904) and story "The Unparalleled Invasion" (1906). Shiel's work thus performed in the UK what London's did in the U.S.,[2] establishing the Asian villain, precursors for Sax Rohmer's more famous Dr. Fu Manchu.[3] The longevity of such fears led to the republication of Shiel's 1913 novel, *The Dragon*, in 1929 as *The Yellow Peril*, also a sign of widespread acceptance of the term itself.

Shiel's three Yellow Peril novels are strikingly similar, offering variations on a theme: an Asian villain secretly plots to undermine peace in Europe; with the European powers at war amongst themselves, he plans to step in and take over the world. A romantic subplot allows for the eroticization of racial tensions. In spite of the villain's exceptional intelligence and determination, supported by seemingly endless hordes of Chinese combatants, a conflicted (generally white) hero steps in to save the white race, sometimes with the help of science-fictionally advanced technology. The following brief synopses contextualize the analysis that follows.

The Yellow Danger (1898)

Set only a year into the future (the date March 16, 1899, is mentioned), Shiel draws upon Great Britain's contemporary climate of fear as his omniscient third-person narrator asserts: "that phrase, 'The Yellow Danger,' had become quite common in every one's ears" (*YD*).[4] The novel's invention of the Westernized Asian nemesis, Dr. Yen How, who sows discord in Europe and then attacks with a combined Japanese and Chinese force supports such anxieties. As the point farthest west, but also because of her own merits, Great Britain represents a linchpin in the success or failure of Yen How's white genocide. Fortunately, an English Everyman hero, John Hardy, eventually rises to the rank of Admiral of the English Navy. He counters with his own genocidal plot, unleashing germ-warfare via a plague seeded in Asian capitals with infected prisoners of war. Although the complete erasure of the "yellow races" fails, Shiel's novel allows the ultimate militaristic fantasy to play out as the Continent of Europe was British territory. This meant that all Asia and Africa were British too. And if Europe, Asia, and Africa, then, beyond doubt, America also; for no two Powers, one so vast, the other so comparatively small, could coexist side by side without a formal or informal acknowledgment of the suzerainty of the greater by the smaller. The sceptre of Britain, therefore, stretched from pole to pole, and from the river to the ends of the earth. (*YD*)

The Yellow Danger thus reflects "the primary fantasy of global supremacy, with the Anglo-Saxon left as supreme ruler" found in late Victorian British fiction (Worth 100), and establishes the tropes of the Yellow Peril narrative.

The Yellow Wave (1905)

Once again Shiel draws on current headlines; the novel remains coy about the exact year but opens on January 11, "when the war was a year old," a war clearly coded as the Russo-Japanese War of 1904–5. The novel's secret history plotline stages an Asian nemesis's attempt to escalate that conflict into a pan-European war, opening the door for conquest by a secret pan-Asian alliance. The plot's ultimate failure leads to the end of the Sino-Japanese War as history wrote it. This time, a Japanese mastermind, Baron M__, is aided by a tightly knit secret society called the Tiger Hunters, which includes two Orientalized white men. The virulence of Shiel's construction of an evil Asian menace to the West and the need to use ultimate force to combat it appears to evolve over time, however, as he depicts an Asian hero in the form of the pacifist Yoshio, Baron M__'s son. Furthermore, the novel's militaristic plotline is largely overtaken by the extraordinary Romeo-and-Juliet romance between Yoshio and the novel's Russian villain's daughter, who is disguised as a soldier. Although it lacks the same level of racial hatreds expressed in *The Yellow Danger* because of its Japanese hero and focus on the lovers' narrative, Shiel nonetheless recounts with relish the details of the inner workings of an Asian terrorist cell whose aims appear to justify Western fears as they, like Dr. Yen How and Li Ku Yu in his third Yellow Peril novel, also seek Asian supremacy at the planetary level.

The Dragon (1913), a.k.a. *The Yellow Peril* (1929)

Returning to the earlier device of an Asian villain pitted against a heroic Englishman, Shiel's third and final instalment in the "yellow peril" cycle raises the stakes. Here the Asian genius Li Ku Yu (which translates as "Sky Blue" according to Shiel) meets none other than Edward, Prince of Wales, while both are at school. Although this "Teddy" may have been modelled on the contemporary prince of that name (the future Edward VIII was born in 1894 and would have been almost twenty at the book's original publication), Shiel distances his character from this model in a number of ways, most clearly by naming him as the son of Prince John (there has, of course, been no King of England by that name since the twelfth and thirteenth centuries) and a commoner. The youths leave school and Li Ku Yu returns to China and Japan, meteorically rising to power and successfully engineering a Sino-Japanese alliance. In the meantime, Teddy continues his training to assume the British crown, but falls in love with a commoner and is secretly married (echoing Yoshio in *The Yellow Wave*). He rises to the challenge of the Asian threat, saving England with the help of the science-fictional inventions—an air-boat and a powerful weapon called the Redlike Ray—of his school-days friend Richard Chinnerly. This novel introduces a Mata Hari-like Asian seductress in the form of Li Ku Yu's beautiful agent, Oyone, sent to distract Chinnerly from his work.

Thus, all largely variants on a theme, Shiel's yellow peril novels stage world-scale military conflicts inspired by race hatreds. As we shall see in the following analysis, Shiel's characters frequently spout the truisms of the racist racial ideologies of the day, which demonize Europe's racial others and attempt to establish a hierarchy of races with the white man at its apex. And yet, a close reading reveals a certain ambivalence to that ideology, as Shiel allows Asian characters to express their own opinions about whites, going so far at times as to suggest the abolition of the white race either by genocide or eventual dilution through racial mixing.

Racialist Discourses in the Yellow Peril Novels

Shiel's ambivalence about his own mixed racial heritage translates into a bizarre mixture of regurgitations of contemporary pseudo-scientific racialist theories, beginning with Cesare Lombroso's anthropometric criminology and the developing field of eugenics.[5] The "racist terrors" expressed in his work link it to contemporary racialist theories of degeneration and its roots in the Decadent and Symbolist writing with which Shiel was associated earlier in his career (Keep 29–30; Svitavsky; Worth 99–101). His fictional works indicate an apparent acceptance of the supposed hierarchy of races, include outright hateful descriptions of racialized others, and express fears of racial degeneration. At the same time, however, they also allow for the erasure of the white race from the planet, either through genocide or through the future "browning" of humanity through racial mixing, subversive, if not visionary attitudes for their time. In the novels' present tense, the overt message is nonetheless that within the hierarchy of races, "the brown does not count" (*YD*) and only the yellow can rival the white. Drawing from Darwin's *The Descent of Man* (1871) (Sharp 91–92), Arthur de Gobineau's *The Inequality of Human Races* (1853–55), and Max Nordau's *Degeneration* (1892) among other contemporary texts (Glover 52–54), Yellow Peril fictions, including Shiel's three novels, nonetheless envision the possibility that the white race may be forced from its presumed position at the apex of human development. This very notion, then, subverts the dominant discourses of white supremacy upon which contemporary colonialist movements were premised and whose wisdom is questioned in Shiel's novels, thus aligning these otherwise reactionary fictions with the interrogation of dominant ideologies of race that twenty-first century critics like De Witt Douglas Kilgore and Stephen Hong Sohn offer.[6]

Hierarchies of Race and the Racial Origins of Human Conflict

The Yellow Danger introduces the notion that subtends all three of these novels, namely that global politics essentially mirror a racial struggle for survival of the fittest, as Dr. Yen How explains to a potential French ally:

> "Look forward five hundred, a thousand years, Marquis, and what do you see?" answered Yen How. "Is it not this?—the white man and the yellow man in their death-grip, contending for the earth. The white and the yellow—there are no others. The black is the slave of both; the brown does not count." (*YD*)

Yen How parrots contemporary theories about racial hierarchy, also exposing the particular roots of white anxiety at this time: the so-called yellow race is the only potential rival for white planetary supremacy. White heroes hold similar beliefs, as seen in the *Yellow Peril*. Shiel's fictional Queen mother raises her son to fear racial others, in particular Asians, warning that "the only man who can outwit a Jew in business is a Chinaman—don't forget. And, then, there are so many of them" (*YP* 10). She thus plants the seeds in the mind of England's future monarch of belief in the Yellow Peril from his childhood. Shiel draws on two phenomena intensifying this threat at the turn of the twentieth century: Meiji Japan's opening to Western technology and the European realization of the sheer numbers of the Asian masses (coupled with fears about declining birth rates and decadence in the West). As Shiel's characters assert: "the order of the day in China, and especially in Japan, was Western modernity" (*YD*), and "in the world to-day there are 408,000,000 Christians and—mark the figures—1,004,000,000 non-Christians" (*YD*). With superior numbers and advanced technology, Asian powers now represent a threat to European imperial aspirations.

Shiel's fiction intensifies such threats by depicting them not as mere struggles over territory and resources, but as genocidal in intent. Aaron Worth argues that "the theme of racial exitinction, even explicit genocide, is another characteristic feature of future-war fiction" (100), citing his Yellow Peril novels as examples. All three works devote extensive passages to the description of battles, in particular sea battles, and introduce behind-the-scenes espionage intrigues. They suggest something sinister in Asians' purported taste for intrigue, as their villains rely on secret plots to turn Europeans against each other, rather than honest, straightforward conflicts: "'We wish the white races killed,' answered Yen; 'well, there are two ways, are there not? We might kill them ourselves—that, you say, is nonsense. The other way is to get them to kill one another'" (*YD*).

Although in the logic of these novels, one attempted genocide deserves another, it is significant that John Hardy's plan to exterminate the yellow races fails, reinforcing a sense of British moral superiority. *The Yellow Danger* concludes that "after all, John Hardy's idea of the extinction of the yellow man never came to pass. Hardy was wise, but Nature is wiser. The yellow man is in the Scheme: And since God suffers him to be, He, too, is God's minister, and labours for some good" (*YD*). Here, although God has a plan for all of humanity, he nonetheless seems to side with the British who can now dominate the entire planet. Shiel's popular novels thus both fuel and respond to the perceived threat of the Yellow Peril with their repeated shoring up of the dominant ideology of white superiority that subtended the civilizing mission of European imperial pretensions.

White Right: Reinforcing the Dominant Ideology

Assertions of white superiority appear frequently in the novels, most often through positive descriptions of the British character. They participate in Benedict Anderson's notion of the "imagined community," not only as they define whiteness in opposition to yellow, but as they construct Britishness itself as a race, something deeper and more profound than the mere political structure of the nation. In *The Yellow Peril*, while still a youth, the Prince of Wales warns his antagonist: "the boys and men of this land can't be conquered" (19). The third-person narrator of *The Yellow Danger* frequently lauds "that strong and large bounty of our race," assigning the island kingdom a manifest destiny to rule the world from the seas. England remains the last bastion of freedom after Dr. Yen How's hordes overrun the Continent:

> By the end of July, one thing at least had been clearly hinted to the whole of Europe: that if those English could not write music, they could work; if they could not make pretty things, they certainly could fight; if they were not "élégants," they at least possessed the knack, and the secret, and the sword of the Conqueror. "La morgue Britannique !" "la raideur Britannique!"—it was not, then, after all, a mere insolence of semi-savages, but a pride based on a genuine supremacy of racial value and valour. (*YD*)

Placing this admiration for the British character in the mouths of the French, the narrator further validates such assertions. Similarly, in *The Yellow Peril* we read that "we here know that the French are more intelligent and mentally liberated than we, the Germans more organising and orderly; yes, but there are certain world-ideals of conscience, of generosity, of moral pride, which are special to us" (59).

The hierarchy of races functions within each of the larger categories of white, yellow, black, and brown. The British, of course, represent the apex of whiteness, as revealed in the formative description of the hero of *The Yellow Danger*:

> It was necessary for Sub-Lieutenant Hardy, before he could annihilate the navies of Europe, to have behind him a long line of ancestors whose home was the sea. He is the apex of a pyramid, the rest of which consists of centuries of the ocean-life and ocean-culture of a race. It is Blood that tells. (*YD*)

That bloodline is invoked as he readies to attack the Asian navy; Shiel's alignment of the English hero with the Norse pantheon, participates in contemporary constructions of an English national ancestry linked to that of Scandinavian marauders and Norman conquerors[7]: "Here is his element, his day—great Thursday—and he, once more, Saxon Thor, red-handed, swinger of thunderbolts, tosser of linked lightnings. The oil of gladness is on his head. He feels his arm, his soul, his ordination. He knows that he cannot fail" (*YD*). In contrast with British superiority, the Slavs—epitomized by the bestial Prince Davriloff in *The Yellow Wave*—figure at the bottom of the white hierarchy.

Racial Othering of Asian Villains

While on the one hand, Shiel's Anglo-Saxon heroes must confront adversaries worthy of their attention, on the other, white right must be shored up with repeated demonstrations of the racial other's inferiority. Thus, the plotlines of Yellow Peril novels repeatedly stage the rise of an exceptional Asian nemesis who will "advocate a League of the yellow races" (*YD*) with himself at its helm. As with the white races, a hierarchy exists within the yellow races. Japanese officers lead the inferior Chinese hordes: "Japan is the head, China the body" (*YW* 36). Even within China,

> The northern Chinese were a hard, ferocious, and treacherous race—considerably more so than the southern. They were also larger and stronger men—rascals tall, and lean, and brawny, their bony toughness being derived from the Tartar blood with which their tribes were infused. (*YD*)

This Manchu versus Han Chinese distinction recurs in *The Yellow Peril*, but it also attributes the northern Chinese's physical strength to a mixed racial heritage, suggesting the theory of "hybrid vigor,"[8] yet another of the paradoxical concepts of the racialist theories of the late nineteenth century adopted by Shiel.

These Asian geniuses, however, seem to be the exception that proves the rule, since the dehumanization and bestialization of Asian characters, both the individuals and the masses, dominate the novels' racialist discourse. Shiel's ambivalence about Asians, as a threat to Westerners because somehow superior and at the same time clearly inferior—at once likened to animals and demonized—reveals the paradoxes of racist thought. Referencing recent popularizations of human evolution from apes, a notion at the basis of the hierarchy of races, Asians are frequently described as monkeys; for example, Li Ku Yu's guardian A-lu-te is introduced as a "little old woman like a monkey" (*YP* 15). Baron M__ admits that the Russian "looks upon us as a race nearly allied with the ape" (*YW* 12–13); his enemy Prince Davriloff attributes his own soldiers' poor performance against the Japanese to a sense that "our men cannot feel they are fighting with men, but with lower creatures" (*YW* 281). Even when they obtain Western technology it is not certain that Asians have the human intelligence to wield it, as the Japanese are told: "your Navy is like a razor in the hands of an ape which has seen its master use it. The brute may or may not cut its own throat with it" (*YD*).

Li Ku Yu's villainy develops in childhood, revealed when he is caught "trephining a cat not properly anaesthetised!" (12), revealing the early establishment of the tropes of today's serial killer as an animal torturer in his youth. Later he appears almost extraterrestrial, addressing Prince Edward "in that strange voice of his—foreign as an animal's from another planet" (*YP* 18). Elsewhere, Asians generally appear as barbaric, even demonic, as the narrator applies racist generalizations with broad strokes:

> The intensity of the Chinese instinct of Vengeance is a mystery—it is not human—it is not bestial—it may be demonic. To us, at all events, it is incomprehensible.... That sweet lust of cruelty which brings to the Chinaman the same keen delight which bodily forms of enjoyment bring to the Western. (*YD*)

Their bloodlust and ability to strike terror into a "civilized" Western heart appears as the first troops leave China for the European invasion, introducing a leitmotif throughout the final third of *The Yellow Danger*, "the Chinese scream": "as the crowded train moves out westward from the station, a shocking shrill scream of glee and terror from two thousand throats—the shrill glee and terror of a child in its first swing—fills all the air" (*YD*). That such screams seemingly contradict the stereotype of Asian inscrutability is of no matter to Shiel, who attributes almost without exception his individual Asian characters with this trait. The assertion of pro-Asian Mr. England that "those Jap aristocrats, they would not betray an emotion if they saw the moon falling" (*YW* 35) perhaps resolves the apparent contradiction, distinguishing nobleman from commoner. Even Yoshio, whose refinement and sensitivity set him apart from the rest of his race, abides by "that instinct for keeping things dark inborn in Orientals" (*YW* 240).

In addition, the most mundane of activities may be used to render the Asian sublimely other, as seen in the Tiger Hunters' meal, described in the early pages of *The Yellow Wave*, shared as they plot Europe's downfall in a Japanese restaurant hidden away in the heart of London. Shiel details every difference between (his own idea of) Asian cuisine and English, repeatedly establishing their opposition. First, the ingredients of the Japanese meal are served raw and then "cooked" at the table in bizarre ways; the meal is then consumed in a strange manner, as well: "whereas forks are instead of the claws of beasts, chopsticks are instead of the beaks of birds: but forks are better than chopsticks, for beasts are better than birds" (9). Finally, the assertion that, when "dessert came—pickles" (10), "we eat sugar with desert, [but] they ate salt" (10) clinches the impression of Asian alienness. Clearly antedating our era of political correctness and cultural relativism, Shiel has no qualms about using differing table manners as a metaphor for Western superiority. A greater level of ambivalence appears in his racial discourse regarding a question that must, even if unconsciously, have touched him personally: that of racial mixing.

Hybridity, Métissage, and Envisioning the End of the White Race

While Shiel's discourse about racial mixing, particularly when applied to individual villains and their henchmen, often reflects dominant discourses about impurity and degeneration, he occasionally allows surprisingly subversive opinions about the end of the white race via genocide or racial mixing to surface. This ambivalence appears most clearly in Asian antagonists' exceptional status. Dr. Yen How and Li Ku Yu, and also to a lesser extent Baron M__, appear evolved beyond the rest of their race, accomplished largely through their appropriation of Western techno-science, becoming themselves hybrid beings.

Dr. Yen How is first introduced to the reader as physically inferior, even freakish, "a very small man ... he was nearly bald ... there was a brown, and dark, and specially dirty shade in the yellow tan of his skin" (*YD*). Likewise, he embodies two other Asian stereotypes: wearing eyeglasses and having difficulty pronouncing certain English sounds: "He had but two defects—his shortness of sight, which caused him to wear spectacles; and his inability, in speaking without effort, to pronounce the word 'little.' He called it 'lillee'" (*YD*). At the same time, however, he appears as a mental giant:

> But then, besides Knowledge and Race, Yen How had something more: he had Genius—the large Eye—the summoning Voice—the enchanter's Wand. The vastness of his outlook—the world-dimensions of his schemes—were simply fascinating. [Hardy] realised that he was in the presence, not so much of a Chinaman, as of a Mind. (*YD*)

Yen How is also a biological hybrid, and this perceived racial impurity increases the impression of his malevolence and monstrosity:

> He was not really a Chinaman—or rather, he was that, and more. He was the son of a Japanese father by a Chinese woman. He combined these antagonistic races in one man. In Dr. Yen How was the East. He was of noble feudal descent, and at Tokio, but for his Chinese blood, would have been styled Count. Not that the admixture of blood was very visible in his appearance; in China he passed for a Chinese, and in Japan for a Jap. If ever man was cosmopolitan, that man was Dr. Yen How. No European could be more familiar with the minutiae of Western civilisation. (*YD*)

Thus, the logic of the Yellow Peril narrative, founded in the notion that, when the Asian genius appropriates the tools of the Westerner in order to lead the Eastern hordes, he becomes virtually unstoppable, restores the ideological order of dominant narratives of race.

In contrast, the middle novel of the cycle, *The Yellow Wave*, overturns the typical racial dynamic of yellow evil and white right in many ways. Still clearly a Yellow Peril narrative with its secret Asian plot to conquer the West, it nonetheless offers some fascinatingly subversive discourses on race. First, it reverses the antagonists' racial poles, with the Japanese Yoshio as its hero and Russian Prince Davriloff—a white man, albeit one at the bottom of his racial hierarchy—its villain. Furthermore, the only central characters of Anglo-Saxon descent are aligned with the Asian plotters. Shiel's description of the aptly named Mr. Paul England and his American cohort Mr. Allan Petersen undermines notions of the essential relationship between race, nation, and culture established elsewhere in the trilogy, admitting that individuals can be assimilated into other racio-cultural groups: "Both were Japanese citizens, though Western by race, both seasoned 'Tiger Hunters' and Orientals" (*YW* 30–31). Indeed, Mr. England is described as "more Japanese than the Japanese" (31). This strategy of a reverse assimilation, of Westerners who have "gone Native," even joining the pro-Asian secret society, fits the economy of Shiel's yellow peril trilogy as Orientalized Westerners mirror the Westernized Asians in the other two Yellow Peril novels. They, too, represent unnatural figures of hybridity.

It is also in *The Yellow Wave* that Shiel most explicitly addresses contemporary discourses on race, evolution, and human development. In a meta-discursive conversation, England explains to Petersen that Baron M__ was convinced that "the yellow races seem to have no destiny" (*YW* 34) until the Briton convinced him otherwise. England later expresses the astonishing opinion that "we fair types are a temporary accident, only by human courtesy. So I look forward three hundred years to one universal race ... of a flushed brown ... with melting almond eyes, and a thick little coral mouth, with little pearls for teeth" (*YW* 250). With this assertion, Shiel's character both undermines the "natural" status of white superiority and envisions humanity's future as one of racial mixing.

In *The Yellow Danger*, Yen How's ingenious plan for world domination includes a Western and Eastern hybridity to charter a "new civilisation," as he allows some groups of "whites" to survive his massacre:

> These exceptions were Hungary, Turkey, Lapland, Finland ... that these should be left alive to form (the Hungarians especially) the nucleus of a new civilisation,

which was to be neither like the old Western, nor like the old Eastern, and like nothing in the world. (*YD*).

Li Ku Yu also predicts humanity's future as one of *métissage*, in *The Yellow Peril*: "'Nature likes all-of-one-kind!—as the strongest weed in the field either kills or marries the rest. So, in time, one universal world-race—mixed—ruby-coloured—prettier and better than any at present. But before that, we to eat the flesh of half the whites—or they ours" (*YP* 30). Although placed in the mouths of villains and race-traitors (like Mr. England), these passages express a utopian fantasy for a world in which racial mixing will not only be permitted, but actually desired in order to bring about an end to the current conflictual order imposed by social Darwinist conceptions of racially motivated wars as representing the "natural" order for human society. By imagining the elimination of racial difference through interracial sexual relations, Shiel's Yellow Peril narratives subvert the dominant discourses about race of their day.

Furthermore, *The Yellow Peril* allows its antagonist Li Ku Yu to voice explicitly anti-white and anti-British sentiments on a number of occasions, thus undermining their unquestioned superiority. In the first instance, his discourse is reported indirectly by Richard Chinnery to the Prince of Wales, still at school with their Asian nemesis. While Chinnery insults Li Ku Yu, he also acknowledges the seductiveness of his ideas:

"Dumb as a mummy! But one afternoon he began to gas, and, Ted-of-the-Throne, I never knew a speech so fascinating. The things that saffron sack of thoughts vomited out of his chasm! You'd hardly believe.... Said white people are a freak! 'like white mice,' not a permanent type; hence we produce a shudder in the yellow breast" (*YP* 14).

Later Li Ku Yu screams accusatorily at the Prince, "White? the colour of decay!—old hair—the louse," a "sickly, faded" color (20). In addition to his hatred for the white race in general, the British are particularly inimical to him, as seen in a tirade which also allows Shiel to depict his English as faulty:

The Saxon a gross dog—obedient! a slave: as you English aristocrats know with secret glee. William the Conqueror conquered them by one single battle. It took his sons three hundred years to conquer the Scotch, the Welsh. Not conquered the Irish yet. Gross dogs. But for the Celts around who have mixed blood, England still a fifth-rate state.... See if Japan doesn't have Australia-Canada! and be not surprised if before you die you catch sight of the saffron Dragonflag of the Manchus flapping from the staff atop your Parliament house. (*YP* 19)

Perhaps the most provocative assertions in the trilogy appear when Shiel allows his Anglo-Saxon, albeit "Orientalized," characters in *The Yellow Wave* to contemplate the demise of the white races:

> [England]: Here begins to end the white man on both sea and land in Asia....
> [Peterson]: White men have it on the brain ... that it is the white man that matters. It would be such an upset in their way of thinking to see otherwise....
> [England:] China alone is half the world. Man lives in Asia and Africa, and the white races are there to modify Man; but *they* are not Man. They are the bitters in the gin-and-bitters: the gin and water's the thing.
> [Petersen:] ... I wonder what it will all end in!
> [England]: Intermarriage no doubt.... Remember, Petersen, that Man is not a white animal: white men are a freak, like white mice, or white horses, and will soon disappear." (*YW* 249–50)

These white men discussing the white race as "a freak" is even more subversive than the same words mouthed by the *The Yellow Peril*'s Chinese antagonist cited earlier.

Conclusion

How do we explain the strange blend of outright racist, pseudo-scientific racialist ideology coupled as it is with potentially progressive fantasies which destabilize the white order and envision future racial harmony through miscegenation found in Shiel's Yellow Peril trilogy? On the one hand, it should be noted that Shiel uses the first-person plural when his English heroes discuss the racial superiority of the British; as a colonial outsider from the West Indies, a person of color "passing" as white in England, Shiel's implementation of such discourses shores up his own racial identity as white and English. On the other hand, the subversive passages which question white supremacy and which envision a future of "red-brown" harmony offer veiled legitimation for Shiel's actual identity as a person of multi-racial heritage. Close analysis of his popular fiction reveals not only the contradictions underlying the racial discourses of his day, but it also sheds light on the mixed-race individual's personal struggle in an era rooted in a hierarchical value system of either/or, rather than a tolerant one valuing both/and.

Notes

1. For information on this subgenre, see I. F. Clarke's "Future-War Fiction: The First Manin Phase, 1871–1900" (1997) and David Seed's *Future Wars* (2012).

2. See Daniel Métraux's "Jack London and the Yellow Peril" (2009).

3. See Ruth Mayer's *Serial Fu Manchu: The Chinese Supervillain and the Spread of the Yellow Peril* (2014).

4. The following abbreviations will be used to disambiguate citations from the three novels in question: YD (*The Yellow Danger*); YW (*The Yellow Wave*); YP (*The Yellow Peril*).

5. Cesare Lombroso proposed that physical measurements of human beings, *anthropometrics*, would allow criminologists not just to arrest criminals based on evidence left at the crime scene (such as fingerprints, hair samples, blood types and later DNA), but to determine and identify in advance criminal types who should be removed from society. Steven Jay Gould's *The Mismeasure of Man* (1981) remains a classic account of the historical misuse of anthropometry.

6. See Kilgore's *Astrofuturism: Science, Race, and Visions of Utopia in Space* (2003) and Sohn's *Racial Asymmetries: Asian American Fictional Worlds* (2014).

7. See Chris Manias's *Race, Science, and the Nation: Reconstructing the Ancient Past in Britain, France, and Germany* (2013).

8. Extrapolated from botany and animal husbandry, already present in Mendelian genetics, it was felt that crossing two cultivars often resulted in a sturdier offspring—hence "hybrid vigor."

Works Cited

Billings, Harold. *M. P. Shiel: A Biography of His Early Years*. Austin: Roger Beacham, 2005. Print.

———. *M. P. Shiel: The Middle Years 1897–1923*. Austin: Roger Beacham, 2010. Print.

Clarke, I. F. "Future-War Fiction: The First Main Phase, 1871–1900." 1997. *Vintage Visions: Essays on Early Science Fiction*. Ed. Arthur B. Evans. Middlebury: Wesleyan UP, 2014. 96–123. Print.

Darwin, Charles. *The Descent of Man*. 1871. New York: Penguin Classics, 2004. Print.

de Gobineau, Arthur. *The Inequality of Human Races*. 1853–55. Trans. Adrian Collins. London: Heinemann, 1915. Print.

Glover, David. "*Die Gelbe gefahr, le peril jaune*, the **Yellow Peril**: The Geopolitics of a Fear." *Fear: Essays on the Meaning and Experience of Fear*. Ed. Kate Hebbelthwaite, and Elizabeth McCarthy. Portland: Four Courts, 2007. 47–60. Print.

Gould, Steven Jay. *The Mismeasure of Man*. New York: Norton, 1981. Print.

Hashimoto, Yorimitsu. "Germs, Body Politics, and Yellow Peril: Relocation of Britishness in *The Yellow Danger*." *Australasian Victorian Studies Journal* 9 (2003): 52–66. Print.

Keep, C. J. "Cross-Dressing at the End of Time: Orientalism and Apocalypse in M. P. Shiel's *The Purple Cloud*." *Revue Frontenac* 10–11 (1993–94): 129–49. Print.

Kilgore, De Witt Douglas. *Astrofuturism: Science, Race, and Visions of Utopia in Space.* Philadelphia: U of Pennsylvania P, 2003. Print.

London, Jack. "The Unparalleled Invasion." 1906. *The Strength of the Strong.* New York: Macmillan, 1914. 71–100. Print.

———. "The Yellow Peril." 1904. *Revolution and Other Essays.* New York: Macmillan, 1910. Print.

Manias, Chris. *Race, Science, and the Nation: Reconstructing the Ancient Past in Britain, France, and Germany.* New York: Routledge, 2013. Print.

Marchetti, Gina. *Romance and the 'Yellow Peril': Race, Sex, and Discursive Strategies in Hollywood Fiction.* Berkeley: U of California P, 1993. Print.

Mayer, Ruth. *Serial Fu Manchu: The Chinese Supervillain and the Spread of the Yellow Peril.* Philadelphia: Temple UP, 2014. Print.

Métraux, Daniel. "Jack London and the Yellow Peril." *ASIA* 14.1 (2009): 29–33. Print.

Nordau, Max., *Degeneration.* 1892. Lincoln: U of Nebraska P, 1993. Print.

Seed, David, ed. *Future Wars.* Liverpool: Liverpool UP, 2012. Print.

Sharp, Patrick B. "Great White 'Race Adventure': Jack London and the Yellow Peril." *Crossing Oceans: Reconfiguring American Literary Studies in the Pacific Rim.* Ed. Noelle Brada-Williams and Karen Chow. Hong Kong/London: Hong Kong UP/Eurospan, 2003. 89–98. Print.

Shiel, M. P. *The Yellow Danger: or, What might happen if the division of the Chinese empire should estrange all European countries.* London: Grant Richards, 1898. Kindle Edition.

———. *The Yellow Peril.* London: Gollancz, 1929. Print.

———. *The Yellow Wave.* London: Ward, Lock, 1905. Print.

Sohn, Stephen H. *Racial Asymmetries: Asian American Fictional Worlds.* New York: NYUP, 2014. Print.

Svitavsky, William L. "From Decadence to Racial Antagonism: M. P. Shiel at the Turn of the Century." *Science Fiction Studies* 31.1 (2004): 1–24. Print.

Wei Tchen, John Kuo. "The Yellow Claw: The Optical Unconscious in Anglo-American Political Culture." *The Oxford History of Popular Print Culture. Volume 6: US Popular Print Culture 1860–1920.* Ed. Christine Bold. New York: Oxford UP, 2012. 477–500. Print.

Worth, Aaron. "The Reversible Empire: Race, Technology and Irreversible Time in Future-War Narratives." *Studies in Irreversibility: Texts and Contexts.* Ed. Benjamin Schreier. Newcastle upon Tyne: Cambridge Scholars, 2007. 99–115. Print.

FICTIONS OF SCIENCE, AMERICAN ORIENTALISM, AND THE ALIEN/ASIAN OF PERCIVAL LOWELL

■ ■ ■

TIMOTHY J. YAMAMURA

This essay analyzes the representation of Asians and "aliens" in the works of American astronomer and writer Percival Lowell on the "Far East" and the planet Mars. While Lowell's ethnographic writings on "Old Japan" during the 1880s and 1890s are well recognized as foundational texts within the field of Asian studies, and while Lowell's contributions to astronomy continue to be celebrated, little if any consideration has been given to Lowell's significance within the field of science fiction studies. My analysis will examine the paradox that, while Lowell's apprehensions and misapprehensions along the continuum of Asians and "aliens" can be read as happening both with and against the grain of the "style of thought" (2) Edward Said called "Orientalism," Lowell's speculations on other worlds simultaneously functioned as a means to contest the alienating powers of capitalist modernity, however ambivalently. I argue that an analysis of Lowell's writings across the continuum of Asians and "aliens" reveals an important genealogy for contemporary representations of Asia in science fiction, as well as the alienations at play within the context of Lowell's late-nineteenth century moment.

Although the critical connection between Asians and "aliens" in cultural representation may now seem commonplace following important interventions by Stephen Hong Sohn, Mike Davis, John Cheng, and others,[1] arguably it is Lowell's writings that provide us with the origin for scholarly interest in the connections between, and conflations of, two of science fiction's most otherworldly objects of speculation. This idea is suggested by Lowell's contemporary, Lafcadio Hearn, who was the first to comment on the "strange" continuum that was developing in Lowell's life and research (218). Hearn writes, "It is strange that Lowell should have written the very best book in the English language on the old Japanese life and character, and the most startling *astronomical* book of the period—'Mars'—more interesting than any romance." (218; italics in original). Although merely suggestive, Hearn's remarks—"more interesting than any romance"—speak to an emergent problem regarding the representation of Asians and "aliens" in literature.

With Amy Lowell and Robert Lowell among his influential literati family, Percival Lowell's writings as a poet, an ethnographer, and as an astronomer have, perhaps understandably, received less critical attention. Yet, as I contend, part of the reason for this is that, although Lowell's writings on the "Far East" brought him acclaim, and although his astronomical speculations on the existence of the planet Pluto[2] proved accurate, his arguments for the existence of advanced life on Mars were eventually proven invalid, even though they ignited the literary imagination of his time. Thus, while works like *The Soul of the Far East* (1888) established Lowell as the foremost American Orientalist of his generation, he is equally infamous for his false claims of the existence of advanced civilization on Mars.

From our present juncture, Lowell's theories about life on Mars, once considered "science," are meaningful only as science fiction. Although contested during his time, and eventually disproven by future generations of telescopes and astronomers, the circulation of Lowell's claims as part of the "print capitalist" (Anderson 44) markets of the world had a major impact on the "emergence of science fiction" (Rieder 15), providing speculative material for future generations of writers and readers. Of course, one important genealogy that follows Lowell is what critic Takayuki Tatsumi has termed the "pre-wellsian, post-wellsian shift" ("Preface" xiv) in science-fictional representation, namely the string of adaptations, appropriations, and alternative conceptualizations of "world war" that followed in the wake of Well's *War of the Worlds* (1897). This includes the perilous associations of Asians with "aliens" endemic to the Yellow Peril tradition of writing, from geostrategist and sea power "prophet" Alfred Mahan's depictions of Asian immigrants as the "vast, outside, masses of aliens" ("Possibilities of an Anglo-American Re-Union") threatening to flood the U.S. West Coast, to Pacific future-war novels like Homer Lea's *The Valor of Ignorance* (1909) and Hector Bywater's *The Great Pacific war: a history of the American-Japanese campaign of 1931–1933* (1925), or even adaptations of alien invasion by Japanese writers by Unno Juza's *Kasei Heidan* (*Mars Army Corp*) (1939), adapted to Japan's own imperialist ambition as an Asia-Pacific empire.

Yet Lowell's influence can even be traced to the very origins of the science fiction genre, for his astronomical writings provided inspiration for a young Hugo Gernsback in Luxembourg, who committed himself to science, fiction, and eventually, "scientifiction" in the United States, after learning of Lowell's claim about an advanced civilization on Mars.

While Lowell's writing on Asia and Mars may seem worlds apart, I find they are best read within a continuum of science-fictional thinking across two of the genre's most prominent objects of speculation. In what follows, I trace this continuum, considering some of the ways in which Lowell's posture as an Orientalist may have influenced his apprehensions, along with his misapprehensions, as a "Martianist." While aspects of Lowell's work, particularly his professed fascination with Old Japan, may seem readable in the traditional Saidian vein of Orientalist othering, as I will argue it is more productive to read Lowell through the techno-Orientalist lens of mirroring. By tracing the technologized metaphors across the alien/Asian continuum in Lowell's writings on other worlds, we see that Lowell's speculations on the Far East and Mars alike reflect the anxieties of a turn-of-the-century era that was encountering what we now call globalization.

Orientalist Apprehensions and the American "Far East"

Lowell was raised in privilege, born a member of a prominent "Boston Brahmin" family.³ Yet it was the privileges and experiences offered by the life of an Orientalist that Lowell pursued following his graduation from Harvard. He first traveled to Asia as a foreign secretary and counsellor for a special diplomatic mission on behalf of the Korean government to the United States in 1883. As Lowell remarked, he is one of the few Americans to have "entered [his] native land as a foreigner"—that is, as a de facto Korean (*Chosön* xv). This suggests that Orientalism afforded Lowell the unique, and potentially transformative, privilege of encountering, but also speaking on behalf of, the position of the other. Yet insofar as Lowell's work as an Orientalist was occasioned by his role in geopolitical dealings, we can also say that Orientalism also involved the arbitration of borders—and hierarchies—both within Asia and between East and West.

After his experiences as a Korean representative, Lowell moved to Japan, where he lived for ten years, producing during that time the first major works by an American writer on the subjects of Korea, Japan, and the Orientalist category of the Far East; they included *Chosön: The Land of the Morning Calm* (1886), *Noto: An Unexplored Corner of Japan* (1891), *Occult Japan, or the Way of the Gods* (1894), and his best known work, *The Soul of the Far East*, (1888)—one of the books that inspired writers like Hearn to journey to Japan.

As Lowell believed, Asian countries like Japan offered something of a paradise for Orientalists looking for material to analyze in the name of science. As an object, Japan's allure is twofold: "the fact is that Japan is still very much an undiscovered country to us.... Japan is scientifically an undiscovered country even to the Japanese" (*Occult Japan* 4). Lowell's metaphor comparing Japan to an "undiscovered country" relies on a post-Columbian maritime narrative of "alien" contact. It also rhetorically establishes scientific study as its own kind of historical marker, one occasioned by the Orientalist's arrival. Finally, Lowell's claim that Japan is, scientifically speaking, an "undiscovered country even to the Japanese," while dubious given the context of his 1894 publication, reveals a belief that Japan, as an Oriental specimen, is untainted by science or modernity. Thus, he inscribes his Oriental objects with a kind of objective "purity," for the Japanese are seen as a prescientific people, both to Western Orientalists and also to the Japanese themselves.

East Mirrors West

Lowell's naive belief in the authenticity of his object allows him to imagine something akin to what Said called "the Orientalist stage," a mode of knowledge production which functions to "exert a three-way force, on the Orient, on the Orientalist, and on the Western 'consumer' of Orientalism" (67). Through discourse and circulation, the Oriental object functions to reify distinctions between East and West, object and interpreter, as well as object and Western consumer, or as Said writes, "The Orient is thus Orientalized, a process that not only marks the Orient as the province of the Orientalist but also forces the uninitiated Western reader to accept Orientalist codifications as the *true* Orient" (67; italics in original).

What Lowell adds to the practice of Orientalist staging is the idea that "the Oriental" functions as a *mirror* for the Western observer. That is, in staging the East-West encounter, Lowell's (techno-)Orientalism promoted the Far East as a mirror by which the West can regard itself in new ways, and thus as a unique object of consumption. He writes:

> It is because the Far East holds up the mirror to our civilization,—a mirror that-like all mirrors gives up back left for right,—because by her very oddities, as they strike us at first, we truly learn to criticize, to examine, and realize our own way of doing things, that she is so interesting. It is in this that her great attraction lies. It

is for this that men have gone to Japan intending to stay for weeks, and have tarried for years. (*Chosön* 137)

In contrast to a simple logic of racial othering, Lowell's image of East-West mirroring offers an alternative conceptualization to modern forms of Orientalism: by presenting an inverted mirror for "our civilization," the Oriental object functions to unsettle the perspective of the Western observer. This effect produces the possibility of self-reflective insight, revealing to the Orientalist the nature of the world from which he comes. As in the case of Said's "Orientalist staging," Lowell's metaphor of the mirror suggests that the East-West encounter functions to facilitate a kind of narcissistic self-reevaluation. He then offers his experience to readers for their consumption and (self-) reflection, thus producing, to invert Said's formulation, the image of a "true" *West(erner)*.

While criticism in the Saidian vein has tended to figure Orientalism in terms of an imperialist will to power, or in Said's articulation, "as a Western style for dominating, restructuring, and having authority over the Orient" (3), Lowell's posture towards his Far Eastern object, while perhaps still uneven, is not necessarily a form of American imperialism. In fact, Lowell seems to have regarded the study of the Orient as a utopian calling. However "alien" Asia may have seemed, Lowell's embrace of Orientalism was informed by the desire to "realize humanity" (*Soul* 4), for the fact that the world seemed divided also presented the possibility of a universalized humanity.

Lowell elaborates by utilizing another technological metaphor, writing, "regarding, then, the Far Oriental as a man, and not simply as a phenomenon, we discover in his peculiar point of view a new importance,—the possibility of using it *stereoptically*" (*Soul* 4; italics added). When the Oriental character is captured, "his mind-photograph of the world can be placed side by side with ours, and the two pictures combined will yield results beyond what either alone could possibly have afforded" (*Soul* 4). Lowell refers to the process by which two photographs of the same object, taken at different angles, can be transposed to create a sense of depth—an early 3D technology. While Orientalism is generally critiqued for promoting *stereotypical* representations of Asia, Lowell suggests a *stereoptic* poetics, one which produces a kind of techno-racial prism-effect in the staging of East and West. Thus, through acts of transposition and layering, Lowell believed that when East and West are "harmonized, they will help us to realize humanity" (*Soul* 4).

Although the utopian aspirations that informed early American Orientalist studies of Asia are worth taking seriously, it is nonetheless undeniable that Lowell's vision of a future humanity suggests an uneven, discrepant vision of a "harmonized" world. Lowell's possessive phrasing suggests such a vision: for just as the Orient exists to help the West understand itself better, *"they"* also exist to "help *us* realize humanity" (*Soul* 4; italics added). Furthermore, while the image of stereoptic mirroring may seem an alternative to racial othering, Lowell's techno-Orientalist posture is also fraught in its own way: the ambivalence and unevenness in Lowell's apprehensions suggest the inevitable ironies, misrecognitions, and obfuscations conditioned by his staging of the Oriental mirror. After all, the self-other mirroring is a product of a "special effect," rather than being inherent to either Oriental or Occidental. While such encounters can be a source of delight and insight, those who seek their reflection in the mirror are also prone to mystifications and misinterpretations. Thus, while Lowell's stereoptics may suggest a mode through which the confusions produced by East-West staging might be clarified, they also reveal that the apprehensions of the Orientalist may actually reflect a deeper problem.

Orientalist "Time Lag" and Space-Time Homogenization

While the fictionalized nature of Orientalist representation is well acknowledged, what remains to be reconciled is another kind of fiction, however related, one which Lowell's techno-Orientalism also foregrounds for critical inquiry: namely, the decisive impact of the hemispheric constructs derived from global longitude, the fiction of capitalist temporality. Significantly, Lowell, as an Orientalist, can also be read as one of the early ethnographers of the East-West hemispheric divide created by the emergence of the hundred and eightieth meridian, across which the Trans-Pacific traveler must warp when crossing the ocean.

Lowell's writing suggests the way in which modern notions of Western and Eastern (or Oriental) hemispheres are rooted in the arbitrary system of longitudinal measurement, a system which homogenized capitalist space-time in the world. As analyzed by Elizabeth Deloughery, "Longitude, particularly the zero-degree meridian at Greenwich, is a political construct, created to protect colonial trade and based on the difference in *time* between a British ships's departure and arrival point" (55; italics in original). While historically derived from the history of maritime trade, British colonialism, and practices of transatlantic slavery, the Greenwich meridian was universalized at the International Greenwich Meridian Conference in Washington, D.C., in 1884, two years before Lowell's first publication on his journeys to the Far East.

As Lowell explains, the Pacific meridian has a unique function within the world system as a border which mediates two discrepant temporalities. Unlike latitudinal measurements, which are based on the natural rotations of the equator, longitude "is not only imaginary; it has not even an astronomical reason for its existence" (Lowell, *Chosön* 1). Thus, although "purely and entirely an arbitrary convention" (*Chosön* 1), the one hundred and eightieth meridian has a dramatic impact on the apprehensions of the transpacific Orientalist. As Lowell writes:

> It (the meridian) sets, not the time of day merely, but the day itself. At the line two days meet. There, though time flows ceaselessly on, occurs that unnatural yet unavoidable jump of twenty-four hours; and no one is there to be startled by the fact,—no one to be perplexed in trying to reconcile the two incongruities, continuous time and discontinuous day. There is nothing but the ocean. (*Chosön* 1)

Lowell describes the meridian as a marker for an irreconcilable paradox of time flowing "ceaselessly on," and yet at the line "two days meet." Although designed to homogenize the experience of time, the westerly transpacific traveler, Lowell explains, actually loses a day "into the depths of the Pacific Ocean" (*Chosön* 3).

In other words, the universalization of capitalist temporality through the standardization of Greenwich as the Prime Meridian has a particular significance on the apprehension of space and time for the transpacific traveler, who warps across time when traversing the "International Date Line," the antipode of the Greenwich meridian. Lowell describes how "we fall asleep one night in the new world to awake on the after-morrow's morning in the old. The day that knows no to-morrow—was yesterday" (*Chosön* 3). However paradoxically, the Westerly journey into the Far East is—like in science fiction—a journey into the future. Those crossing the Pacific meridian, then, are subject to the defining temporal paradox of capitalist modernity (today commonly called "jet lag").

But if Lowell's description of the uncanny nature of transpacific temporality may sound romanticized, it is because the "arbitrary convention" (1) of global longitude can be read as the sustaining myth of his Orientalism. Arguably, the establishment of the Greenwich meridian also naturalized the perceived division between hemispheres, of the world divided into mirroring opposites. Thus, the International Date Line is "of exceeding importance to mankind" (Lowell, *Chosön* 1) not just for its homogenization of space-time, but because it reified the divisions between Western and Eastern worlds.

In spite of Lowell's professed fasciation for Old Japan, we see that his brand of Orientalism is already a kind of techno-Orientalism—that is, both the strand of economic alienation and the racialization that Sohn associates with the figuration of the "Alien/Asian" (6). Lowell's writing reveals how the modern construction of the East-West divide is rooted in the global proliferation of clocks and the fiction of what Walter Benjamin called "homogeneous, empty time" (261). For this reason, we must read Far East Orientalism, or more broadly, the science fiction of what Collene Lye has called "Asiatic racial form" (5), as one of the most perceptible, and pernicious, forms of modernity's dehumanizations. In other words, the fiction of hemispheric division in the Pacific is itself rooted in the deeper myths of our time, made manifest by the apprehensions of the traveler who crosses the International Date Line. Thus, we can read the (mis)apprehensions of the "time-lagged" Orientalist as a reflection of the mystifying effects of capitalist modernity.

In fact, the way Lowell describes his own encounter with the Oriental mirror also suggests this very mystification. Lowell writes that "like us, indeed, and yet so unlike are they that we seem, as we gaze at them, to be viewing our own humanity in some mirth-provoking mirror of the mind,—a mirror that shows us our own familiar thoughts, but all turned wrong side out" (*Soul* 3). Lowell's staging seems to have cast him into a condition similar to the colonial ambivalence theorized by Homi Bhabha, where the Far East Oriental—"like us ... and yet so unlike"—marks the anxiety of encounter with an uncanny object that is "almost the same but not quite" (127). Of course, Lowell, who believed that Far East Orientalism was a utopian project, finds the mirroring effect a source of delight and possibility. Yet it is also a source of anxiety and consternation, for when regarding the mirror of the Oriental, "we become the sport of our own reflections" (*Soul* 3). Thus, the Orientalist finds that his observations may be tainted by his very own perspective.

In his last writings on Japan, Lowell seems to have resigned to the failure of his Orientalist project, for he realizes that, "the farther the foreigner goes, the more he perceives the ideas in the two hemispheres to be fundamentally diverse" (*Occult Japan* 14). In other words, Lowell seems to question whether "East" and "West" can ever be reconciled, for the staging of Orientalist mirroring seems to produce a deeper recognition of incommensurability.

Martian Orientalism and the "Canali" of Mars

After ten years living in Asia, Lowell performed one of the most infamous, yet revealing, field switches of his time—from Orientalism to astronomy. Just as

Lowell was emerging in the publishing world as the foremost Far East Orientalist of his generation, he was also beginning his search for extraterrestrial life in the cosmos, specifically on Mars. Lowell learned of Italian astronomer Giovanni Schiaparelli's discovery of "canali" on Mars while living in Japan. Although Schiaparelli's usage of the word could be read as denoting the presence of "channels" or "grooves" on the surface of the Martian planet, the text that Lowell read translated "canali" as "canals," a translation Lowell stuck with for the rest of his life.

The translation of "canali" suggested to Lowell an image of purposiveness, that the planet-wide network of canals on Mars was the work of a highly advanced species inhabiting the planet. When Lowell learned of Schiaparelli's retirement from astronomy (due to failing eyesight) Lowell decided to abandon his studies of Asia and devote himself to the work that remained in Schiaparelli's wake, namely the search for the species that created the canals of Mars. Lowell left Japan to establish the Lowell Astronomical Observatory at Flagstaff, Arizona, in 1894. The following year, Lowell began presenting his evidence for the existence of extraterrestrial life in the universe, writing, "that Mars seems inhabited is the first, not the last, word on the subject" (*Mars* 211). Lowell's books on Mars include *Mars* (1895), *Mars and Its Canals* (1906), and *Mars As the Abode of Life* (1908).

From his Flagstaff observatory, Lowell believed that he had discovered evidence for the existence of an advanced species living on Mars. With the latest nineteenth-century telescopic technology, and with his knowledge of astrophysics and mathematics, Lowell envisioned a "planet wide" (*Mars* 235) system of canals on Mars, designed to facilitate the flow of water about the arid planet. From his perspective, Lowell believed that the canals of Mars evidenced the work of "beings who are in advance of, not behind us, in the journey of life" (*Mars* 235), for "the evidence of handicraft, if such it be, points to a highly intelligent mind behind it" (*Mars* 234).

Was it Lowell's desire as an Orientalist-turned-Martianist to "realize humanity" that led him to (mis)perceive the canals of Mars as artificial constructions, to view the surface of the planet as exhibiting "truly wonderful mathematical fitness" (*Mars* 208–9), when in fact there was nothing of the sort? At this point, I can only speculate to what degree Lowell's mistranslation of Schiaparelli's "canali" may have led him to misapprehend the planet's features. It is, nonetheless, an appropriate explanation for a writer whose first object of study proved to be a source of confusion.

What is clear is that Lowell's Orientalist desires to find a mirror also resonates with his speculations on human-Martian comparability. According to Lowell, Mars, although literally a world away, is "our nearest neighbor in space" (*Mars* 2), thus they are "of our own cosmic kin" (*Mars* 2). As with his Far East Orientalism, Lowell romanticizes the calling to astronomical study, for it allowed him to imagine the universe to be a single cosmic family. And yet, while Lowell's search for "aliens" may have helped him keep alive his dream to realize humanity, arguably his misapprehensions of life on Mars suggest that his astronomical speculations may have replicated the problems conditioned by his Orientalist staging.

Martian Folk and the Human Future

Lowell begins by raising a logical qualification regarding the search for extraterrestrial life in the universe, attempting to preempt the temptation to anthropomorphize Martians by assuming "that extra-terrestrial life means extra-terrestrial human life" (*Mars* 6). At the same time, although Lowell warns his reader that "to talk of Martian beings is not to mean Martian men" (*Mars* 6), he also cannot avoid the inevitable comparison with humanity, particularly from his objective frame of reference as a white American male. Thus, as with his writings on Asia, Lowell's discourse on Martian folk can be read through the techno-Orientalist lens of mirroring—that is, as a means "to criticize, to examine, and realize our own way of doing things" on planet Earth (*Chosön* 137). Yet, as we have seen, such apprehensions are also prone to misapprehension.

Lowell attempts to illustrate the problem of conceptualizing alien life in the universe through a reference to *the Japanese*. Lowell recalls an anecdote about an "innocent globetrotter to a friend of mine in Japan once, a connoisseur of Japanese painting, upon being told that the Japanese pictures were exceedingly fine. 'What!' the globe-trotter exclaimed in surprise, 'do the Japanese have pictures,—real pictures, I mean, in gilt frames?'" (*Mars* 6). Lowell uses the example of the unseasoned globetrotter as a way of commenting on the tendency to transpose one's own cultural frames so as to make the other intelligible. But implicitly, Lowell utilizes the perceived alienness of the Japanese as his comparative reference point for the problem of conceptualizing "Martian beings" (*Mars* 6). Revealingly, his speculations on Martians seem to replicate the civilizational and racial dynamics that Lowell first imagines between East and West—specifically, the fraught logic of techno-Orientalist mirroring.

As with his ethnographic depictions of the Far East, Lowell's speculations on Martian civilization facilitate a discussion on technology, for as Lowell imagines, "quite possibly, such Martian folk are possessed of inventions of which we have not dreamed" (*Mars* 209). For Lowell, the globalized networks of canals that supplied water to the entire planet provide the necessary evidence. Just as Lowell foreshadows the premise of H. G. Wells's colonial satire in *The War of the Worlds* (1898), he also points to the danger of ecological devastation as a unifying force in Martian society. For Martian solidarity seemed to Lowell a response to the harsh, arid ecology of their planet, in which the need to "procure water enough to support life would be the great communal problem of the day" (*Mars* 129).

Lowell's speculations on "beings who are in advance of, not behind us, in the journey of life" (*Mars* 235) reveal that the logic of "alien" mirroring functioned, as with Lowell's Far Eastern object, as a reflection on his own society and western perspective. Lowell lampoons Grover Cleveland, the American President, in his assertion that the Martians must possess a "mind certainly of considerably more comprehensiveness than that which presides over the various departments of our own public works" (*Mars* 235). Further, the planetary unity suggested by the image of global canals suggests to Lowell that "party politics . . . have had no part in them" (*Mars* 235). Lowell's speculations on Martian unity, then, can be read as a commentary upon trends in American politics, divided by "local labor, women's suffrage, and Eastern questions" (*Mars* 129). That is, Lowell identifies gendered, economic, and racial strife as examples of modern anxieties that the Martians seem to have transcended; for in contrast to a hopelessly divided society like America, the canals of Mars suggested that Martians had united in solidarity with members of their species.

Importantly, because Mars represents an older world, it therefore offers humanity a model for the future, for Lowell uses Mars as a mirror for his human world. Lowell waxes nostalgic when speculating on accomplishments of Martian society, for just as Martians have left political strife behind, their "electrophones and kinetoscopes are things of a bygone past, preserved with veneration in museums as relics of the clumsy contrivances of the simple childhood of their kind" (*Mars* 235). Using earthly technologies as comparative examples, Lowell speculates on a Martian planet in which the cutting-edge technologies of earth have become relics of a bygone past. While Lowell's image suggests a subversion of Western techno-Darwinism through the imagination of a species that had surpassed his own society, he also implicitly plots humanity on a course that follows his fictional Martians, towards a future that will transcend the modernity of his time, a future "of which we have not dreamed" (*Mars* 235).

As with his quest for "other-world manifestations" in Asia, Lowell seems to conclude his cosmic search for "aliens" resigned to the failure of his project (*Occult Japan* 14). For the astronomer, like the Orientalist, ultimately "learns that . . . he will probably never find his double anywhere" (*Mars* 212). Lowell's reference to man's search for "his double" returns us to his earlier metaphor of the "mirror," for just as the Orient was the illusion of the Orientalist, as the astronomer of Mars Lowell learns that man's perfect double will never be found. So while his writings, as with much of the science fiction that emerged in Lowell's wake, reveal how the "white man's relentless quest for himself" (Clifford 163) may be projectable even into the cosmos, they also suggest that alien worlds may leave him unsatisfied. Nonetheless, the fact that Lowell's speculations on Mars tended to replicate the problems structured by his Orientalism further suggest the ways in which Lowell's alien/Asian continuum can be read as a reflection on an earthly world going through its own form of emergent globalization.

Haunted Mirrors and the Alien/Asian Legacy

Lowell's writings on the Far East and Mars offer an important genealogy for the grave (mis)apprehensions of a late-nineteenth century moment in which the "War of the Worlds" model would become ubiquitous as a mode of apprehending the future of nations and races in the science fiction and geopolitics of the twentieth century.

And yet, within the context of Lowell's own life and work, we can also acknowledge a kind of utopian desire for mutual transformation as a result of alien encounter, however incomplete the conditions of imagination. Although Lowell's science turned out to be fiction, it is significant as science fiction insofar as Lowell's (mis)apprehensions of Mars, like his apprehensions of the Far East, were clearly rooted in the anxieties of his era as well as the material conditions of his late-nineteenth century moment. And while (techno-)Orientalism remains a discrepant archive, one that includes some of the worst racial and economic violence of our time, it was also a project that Americans like Lowell pursued out of a dream that somewhere in the universe there might be an alternative to the capitalist modernity of his era, and that someday we might learn to render the hemispheric fictions of East and West obsolete.

Notes

1. See Sohn's "Alien/Asian: Imagining the Racialized Future" (2008); Davis's *Ecology of Fear: Los Angeles and the Imagination of Disaster* (1999); and Cheng's *Astounding Wonder: Imagining Science and Science Fiction in Interwar America* (2012).

2. The initials designated to the planet Pluto, "PL," were chosen in Percival Lowell's honor.

3. Boston's traditional upper class dating back to the establishment of the Massachusetts Bay Colony.

Works Cited

Benjamin, Walter, Hannah Arendt, and Harry Zohn. *Illuminations*. New York: Harcourt Brace, 1968. Print.
Bhabha, Homi K. *The Location of Culture*. New York: Routledge, 1994. Print.
Clifford, James. *The Predicament of Culture: Twentieth-Century Ethnography, Literature, and Art*. Cambridge: Harvard UP, 1988. Print.
Deloughrey, Elizabeth M. *Routes and Roots: Navigating Caribbean and Pacific Island Literatures*. Honolulu: U of Hawaii P, 2010. Print.
Hearn, Lafcadio. *The Writings of Lafcadio Hearn. Life and Letters of Lafcadio Hearn Including the Japanese Letters*. Vol. 3. 15, 15. Boston: Mifflin, 1923. Print.
Lowell, Percival. *Chosön: The Land of the Morning Calm; a Sketch of Korea*. Boston: Ticknor, 1886. Print.
———. *Mars*. Boston: Houghton Mifflin, 1895. Print.
———. *Occult Japan, Or, The Way of the Gods: An Esoteric Study of Japanese Personality and Possession*. Boston: Houghton Mifflin, 1894. Print.
———. *The Soul of the Far East*. Boston: Houghton Mifflin, 1888. Print.
Lye, Colleen. *America's Asia: Racial Form and American Literature, 1893–1945*. Princeton: Princeton UP, 2004. Print.
Mahan, Alfred Thayer. "Possibilities of an Anglo-American Reunion." *The Interest of America in Sea Power: Present and Future*. New York: Little Brown, 1898. Digital File.
Said, Edward W. *Orientalism*. New York: Vintage, 1979. Print.
Sohn, Stephen Hong. "Special Issue: Alien/Asian—Editor's Introduction: Alien/Asian: Imagining the Racialized Future." *MELUS* 33.4 (2008): 5–22. Print.
Rieder, John. *Colonialism and the Emergence of Science Fiction*. Middletown: Wesleyan UP, 2008. Print.
Tatsumi, Takayuki. "Preface." *The Great War of 189-: A Forecast*. By. Philip H. Colomb. London: Routledge/Thoemmes Press, 1998. Print.
Wells, H. G. *War of the Worlds*. 1898. New York: Dover, 1997. Print.

TECHNO-ORIENTALISM AND THE END OF HISTORY IN GARY SHTEYNGART'S *SUPER SAD TRUE LOVE STORY*

■ ■ ■

STEPHANIE LI

American fears of a rising China have animated a number of dystopian visions of a near future. Such fears have been described by social scientists like Madison Grant and Lothrop Stoddard at the start of the twentieth century and further reimagined by such authors as Maureen McHugh and Chang-rae Lee, among others, at the end of the twentieth century and into the twenty-first century.[1] The military and economic clout newly posed by China has reignited familiar threats associated with Asian dominance. What will come of China's position as the largest holder of U.S. debt?[2] Such concerns continue to feed anxieties about Asian power that operate on both a global financial scale and a more personal level. Four years ago, the harsh disciplinary tactics of Amy Chua's "tiger mom" initiated a national conversation on the seemingly superior childrearing techniques of Asian American parents. Will aggressive tiger moms produce math and science prodigies that leave American students unemployed or at least denied admission to the Ivy League college of choice?[3] Against such a backdrop, Gary Shteyngart's third novel tells the story of Lenny Abramov and his doomed love for twenty-four-year-old Korean American Eunice Park.

Set in a familiar but exaggerated America, *Super Sad True Love Story* (2010) satirizes many of the trends that have come to define contemporary life while also speaking directly to techno-Orientalist fantasies. The characters in Shteyngart's often hilarious novel obsessively check their äppäräts, glorified smart phones that rate the attractiveness and credit scores of everyone they encounter. In this world, images threaten to overtake words as the primary means of communication, as an advertisement for GLOBALTEENS, a kind of advanced version of Facebook, proclaims, "Switch to Images today! Less words = more fun!!!" (27). This emphasis on images represents the fulfillment of Jean Baudrillard's claim that the simulacrum is not merely a copy of the real but becomes its own form of truth. In Shteyngart's troubling world, there is no authentic reality, only the performance of reality. Old people are made to look like teenagers and images proliferate with overwhelming force, producing what Frederic Jameson describes as, "a consequent weakening of historicity, both in our relationship to public History and in the new forms of our private temporality" (6). Just as age is erased through advances in plastic surgery and medicine, history becomes a thing of the past, a story that need not be told as the urgent, exciting world of images dominates all aspects of social life.

Shteyngart imagines an America so infatuated with the present that history is not only weakened but actively negated. Lenny's profession effectively represents the end of history. He works at a company named Post-Human Services where he is tasked with identifying High Net Worth Individuals or HNWIs, individuals who have the formidable assets necessary to purchase various procedures that promise "indefinite life extension." The term "post-human" suggests that those who engage the company's services sacrifice their humanity, becoming cyborgs living in an infinite present.[4] Immortality and an obsessive focus on youth makes history seemingly irrelevant. The main character, Lenny, proves to be ambivalent about such technologies and their consequences. Though he vows to live forever after he falls in love with Eunice, a recent college graduate who majored in Images and minored in Assertiveness, Lenny is often unfamiliar with the latest äppäräts functions and he must hide his antiquated love of books. Lenny's uneasy relationship to images and history is reflected in his infatuation with Eunice as she becomes for him a racialized simulacrum, promising an infinite present. Though his feelings for her are strong, he approaches her more as an image, tied to a specific set of racial stereotypes and prejudices, than as a person. Their relationship fails as America's economy crumbles due to its reliance on Chinese capital. In the novel's final chapters, the nation is paralyzed by a Nonnuclear Electromagnetic Pulse that disrupts the nation's internet technology. Lenny and Eunice's break-up highlights the dangers of aspiring toward ahistorical images and failing to recognize how any future is necessarily based upon the past.

Lenny's adoration of Eunice reflects what David Morley and Kevin Robins first termed techno-Orientalism. Greta Niu has usefully refined the definition of techno-Orientalism to refer to the "practice of ascribing, erasing and/or disavowing relationships between technology and Asian peoples and subjects" (74). Since the beginning of the twentieth century, science fiction writers have employed images of Asians to express anxieties about dystopian futures in Yellow Peril stories. Techno-Orientalist texts merge fears of a new Asian imperialism generated through late capitalism with the threat of alienating technologies that dehumanize and even enslave the individual. From Jack London's short story "The Unparalleled Invasion" (1906) to Ridley Scott's film *Blade Runner* (1982), Asian countries and cultures have figured as the dangerous if inevitable heirs to American society. This fascination with Asia and Asian images represents a simultaneous admiration and dread of Asian economic, intellectual and technological power.

Techno-Orientalism operates in multiple ways in *Super Sad True Love Story*. While the novel is primarily focused on Lenny and Eunice's fraught relationship, Shteyngart's novel occurs on the eve of a violent "Rupture" in the United States caused in part by a state visit from the Chinese Central Banker. The "Rupture," first instigated by a rebellion of homeless activists against the government's broken promises, leads to an attack by Venezuela that destroys America's electronic networking. Following the subsequent information blackout, the United States is eventually occupied by China, Saudi Arabia, and Norway. This peculiar trio of countries represents a constellation of national concerns: the consolidation of Asian financial power, continued American reliance on foreign oil, and the rise of a new European leader with little obligations or historical ties to the U.S. Shteyngart imagines the frightening consequences of America's staggering debt to China. The new superpowers seize the United States, which becomes a wasteland punctuated by the possibly lucrative fortunes of New York City's rebranding as a "Lifestyle Hub, Trophy City," part of "America 2.0: A GLOBAL Partnership" (322). A new subsidary of China, "America 2.0" suggests the triumph of a more technologically sophisticated nation. The United States literally becomes a simulacral nation, a copy defined by what Jameson characterizes as a "new depthlessness" (6). America 2.0 is America stripped of its history and culture, a commodity composed purely of flat images.

The more nuanced and intriguing form of techno-Orientalism in *Super Sad True Love Story* involves Lenny's understanding of Eunice. She offers an especially personal variation of national fears, anxieties and fantasies mapped onto a pretty Asian face. For Lenny and many of the other men who encounter her in the novel, Eunice represents a brave new world of eternal youth, the basic goal of Post-Human Services. As such, she is both the perfect lover and the ideal business product. She is the "post-human" sought by Post-Human Services, a status made possible precisely because she is Asian. Eunice represents the ultimate techno-Orientalist fantasy: a gorgeous, seemingly ahistorical body that will fulfill the capitalistic dreams of Lenny and his boss, company founder Joshie Goldmann. Explaining his attraction to Eunice, Lenny muses, "I guess in some ridiculous way I think Eunice will let me live forever" (154). Their relationship is premised upon this misguided dream, which thrives precisely because it is projected onto her racialized body, and the accompanying desire to escape history.

Immortality v. Europe's Old World

Super Sad True Love Story begins with Lenny's declaration, "Today I've made a major decision: *I am never going to die*" (3). He vows to live forever because having just met Eunice the night before, he believes that "she will sustain me forever" (4). Rejecting a future built on either past or future generations, Lenny aspires to a new American legacy based upon his own longevity. He will live in the eternal present Jameson associates with postmodernism and the triumph of "the sphere of commodities" (x) amply demonstrated by Shteyngart's materialist dystopia. Lenny vehemently rejects the notion that one's legacy is passed on through offspring, quoting Whitney Houston from her 1986 album, *The Greatest Love of All*, in order to mock such an outmoded sentiment as "*ah buh-lieve thuh chil'ren ah our future*" (3). This unfortunate use of eye dialect alienates readers from Houston's song, suggesting that she is caught in some antiquated time. Like other African American characters in the novel, Houston represents an inability to adapt to and master new technologies.[5] By contrast, Lenny imagines the future and his personal immortality through the extension of his own life which will occur through his newfound love. This reliance on Eunice establishes one of the key tensions of the novel: how Lenny uses her as a surrogate for his own absent children. Fifteen years separate the lovers, a fact which sometimes causes Lenny to be mistaken for Eunice's father. As the supposed key to Lenny's future, Eunice represents a disavowal of his own past and a desire to merge himself with his seemingly more technologically advanced Asian American girlfriend.

Lenny first meets Eunice in Rome where he has been sleeping with an Italian woman named Fabrizia. This opening Old-World-European setting highlights the marvels that a future with Eunice might provide. Lenny notes that Fabrizia's social circle is composed primarily of forty-year-olds living off the wealth "of their parents' fading fortunes" (14). He continues, "That's what I admire about youngish Italians, the slow diminution of ambition, the recognition that the best is far behind them. (An Italian Whitney Houston might have sung, 'I believe the parents are our future.') We Americans can learn a lot from their graceful decline" (14). Like the Italians, comfortable in their inevitable fall from cultural and economic power, Americans like Lenny are in danger of defining themselves by a once glorious past. Lenny's description of Fabrizia provides a striking contrast to his admiring portrait of Eunice:

> Fabrizia. The softest woman I had ever touched. But maybe I no longer *needed* softness. Fabrizia. Her body conquered by small armies of hair, her curves fixed by carbohydrates, nothing but the Old World and its dying nonelectronic corporeality. And in front of me, Eunice Park. A nano-sized woman who had likely never known the tickle of her own pubic hair, who lacked both breast and scent, who existed as easily on an äppärät screen as on the street before me. (21)

By comparing Fabrizia to the Old World, Lenny vests her with the histories and physical burdens of the past. A diet of pasta and bread has led to Fabrizia's soft curves; her body is literally weighted with Old World culture. Eunice, however, presents the opposite of such historical narratives and indulgent habits. By describing her as "nano-sized," Lenny references the new frontier of nanotechnology which promises to revolutionize our lives through the manipulation of matter on an atomic level. Where Fabrizia is ample and even excessive, Eunice appears as precisely calibrated. Nothing on her slight frame is wasted, as if she is the very model of efficient female design. She is a "sleek digital creature" (153) in comparison to the antiquated analog system of Fabrizia. Lenny's characterization of Eunice clearly indulges in techno-Orientalist fantasies, but his description of Fabrizia is also inflected with certain cultural preconceptions.

Lenny's sexual relationship with Fabrizia is built upon images of the past, a quality in keeping with how he describes all of Rome; it is "a city useful only as a reference to the past" (18). Resolving to have sex with his Italian lover one last time on his final night in Rome before returning home to Manhattan, he "made a few slow gyrating motions toward her and batted [his] eyelashes (that is to say, blinked a lot), trying, with a dose of East Coast irony, to resemble some hot Cinecittà leading lady of the 1960s" (14). Fabrizia responds immediately to Lenny's nostalgic move, shoving her hand down her panties and leading him to her bedroom. However, their plans are thwarted by the apperance of Fabrizia's unattended three-year-old son. They are literally frustrated by the embodiment of Fabrizia's past, suggesting how inconvenient the products of history can be. While waiting for Fabrizia to find her son's nanny, Lenny reflects, "She was the softest woman I had ever touched, the muscles stirring somewhere deep beneath her skin like phantom gears, and her breath, like her son's, was shallow and hard, so that when she 'made the love' (her words), it sounded like she was in danger of expiring" (16). By comparing Fabrizia to her son, Lenny affirms how his Italian lover cannot be disentangled from her past and a future, as demonstrated by Houston's lyrics, mistakeningly intertwined with one's progeny. Her somewhat labored breath suggests the onset of death, again demonstrating how closely Lenny associates Europeans with mortality. Despite presenting Europe as a place of decline, it remains in Lenny's imagination always fundamentally human. By contrast, Asia and Asian American characters are vested with the power of immortality, a power that implicitly denies their humanity.

Despite his eager Italian lover, Lenny is immediately attracted to Eunice when he meets her moments later. In this first encounter, he initiates a long pattern of objectifying her petite body:

> She had full shiny lips and a lovely if incongruous splash of freckles across her nose, and could not have weighed more than eighty pounds, a compactness which made me tremble with bad thoughts. I wondered, for example, if her mother, probably a tiny, immaculate woman humming with immigrant anxiety and bad religion, knew that her little girl was no longer a virgin. (16)

Lenny's musing about Eunice's mother may seem incongruous, but it demonstrates his fantasy that she is unbound by the strictures of family that define him and women like Fabrizia. While Fabrizia dutifully tends to her child, Lenny imagines that Eunice has already rebelled against her mother's rules. She represents the possibility of selfish fulfillment shorn of responsibilities to family. However, this conception proves to be completely misguided as Eunice is actually deeply committed to her family. In fact, she ultimately leaves Lenny because of her concern for her parents and younger sister.

Lenny's repeated reference to Eunice's slim, almost child-like body both infantilizes her and transforms her into a kind of ahistorical blank slate. Lacking "both breast and scent," she seems devoid of the marks of adulthood and human individuality. She has no narrative of her own, but appears like the static icon of a computer screen. One click will connect Lenny to a new app that promises an escape from his own personal difficulties and anxieties. In fact when Lenny purchases a new äppärät, the welcome guide is "an Asian woman of Eunice's caliber" (70), again affirming the techo-Orientalist fantasies of the novel. While Fabrizia represents the inevitable decay of history and the human body, Eunice appears to Lenny as an "obscenely fresh body" (21) upon which he may conjure an entirely new self. In this way, Eunice has the potential to transform Lenny, moving him into the future rather than into the tired past of Fabrizia's history-laden body. When standing before Eunice, or, as Lenny writes, "On Planet Eunice Park," as if she is indeed an alien being, he has no idea who he is: "I didn't know what to say or do," he explains, becoming "some kind of ancient dork" (22). While over a decade separate Eunice and Lenny, their difference is less about age than about what their physical bodies represent. At thirty-nine, Lenny is showing signs of decay. Eunice, however, seems to represent a kind of space age immortality. As Lenny explains to his mentor, Joshie Goldmann, "she's like a poster child for eternity" (127). Reduced to an advertisement readily exploited in the marketplace, Eunice seems to offer a better, more glamorous life.

Although *Super Sad True Love Story* is primarily composed of excerpts from Lenny's diary, it also includes brief chapters taken from Eunice's Globalteens account, an email and instant messaging platform through which she communicates with her best friend Jenny, her mother and her younger sister, Sally. Eunice's correspondence provides an important corollary to Lenny's version of events. She emerges as hardly "young" and "stoic" as Lenny characterizes her, but instead as deeply concerned about her family and eager to care for them as best she can. Moreover, Eunice describes her irritation at being marked as a racial other. She writes to Jenny, "There were all these Italian girls in Onionskin jeans staring at us, like I was stealing one of their white guys or something. I fucking hate that. If they mention my 'almond eyes' one more time, I swear" (27). Eunice is accustomed to being treated as an alien Asian who is reduced to her pleasing physical features.[6] Although Lenny does not comment on her "almond eyes," he takes part in fetishistic discourse centered on Eunice's body. Her writings also indicate how little she is concerned with Lenny in the early part of their relationship. Her first messages to Jenny focus almost exclusively on another man she meets in Rome; Lenny is referenced only in the P.S. section. Eunice's primary concern is with her mother and sister, who are both subject to the violent wrath of her podiatrist father. Eunice ultimately decides to leave Rome because she is worried that her mother is being physically abused and that Sally is becoming too politically active, a dangerous pursuit in the novel's militarized world. She contacts Lenny who lives in New York City because she needs a place to stay, not because she is emotionally moved by their short time together in Rome. Although Lenny reads her visit as an important development in their relationship, for Eunice, the visit is a calculated and self-interested means to be closer to her family. Eunice eventually develops genuine feelings for

Lenny, but their affair is premised on her familial obligations, not some fundamental attraction between them. Lenny is certainly aware of this dynamic but, in a move characteristic of his disregard of history, he chooses to ignore how Eunice uses him for her own purposes.

Post-Human Services and the End of History

Lenny's refusal to consider Eunice's self-interested aims in furthering their relationship is consonant with the kind of denial of reality at the center of Post-Human Services. Lenny's employer promises indefinite life extension. Theoretically, the company offers its services to anyone, but their clientele represents an exceptionally exclusive group that reflects the racial dynamics of Shteyngart's new America. While reviewing the files of prospective "Life Lovers," Lenny notes that they are all composed of "white, beatific, mostly male faces" (121). Immortality is a goal available primarily to white men and as such it reinforces the entitlements of such a privileged social position. However, the nation's dependence on foreign loans and investments soon makes Americans of any kind unlikely clients for Post-Human Services. Signs advertising a new living complex targeted at foreign residents with massive financial resources horrify Lenny, who believes that "the whole philosophy" of his company is irrevocably compromised by this shift in consumer base. He reasons that his job of finding the most exclusive American clients is negated if "they were going to bestow immortality on a bunch of fat, glossy Dubai billionaires who bought a Staatling Property 'TRIPLEX Living Unit'" (151). Lenny's anger and despair highlights how his work at Post-Human Services is fundamentally about instantiating America's social, racial, and economic elite. If non-citizens are allowed access to indefinite life-extension technologies, his position as the arbiter of power is severely jeopardized.

This realization nearly induces a panic attack for Lenny. He is suddenly reminded of Fabrizia and "My betrayal," reflecting, "What had I done to her?" He then turns to Eunice and wonders, "What was I even doing with this sleek digital creature? I felt, for the first time since her arrival in my life, truly mistaken" (153). Lenny's anxiety links Eunice to the "glossy Dubai billionaires" as if his girlfriend is a foreign national while Fabrizia represents the decline of American power. Though Fabrizia is Italian, her European cultural heritage offers a more direct link to Lenny's understanding of American identity. Fabrizia, once perceived as antiquated and hopelessly corporeal, provides the grounding for Lenny's own sense of self. By contrast, Eunice as the ever alien Asian represents the danger of foreign invasion.

Unlike Lenny, Joshie never doubts his own infatuation with Eunice. Soon after meeting her, he woos her away from Lenny, though he is successful primarily because he offers more security for her family. Even before he meets Eunice, Joshie is caught in a techno-Orientalist fantasy. He has dedicated most of his life to the pursuit of eternal youth, a passion that leads him to travel and study a wide range of Asian countries. Although he has avoided serious relationships in his quest for longevity, Joshie's younger days indicate a serious romance with all things Asian. His desk contains numerous pictures of himself: "young Joshie dressed up like a maharajah during his short-lived one-man Off Broadway show, happy Buddhists at the Laotian temple his funds had rebuilt from scratch beseeching the camera on their knees, Joshie in a conical straw hat smiling irresistibly during his brief tenure as a soy farmer" (65). Joshie's Asian adventures culminate in his commitment to Post-Human Services, as if through immortality he can capture the seemingly timeless appeal of his Orientalist fantasies.

The pictures that adorn Joshie's desk reflect the rejection of history prized by Post-Human Services. The "young Joshie" that Lenny observes in his Off Broadway show appears even younger than the decades-older Joshie that stands before him: "he looked thirty years younger today than in the Image, which was at least ten years old" (219). Lenny notes how Joshie's "body run through with new muscles and obedient nerve endings, leaned forward like a missile in mid-arc, his mind likely flooding with youthful instincts," and wonders, "heretically, if he would ever miss being older, if his body would ever long for history" (222). The dramatic physical treatments that Joshie has undergone, including blood replacement and something called dechronification, erase the marks of history. Moreover, Lenny's reference to a "missile in mid-arc" suggests that without the grounding of the past, Joshie is a danger to others. His quest for eternal youth is inherently destructive because it obliterates the past. Lenny and Joshie's infatuation with Eunice maps this desire to erase history onto a racial subject. Their techno-Orientalist fantasies of eternal life also demand the perpetuation of an infinite present oblivious to prior narratives. James Baldwin understood such a problematic approach to history as a racialized construction. He explains in "On Being 'White' . . . and Other Lies" that whiteness is a choice against the revelation of truth: "Because they think they are white, they do not dare confront the ravage and the lie of their history. Because they think they are white, they cannot allow themselves to be tormented by the suspicion that all men are brothers" (180). Just as Lenny and Joshie implicitly deny the humanity of African Americans, Latinos, and any other "low-credit individuals" (as they are termed in the novel), they deny their own history, fashioning an eternal present built on depthless simulacrum.

For both Lenny and Joshie, Eunice seems to offer the promise of youth everlasting. After meeting Eunice in person, Joshie begins a campaign to make her need him as much as Lenny needs him. He starts by sending her seemingly harmless email messages that he asks be kept secret from Lenny for indeterminate reasons. Though Eunice is initially reluctant to communicate with Joshie privately, the Rupture leads her to exploit the older man's infatuation. Although he is over four decades older than Eunice, Joshie attempts to match his remarkably youthful looking body with a corresponding exuberant approach to life. He bemoans how Lenny is "just really focused on his parents and worried about THEIR death, without really understanding what it means to want to live life to the fullest, to the freshest, to the youngest. In some ways, you and I are really from the same generation of people and Lenny is from a different world, a previous world that was obsessed with death and not life" (268). According to Joshie, youth has an ahistorical quality; it is defined by a disregard for parents and a singular focus on a narcissistic now. He explains to Eunice that in their first encounter, he felt released from the traumatic moments of his past:

> When I saw you, I remembered some of the worst parts of my life, some things I shouldn't really be talking about over this emergency signal. Let's just say there were some difficult moments, moments that it may take several more lifetimes to get over (which is why I simply cannot die), and when I saw you, AFTER I started breathing again (ha ha), I felt some of that weight lift off my shoulders. (268–69)

The very image of Eunice seems to banish the past for Joshie. Rather than inspiring a way to process and understand these difficult moments, she makes them disappear. All that remains is the seductive promise of an eternal present symbolized by her Asian body. Shorn of personal attachments and existing in a manufactured state of permanent youth, Joshie's life and business represent an abdication of the past.

The Rupture and the Return of History

Although Joshie's newfound infatuation with Eunice poses the greatest threat to her relationship to Lenny, the super sad part of this love story begins with the first signs of violence against the Low Net Worth Individuals (LNWIs). This elaborate acronym refers primarily to African American and Latinos with low credit ratings. The arrival of the Central Chinese Banker inspires the American Restoration Authority (ARA), a merger of the Democratic and

Republican parties, to institute "Harm Reduction" measures in which LNWIs are removed from public areas. This absurd euphemism equates LNWIs with harm though the ARA violence only perpetuates harm against others. During the two key moments of violent attack, Lenny is out socializing with friends, demonstrating how far removed he is from political matters. At a fashionable bar, Lenny, along with his collection of Asian American and Jewish companions, watch as National Guards attack the squatters in Central Park. The soldiers kill Aziz, a black man he and Eunice encountered on their first day together in the city. Horrified by the images of helicopters strafing the poor, Lenny imagines the panic and fear of his "fellow New Yorkers." However, such feelings quickly pass: "the fear and empathy were replaced by a different knowledge. The knowledge that it wouldn't happen to us. That what we were witnessing was not terrorism. That we were of good stock. That these bullets would discriminate" (157). Safe among his exclusive friends, Lenny imagines that they are immune from such violence. The language here echoes with racial exceptionalism: he and his cohort are of "good stock" like the biologically pure and the bullets will only "discriminate" against the "naked black arms thrown wildly across their bodies" (156).

Following the massacre, Lenny resolves to "never visit those poor people in Tompkins Square Park," concluding, "'Safety first,' as they say around Post-Human Services. Our lives are worth more than the lives of others" (165). Repeating the scorn that his parents hold for dark-skinned poor people, Lenny isolates himself from the troubles of the disenfranchised. Eunice, however, has a radically different response to the violence, and it is here that the two begin to grow apart. She volunteers her time and donates money to the people in Tompkins Square Park. The day after the attack on Central Park, she brings cases of water to the LNWIs and speaks at length with David, one of the movement's primary leaders. A former Guardsman with "Germanic-looking" features (146), David shows Eunice the camp with its limited, but carefully structured medical and sanitation facilities. Eunice notes, "They're so organized here, it kind of reminds me of my family growing up. Everyone's assigned a role, no matter how young or old, and everyone has to do their part" (174). Although Lenny repeatedly stresses how he and Eunice share a hard-working immigrant background, such collective ethos has disappeared for Lenny in his pursuit of American status symbols.

By contrast, this emphasis on the power of the group is foundational to Eunice and her family. Even her father, who is largely described as a fearsome, violent presence throughout the novel, joins the effort in Tompkins Square. Eunice brings him there so that he can offer his medical services to the LNWIs. He quickly softens around the children in the camp and is especially impressed by David with whom he discusses Scripture. Surprised and pleased by this constructive harmony, Eunice is struck by the notion that "maybe this could be my family" (229). Importantly, Lenny remains absent from this group as Eunice notes, "all these poor people sound like saints, much better than the stuck-up Media jerks Lenny hangs around with" (229). Although Eunice does not distinguish these groups racially, there are clear racial divisions at work: the snobbish Asian Americans and Jews that Lenny associates with are sharply opposed to the multiracial gathering in the park. Of course, Eunice and her father are also Asian American and thus their presence among the LNWIs negates this racial division. Their choice to identify themselves with the underclass demonstrates the flexible social hierarchies of the novel. This degree of agency makes Lenny's refusal to associate with the LNWIs all the more disappointing.

When the Rupture begins, Eunice's first response is to go to Tompkins Park. She is anxious to help David and to see if her sister, who has been volunteering among the LNWIs, is safe. Lenny refuses, claiming that it is too dangerous. This response prompts a sharp transformation in Eunice; Lenny observes, "The dead smile came on with such full force that I thought a part of her cheekbone had cracked. 'That's fine,' she said" (240). Eunice's stony turn signals a definitive change in their relationship. The façade of beauty has cracked, splintering their romantic idyll. As they begin the treacherous journey back to Manhattan, per Joshie's instructions, Lenny observes, "A sickening Caucasian fear, mowed grass and temperate sex mixed with a surprising shot of third-world perspiration, crowded the borough's most elegant street, the hipsterish white young humanity rushing back toward the Staten Island Ferry toward Manhattan and then Brooklyn" (244). Lenny racializes the fear of the crowd, suggesting how the ensuing conflict presents a stark opposition between the white/Asian elites and the brown/black underclass. The "mowed grass" and "temperate sex" of the whites implies the end of a suburban dream, and the explosive move toward "third-world" anxiety and chaos.

Eunice's best friend concludes that the Rupture and the destruction of the American economy is based upon the problems of whiteness. Jennie tells Eunice, "This country is so stupid. Only spoiled white people could let something so good get so bad" (201). While Jenny's pronouncement simplifies the political and social upheaval of the Rupture, its causes are amply reflected in characters like Lenny and Joshie. Lenny is utterly content to live isolated from those who are not Asian or Jewish. He avoids the LNWIs and the racial groups they represent. Joshie is even more exclusive in choosing social companions. He interacts only with Lenny and Eunice. This deliberate seclusion fosters a lack of communication and failure to empathize with others. In his last email to Eunice, David describes how the final message he received from his father elucidates why the country fell apart. He states, "I think that's where we went wrong as a country. We were afraid to really fight each other, and so we devolved into this Bipartisan thing and this ARA thing. When we lost touch with how much we really hate each other, we also lost the responsibility for our common future" (177). Lenny and Joshie refuse to engage with anyone different from themselves. People who they hate or with whom they disagree are nonexistent in their lives. Happy in their cloistered enclaves, they perceive the future solely in narcissistic terms, never as a "common" destiny premised upon difference and conflict.

In the aftermath of the Rupture, Lenny's primary relationships break down. He and Joshie come to blows as the latter describes the country's chaos as an important business opportunity if only the remaining LNWIs can be evacuated. At home, Lenny and Eunice hardly speak. Returning home from his fight with Joshie, Lenny finds Eunice shaking on the bathroom floor. Confronted with her unrestrained anguish, Lenny at last realizes that she has a history and narrative of her own:

> She wailed from a place so deep that I could only connect it with somewhere across the seas, and from a time when our nations were barely formed. For the first time since we'd met, I realized that Eunice Park, unlike others of her generation, was not completely ahistorical. I cradled the softness of her behind, her one concession to being a woman. (261)

Finally aware that Eunice is deeply influenced by her parents, their immigrant experiences, and her own encounter with the United States, Lenny at last recognizes that she is not a blank screen upon which to project his sexual and emotional fantasies. She does not represent a rejection of history, but is, like Lenny himself, a composite of her family's past. Touching her behind, Lenny for the first time realizes that Eunice is soft. Like Fabrizia, she has vulnerabilities and human qualities. She is not a techno-Orientalist fantasy but a woman with a complex history and a frightening, uncertain future.

Eunice channels much of her grief into helping the elderly residents of their apartment building. Bewildered by this generosity, Lenny exhibits a general fear of his older neighbors. Eunice, however, carefully bathes them and brings them water. She watches a woman die, unlike Lenny, who leaves because he "couldn't bear to rekindle the memories of [his] own grandmother after her final stroke" (273). Lenny proves too cowardly to confront his own history and mortality. By contast, as Eunice honors her missing parents by caring for the elderly, she recognizes her true identity: "I was never really an American. It was all pretending.

I was always a Korean girl from a Korean family with a Korean way of doing things, and I'm proud of what that means. It means that, unlike so many people around me, I know who I am" (297). Eunice admits that until this point, her identity has largely been a performance. Her Americanness was no more than an image, albeit one she strategically deployed in service to her family.

As Eunice draws closer to her family by tending to her elderly neighbors, Lenny flees from reminders of his personal history. The only link to the past that he values is his bond with his parents. When internet service is finally restored, he visits them on Long Island and finds that they are starving. Their fragility and desperation force Lenny to recognize that amid the turmoil of the Rupture and the breakdown of his relationships, he remains "little more than my parents' son" (294). The realization of this abiding identity kindles a desire to understand his father's history: "I tried, unsucessfully, to see the country around me not just through my father's eyes but through his *history*. I wanted to be a part of a meaningful cycle with him, a cycle other than birth and death" (290). The cycle that Lenny craves is the cycle of history, a way to understand the crumbling of his father's Russian homeland as a corollary to America's demise.

Like his parents, Lenny leaves the country of his birth, fleeing with the hope of a better life. He ends the novel where he began, in Rome; once maligned as the symbol of decaying antiquity, it now promises a degree of comfort and peace. Resolving to die rather than struggle for eternal youth, Lenny explains, "I wanted to be in a place with less data, less youth, and where old people like myself were not despised simply for being old, where an older man, for example, could be considered beautiful" (328). Lenny does not state that he finds himself or other older people beautiful, but only expresses the hope that a new aesthetic, one affirming age and death, might take hold. By returning to Rome, Lenny also puts an end to his techno-Orientalist fantasies. He immerses himself in a European past, one far removed from the media-saturated world he inhabited and imagined with Eunice. That vision of eternal youth is replaced by a new respect for age and the passing of time. But Lenny's exile also suggests that he cannot reconcile his image of Eunice with her own messy, complicated history. Although he may reflect upon his past in Rome, Eunice remains inaccessible to him, a fantasy he will never capture.

Notes

1. See Grant's *The Passing of the Great Race* (1916) and Stoddard's *The Rising Tide of Color against White World-Supremacy* (1920) as well as McHugh's *China Mountain Zhang* (1992) and Lee's *On Such a Full Sea* (2014).

2. In June 2015, the U.S. Treasury reported that China owns $1.271 trillion worth of U.S. government securities. http://www.treasury.gov/ticdata/Publish/mfh.txt.

3. Chua popularized the term "tiger mom" in her memoir *The Battle Hymn of the Tiger Mother* (2011).

4. For further dicussion of the post-human, see N. Katherine Hayles's *How We Became Posthuman: Virtual Bodies in Cybernetics, Literature, and Informatics* (1999).

5. This depiction of the limited access and mastery of African Americans to technological advancements reflects a "digital divide," the gap in access to the Internet and other forms of technology among all demographics. For further discussion of the digital divide see *Race in Cyberspace* (2000), edited by Beth E. Kolko, Lisa Nakamura and Gilbert B. Rodman.

6. See Stephen Hong Sohn's "Alien/Asian: Imagining the Racialized Future" (2008), where elaborates on the Alien/Asian conflation.

Works Cited

Baldwin, James. "On Being 'White' . . . and Other Lies." *Black on White: Black Writers on What It Means to be White*. Ed. David R. Roediger. New York: Schocken, 1998. 177–80. Print.

Blade Runner. Dir. Ridley Scott. Warner Brothers, 1982. DVD.

Chua, Amy. *Battle Hymn of the Tiger Mother*. New York: Penguin, 2011. Print.

Hayles, N. Katherine. *How We Became Posthuman: Virtual Bodies in Cybernetics, Literature, and Informatics*. Chicago: U of Chicago P, 1999. Print.

Houston, Whitney. "The Greatest Love of All." 1985. By Michael Masser and Linda Creed. *Whitney Houston*. Arista Records

Jameson, Frederic. *Postmodernism, or the Cultural Logic of Late Capitalism*. Durham, NC: Duke UP, 1991. Print.

Kolko, Beth E., Lisa Nakamura and Gilbert B. Rodman, eds. *Race in Cyberspace*. New York: Routledge, 2000. Print.

London, Jack. "The Unparalleled Invasion." 1906. *The Complete Short Stories of Jack London*. Eds. Earle Labor, Robert C. Leitze, III and I. Milo Shepard. Stanford: Stanford UP, 1993. Print.

Morley, David and Kevin Robins. "Techno-Orientalism: Japan Panic." *Spaces of Identity: Global Media, Electronic Landscapes, and Cultural Boundaries*. New York: Routledge, 1995. 145–73. Print.

Niu, Greta. "Techno-Orientalism, Nanotechnology, Posthumans, and Post-Posthumans in Neal Stephenson's and Linda Nagata's Science Fiction." *MELUS* 33.4 (2008): 73–96. Print.

Shteyngart, Gary. *Super Sad True Love Story*. New York: Random House, 2010. Print.

Sohn, Stephen Hong, "Alien/Asian: Imagining the Racialized Future." *MELUS* 33.4 (2008): 5–22. Print.

"RACE AS TECHNOLOGY" AND THE ASIAN BODY IN *THE BOHR MAKER* AND *SALT FISH GIRL*

■ ■ ■

MALISA KURTZ

This essay examines the relationship between race and technology, particularly biotechnologies and genomics, in Linda Nagata's *The Bohr Maker* (1995) and Larissa Lai's *Salt Fish Girl* (2002). I argue that the representation of Asian bodies and their modification through genetic engineering constructs "race as technology" (Coleman 177), a move that enables each novel to explore the promises and perils of understanding race through genomics. Asian characters in *The Bohr Maker* and *Salt Fish Girl* are differentiated by their genetics rather than visible physical traits, and both novels question how genomic research might lead to the re-emergence of racist assumptions about biological "destiny." In this respect, *The Bohr Maker* and *Salt Fish Girl* explore how the genetics of certain bodies continue to be seen as more valuable while others are deemed expendable and easily exploited, even if processes of racialization may no longer be premised upon visible physical traits. The identification of this difference in value on a molecular, genetic level is symptomatic of new biopolitical regimes that organize and divide bodies through a variety of processes, including scrutiny over one's conception (natural versus unnatural birth), the ability to access technological resources to attend to one's body, and the ability to make decisions about one's body. Tellingly, Asian bodies in these narratives are "owned" and acted upon by other characters in the scientific community. By specifically using techno-Orientalist tropes, both novels reveal the ways in which the bodies of people of color are doubly racialized in science fiction, reduced to instruments of both science and narrative exoticism.

Despite their somewhat different subgenres—Greta A. Niu calls *The Bohr Maker* nanopunk and *Salt Fish Girl* is often examined in relation to postcolonial science fiction—both novels share many thematic concerns. To briefly summarize the plot of each, Nagata's novel follows the separate (but soon to be intertwined) lives of Nikko, a genetically engineered man, and Phousita, a genetically altered woman. An illegal nanotechnology known as the "Bohr Maker" (described as a kind of molecular genetic technology) brings them together when Phousita is unintentionally injected with it and the Maker begins to alter her physiology, giving her access to technological resources previously unavailable to her in the poverty stricken community of Sunda. Nikko and Phousita have ambiguous "origins," in the sense that while described and characterized according to their Asian features, they are not explicitly linked to a specific ethnicity or nation. This ambiguity is characteristic of both novels and their interrogation of the shifting relationship between race, anxieties about the body, contemporary genomics, and processes of racialization premised upon new divisions.

Like *The Bohr Maker*, Lai's novel depicts a future where the human genome sequence can be altered and cloned. *Salt Fish Girl* is set in the near future along the western coast of Canada, and one of its primary narrative arcs is about the relationship between Miranda and Evie, both characters of Asian descent. During a critical moment in the novel, Miranda discovers that Evie's genes have been spliced with those of freshwater carp in order to render her "nonhuman."[1] Though it is considered illegal, multinational corporations are revealed to be creating genetically altered humans like Evie for work in their factories, a future rendition of contemporary sweatshops.

My purposes in this essay are twofold: first, I examine the ways both novels critique the ways Asian bodies are constructed as genetic "others." By foregrounding difference at the micro-level of genetics, both texts interrogate the biopolitical reassertion of racial "markers" through genomics and critique the ways this difference continues to position certain bodies as more expendable and exploitable than others. Second, I examine how science fiction may provide the conceptual tools for imagining an engagement with race beyond its negative history as lack and abjection. That is, rather than offering critique only, I suggest that *The Bohr Maker* and *Salt Fish Girl* also construct alternative frameworks for seeing race as a tool of ethical deliberation. Using Beth Coleman's influential work on race as technology, I argue that the use of techno-Orientalist tropes in these narratives might also be seen as opening up a space, or gap, that can "be exploited to liberate race from an inherited position of abjection toward a greater expression of agency" (177). Because techno-Orientalism positions the Asian body itself as technological, it becomes a particularly potent medium through which processes of racialization can be interrogated, critiqued, and reimagined.

By doing, so Asian characters in the novels move towards greater expressions of agency, as they utilize "race as levered mechanism" against the systems that attempt to contain them by "mov[ing] discourses of race from the field of science into that of ethics" (Coleman 182). Rather than framing discussion of race and what qualifies as "Asian" through the dichotomy of science versus ideology, *The Bohr Maker* and *Salt Fish Girl* shift the discussion towards questions of process, asking instead *why* certain modes of representation are generated and *who* they benefit. Both novels are therefore more interested in interrogating the social and ethical implications of genomics than its accuracy or "truth"; as Jenny Reardon argues, "we may never resolve questions about the biological meaning of race, but we can make more reflective choices about whether and how we engage the debate" (59). Shifting arguments away from the divide between biology and culture that often defines Asian Americanist critique, positioning race as technology means that *The Bohr Maker* and *Salt Fish Girl* embrace the technoscientific discourse of science fiction to highlight the fragmented and relational terms (epistemological, material, and economic) upon which Asian and Asian American identities have historically been constructed.

Critique: Techno-Orientalism and the Asian Body

A central concern that unites *The Bohr Maker* and *Salt Fish Girl* is their interrogation of the biopolitcal reassertion of racial "markers" through genetic technologies. By focusing on genetically altered posthuman characters who are of Asian descent, or who are represented as "Asian" in appearance, both novels inevitably draw on techno-Orientalist tropes. In one of the earliest theorizations of the term, David Morley and Kevin Robins define techno-Orientalism as the integration of racist assumptions into representations of technology itself; thus, Morley and Robins contend that "the alienated and dystopian image of capitalist progress" (170) is represented through dehumanized, emotionless Asian robots who also signify Western fear over loss of technological hegemony. While scholars such as Morley, Robins, and Toshiya Ueno[2] focus primarily on the ways techno-Orientalism articulates anxieties about the West's economic status in the future, in this section I focus on the ways representations of Asian characters in *The Bohr Maker* and *Salt Fish*

Girl express anxiety over the ways race *is* technology precisely because racial difference is established through genomics and new scientific practices. Techno-Orientalism in these narratives is therefore not representative of fear over technological hegemony, but fear of increasingly unstable definitions and understandings of race in a supposedly "post-racial" scientific age. Specifically, developments in mapping the human genome have led to increasing tension between genetic racialists and racial constructionists over the value of using genomics as a basis for understanding and discussing race. *The Bohr Maker* and *Salt Fish Girl* reveal the dangers of searching for "truths" about race through genomics, even when such scientific discourse appears to affirm the meaninglessness of race. In this way, they make evident Reardon's claim that in the early twenty-first century, "subtle differences among statements about the biological meaninglessness of race acted to shore up the power of biological experts and political actors to differentiate humans racially for the purposes of knowing and governing them" (40). In the novels examined here, the manipulation of human genetic material means that people can change their physical appearances (*The Bohr Maker*), or science has confirmed the equality of all people and "stuff like that is not supposed to happen anymore" (Lai 160). However, even in these supposedly post-racial scientific futures, racializing techniques continue to segregate and construct as abject certain bodies. This racialization occurs through the ways in which certain bodies are genetically modified without consent (positioning them as instruments of science), or through the ways in which access to biotechnology and scientific resources limits the ability of certain people to live according to the same standards of life granted to those in the Global North. *The Bohr Maker* and *Salt Fish Girl* therefore articulate contemporary anxieties around the meaning of "difference" in an age when bodies can be examined, probed, and modified at the very micro-scale of genetics.

In *The Bohr Maker*, for instance, it is significant that Nikko is the only character specifically racialized as Asian while other characters are described primarily through phenotypic characteristics (through skin or hair color). Nikko's face is "half-masked, his flat Asian nose and petite ears barely visible," and the platelets that characterize his skin are frequently called "china-blue" (16). Furthermore, Nikko's genetic alterations mean his face is defined by a "cold stare" and "lack of expressions" (16). These physical characteristics, however, indicate a greater biological difference. To Kirstin, Nikko's secret lover and "Chief of the Commonwealth Police, charged with enforcing the laws that limited the use of nanotechnology" (20), Nikko is an "animal" (17) and "freak" (28) because he is genetically engineered. Though she fetishizes his difference as a "china statue" (20), Kirstin considers it "one of her duties to ensure that society remained human" (20), and she sees Nikko as a decidedly animalistic, "feral" (17), and inhuman statue; thus, Nikko's physical "Asian" qualities come to be associated with the subhuman. In a future where people with money can change their physical appearances, identifying the novel's only subhuman character with a specific racial category could be seen as an instance of techno-Orientalism in which Nikko's "half-masked" face and "flat Asian nose" symbolize the fear of "dehumanised technological power" (Morley and Robins 170). Put another way, Nikko represents western anxieties around unfettered technological and capitalist expansion in Asia.

However, Nagata's novel does not simply reiterate techno-Orientalist tropes; instead, it critiques them specifically, and paradoxically, by constantly describing Nikko's body through racialized terms, a move that makes legible the ways Nikko's genetic difference is established with recourse to traditional racial taxonomies. Nikko's genetic alterations make him subhuman in the novel, not his epidermal characteristics; by making this invisible difference visible through the characteristic markers of techno-Orientalist discourse, Nagata's novel highlights the dangers of reading biological "meaning" through genomics. For instance, despite Nikko's claim that, "I am *not* an animal!" (18), he is considered to be first and foremost a scientific experiment, not a person with rights and agency. Though mixing human genetic material is allowed, the global government body known as the Commonwealth bans the combination of "human inheritance with nonhuman or artificial instructions" (22). Because Nikko's genomic structure results from artificial instructions that create additional body parts and an "enameled hide" (16) which allow him to exist in space, he is not considered human. Instead, he is "an *experimental model*, a singular prototype of an artificial human variant that had since been banned" (16; italics added). Just as the bodies of people of color have always been used as instruments of science,[3] Nikko's body is a tool, valued for its utility as a scientific experiment. Accordingly, his right to live is premised upon the will of others, in this case the "authority of a research permit" granted by the Congressional science advisory committee that also includes an "expiration date" (19) for when he must be shut down. In order to make Nikko's difference matter and to enforce his position as object rather than human subject, Nikko's physical characteristics (as Asian) therefore "signify" the invisible processes at the micro-level of genetics.

Additional means through which certain bodies are marked as subhuman include access to genetic technologies and the agency to use them (something Nikko also does not have). Put another way, genetic differences are not the only determining factors to qualify as "human" in the novel. Because Phousita cannot afford body modifications that would enable her to have "ghosts" and additional cloned bodies, Niu argues that she "lacks the modifications that make one recognizably human to the Commonwealth" (86). The lack of agency of Phousita, who is not specifically described as Asian like Nikko, represents Orientalist terms. Not only is she from the "primitive political entity" of Sunda (84)—a reference to islands in the territory of Indonesia—Phousita is described through stereotypes typically associated with Asian women as petite and passive. She is "unnaturally small" and "stood no taller than a petite child of seven or eight" (8). Her physicality, like many racialized stereotypes, serves to initially indicate a passivity, as we are told that she "belong[s] to Arif" (40) and depends upon his direction. Furthermore, Nagata implies that Phousita's modified body is part of what subjects her to the sex trade, positioning her as part of what Kirstin calls the "scourge of human rats" who live in poverty outside the Commonwealth (85). Despite their different backgrounds, Nikko and Phousita both exemplify the ways genetics are a determining factor in this future. One's genomic structure not only defines who has the "right" to live but also who has access to technologies that would enable this kind of subjectivity. Agency in the novel indicates the right to live, thrive, and move as a free being, abilities denied to both Nikko and Phousita.

Like Nikko, Evie in *Salt Fish Girl* is represented as Asian, though the use of racial taxonomy serves primarily to indicate a greater, genetic difference. Evie and her sisters (the other women in the factories, known as *Sonias*) all have "brown eyes and black hair" (160), and there are rumors that they descend from "a woman called Ai, a Chinese woman who married a Japanese man" (160). Importantly, these physical characteristics do not matter until Evie reveals that she is "not human" because her "genes are point zero three per cent *Cyprinus carpio*—freshwater carp," designating Evie as a "new fucking life form" (158). Upon learning Evie is a clone, Miranda notes, "She creeped me out . . . there was something sordid about her origins" (158). Indeed, prior to this revelation, Miranda did not see anything different about Evie. Miranda's shift in perspective underscores the immateriality of race—Evie's body is not raced until the scientific "truth" of her origins as being composed of non-human genetic material emerges. This genetic indicator marks Evie as a biological other and provides the reason Nextcorp can exploit the labor of women of color—where early colonialism used phenotypic characteristics to indicate the inherent inferiority of people of color,[4] Nextcorp uses genetic difference to assert that Sonias are subhuman. In *Salt Fish Girl*, race *is* technology, not only because it is purposely and culturally engineered, but also because the supposedly neutral scientific field of genomics establishes race.

What racializes the "brown eyed, black haired" bodies in *Salt Fish Girl*, then, is not their phenotypic difference but the ways in which their bodies become instruments of science, reduced to biomaterial that can be manipulated, commodified, and controlled. While the origin story about Ai is a rumor only, Evie suggests the greater likelihood that the genetic material for the Sonias was acquired from the Diverse Genome Project which "focused on the peoples of the so-called Third World, Aboriginal peoples, and peoples in danger of extinction," a project that was purchased by Nextcorp (160). Regardless of the origin story, in both cases the genetic material of people of color gets treated as a commodity to be bought and sold for scientific practice. This process not only replicates but *constructs* racist assumptions about biological difference and inferiority—by selling the biomaterial of only certain populations, specific bodies are targeted for their "bioavailability." Rachel Lee argues that, "At the turn of the twenty-first century, an epidermal notion of race rubs against and in tension with other modes of aggregating populations" (210). One primary mode of segregating populations emerges from what Lee calls "a biomodification regime of primary class or economic stratification in which wealthier sectors of society supplement and extend their optimized bodily transformations, while poor and perpetually debt-ridden sectors of society become bioavailable to service this sector's amplified transformations" (210). Lee offers the example of organ donors from the Global South as an example of such bioavailability, alongside other examples such as the biopsied tissue of Henrietta Lacks and ensuing racialization of the cell line HeLa.[5] In a supposedly post-racial world where "stuff like that is not supposed to happen any more" (160), the segregation of populations in *Salt Fish Girl* according to biological difference reveals that understanding race through genetics is a difference in degree and not kind from the overtly racist ideologies of colonialism.

Accordingly, while Evie and Miranda look exactly alike—indeed, when Evie suggests she is not human, Miranda "looked at her blankly" (156)—what comes to matter is "the neoracializing mode of cloned or ontogenetic marking" (Lee 61). By focusing on processes of racialization, Lai's novel avoids framing race as purely scientific fact or social ideology. Instead, *Salt Fish Girl* more interestingly examines what the ethical, social, and political stakes are of biological definitions of race. For Evie, part of the danger of identifying race at the micro-level of genetics lies in the hand of a corporation, Nextcorp, which defines the distinction between human and non-human as well as who can live and how through labor. Evie and the Sonias are therefore intentionally racialized for their labor and enslaved because they are, after all, not human according to the ideological divisions propagated by Nextcorp's genomic research. Lai's novel also highlights the ways in which ideological divisions between civilization and savagery or human and nonhuman are central structures of racialized capitalism where the exploitation of people of color continues to be a reality. Just as the colonial gaze is premised upon the binary between the one who looks and the one who is looked at, John Rieder points out that "the apologetic function of the concept of race does not depend on precise categorization ... but simply on division itself" (110). By defining "human" and "nonhuman" difference through genetic variation, Nextcorp can continue to use cheap labor and exploit their workers with little regard for their well-being.

In different ways, then, both *The Bohr Maker* and *Salt Fish Girl* present the racialized Asian body as a biological resource, distinguished by their supposed biological "inferiority," and useful only for the purposes of scientific advance (Nikko) or fulfilling the desires of a biologically superior race (Phousita and Evie). Racism has not disappeared in these novels, and genomics justifies not only the difference and "subhuman" qualities of these characters, but also the wholesale killing of their communities. With little ethical consideration, Kirstin decides to destroy Phousita's community by burning it down to draw out Phousita and the Bohr Maker. The extermination of Sonias in *Salt Fish Girl* is equally brutal, as the safe house Evie formed with the Sonias gets destroyed when their nascent, self-governed community is discovered. Sonia 14 finds her murdered sisters in a field, where "she recognized Sonia 148 by her hand, still wearing a ring cut from a bit of copper pipe" and "Sonia 116 by a mole on her heel" (250). The brutality of these murders reveals that racialized bodies are not only exploited but expendable. As Lee claims, "race operates as a mode of class—labor exploitation ... but racism as it engenders moral repugnance refers to genocidal obliteration (necropolitics), including the keeping of half-alive dehumanized others as bioemporiums and as scientific/clinical resources for the biopolitical elect" (217). The Sonias are kept "half-alive" as exploitable labor for the benefit of a biologically superior race, but once they challenge their limited agency, they are killed with little regard as they have no political rights and are not legally considered human. By foregrounding the emergence of new modes of racialization in these technological futures, both *The Bohr Maker* and *Salt Fish Girl* clearly see dangers in the ways changing biopolitical regimes will understand and regulate difference.

Constructivism: "Race as Technology"

The Bohr Maker and *Salt Fish Girl* draw on techno-Orientalist tropes, but they do so in order to critique the ways processes of racialization continue to function at the subdermal level, even if in a supposedly post-racial age visible physical difference is no longer seen as meaningful. Instead, genomics posits difference at the micro-level, presenting a whole new set of dangers for people who are already in situations of economic and social precarity. By using techno-Orientalist tropes to exemplify the ways certain bodies are constructed as Asian, however, both novels also open up the space for understanding race itself as a technology. While this observation may seem obvious, as race is often discussed as a tool of subjugation, Coleman contends that seeing race as technology can also function productively rather than "continu[ing] to naturalize racial difference as lack" (182). Coleman declares, "the adjustment suggested by the concept of race as technology is one away from race as information (i.e., race considered only in terms of quantifiable—and thus reessentialized—data) and one toward race conceived as tool (as the possibility for *production and creativity*)" (193; italics added). Seeing race as "tool" or technology recognizes, as Wendy Chun notes, that "race has never been simply biological or cultural, but rather a means by which both are established and negotiated" (44). Race thus becomes a tool of ethical deliberation, in which thinking about, using, and negotiating the terrain of racial representation develops into a form of agency rather than a predetermined position of "lack." In *The Bohr Maker* and *Salt Fish Girl*, it is precisely by using their position as Asian "others" that characters challenge the structures that confine them and form new understandings of community.

In Nagata's novel, Phousita's embrace of the Bohr Maker challenges the dichotomy of biology and culture in understanding the genomic "truth" of race. Though the Bohr Maker is a nanotechnology in the novel, its representation as a microscopic tool that can alter biological material means the Bohr Maker also symbolizes a broader discourse about the genetic realities of human difference. In the novel, the anxiety of understanding the "truth" of this difference manifests as anxiety over what is "natural" biology or not. This anxiety becomes discernable during a conversation between Phousita and Leander Bohr, the inventor of the Maker. Leander warns Phousita that if she allows everyone access to the Maker people will only continue to utilize it for harm as "they want to be more than human. They want to remake the world. They will murder the spirit of our Mother" and thus destroy the "biological continuum" (221). By "Mother," Leander means the "natural" realm of creation and genetic evolution, "the billions of years of change, the billions of deaths of human and nonhuman entities, the constant unconscious improvisation of a trillion genetic lines" (222). As someone from Sunda whose life was spent trading sex for food, Phousita questions the "unconscious" nature of this evolutionary process. She asks, "The continuum. What was that but pain passed from one generation to the next?" (222). Where Leander appeals to the supposedly rational scientific knowledge of genetic inheritance as natural evolution and fears the erosion of this process because of the Bohr Maker, Phousita identifies not the tool itself as problematic but the logic that underlies it as ethically questionable. Thus, when Leander asks for Phousita to destroy the Maker, she retorts, "I've heard that gods are stingy with their gifts, that they enjoy the suffering of the people ... it makes their own lives more sweet" (221), recognizing that not only has nanotechnology been kept out of reach for the people in the Spill, but that doing so has enabled the life of plenitude for citizens of the Commonwealth. For Phousita, the Bohr Maker and its technology does not represent the struggle between biology and culture—rather, it represents an *ethical* struggle between who has the right to prosper and who must suffer for this.

Where Leander believes that the Bohr Maker would disrupt the natural process of evolution, or the "continuum of life" (222), Phousita recognizes that "nature is always already culturally altered; culture is always already composed of material nature" (Lee 11). That is, science's claim to knowledge divested of ideological interest is problematic, particularly when an exclusive group of "experts" produce this knowledge and benefit from it most. As a molecular designer, Leander believes his objective scientific approach can be distinguished from social ideologies, but Phousita challenges this belief, asking Leander, "who are you to command the world?" (223). Indeed, Phousita's challenge highlights a history of scientific knowledge that has produced racialized claims. As Reardon argues about the supposedly "color-blind" claims made by geneticists in the late twentieth century, by positioning geneticists as the only people with the "molecular tools that could pierce the ideological veil of the skin to view the truth that lay beneath it in the DNA" (52), biological definitions of race continue to "invest one group with the expertise to define race ... circumscrib[ing] vital public debate about what we want to know about our differences and how those differences should matter" (58). Phousita, however, recognizes that the value and utility of the Bohr Maker must be a communal and public conversation, and she decides to share the Bohr Maker with the people of the Spill. Ultimately, Phousita cares less about whether the Bohr Maker will alter the nature of genetic development and more about how it will affect her people.

Similarly, *Salt Fish Girl* is less concerned with the reality of human difference and its genetic constitution, and more concerned with ethical questions, asking, "What relations does race set up?" (Chun 57). This concern first arises when Evie reveals to Miranda that she is a genetically modified human. Indeed, this encounter foregrounds race for the first time in *Salt Fish Girl*, but the novel shifts race from a tool of subjugation (in which Miranda was "creeped out" by Evie) to a tool which challenges Evie's supposedly nonhuman status, making Miranda question her previous assumptions about the relationship between ideology and truth. Evie uses the signification of her body—her "brown eyes and black hair" (Lai 160)—as prosthesis which "adds functionality to the subject, helps form location, and provides information" (Coleman 194). In other words, Evie's raced body serves as a prosthesis that asks the ethical consequences of certain modes of signification, or why certain bodies are "raced" in certain ways. Her story helps Miranda realize her ignorance and complicity in failing to question the surface appearance of what she has been taught to believe. When Evie asks if "everyone in this town [is] as out of it as you" (161), Miranda is offended by the implication, but she soon realizes Evie is right. As Miranda ponders the implications of her newfound knowledge that certain people continue to be dehumanized for the profit of others, she notes how Evie has changed her: "My world had suddenly become something quite different from what it had been mere moments ago" (161).

Despite the novel's emphasis on the "dark forces of biotechnology" (as the back cover states), *Salt Fish Girl* does not condemn Evie or necessarily care about the implications of Evie's genetic difference for understanding "human" genetics. Instead, the novel elides ontological questions of race to foreground the ways "race as technology recognizes the proper place of race not as a trait but as a tool—for good or for ill—to reconceptualise how race fits into a larger pattern of meaning and power " (Coleman 184–85). Miranda's shift in perspective from viewing Evie as something unnatural to viewing Evie's difference as revelation represents a moment at which the question of ethics is at work, tracing "larger pattern[s] of meaning and power." For instance, Miranda sees beyond Evie's supposed difference to question the epistemological frameworks that she has unquestionably accepted. These frameworks have led her to believe what "the newspapers say," to "respect private property," that "there must be laws governing human biomaterial," and as previously mentioned, that "stuff like that is not supposed to happen anymore" (161). Furthermore, the novel's final section ends with the birth of a child and the development of a new form of family for Evie and Miranda. Tellingly, this section is titled "zero point three per cent" (252), suggesting that while Evie is still legally considered non-human, her future promises to be much different than the one of racialized labor she was subjected to. Accordingly, Evie might represent Chun's claim that "although the idea and the experience of race have been used for racist ends, the best way to fight racism might not be to deny the existence of race, but to make race do different things" (57). Evie may be different, not because of her genetics, but because she constructs an alternative future in which race 'does different things.' Though Lai's novel takes a firmly historical approach to understanding the shifting material and epistemological frameworks that define the realities of human difference, it ends on an ambiguous note about what will be done in the future and what will happen the "next time" (269) determinist readings of race emerge.

Biopolitical Articulations of Racialized Labor

Wendy Chun notes that rethinking race as technology raises the question, "can the abject, the Orientalized, the robot-like data-like Asian/Asian American other be a place from which something like insubordination or creativity can arise?" (51). Nagata's and Lai's novels suggest yes, as *The Bohr Maker* and *Salt Fish Girl* use techno-Orientalist tropes, but they do so in order to critique a history of racialized labor and its new biopolitical articulations in fields such as genomics, which problematically divest science from ideological values. This critique makes all the more clear *why* Lai and Nagata represent their characters as Asian, bodies that have stereotypically been associated with mechanical, dehumanized labor. Furthermore, Phousita and Evie, by being characterized in specifically techno-Orientalist terms, reorient the idea of race as prescriptive and determinist, engaging instead with race as a point of departure for critically examining the implications of reinscribing human difference at the level of genetics. Both novels thus use the idea of mechanical or mechanized Asian bodies in a manner that highlights the ways race can be used as a tool towards more productive endeavors, enabling, as Coleman puts it, the "critique of racial instrumentalization, but in a fashion that exploits the nature of technology toward the human and the affective as opposed to toward dehumanization" (199). Paradoxically, then, through techno-Orientalist tropes that dehumanize Asian characters, Phousita and Evie bring to light questions about the way in which we continue to classify, use, and appropriate the meaning of human difference.

By addressing the history of racialized violence against Asians and Asian Americans while using the conceptual tools of science fiction to disrupt these occurrences, *The Bohr Maker* and *Salt Fish Girl* exemplify Coleman's call for a renewed engagement with race beyond determinist attempts to define human difference. That is, *The Bohr Maker* and *Salt Fish Girl* displace the question of biology versus culture all together, asking instead if race might be used as "an aesthetics and ethics" in which "an agent can judge the strategic value of one mode of representation over another" (Coleman 199). Importantly, Coleman notes that seeing race as a tool in this regard does not mean erasing the very real, material experiences faced by people of color—instead, Coleman argues that seeing race as technology supplements critique by arguing for a dislocation of race from the biological that can function through the work of ethics, in which "how we engage race as an extension of ourselves constitutes a key question" (199). Thus, race changes from something that predetermines the agency of racialized bodies into a tool that raced bodies such as Phousita and Evie can use towards challenging the repressive systems that attempt to define them.

Both Phousita and Evie share central roles in changing the communities they are a part of, and they do so not despite their difference but because of it. For *The Bohr Maker* and *Salt Fish Girl*, engaging with race is not a matter of overcoming stereotypes about Asians as "model minorities" or presenting more "emotionally" complex Asian characters—it is instead about asking how our understanding of Asian and Asian American identities can illuminate the entangled networks of power that are continually inscribed on the bodies of people of color. Mediating the boundaries of past and present, science fiction provides the ultimate space for this project of critiquing the historical processes of racializing while imagining a future in which race functions differently. Miranda says it best, perhaps, noting at the end of *Salt Fish Girl*, that her growing family with Evie represents, "the new children of the earth . . . out of DNA both new and old, an imprint of what has gone before, but also a variation. By our difference we mark how ancient the alphabet of our bodies is. By our strangeness we write our bodies into the future" (259). These bodies of the future may be marked by histories of racialization, but their "strangeness" will also function differently than the assumptions of racial essentialism that preceded them. Like the engineered bodies of their posthumans, *The Bohr Maker* and *Salt Fish Girl* ask how conceptions of race might be engineered differently in the future, such that processes of racialization change from tools of subjugation to tools of communication and ethical deliberation.

Notes

1. Two primary narrative arcs occur in *Salt Fish Girl*: the first narrative, set in nineteenth century China, focuses on Nu Wa and the salt fish girl, while the second, set in the near-future, features Miranda and Evie. For the purposes of this essay, I only discuss the second narrative as it most clearly exemplifies the intersection between science fiction, techno-Orientalism, and biotechnologies.

2. See Ueno's essay "Techno-orientalism and media-tribalism: On Japanese animation and rave culture" (1999).

3. The Tuskegee Experiment, where the U.S. government infamously conducted a syphilis experiment on African American men in Alabama between 1932 and 1972, quickly comes to mind.

4. See, for instance, *The Exquisite Corpse of Asian America* (2014), where Rachel Lee points out the ways "comparative anatomy and the equation of colored bodies with primitive sexuality and infectious disease were used to justify ... colonial policies" such as those "in the Philippines and Asian exclusion legislation in the United States" (260).

5. For more information, see Rebecca Skloot's *The Immortal Life of Henrietta Lacks* (2010).

Works Cited

Chun, Wendy Hui Kyong. "Race and/as Technology or How to Do Things to Race." *Race After the Internet*. Eds. Lisa Nakamura and Peter Chow-White. New York: Routledge, 2012. 38–60. Print.

Coleman, Beth. "Race as Technology." *Camera Obscura* 24.1 (2009): 177–207. Print.

Lai, Larissa. *Salt Fish Girl*. Toronto: Thomas Allen, 2002. Print.

Lee, Rachel. *The Exquisite Corpse of Asian America: Biopolitics, Biosociality, and Posthuman Ecologies*. New York: NYUP, 2014. Print.

Morley, David, and Kevin Robins. "Techno-Orientalism: Japan Panic." *Spaces of Identity: Global Media, Electronic Landscapes and Cultural Boundaries*. Eds. David Morley and Kevin Robins. London: Routledge, 1995. 147–73. Print.

Nagata, Linda. *The Bohr Maker*. Kula: Mythic Island, 1995. Print.

Niu, Greta A. "Techno-Orientalism, Nanotechnology, Posthumans, and Post-Posthumans in Neal Stephenson's and Linda Nagata's Science Fiction." *MELUS* 33.4 (2008): 73–96. Print.

Reardon, Jenny. "Decoding Race and Human Difference in a Genomic Age." *Differences: A Journal of Feminist Cultural Studies* 15.3 (2004): 38–65. Print.

Rieder, John. *Colonialism and the Emergence of Science Fiction*. Middletown: Wesleyan UP, 2008. Print.

Skloot, Rebecca. *The Immortal Life of Henrietta Lacks*. New York: Crown, 2010. Print.

Ueno, Toshiya. "Techno-orientalism and media-tribalism: on Japanese animation and rave culture." *Third Text* 13.47 (1999): 95–106. Print.

ENGINEERING THE TECHNO-ORIENT
The Hyperrealization of Post-Racial Politics in *Cloud Atlas*

■ ■ ■

HAERIN SHIN

In the spring of 2014, the American media became the seat of a heated debate[1] over writer Suey Park's #CancelColbert campaign and her subsequent interview with *Huffington Post Live* host Josh Zepp ("Park"). The militant approach Park took towards *The Colbert Report*'s attempt at commenting on the Redskins controversy with an alternative team name that onomatopoeically pokes fun at Chinese stereotypes ("Ching-Chong Ding-Dong") engendered a fair share of detractors. Meanwhile, Zepp ironically and effectively enacted Park's charge, insulting Park by questioning whether she even knew the meaning of "satire," and summarily dismissing her claims as a "stupid opinion" in his response. Zepp's patronizing tone and attitude aside, this problematic correspondence brings to light two long-standing issues concerning the discourses of alterity in their representation—the legitimacy of (if not always critical) conscious appropriation, and the hyperreal afterlife of Orientalism as a sustained mechanism of othering. Edward Said's notion of the Orient as a backwards civilization caught in a timeless limbo of non-progress may, as Zepp insinuated, indeed sound defunct in a time when cutting-edge Asian electronics dominate the market and affluent tourists flood high-end boutiques across the Eurozone. In the 2013 film *Cloud Atlas*, future Seoul even becomes the ground zero for a revolution that fundamentally reshapes social ontology, with a Korean heroine preaching on a transracial ethics of subjectivity and asserting that "to know thyself is only possible through the eyes of another" (2:25:45).

Set in the year of 2144, Neo Seoul is a bio-racially segregated society where human clones serve as indentured slaves for natural-borns called purebloods.

Indoctrinated into the belief that their dedication will be eventually rewarded through a quasi-religious sublimation process called Xultation, and deprived of access to any and all information that may reveal their abject status, the clones endure abuse without even being aware of their abject status. This dystopian vision of Neo Seoul is part of a spatiotemporal constellation of oppressions mapped out in the overarching narrative, ranging from the trans-Pacific slavery trade to corporate conspiracies and systematized erasures of the disenfranchised such as those deemed mentally and physically incapable, sexually marginalized, or economically disadvantaged. The film presents a complex montage of past, present, and future moments whereby recurring characters manifest themselves in disparate incarnations, producing a symphonic resonance of cosmic fate. Their relational ties crystalize around a central figure whose spiritual continuity becomes physically transmediated in the form of a comet-shaped birthmark with each rebirth. The visionary clone who breaks free of her congenital bond and calls for emancipation is none other than this transcendental protagonist; embodying the legacy of her previous lives, she becomes a martyr for the cause. In the wake of her execution, the resounding notes of her Levinasian swan song—to know thyself is only possible through the eyes of an other—quietly infiltrates the shaken rulers of Neo Seoul, foreshadowing the apocalyptic downfall of its civilized façade in the years to come.

However, this seemingly redemptive message comes through a confusing array of conflicting signifiers that refute rather than represent the signified. While the bird's-eye view of the hyper-technologized cityscape remains immune to the geo-cultural specificity of Seoul, the narrative itself professes to be anchored in, save for intermittent neon signs bearing Korean text in archaic font, the walls of the rebels' secretive refuge chamber, which is plastered with Japanese cherry blossom designs, and the backstreets bustle with a Pan-Asian jumble of artifacts that conflate and in turn reinforce the Orientalist gaze. The lowermost tier of the social strata features commodified, literally "engineered" robotic female Asian clones who embody a myriad of stereotypes, including model minority, techno-Orientalist, and china doll, in contrast to the "purebloods" performed by Caucasian actors whose facial contours are obscured in their yellowface reincarnate.[2]

The disjuncture between the film's intended message of cultural, ethnic, and racial transcendence and its mimetic delivery and the role technology (visual remediation in particular) plays in its process urgently demand a deeper look into the evolution of Orientalism in the contemporary context, in which the double-bind of economic prestige and ethno-racial subjugation weigh down on Asian subjecthood. The misaligned cultural cues we see in *Cloud Atlas* for instance, in the hideaway room—demand further scrutiny in that they are the products of transmedial visualization rather than faithful renderings of any comparable locale in David Mitchell's original novel.[3] Excluding intermittent culture-specific references such as food, locations, and appellations, the novel paints a cosmopolitan futurity, focusing its descriptive force on the intrigues of a corpocratic society where common nouns are replaced by brands and corporate names; for instance, Fords (but with a lowercase "f") stand in for cars and Sonys for media content players. While the novel takes the luxury of leaving characters' transitions from one timeline, race, country, and gender to another to the readers' imagination with its undergirding theme of reincarnation, the film takes on the challenge of embodying these shifts, consequently producing an incoherent patchwork of stereotypes that invokes an imagined "Orient" while erasing its referent.

Admittedly, the directors of *Cloud Atlas* seem to have hardly been intending disrespect. On the contrary, they took the rare initiative of casting a Korean actress for the role of the heroine (although that courtesy did not extend to the other fabricants or her male counterpart Hae-joo Chang).[4] However, can the use of cultural, racial, and ethnic stereotypes and their conflation be justified when framed as critical commentary, and if so, how are we to demarcate the thin line between appropriation and inordinate reproduction? What happens when 'otherness' as concept becomes sense-perceptively translated (in other words, technologized) across mediums, and how may we understand the gaps and misalignments that occur in this process? How does technology, whether in terms of its telecommunicative effectiveness in representing intuitively graspable cues of otherness or its role as a signpost of power in the age of global capital—with Asian countries figuring prominently among those ahead of the race toward progress—serve to address issues of othering when specifically applied to the Asian context? This essay poses the above questions by looking at visions of technologized Asia and Asian bodies in the Philips TV commercial *Robotskin* (2007) and the film *Cloud Atlas* (2012), focusing on specific scenes that attempt to visualize the motif of crossing but instead deteriorate into problematic instances of conflation. Exploring the appropriative use of stereotypes in transmedia augmentations that produce signs and meanings that are absent in or even expunge the original object of mimesis, I position *Robotskin* and *Cloud Atlas*'s techno-Orientalism, with regard to the more nuanced substructures of othering in our time, as a hyperreal afterlife of its progenitor under the veneer of post-racialist politics. I claim that the fearful realization we must face in reading speculative imaginations that conflate cultural, ethnic, and racial stereotypes in their transmedial delivery, is what cultural theorist Jean Baudrillard may call the ultimate precession of the simulacra: representations that proceed from masking authenticity to veiling the very absence of such, going on to produce signs that semantically hollow out their original object of mimesis while creating precarious new meanings of their own, becoming cyphers that erase out rather than deliver that which they pose to speak for.

The Technologized Orient as a Hyperreal Afterlife of Orientalism

Techno-Orientalism, a concept that has been gaining a robust degree of renewed traction of late since its 1995 introduction by David Morley and Kevin Robins,[5] brings to light two long-standing issues concerning discourses of the alterity: the function of transmediation as (if not always critical) conscious appropriation, and more specifically, the hyperreal afterlife of Orientalism as a sustained mechanism of othering. By transmediation, I mean various ways in which imageries of technologically suave, exotically alluring, yet cognitively alien, politically acquiescent, and aesthetically antiquated Asia become transmitted (or rather, created) across mediums and agents, from sheer imagination and textual narratives to films, video games, animations, or commercial advertisements. Telemediation technology plays a crucial role in this process as the drive and conduit of such indoctrination, as much as the infrastructural advancements that pulled certain countries in Asia up amongst the top ranks of global economic powers.

The basic tenet of the Saidian Orientalism, namely that the Eastern hemisphere is where the past lingers on, may no longer hold against the relentless flow of global capital revolving around the regions that have been categorically called the Orient or Asia.[6] However, there persists the more insidious theorem underlining this defunct supposition: that the Orient (or Asia) must always remain an epistemically benighted and therefore ontologically inferior counterpart of the Occident or West regardless of the rationale behind such a stance or even the affective or aesthetic appeal of its stylized image. In Said's words, "Orientalism depends for its strategy on this flexible *positional* superiority, which puts the Westerner in a whole series of possible relationships with the Orient without ever losing him the relative upper hand" (8). This is precisely how Orientalism acquires a state of hyperreality in its precession toward techno-Orientalism in transmediated imaginaries. Even as the original referent of the imagined Orient recedes into obscurity, signifiers that arise from and gesture back to the position rather than the content of the mimicked object come into a life of their own, erecting new facades of an unnegotiable alterity.

Earlier iterations of techno-Orientalism frame the Orient or Asia in light of its technological capacity, seemingly counteracting the negative connotations of exoticism with the redeeming light of progress. The disparaging insinuations of its subtext could be roughly summarized as follows: while the Orient or Asia appears to have caught up with the material abundance and operational efficiency of the West, their industrality is more akin to bestial or mechanical conformity than the manifestation of an enlightened subject. As David S. Roh, Betsy Huang, and Greta A. Niu cogently point out in their introduction to the groundbreaking collection *Techno-Orientalism: Imagining Asia in Speculative Fiction, History, and Media* (2015), "Techno-Orientalism, like Orientalism, places great emphasis on the project of modernity—cultures privilege modernity and fear losing their perceived 'edge' over others" (3). Think back to the Japanese woman dressed and made up in a noticeably alien (traditional) attire, smiling and beckoning out of a giant holograph advertisement floating about in the dreary monotone nightscape of Ridley Scott's *Blade Runner* (1983). Or the enigmatic backstreets of Chiba City, its deep recesses harboring cutting-edge black market bio-gears and neurosurgical wonders in William Gibson's *Neuromancer* (1984). These iconic images are indicative of the threatening alterity attributed to Asia in its technologized form, as embodiments of the inassimilable, unfamiliar, often illegitimate, obsequious, and devious who haunt the dark alleys of Western civilization.

While the above archetypes strictly adhere to the stance of the Eastward gaze, techno-Orientalist fantasies have also found their way into the cultural spheres of its very object, at times reproducing hegemonic hierarchies, but also occasionally redrawing the maps of the global power structure, and in turn influencing its original imparters. Again, Roh, Huang, and Niu's introductory remarks to *Techno-Orientalism* provide a useful historiography of this bidirectional dynamic, as does Lisa Nakamura's book *Cybertypes* (2002). Stephen Hong Sohn offers a most insightful complication of the East-West binary by transposing the liminality of Asian American discourse onto the Yellow Peril framework in his introduction to the *MELUS* special issue (Winter 2008) on Asian American literature, entitled "Alien/Asian." Baryon T. Posadas's essay on *Venus City* in this very volume addresses the larger issues of coloniality at stake by expanding the subfield of techno-Orientalist studies to that of subversive transcultural and transgender landscapes. Toshiya Ueno highlights the ramifications of globalization through newly emergent communities of identification called "tribes" in articulating the evolution of Orientalism, and Christopher T. Fan places the prefix "techno-" under a microscope in his reading of Ted Chiang's works, elucidating the reflexive persistence of the bypassed other in its representational occlusion. These varying perspectives paint a multi-focal portrait of techno-Orientalism's varying incarnations across mediums and cultures, seeking measures of reclamation or perhaps even reparation. In the following sections, however, I will redirect our attention to what I call the "Eastward gaze," because there still remains much to be explored in the particularities of its fictional representations. More specifically, I focus on two tendencies that correspond to the post-racial fantasia of our time's milieu, the combination of which harbors the potential of becoming a lethal formula that serves to erect a simulacrum of the techno-Orient in their mediated forms: the supposition that favorable appropriation connotes or even supersedes a critical awareness of the object of representation, and conflation (whether it be ethnic, cultural, racial, or even ontological) as the mechanism of its delivery.

Empty Signs and Self-Erasing References: The Techno-Orientalist Aesthetics of *Robotskin*

I find one such prominent example in the 2007 Philips *Robotskin* moisturizing shaving system advertisement.[7] The short film opens with a close-up of a slick metal entity in crouching stance, which reveals itself to be an android donning a female physique as the camera pans out and captures the robot's awakening. Its head is shaped in the style of Shimada Mage, a traditional women's hairdo in Japan. Single-lidded eyes, highly sculpted cheekbones, and the low but straight nose complete the stereotypical Asian features, while the voluminous curves of its body plays up to the male gaze of the target consumers. As a seductive melody chimes on like droplets of water softly falling around and caressing the viewers' ears, the robot unpacks itself from a fetal position and disconnects its umbilical cord. Its fluid but segmented movements convey an insectile feel, an impression further amplified by the triangular, hymenopteran head and the pair of feeler-like cords that fall off the back. Having collected itself, the robot paces its way through the corridors of a futuristic pod, its design again invoking the imagery of an intricately constructed insect hive. Laying out a towel and inserting the Philips razor into its hand, its phallic symbolism apparent, the robot awaits the hero (a white man, no less) in the shower, and begins to stroke (shave) his face. The man's eyes are closed throughout the entirety of the ritual, rendering the robot's presence and service not only invisible but completely unacknowledged. Once the deed is done, the man walks away in a freshened gait, leaving the robot behind to stare yearningly at his back.

Upon further research, I found out that there was an entire flash animation franchise built around the Robotskin (which happens to be the name of the robot in addition to the product) character. Apart from the problematics of subservience in the sexual overtone, what intrigues me most is the lack of critical commentary on the strikingly disturbing visuals of this commercial, despite the obviousness of its techno-Orientalist aesthetics. 'Aesthetics' is an important keyword to consider in unpacking *Robotskin*, for it is all about stylization. The robot is the embodiment of techno-futuristic excellence, every detail of its features meticulously engineered for fetish, which in turn positions it as a paradox in and of itself. Simultaneously an object of appreciation and a practical tool, the robot's seamless service cancels out its elaborately constructed looks and moves. The robot's aesthetics is also crucial, meanwhile, to its utility outside the diegetic framework; the objective of its existence and its effectiveness as an advertisement for a commercial product heavily rely on sensorial appeal. Serving the function of an interface between product and consumer, as well as utility and aesthetics, Robotskin is a prime instantiation of the cutting-edge design scheme Apple has established as the standard for advanced technological gadgetry—functionality must be escorted by style, staying latent until summoned and used on a need-only basis. Seen but also unseen, subjugated but also manipulating (the viewers into, hopefully, purchasing the product), Robotskin is the quintessential technology all apparatuses aspire to.

This feat is achieved, however, at the cost of an alienated, objectified, subservient, yet (purportedly) devious, Asian female body. The "Asianness" of the robot is not merely spice to its fetish-inducing features, but a central repository of meanings the skin-like robot carries as a sign. The problematic implications of this appropriation appears to have eluded ethno-racial critique, because in principle, the subject in question is in fact not a subject, but a lifeless object made of cords and metal. The alien, insectile (bestial), and subservient otherness of the robot is therefore safely vacated from the premises for two excuses that hype up the prefix "techno" in its techno-Orientalist composition. Firstly, the stereotypical enlistment of Asian female sexuality is shielded from critique by being conflated with positive indications, such as functional effectiveness and aesthetic sophistication. Secondly, the problematic intersection of race, gender, ethnicity, and culture we see in the robot is a non-sequitur because there is no personhood being exploited. The Asian (Japanese) woman subject is, in this fashion, denied its agency in a four-step precession of hyperrealization. Baudrillard conceptualizes hyperrealization, or in other words simulation, as "the generation by models of a real without origin or reality" (1). Simulation differs from representation in that it "stems from the Utopia of the principle of equivalence, from the radial negation of the sign as value, from the sign as the reversion and death sentence of every reference" (6). The resultant copy, model, or image, which he calls the simulacrum, is produced through the successive phases of reflecting a profound reality, masking and denaturing a profound reality, masking the absence of a profound reality, having no relation to any reality whatsoever, and then becoming its own pure simulacrum (6).

The image on the screen purports to represent, but in actuality *abuses*, the coded meanings of the sexualized "Oriental" subject. Then, the actions that subsequently unfold mask the "Orient" by foregrounding the functional utility of its technologized application. Moreover, as the subject's true reason for existence (as commodity) becomes clearer, the instrumentality of its object-status, meaningful only so far as it fulfills the role it was made to play, implies that its "Oriental" identity is but an illusion, for the entity in question does not qualify for any kind of subjecthood to begin with. The resultant being is a cypher, neither a mere instrument nor a culturally, sexually, and racially coded human subject—the ultimate hyperreal—leaving the imagery of the Japanese woman it set out to mimic in a vacuum of denied presence.

When Transcendence Precedes Articulation: The Hyperreal Afterlife of Techno-Orientalism in *Cloud Atlas*

The human clones called fabricants in the Neo Seoul sections of *Cloud Atlas* are subject to a similar state of abjection, their bodies exploited for labor and sexual pleasure while their minds are constantly emptied out by chemical means to ensure robotic servitude. Engineered to the controlling class's taste and need from birth to death, the fabricants are neither human nor machine, disqualified from and made invisible to the social fabric they operate in. Given the geographic setting and the need for consistency in the characters who play the central roles (none of whom happen to be a fabricant save for Sonmi-451), all the fabricants we see on the screen consist of, understandably, Asian female bodies (or female bodies of Asian descent). As in *Robotskin*, aestheticism persists (the futuristic cityscape of Neo Seoul is awe-inspiring to say the least), the "techno" and the "Orient" at once augmenting and cancelling out each other. What further abjects the techno-Orientals in its hyper-realization in *Cloud Atlas*, however, is the proposed narrative framework that betrays itself through visual cues. Sonmi-451, an oppressed Asian female sub-human, is supposed to be the instigator of a revolutionary shift that abolishes the dystopian regime and tears down the exploitive master-slave dynamics of a racialized society. Ironically, the very place and people who catalyze her awakening are mottled with misappropriated signs of colonialism, exhibiting a disturbing instance of ethno-cultural conflation.

The sequences that describe Sonmi-451's initiation into the rebels' cause are most indicative of this categorical dismissal of Asia as a region comprising heterogeneous cultures, people, and historical legacies that are not only different but also at times on contending ends. After witnessing the unsuccessful resistance and execution of a fellow fabricant, a pureblood man called Hae-joo Chang whisks away Sonmi-451 to a safe haven. Telling the bemused clone how she is destined to be a messiah, and unveiling a conspiracy to upturn the ruling party, he walks her into a dark room hidden behind formidably thick metal doors, which then instantly transforms into a neat parlor at his wave of a remote controller. The interior design is of particular note. The floor tiles unfold piece by piece in red, gridded in thick black lines, and the left side of the wall fills up with rectangular lattices encasing white rice-paper-like panels. These minimalist features are offset by the right wall, which rolls out a Sakura (cherry blossom) tree in full bloom, with a crescent moon sitting atop and pink petals gracefully dancing down its branches. Breaking the news that Sonmi can have this (beautiful) room all to herself while she awaits her destiny, and calling up a shimmering view of Neo Seoul from up high to replace the Sakura tree, Hae-joo Chang opens the screens on the left wall and reveals a row of colorful gowns adorned with large bright patterns and ornately corrugated fabric. But something is wrong here. At first glance, this refuge chamber appears to be an ideal place for repose and recuperation, quaintly "Asian" in style yet high-tech with its fancy contraptions. However, the impropriety of the situation should grate against the sensitivity of not only the expectant Korean viewership but also anyone attuned to the colonial history between Korea and Japan in their modernity.

The Sakura blossom unequivocally symbolizes Japan. In addition to being a popular seasonal marker, its disciplined pattern of bloom and fall has been widely used as the emblem of the Samurai spirit and the militarist regime throughout Japan's colonialist expansion.[8] The latticed wall, with its white paper screens and wooden gratings, takes after traditional Japanese doors.[9] Although this detail about screen door patterns may seem trivial, such minor details are still clear indexes of significant cultural variations. For instance, Japan's wooden chopsticks and Korea's metal utensils, despite their formal and functional similarity, reflect difference in climate, agriculture, and subsequent culinary practices. Likewise, the intervals and arrangements of the grate patterns reflect cultural particularities that cannot be readily interchangeable.

The dark red tiles on the floor are also heavily reminiscent of the central (or rather, aside from the white in the backdrop, the only) color in Japan's current national flag as well as the Imperialist flag of the Rising Sun. Old or new, "Seoul" is nowhere to be seen in this room,[10] while the "Asianness" associated with Korea hangs over its quarters through transplanted Japanese imageries, which attests to a general disregard for the historical implications of coloniality, trauma, and even currently ongoing conflicts between the two distinct national, cultural, and ethnic communities.

The yellowface controversy evidences the width and depth of such oversight that mars the film. While welcoming, and even laying claim to a critical awareness of the race issues involved, the directors nevertheless refute charges of disrespect by pointing out that the premise of incarnation makes cross-racial representation inevitable, the execution of which involves not only white actors posing as Asian but also Asian and black actors dressed up as white. The Wachowskis also assert that the film goes beyond race in its ambition to build a cosmic connection among the characters and their settings: "there is a humanity that is beyond our tribe, our ethnic features. A humanity that is beyond our gender. A humanity that unites all of us and transcends our tribal differences" (Rosen). The "transcendence" they aspire to is a commendable ideal, but such prospects could easily deteriorate into a post-racial disregard for the feelings and experiences of actual subjects who suffer from extant mechanisms of othering. When their heterogeneity, rather than its misappropriation, becomes the object of transcendence, crossing becomes erasure instead of emancipation; that which must be overcome, in other words, is not difference itself, but its abuse as a metric of othering.

The Post-Racialist Politics of Engineering a Hyperreal Techno-Orient

In light of the film's post-racial and cosmopolitan politics, then, what *Cloud Atlas* engineers with its misled critical intent is the hyperreal afterlife of techno-Orientalism rather than Orientalism itself, as we have seen in *Robotskin*. Whereas the stance the film takes towards all forces of oppression may frame the monstrous projection of Imperial symbolism on to the advocates of the oppressed as yet another attempt at "crossing" the tribal barriers to which the Wachowskis allude, the lack of respect for both the affective and political dimensions implied in the referents of the cultural, racial, and ethnic signs mask, and then in turn erase, the reality from which they spring. The juxtaposition of *Robotskin* and *Cloud Atlas* is crucial to understanding the problematics of the latter's recuperative project, for the object of emancipation in *Cloud Atlas* is not the antiquated imagery of Asia and its people as uncivilized and therefore subhuman negatives of the West, but an uncanny reflection of the Eastward gaze itself, as technology—the mechanism of alienation that undergirds both Orientalism and techno-Orientalism as its afterlife—stares back at its creator through an embodied presence.

The process of hyperealization, to return to and elaborate on what I wrote above, thus unfolds as follows. While the original referent of Orientalism recedes into obscurity in the film's problematic attempt to create a categorical image of otherness in a future Korea where anti-colonial forces rely on the style (and thereby implicitly, the politics) of the colonizer, the signifiers that originate from and seemingly gesture back to the object of mimesis, namely the misaligned references to ethno-cultural specificities seen in the interior design of the rebels' refuge chamber, acquire a life of their own in erecting new facades of an unnegotiable alterity. The resultant product is an Orientalist vision of Asia (or to be more specific, East Asia) as a technologically sophisticated and aesthetically pleasing fantasy that is still, despite all its guises of progress, moored in premodern despotism. The Neo Seoul in *Cloud Atlas*, therefore, is painted as epistemically benighted, and therefore ontologically inferior under the Eastward gaze, which erases out the quiddity (the "whatness") of the actual subjects that constitute the imagined Asia in lived reality.

Simulated as such, the gaudy futurity of Neo Seoul appears to mask what Korea really is like or about. Of course, what purportedly lies beneath this façade is but an illusion, for no culture, country, or people could be petrified into a fixed set of identities, but the performativity of this masking mechanism imparts the impression that an authentic model actually exists, assigning value and credibility to the misguiding visual cues. The validity of these markers of (an imagined) reality, however, becomes null as the simulation progresses towards its ultimate goal of transcultural (not crosscultural) singularity where all forms of distinctions no longer matter. What is occluded in this precession of hyperrealization is that culture, ethnicity, and race are about heterogeneity not only in their transient manifestations but also in what they mean to the involved subjects. The empty space left behind by discluded historicity is, then, taken over by the paradoxical image of a post-racial, pan-cultural and ahistorical Asia.

Acknowledgments

Special thanks to members of my Spring 2015 Asian American Literature course at Vanderbilt, whose academic rigor and enthusiasm made sharing my observations on this film a true joy. Also, I am immensely thankful to Jung

Min Shin, my amazing undergraduate research partner in the Littlejohn Fellowship, for her light-speed assistance in compiling the sources for this essay. Likewise, thanks to Aimee Bhang, who first introduced me to this commercial at a talk she gave on techno-Orientalism as part of an Asian American Comics Symposium in 2012.

Notes

1. Reddit provides some examples of the reactions Suey Park's campaign gave rise to in the social media world (rentonwong) (this came to my attention thanks to Joanna Zhang from my Representations of Asian Americans class in Spring 2014).

2. The yellowface controversy persisted in spite of the across-the-board application of cross-racial performance throughout the film, such as African American and Asian actors and actresses playing white characters.

3. Following her extrication from Papa Song's (the fast food restaurant where fabricants are being exploited), David Mitchell's Sonmi-451 is kept in a university lab.

4. In light of the post-racial politics of *Cloud Atlas*, Hae-joo Chang and Sonmi-451's relationship of mentor-mentee turned lovers becomes a problematic reproduction of the colonial dynamic. Hae-joo Chang's obvious whiteness (ironically accentuated by the yellowface makeup Jim Sturgess wears), paired with Doona Bae's type-casted Asianness, invokes the specter of the white (male) savior narrative instead of intimating a transracial (or cross-racial, in this case) consummation.

5. See *Spaces of Identity: Global Media, Electronic Landscapes and Cultural Boundaries* (1995).

6. As Said noted, the referent of the "Orient" may vary (meaning the Middle East or the subcontinent of India for Europe, and Asia proper including Southeast and East Asia for the U.S.), as is the case for the word "Asia."

7. Although the campaign webpage (www.robotskin.com) is no longer active, the full commercial is still available on YouTube (Aveillan).

8. For more on the symbolism of cherry blossoms, see Emiko Ohnuki-Tierney's *Kamikaze, Cherry Blossoms, and Nationalisms: the Militarization of Aesthetics in Japanese History* (2002).

9. For further information on Korean screen door patterns, see Chae-wŏn Yun's "A Study on the Development of CAD Digital Jewelry Design Applying the Korean Traditional Window Patterns" (2011).

10. In contrast, outside the room, Neo Seoul is still clearly framed as "Korea" despite having been fast-forwarded across centuries into a fictive future, with street signs and product labels written in Hangul (the Korean alphabet) and people speaking the Korean language. Such subsistence, however, seems but another form of occlusion, for all things ethnically and culturally Korean are associated with decline and retardation. Korean is the low speech the purebloods refuse to use, the Hangul fonts occasionally popping into sight are anachronistic, and the greater majority of the figures who appear to be ethnically Korean or Asian are deemed subhuman (in other words, are fabricants).

Works Cited

Aveillan, Bruno. "Phillips 'Robot skin' (LONG VERSION)." Online video clip. *YouTube.* YouTube, 31 Jan. 2008. Web. 15 April 2014. <https://youtu.be/boSVIA5SaLg>.
Baudrillard, Jean. *Simulacra and Simulation*. 1995. Trans. Sheila F. Glaser. Ann Arbor: U of Michigan P, 2010. Print.
Cloud Atlas. 2012. Dirs. Lana Wachowski, Tom Tykwer, and Andy Wachowski. Warner Home Video, 2013. DVD.
Fan, Christopher T. "Melancholy Transcendence: Ted Chiang and Asian American Postracial Form." *Post45.* 5 Nov. 2014. Web. 2 Feb. 2015.
Huang, Betsy, Greta A. Niu, and David S. Roh, eds. *Techno-Orientalism: Imagining Asia in Speculative Fiction, History, and Media*. New Brunswick: Rutgers UP, 2015.Print.
Mitchell, David. *Cloud Atlas*. New York: Random House, 2004. Print.
Morley, David and Kevin Robins. *Spaces of Identity: Global Media, Electronic Landscapes and Cultural Boundaries*. New York: Routledge, 1995. Print.
Nakamura, Lisa. *Cybertypes: Race, Ethnicity, and Identity on the Internet*. New York: Routeledge, 2002. Print.
Niu, Greta Aiyu. "Techno-Orientalism, Nanotechnology, Posthumans, and Post-Posthumans in Neal Stephenson's and Linda Nagata's Science Fiction." *MELUS* 33.4 (2008): 73–96. Print.
Ohnuki-Tierney, Emiko. *Kamikaze, Cherry Blossoms, and Nationalisms: The Militarization of Aesthetics in Japanese History*. Chicago: U of Chicago P, 2002. Print.
Park, Suey. "Josh Zepp Interviews Suey Park." *Huffington Post Live.* Huffington Post, 28 Mar. 2014. Web. 2 Feb. 2015. <https://youtu.be/MNK-e6nnFGY>.
Posadas, Baryon T. "Beyond Techno-Orientalism: Virtual Worlds and Identity Tourism in Japanese Cyberpunk." *Dis-Orienting Planets: Racial Representations of Asia in Science Fiction*. Jackson: UP of Mississippi, 2017: 144–59. Print.
rentonwong. "Josh Zepp Interviews Suey Park." *Reddit.com*. N. pag., 31 March 2014. Web. 7 April 2014. <https://redd.it/21t8hl>.
Rosen, Christopher. "'Cloud Atlas': Andy & Lana Wachowski and Tom Tykwer On the Problem with Hollywood." *Huffington Post*. 22 Oct. 2012. Web. 12 Mar. 2015.
Said, Edward W. *Orientalism*. 1979. London: Penguin, 2003. Print.
Sohn, Stephen H. "Introduction: Alien/Asian: Imagining the Racialized Future." *MELUS Asian/Alien: Special Issue on Asian American Literature* 33.4 (2008): 5–22. Print.
Ueno, Toshiya. "Techno-Orientalism and Media-Tribalism: On Japanese Animation and Rave Culture." *Third Text* 13.47 (1999): 95–106. Print.
Yun, Chae-wŏn. "A Study on the Development of CAD Digital Jewelry Design Applying the Korean Traditional Window Patterns." *Journal of Communication Design* 37.10 (2011): 251–59. Print.

BEYOND TECHNO-ORIENTALISM
Virtual Worlds and Identity Tourism
in Japanese Cyberpunk

■ ■ ■

BARYON TENSOR POSADAS

Translating Techno-Orientalism

Since the 1980s, especially in the wake of William Gibson's groundbreaking novel *Neuromancer* (1984), a characteristic feature of many science fiction (SF) works identified under the moniker of "cyberpunk" is the tendency to meld images of cyborgs and high tech information networks with racialized and gendered conceptions of a futuristic, imagined "Orient." This pattern of discourse has been termed techno-Orientalism: "the phenomenon of imaging Asia and Asians in hypo- or hyper-technological terms in cultural productions and political discourse" (Roh, Huang, and Niu 2). While the term saw its first articulation in the work of David Morley and Kevin Robbins, wherein they extend Edward Said's conception of Orientalism to consider the production of new stereotypes and imagery of Japan in response to the global dominance of Japanese high-tech companies (141), other cultural critics have subsequently developed the concept further. One such critic, Toshiya Ueno, characterizes techno-Orientalism as the late twentieth century mutation of an older colonial Orientalism for a new global capitalist information age (228–29). Another critic, Stephen Hong Sohn, traces the lineage of contemporary techno-Orientalist representations to the history of Yellow Peril narratives, functioning similarly in response to the perceived threat to Western military and economic dominance (7). Indeed, the mediation of techno-Orientalist imagery enables the treatment of the contemporary experience of dislocation in late capitalist modernity by rendering it graspable as something quintessentially Asian.

In this respect, the proliferation of techno-Orientalist representations in SF may very well be understood as a contemporary manifestation of the genre's long-standing historical linkage with colonial discourse. It should no longer be at all novel or controversial to contend that the formation of the genre of SF is intimately intertwined with the history of colonial conquest. Several recent studies have posited precisely this argument. For example, John Rieder cogently argues that colonialism served as a crucial historical condition of possibility for the very emergence of the genre in the first place. In Rieder's words, it serves as a "part of the genre's texture, a persistent, important component of its displaced references to history, its engagement in ideological production, and its construction of the possible and imaginable" (15). Not only do the central tropes and images of early science fiction—exploration and the frontier, the encounter with alien cultures, eugenic theories and racial discourses—derive from a colonial gaze, but also, the appearance of a class of technocratic consumer-subjects. This class would constitute the SF readership requiring the concomitant development of an advanced industrial economy organized around the commodification of leisure time, which is itself a historical process dependent upon the exploitation of the colonial periphery (Rieder 27–28). Yet while Rieder's focus is on the historical emergence of the genre, the persistence of techno-Orientalism in contemporary SF writings indicates that the colonial underpinnings of the SF genre is not merely an historical issue but one that pervades the genre's continued production of an imperial imagination in the present. At issue is how exactly the very history of colonialism continues to be a constitutive component of the present, and as such continues to play a formative role in the conditions of possibility for thinking about the politics of futurity.

This question serves as the point of departure for my discussion of techno-Orientalism in this essay. To date, much of the existing scholarship on techno-Orientalism has placed its focus primarily on the problems with Western (mis)representations of Asia and Asian people in Anglophone SF texts. In contrast, the question of the consequences for SF writing emerging from those locations that have become the objects of fetish and fantasies of difference—in particular, Japan—has garnered relatively less attention, despite the fact that, as Ueno points out, techno-Orientalist discourse functions as a kind of two-way mirror, by which "Western or other people misunderstand and fail to recognize an always illusory Japanese culture, but it also is the mechanism through which Japanese misunderstand themselves" (228). Ironically, as valuable as it may be, critical writing about techno-Orientalism would largely appear to still be enclosed within a techno-Orientalist frame in its seeming blindness to texts outside of the Anglophone tradition. Yet I argue that the examination of the impact of techno-Orientalism on Japanese SF opens up an important space to articulate the larger stakes of the critique of techno-Orientalism beyond the cataloging of misrepresentations or the seeking of alternative or counter-Orientalist visions. I contend that at stake in the question of techno-Orientalism is more than matters of mere cultural misrepresentation, but the larger issue of how the mechanisms of colonial cognitive estrangement continue to set the terms for the imagination of futurity. While SF texts often employ colonial or Orientalist imagery with an eye towards its subversion or reversal, attending to Japanese SF texts reveals the limitations of this gesture by bringing to attention the structural pervasiveness of the gendered and racialized infrastructure that sets the terms of the genre's attempts to imagine other worlds and futurities.

Identity Tourism in Venus City

In the spirit of attempting to account for SF as a site of contestation, as a space for addressing the heterogeneity of possible positionalities in relation to the imagination of futurity, I take up the work of Japanese author Gorō Masaki (b. 1957).[1] What makes Masaki's SF writing particularly illustrative for my purposes is its extensive employment of motifs closely associated with cyberpunk—for instance, the now familiar formula involving cybernetic technologies, console cowboys, and a hard-boiled thriller plotline set in a dystopian late capitalist world—in a way that calls attention to the techno-Orientalizing tendencies of such settings. In doing so, his work raises the question of envisioning a futurity that does not simply reproduce the terms of the present, not only within the science fiction genre, but also in the cultural politics of the contemporary conjuncture, whose very conception is already inflected by the language of science-fictionality.

As early as the publication of his first major work of fiction, *Evil Eyes (Jagan,* 1988), whose story revolves around the conflict between a New Age cult and a multinational music conglomerate over a piece of mind-control software with the capacity to brainwash a whole population, Masaki developed a reputation as a kind of Japanese clone of William Gibson, (Gregory, McCaffery, and Masaki 78). His reputation indicates the relative ease in which the cyberpunk sensibility translated to the Japanese context. Although *Evil Eyes* does not directly take up the techno-Orientalist tendency to produce fetishized images of a futuristic Japan, such is certainly not the case in Masaki's second major work of fiction, his post-cyberpunk novel that won the Seiun and Nihon SF Taisho awards, *Venus City* (*Viinasu Shiti*, 1992), which arguably foregrounds precisely this problem. This latter novel is set in an alternate future world wherein Japan has become the dominant global economic power with much of its industrial manufacturing outsourced to other nations, most of which are in the midst of a recession. Migrants from these other nations seeking better fortunes steadily arrive in Japan, with the consequence of exacerbating existing racial tensions and xenophobic anti-immigrant sentiments among the Japanese population.

The story of the novel revolves around one such individual with xenophobic attitudes: a young woman by the name of Sakiko Moriguchi. A self-professed delinquent employee, who is perennially tardy and unfocused, Sakiko resents that she has to work under a white American male boss in a multinational Big Data conglomerate known as Arc Corporation. She instead spends much of her idle time in the titular "Venus City," which is the name for a massive multi-user virtual space. In Venus City, Sakiko dons the identity of Saki, her ethnically ambiguous male avatar. The plot unfolds when Saki encounters and begins a sexual relationship with Junko, whose avatar is the living embodiment of a Japanese doll. At this point, the novel shifts its perspective to that of Junko, who turns out to be none other than Sakiko's boss Jim Bradley. The story subsequently reveals that Jim's Venus City avatar of Junko is being subjected to sexual abuse as a form of blackmail by a nebulous group of conspirators who seek access to classified material from the digital archive of Arc Corporation. This information would give them the ability to control Venus City by reconfiguring the neural networks of its users such that they will recognize virtual reality as actual, in effect making Venus City appear to be the actual world to its users. Although the novel initially suggests that the conspiracy is a part of an information terrorism plot to cripple the Japanese information economy, in the end, the author reveals that the conspiracy emerged from the collective unconscious of Venus City itself, which has become sentient and seeks to fulfill the unconscious desires of all its users to permanently replace their material world with the virtual world of Venus City.

Immediately evident from the above summary, the world of *Venus City* features key elements of the paranoid techno-Orientalist fantasies vis-a-vis Japan that widely circulated during the heyday of cyberpunk in the 1980s, seeing the extent to which the novel sets up Japan as a new global hegemon dominating the economies and industries of other countries. Indeed, as a number of critics have noted, the novel appears to take as its point of departure the widely circulating "Pax Japonica" nightmares of American commentators about the existential threat of a Japan poised to take over the global economic system during the peak of the Japanese economic bubble.[2] On its face, this reproduction and reiteration of such techno-Orientalist tropes could be read as indicative of the pattern wherein Japanese cyberpunk texts often present a science-fictional "Japan" that is in alignment with the "Japan" imagined in Anglophone cyberpunk. As Takayuki Tatsumi puts it, "Anglo-American writers, through their own logic of mimicry, imitated and reappropriated 'Japanesque' images, that is images that at once draw on and distort Japanese culture" (*Full Metal Apache* xv). Tatsumi continues, "their Japanese counterparts came to realize that writing subversive fiction in the wake of cyberpunk meant gaining insight into the radically science-fictional 'Japan'" (*Full Metal Apache* xv).

That said, the explicit foregrounding of these representations, arguably even to the point of satirical excess, hint at a desire to trouble these techno-Orientalist visions. Specifically, the multiple scenes depicting racial and gender passing in virtual spaces in Masaki's novel provide a commentary on the conventional conceptions of the relationship between information technologies and gendered and racialized bodies. The very opening lines of the novel establish this interest in the cultural phenomenon of virtual passing in cyberspace, which begin with the narrator Sakiko's words "I've made up my mind. Tonight, I will change my sex" (Masaki 9).[3] The subsequent chapters reveal just what is entailed in such a so-called "sex change," with an extended sequence of Sakiko preparing her brand new highly customized masculine-presenting avatar just before once again accessing the Venus City multi-user network. These customizations include not just a change in the sexual characteristics of the body itself, but also various options for clothing, hairstyle, and all manner of other accoutrements. Through this process, Sakiko takes on the form of Saki in Venus City, a six-foot tall man dressed in "Designer Punk" fashion whose body has been custom-designed to be "androgynous from an overall appearance, combining the active dynamism of a man's muscle and the delicate charm of a woman" and to be "very plastic, very streamlined" in look (Masaki 17).

Such a desire for experimentation by way of the meticulous designing and inhabiting of another body by no means restricts Sakiko's desire to just an idiosyncratic quirk, either. On the contrary, in the world of Masaki's *Venus City*, it would appear that there is nothing at all considered transgressive or unusual about using an avatar whose gender presentation and appearance is markedly distinct from one's body in the material world. Rather, as Sakiko's account suggests, it is treated as a logical step in the typical progress of a new user of Venus City towards system mastery. Sakiko believes that "when you first set foot in Venus City, initially . . . your form in this world (otherwise known as the physical world) will appear in that world (conversely, known as the mental world) unchanged," but that "soon enough, as an inhabitant of Venus City, you'll want a new Self-Image as distinct as anyone else's" (Masaki 41). Indeed, all the characters encountered by Sakiko (in her virtual form as Saki) within Venus City similarly make use of meticulously designed custom avatars that bear little resemblance to their appearance in the physical world. For example, the TRB (trans-reality brothers), a group of four friends who later serve as her posse, all have androgynous (but primarily male-presenting) avatars clad in fetish wear within Venus City, but are later revealed to be fairly ordinary housewives and young computer science students. If all these other users of Venus City are any indication, Sakiko's explanation of the motivations behind her desire to adopt a masculine presenting avatar in Venus City—with the words "wrapped within the flesh of a vigorous man, I am able to discover another me" (Masaki 23)—could perhaps be extended to a broader social desire for acts of race and gender in the world of Masaki's novel.

In his analysis of Masaki's novel, Torahiko Ichikawa suggests that the popular desire for exploring other identities in the virtual world of Venus City expresses dissatisfaction with the stifling rigidity of contemporary Japanese social and cultural life. In his words, Venus City functions as a "pressure valve for the elaborate system of social discipline, an electronic carnivalesque place" (150). However, it should be noted that Sakiko's place of employment is not a Japanese company, but instead a multinational tech conglomerate. Moreover, the impetus behind her desire to take on the body of a masculine-presenting avatar is her dislike of working for a white male boss. For this reason, I would argue that her desire to gender-bend cannot simply be ascribed to the stifling corporate culture and social structures of Japan. Famously, Donna Haraway identifies women of color as the quintessential cyborg figure, pointing specifically to "the cyborg women making chips in Asia" (7) in a gesture indicative of how the melding of machinic alterity with a racialized and gendered otherness marks the historical changes in the organization of global labor in the form of the displacement of the labor of mechanized production onto Asian women. In this context, her actions may also be understood as a response to the Orientalist eroticization of Japanese women as docile and subservient, stereotypes that also often overlap with notions about Japan's docile and robotic workforce that began to circulate as Japan increasingly came to be seen as an economic threat to the West (Morley and Robbins 170). Indeed,

Sakiko's persistent repetition of her self-proclaimed status as a delinquent worker (*furyo shain*) points towards such motives.

Given the novel's depiction of the potential of virtual worlds to facilitate cross-racial and cross-gender passing, *Venus City* seemingly presents a scenario in alignment with the more techno-utopian fantasies *vis-à-vis* online interactions that characterize it as space wherein users' racialized and gendered identities can be suspended to create a discrimination-free space. Yet while the act of gender passing appears unremarkable in the novel at first glance, insofar as these gender performances depend on existing stylistics of enactment for their legibility, such acts run the risk of reinscribing rather than disrupting existing cultural codes surrounding gender. In the case of *Venus City*, while androgynous and other characters who transgress the gender binary do occasionally appear in the background, the central storyline between Sakiko/Saki and Jim/Junko largely follow conventional codes that map vigor onto the masculine and innocence onto the feminine. Furthermore, the racial distribution of users' avatars within the virtual world of Venus City is revealing. Despite the fact that most users are Japanese, "close to half of all users who come to Venus City do so with a self-image that mimics a Caucasian body. Another twenty percent have a black-looking self-image. And almost all of the remaining thirty percent use a self-image borrowed from Japanese manga or animation." (Masaki 150). Taken together, these details hint at a recognition of the continuing normativity of an unmarked white masculinity.

In this respect, the depiction of online world in *Venus City* appears to be closer in alignment with more recent scholarship that have challenged such techno-utopian characterizations of online spaces, instead emphasizing the point that overlooked in such readings are the racialized and gendered infrastructures that still undergird these more utopian valorizations of the virtual. The work of Lisa Nakamura, for instance, offers a thorough interrogation of the dynamics of what she terms "identity tourism," which in her analysis results not in a radically democratizing post-racial or post-gender space (as digital utopians would have it), but instead as a site that reinscribes all manner of identity-based oppressions (40). With the unmooring of identity from the physical body, "users are drawn to create personae that are culturally coherent and intelligible, and racial cybertypes provide familiar, solid, and reassuring versions of race which other users can readily accept and understand since they are so used to seeing them in novels, films, and videogames" (Nakamura 40). Considering how cyberpunk fictions have served, in the words of Nakamura, to "supply the specific imagery, tropes, and ways of representing race that provide the racial templates for online interactions"

(61), the thematic echoes between the narrative staging of various acts of racial and gender passing in the virtual world of *Venus City* and the critical writing on contemporary digital cultures that have subsequently appeared in its wake should not be surprising. Nonetheless, the writing and publication of Masaki's novel predates the mass popularization of the Internet. As such, the significance of the novel cannot be reduced to merely an allegory or reflection of the contemporary cultural politics of the Internet. Rather, it seems that the object of its commentary is more productively identified as their common point of reference in the genre of cyberpunk SF itself. In this sense, parallel to Nakamura's unpacking of the question of whether the Internet can "propagate genuinely new and nonracist (and non-sexist and nonclassist) ways of being, or does it merely reflect our culture at large" (xii), I believe that Masaki's novel can be better understood as a text concerned with the specific ways in which the imagination of alterity and futurity within the structural constraints of SF world-building mediate (and are mediated by) racialized and gendered dynamics.

Satirical Reversals

Viewed in these terms, the virtual world envisioned in Masaki's *Venus City* precisely makes use of these scenes of racial and gender passing to call into question their fetishization in cyberpunk. As a genre, cyberpunk "offers a uniquely fluid capacity to change gender, name, age, culture, race, role, and personality in the process of moving from one world into another" (Heuser 64). However, Masaki's novel calls attention to the racialized and gendered infrastructure of techno-Orientalism that often undergirds these more utopian valorizations of the virtual in cyberpunk. Indeed, Timothy Yu contends that the disembodied and deterritorialized character of cyberspace explicitly contrasts with the postmodern globalized city that remains marked by the traces of history and racialized and gendered dynamics. Taking up William Gibson's classic cyberpunk novel *Neuromancer* as one of his illustrative examples, Yu argues that the novel is structured as a movement from the Orientalized space of Chiba City to the deterritorialized domain of cyberspace, with the former prefiguring the latter, such that "Chiba City remains necessary in Gibson's narrative only so long as Case remains tied to his physical body, incapable of jacking into cyberspace; once he regains those abilities, the narrative shifts to the disembodied realm of cyberspace" (62–63). Yet at the same time, this movement into cyberspace is also a reterritorialization in that it enables Case to end his exile in Japan and return home to the West, in effect reasserting his position as a white Western subject against the Japanese other. Wendy Chun has also raised similar arguments. For Chun, a salient feature of Gibson's conception of cyberspace is its evocations of the imagination of the frontier. While Chiba City overflows in material signifiers—corporate names, technical jargon, ethnic markers—the most significant characteristic of cyberspace is its perceived emptiness. In effect, cyberspace functions as the negation of the techno-Orientalized Japan, enabling its transformation into a frontier, and with that, a site of sexual and colonial conquest: As Chun puts it, "cyberspace—unlike the physical landscape—can be conquered and made to submit: entering cyberspace is analogous to opening up the Orient.... Cyberspace as disembodied representation rehearses themes of Oriental exoticism and Western penetration" (188).

Venus City takes these organizing oppositions between West and East, the virtual and the physical, or the masculine and feminine, and turns them on their heads. In contrast to Gibson's take on cyberspace as a kind of empty electronic frontier space populated only by AI constructs and raw data represented as abstract shapes, the titular Venus City of Masaki's novel bustles as a virtual metropolis with both established and emergent social conventions, cultures, and practices. Following this pattern, in place of a depiction of virtual space as an enabler of a disembodied and deterritorialized experience, the novel emphasizes corporeality of the body repeatedly. Consider, for example, that it does not follow the genre convention of "jacking in" directly into the cerebral cortex (and hence bypassing the body in the process) as the mechanism for accessing the virtual world, but instead makes the interface for entering Venus City an almost lycra-like body-fitting "data suit," thus emphasizing the bodily sensations of the user experience. Indeed, when Sakiko first tries out her masculine-presenting avatar, it is the corporeal experience inhabiting another body that is foremost on her mind: "From a perspective a foot higher than the usual, I gazed at the world around me. Just this extra foot of height somehow gave me the feeling a great strength [. . .] Wrapped in this body, my state of mind shifted to something akin to the protagonist of a hard-boiled novel—tough and vigorous" (Masaki 18). Conversely, parallel to Saki's transformation into a hard-boiled hero, Jim Bradley in turn becomes the damsel in distress Junko, a Japanese girl whose exquisite custom-built features are often compared to the appearance of a traditional Japanese doll (Masaki 32). Not only is Junko one of the only explicitly racialized avatars in the novel, the marking of her identity as a young Japanese woman is interwoven with her sexualization and objectification. Unlike other characters who design their own avatars, the virtual identity of Junko is imposed upon Jim Bradley, forced on him as a part of the plot to compel him to reveal the secrets of Arc Corporation. The fact that the only character whose avatar is marked as a Japanese woman in the novel is compelled to enact the stereotypical role of a submissive hypersexualized girl highlights the circumscription of the possible roles she is permitted to perform. Chun's diagnosis is that "cyberpunk's twin obsessions with cyberspace and Japan as the Orient are not accidental.... Rather, the Japanese Orient is a privileged example of the virtual" (195); if she is correct, then what appears in *Venus City* is the literalization of this gesture, such that the imagination of techno-Orientalized Japan no longer merely prefigures but has instead become cyberspace itself. Put differently, Masaki presents the virtual world of *Venus City* as something other than as a site for the recuperation of Western fantasies of sexual and colonial conquest. Instead, it is presented as the opposite, as a space that compels the white Western subject to become precisely the embodiment of techno-Orientalist fetishization. In doing so, the novel resists the desire to present cyberspace in techno-utopian terms as a disembodied and post-racial site and instead compels the recognition of it as a site of struggle, as a concept that is haunted by the subtext of techno-Orientalist discourse.

These gestures of reversal ask more than the simple question of representation of Asian bodies and spaces within the virtual worlds of cyberpunk fiction. More than that, they take up the persistent problem in the SF genre of imagining radically different worlds and futurities whose terrains are not already mapped out in advance by existing racialized and gendered imaginaries, especially given how the most characteristic motifs of cyberpunk texts often already foreground metafictive questions. As Brian McHale observes in his analysis of the poetics of cyberpunk, "the paraspace motif, including cyberspace and its functional equivalent, the myth-world, not only serves to bring into view the 'worldness' of world; it also offers opportunities for reflecting on world-making itself, and on science fiction world-making in particular" (12). Consequently, the question at the heart of the novel is how, as Chun puts it, techno-Orientalism "seeks to orient the reader to a technology-oriented present/future ... through the promise of a readable difference, and through a conflation of information networks with an exotic urban landscape" (177). In other words, even as SF texts evoke a sense of disorienting alterity in the futuristic worlds it presents, this defamiliarization is also matched by the employment of familiar cultural images that serve as signposts with which to literally orient oneself within the otherness of the imagined world of the text. Because of the wide circulation of standard images of the colonial or racial or ethnic other, they become an easy stand-in for depicting alienness in general.

The techno-Orientalism of cyberpunk writings represents but another instantiation of SF's long history of employing colonial codes as allegorical devices or metaphors—ideologies of progress, space colonization, the exploration of the frontier, the discovery of lost worlds, or the encounter with alien cultures—and thus functions as an important device for making legible its speculative fantasies (Rieder 2). Or, to build upon Darko Suvin's pioneering theorization of the genre, if SF operates on the basis of a mechanism of "cognitive estrangement," then it necessarily accounts for how coloniality—understood not only as a historical period that is now over, but as a set of social technologies that persist into the present—works as one of the mechanisms through which the cognition effect is generated (4). Put simply, readers must recognize that SF operates on a principle of *colonial* cognitive estrangement in order to fully open up a space to articulate critical questions about the politics of futurity.

With this critical context in mind, what makes Masaki's novel noteworthy in its engagement with techno-Orientalist discourse is its attempt to interrogate its own historical conditions of production within the particular position that Japan occupies vis-à-vis the colonial gaze of the SF genre. I find Rieder's identification of a structure of satirical reversal as one of the critical possibilities offered by the SF genre's engagement with colonial discourse relevant here. Even as he recognizes that such a gesture does not go beyond the logic of empire itself, Rieder nonetheless contends that "the science fiction novel, while staying within the ideological and epistemological framework of the colonial discourse, exaggerates and exploits its internal divisions [that] it estranges the colonial gaze by reversing the direction of the gaze's anachronism" (10). Yet is it not the case that this reversal of colonial anachronism is precisely what is already performed in the techno-Orientalist habit of locating the site of futurity onto the Japanese other? Such a reversal emerges as a constellation of imagery and rhetoric in response to the fear of Japan's geopolitical successes in the latter half of the twentieth century. Here, Stephen Hong Sohn contends that techno-Orientalism is a contemporary reworking of older Yellow Peril fictions of an earlier historical moment. If Yellow Peril narratives were a product of the "reorientation and reconsideration of Asia more broadly as a location from which to mold futuristic representations and alternative temporalities" resulting from Japan's victory in the Russo-Japanese War, then it appears that techno-Orientalism's formative role in the emergence of SF as a coherent genre is more pervasive than would initially seem (Sohn 5). Even as Japan has become the object of all manner of science-fictional fantasies of difference, be it in the form of earlier Yellow Peril images or more current modes of high tech cultural exoticism, it is nonetheless crucial to recognize that Japanese SF, too, emerged out of the nation's history of imperial conquest and expansion (Mizuno 156–59). While it was no less brutal or violent than other imperialist projects, as Naoki Sakai points out, Japanese imperialism was remarkable for its employment of a rhetoric of opposition to imperialism (or, at the very least, European imperialism) as an important ideological buttress (817). In effect, Japan already serves as a kind of satirical reversal of the Western colonial gaze by becoming a colonial power itself. This pattern that is only repeated in the contemporary moment, manifesting in the interplay between cyberpunk post-humanist rhetoric (with all its attendant techno-Orientalizing overtones) that then becomes the basis for the development of a Japanese cultural nationalist discourse (Sato 336).

Masaki's *Venus City* brings attention to this problem of staging all manner of reversals of cyberpunk motifs. Despite the foregrounding of the techno-Orientalist underpinnings of cyberpunk concepts that these reversals enact, ultimately, the novel does not offer a corrective or counter-Orientalist gesture beyond this satirical reversal itself. In fact, at times, the novel almost appears to actively reject such a move. While the virtual world of Venus appears at first glance to allow its users to freely adopt avatars and identities of all kinds, all too often these identities still fall into recognizable types, from the leather-clad hard-boiled hero to the fetishized Japanese doll. Indeed, while Sakiko and Jim Bradley switch their gender presentations when they don their respective avatars of Saki and Junko, the gender roles and sexual politics within Venus City depicted in the novel remain largely conventional. The Japanese doll Junko remains the object of fetishized desire and the leather-clad masculine figure of Saki remains the hardboiled hero. Moreover, despite the seeming prevalence of racial and gender passing in the virtual world of Venus City, at no point in the novel do the interrelationships between the characters transgress socially circumscribed heteronormative desires. These unchanged identity politics point towards a seeming resistance to articulate a virtual world—and by extension, a science-fictional vision—beyond an extrapolation of existing norms of what Lee Edelman has termed reproductive futurism (2).

Japan and SF

At the end of *Venus City*, Sakiko and Jim Bradley race back to Arc Corporation to cut it off from access to all networks. Their goal is to prevent access to a classified archive that contains research on techniques for reconfiguring the human brain such that it would no longer be able to distinguish the virtual world from the physical world. Although they initially assume that foreign anti-Japanese elements are behind the plot—thinking that the ultimate objective is to cripple the Japanese economy by locking its citizens in Venus City, turning it into a virtual prison that they believe to be their actual world—at the novel's conclusion they finally learn the truth. The collective unconscious of Venus City itself has gained sentience. Taking on the avatar of Venus, the city uses the secret desires of its users to replace their actual world with the virtual one made manifest, telling Sakiko "Do you not desire a body that could overcome any other man?" and Jim, "In the city, no one will ever know that you are a foreigner" (Masaki 303). Here, both characters are offered the possibility of going beyond mere mimicry, of fully assimilating into the dominant culture across the respective axes of gender and nationality. Of course, assimilation does not ultimately entail any real disruption of existing structures of exclusion, instead serving only to reinforce and naturalize them. Could this be why Sakiko and Jim, despite their inability to deny having such desires, nevertheless hold the gate and prevent Venus from accomplishing her goal?

At the level of the story, the narrative ends with a return to the status quo, suggesting a failure of imagination, a failure of will to leap forth into a world that both characters evidently desire. Yet, at another level, perhaps such a conclusion precisely reflects the point. The novel enacts a metafictive autocritique of SF's world-making techniques through its interrogation of the techno-Orientalist underpinnings of cyberpunk's virtual worlds. This reading provides an illustrative example of SF's failure itself to imagine a future not already colonized in advance by the terms of the techno-Orientalized present. It illustrates, in other words, Fredric Jameson's famous claim that the genre's "deepest vocation is to over and over demonstrate and to dramatize our incapacity to imagine a future" (288–89). In doing so, it calls attention to the horizons of the genre's political engagement and expression, revealing the limits of techniques such as estrangement or satirical reversal that may appear to be a locus of critical potential. In this sense, Japanese SF's reversal of the colonial gaze exposes how the politics of the genre take the form not of the imagination of the future per se, but instead the cataloguing of the ideological limits that shape what futures are imaginable at particular historical conjunctures.

If techno-Orientalism's language is woven into the texture of the genre, then how SF might begin to exceed these logics becomes a relevant question to address. SF articulates imagined futures and alterities that present a radical alternative to the structures and logics of coloniality; futures that have not been colonized by (and in effect, rendered docile to) the terms of the present, reduced to merely its extension (Jameson 232). This challenge takes on even greater resonance in light of Istvan Csicsery-Ronay Jr.'s claim that the "widespread normalization of what is essentially a style of estrangement and dislocation has stimulated the development of science-fictional habits of mind, so that we no longer treat SF as purely a genre-engine producing formulaic effects, but rather as a kind of awareness we might call *science-fictionality*, a mode of response that frames and tests experiences as if they were aspects of a work of science fiction" (2). Paradoxically, the loss of a sense of historicity and futurity appears to be the most pressing political problem marking the condition of science-fictionality of the contemporary conjuncture; that is to say, the very inability to imagine a radically different future not already determined in advance by colonized habits of thought.

Oddly enough, SF persists despite these failures of imagination, perhaps indicative of the existence of a form of "cruel optimism" about SF's utopian potential (Berlant 2). While SF's other worlds and other futures might themselves be discredited, the persistence of an attachment to these texts (and to the genre as such) nonetheless engenders models of social belonging through their practices of collective production and consumption. I wonder if the *affective attachments* to this archive of unrealized utopias might not also be an important object of inquiry. Such an approach would demand an analysis of SF attentive to the affective intensities, the interpretative techniques, the social institutions, and the participatory practices of SF culture as a kind of social movement devoted to world-building, not only of a science-fictional universe, but also, potentially, an alternative sociopolitical order that forms the basis of a set of political demands.

Given that popular techno-Orientalist representations often still imagine "Japan" as a locus of science-fictionality, as a site signifying the future as such, might this critique also open up ways of reframing the critical practice of Japan Studies as well? Might it be productive to consider Japan Studies as a branch of Science Fiction Studies? Indeed, just as SF in the contemporary conjuncture must operate in an environment after the end of the future, Japanese Studies today must operate in an environment after "Japan" has ceased to be all that meaningful as an organizing or disciplinary category of analysis, what with all the conceptual baggage of the nation form, the intellectual history of area studies, and the logic of Orientalism that structures the field as such. After all, with the field's origins as an artifact of Cold War era attempts to produce knowledge of other places in the name of national (particularly American) interests, H. D. Harootunian and Masao Miyoshi have rightly declared that area studies is now in its "afterlife" as the original historical conditions of its coming into being no longer exist. In their words, "the world we now live in has already exceeded the original horizon of area studies programs.... We must begin the labor of reconstituting strategies to secure knowledges of regions of the world that are no longer the outside of Euro-America" (Harootunian and Miyoshi 14). Yet at the same time, "Japan" remains a persistent object of affective attachment. Rather than simply rejecting these attachments, I believe the challenge is to engage with the affective fact of "Japan," and to take seriously the attachments it engenders. This approach entails going beyond the tired moralizing criticisms of the misrepresentations of techno-Orientalisms and fetishisms, and instead requires a consideration of how it may very well precisely be these techno-Orientalisms that create sites of belonging, and potentially, sites of struggle.

Notes

1. The name "Gorō Masaki" is a pseudonym, and little else about the secretive author's background has been officially confirmed. To date, only two of his works are available in English translation. The first is the short story "With Love, To My Eldest Brother," which appeared in *Fictional International* 24 (1993), and the second is an excerpt from the novella *Evil Eyes* titled "The Human Factor," which appeared in *The Review of Contemporary Fiction* XXII No. 2 (2002).

2. For example, in his *Japanoido Sengen* (*A Japanoid Manifesto*, 1993), Tatsumi describes the novel's setting as follows: "The stage is set in a 21st century 'Pax Japonica' society that has consolidated a massive information network. Japan's industrial manufacturing base has been outsourced to every other Asian nation, leaving only the headquarters in the Japanese archipelago itself. While Japan itself refuses any internal reforms, it exports its technology, capital, and business practices around the world, subordinating factories in different countries and exercising a power to control manufacturing plants all over the world" (216–17).

3. All translations from the novel and other Japanese language materials are my own.

Works Cited

Berlant, Lauren. *Cruel Optimism*. Durham: Duke UP, 2011. Print.
Chun, Wendy Hui Kyong. *Control and Freedom: Power and Paranoia in the Age of Fiber Optics*. Cambridge: MIT P, 2006. Print.
Csicsery-Ronay, Istvan, Jr. *The Seven Beauties of Science Fiction*. Middletown: Wesleyan UP, 2008. Print.
Edelman, Lee. *No Future: Queer Theory and the Death Drive*. Durham: Duke UP, 2004. Print.
Gregory, Sinda, Larry McCaffery, and Goro Masaki. "Not Just a Gibson Clone: An Interview with Goro Masaki." *Review of Contemporary Fiction* 22.2 (2002): 75–81. Print.
Haraway, Donna. "A Manifesto for Cyborgs: Science, Technology, and Socialist Feminism in the 1980s." *Socialist Review* 80 (1985): 65–108. Print.
Harootunian, H. D., and Miyoshi, Masao. "Introduction: The 'Afterlife' of Area Studies." *Learning Places: The Afterlives of Area Studies*. Eds. Masao Miyoshi and Harry D. Harootunian. Durham: Duke UP, 1–18. Print.
Heuser, Sabine. *Virtual Geographies: Cyberpunk at the Intersection of the Postmodern and Science Fiction*. Amsterdam: Rodopi, 2003. Print.

Ichikawa, Torahiko. "Pakkusu Japonika-to Shūsei-Shugi: Viinasu Shiti-Ron" ["Pax Japonica and Revisionism: On *Venus City*"]. *Matsuyama Daigaku Ronshū* 9.3 (1997): 141–57. Print.
Jameson, Fredric. *Archaeologies of the Future: The Desire Called Utopia and Other Science Fictions*. New York: Verso, 2005. Print.
Masaki, Gorō. *Viinasu Shiti [Venus City]*. Tokyo: Hayakawa shobō, 1992. Print.
———. "With Love, to my Eldest Brother." *Fiction International* 24 (Spring 1993): 30–35. Print
———. "The Human Factor (from *Evil Eyes*)." *The Review of Contemporary Fiction* 22.2 (2002): 82–90. Print.
McHale, Brian. "Towards a Poetics of Cyberpunk." *Beyond Cyberpunk: New Critical Perspectives*. Eds. Graham J. Murphy and Sherryl Vint. New York: Routledge, 2010. 3–28. Print.
Mizuno, Hiromi. *Science for the Empire: Scientific Nationalism in Modern Japan*. Stanford: Stanford UP, 2009. Print.
Morley, David, and Kevin Robbins. *Spaces of Identity: Global Media, Electronic Landscapes, and Cultural Boundaries*. New York: Routledge, 1995. Print.
Nakamura, Lisa. *Cybertypes: Race, Ethnicity, and Identity on the Internet*. New York: Routledge, 2002. Print.
Rieder, John. *Colonialism and the Emergence of Science Fiction*. Middletown: Wesleyan UP, 2008. Print.
Roh, David S., Betsy Huang, and Greta A. Niu. "Technologizing Orientalism: An Introduction." *Techno-Orientalism: Imagining Asia in Speculative Fiction, History, and Media*. New Brunswick: Rutgers UP, 2015. 1–19. Print.
Sakai, Naoki. "'You Asians': On the Historical Role of the West and Asia Binary." *South Atlantic Quarterly* 99.4 (2000): 789–818. Print.
Sato, Kumiko. "How Information Technology Has (Not) Changed Feminism and Japanism: Cyberpunk in the Japanese Context." *Comparative Literature Studies* 41.3 (2004): 335–55. Project MUSE. Web. 25 Apr. 2014.
Sohn, Stephen Hong. "Introduction: Alien/Asian: Imagining the Racialized Future." *MELUS* 33.4 (2008): 5–22. Print.
Suvin, Darko. *Metamorphoses of Science Fiction: On the Poetics and History of a Literary Genre*. New Haven: Yale UP, 1979. Print.
Tatsumi, Takayuki. *Full Metal Apache: Transactions between Cyberpunk Japan and Avant-Pop America*. Durham: Duke UP, 2006. Print.
———. *Japanoido Sengen: Gendai Nihon SF o Yomu Tameni [A Japanoid Manifesto: Towards a Reading of Contemporary Japanese SF]*. Tokyo: Hayakawa shobō, 1993. Print.
Ueno, Toshiya. "Japanimation and Techno-Orientalism." *The Uncanny: Experiments in Cyborg Culture*. Ed. Bruce Grenville. Vancouver: Arsenal, 2002. 228–31. Print.
Yu, Timothy. "Oriental Cities, Postmodern Futures: *Naked Lunch*, *Blade Runner*, and *Neuromancer*." *MELUS* 33.4 (2008): 45–71. Print.

MANY PATHS, ONE JOURNEY
Cixin Liu's Three Body Problem Novels

■ ■ ■

BRADFORD LYAU

By now it is almost trite to declare science fiction a global phenomenon. It is equally obvious that American genre science fiction dominates the field. Its tradition of credible extrapolation of new science and technology in well thought-out and well-written fictional futures provides the basis of its global attraction. However, there do exist other prominent traditions in the field. In France the adaptation of Voltaire's philosophical tale (*conte philosophique*) plays a significant role in France's science fiction history.[1] Even in English-language science fiction variations of this genre have emerged, including H.G. Wells's *The War of the Worlds* (1898) and Ursula K. Le Guin's *The Word for World is Forest* (1972). Furthermore, there are examples of works which blend the two traditions together. Kim Stanley Robinson's trilogy dealing with human settlement on Mars (*Red Mars* [1993], *Green Mars* [1994], and *Blue Mars* [1996]) comes to mind.

Cixin Liu's[2] trilogy dealing with Earth's struggles against an alien race, titled *Remembrance of Earth's Past,* but often referred to merely as the Three Body trilogy (*The Three-Body Problem* [2007, English translation 2014], *The Dark Forest* [2008, 2015], and *Death's End* [2010, planned publication for 2016]), is another example of this particular combination. This chapter analyzes the first two novels of Liu's trilogy in light of the literary traditions (both Chinese and Western) present in them, and especially in terms of American genre science fiction and the philosophical tale.

Liu's own published statements about his trilogy supports this observation. In his article, "The Worst of All Possible Universes and the Best of All Possible Earths: *Three Body and Chinese Science Fiction*," he offers some background for his novels. Liu describes his brand of science fiction as very American or, as he puts it, "Campbellian 'science fiction fundamentalism,'" referring to the influential American magazine editor, John W. Campbell Jr. (1910–71). Since this type of story is often not respected by the Chinese literary establishment, Liu states that he wanted to gain wider acceptance of his novels by not only raising the literary quality of his writing, but also by infusing realism and injecting present-day concerns into his stories to give them a contemporary relevancy. When he wrote his third novel of the series (to be released in English in America next year), he found this impossible. So he returned to his Campbellian roots and wrote his fundamentalist science fiction novel. Ironically, as he points out, this novel turned out to be the one responsible for making the series popular among the general reading public. The fact that this trilogy sold well in China and received positive critical reactions (with *The Three-Body Problem* even winning an American science fiction award, the Hugo Award for Best Novel, in 2014) demands attention.

The chapter's title calls to mind Voltaire's *Candide, or Optimism* (1759), the prototype for all modern Western philosophical tales, and its memorable character Pangloss, whom Voltaire employs to be the ever naive Leibnizian optimistic foil to the protagonist Candide. Pangloss's often cited explanation in the face of the real world's sadness and tragedies that this existence remains the best of all possible worlds comes under constant attack. The application of this quote is not only in the article's title, but Liu also uses it as a concluding remark, "I wrote about the worst of possible worlds in *Three Body* out of hope that we can strive for the best of all possible Earths" ("Worst"). These two resonances with Western literature, both popular and elite, invites the reader to consider Liu's novel's different literary roots: 1) American genre science fiction, 2) the philosophical tale as it emerged in the West, 3) the role of philosophy in Chinese literature, and 4) Chinese science fiction.

American Genre Science Fiction

Science fiction has existed in American mainstream literature since at least the days of Edgar Allan Poe. As for the beginning of the genre, most scholars and historians agree that it began in April 1926 with the first issue of *Amazing Stories*, founded by Hugo Gernsback, also its first editor. Labeling the magazine's stories as "scientifiction" (the familiar term *science fiction* would not be coined until 1929 by Gernsback), *Amazing Stories* became the first periodical specializing in science fiction. In this issue's first editorial column Gernsback described the magazine's stories as in the vein of those written by Jules Verne, H. G. Wells, and Poe (3). In fact many of the early issues were composed of reprints by these and other well-known writers. The original stories, meanwhile, were written by new writers whose output really defined the nature of American genre science fiction.

In order to identify this new type of popular fiction, one would have to go back almost two decades prior, when Gernsback introduced in 1908 the first radio specialty magazine, *Modern Electrics*, which was first retitled *Electrical Experimenter* and then finally *Science and Invention*. In addition to the latest news about radio, Gernsback began publishing fiction speculating about the impact of new science and technology on society. These new tales stressed above all the extrapolation of new technology in future societies and soon became one of the most popular features of the magazine. The demand for these type of stories was so great that Gernsback eventually decided to publish a specialty magazine devoted entirely to this fiction; thus, *Amazing Stories*.[3]

While focusing on technical extrapolations, these new stories—as with most pulp fiction—were often stylistically clumsy (while still containing an energetic prose), simple in plot, heavy in action, and lacking depth in character. However, this situation would change soon. Soon after *Amazing Stories* hit the stands, other competitors joined in the field, most notably *Astounding Tales of Super Science* (1930), whose title went through various changes and since 1991 has been known as *Analog Science Fiction and Fact*. Here is where the aforementioned John W. Campbell Jr. reshaped the whole genre by insisting on a higher quality of stories that went beyond mere technical extrapolation and fast action. During his tenure as editor (1938–71) scores of writers emerged from the pages of this magazine and basically defined twentieth century American genre science fiction.[4] Campbell wielded an immense influence in the genre, which is why Liu identifies American science fiction with him.

The Philosophical Tale

Though philosophy's relation to Western literature goes back to ancient times, most scholars use the term *philosophical tale* (*conte philosophique*) to mean the literary genre developed by Voltaire (François-Marie Arouet, 1694–1778). The *conte*, or tale, claims a rich tradition that goes back to medieval times and one quite familiar to the literate population by the seventeenth century. The tale was not meant to portray life or characters in a realistic manner. It was used for communicating satire or humor in general, making a moral point, or presenting an idea in an allegorical manner. The tales covered all subject matter and could be found in all types of stories.

Meanwhile, Voltaire adds a philosophical dimension to the tale and creates the philosophical tale. As Aram Vartanian writes, Voltaire made this particular form a "sui generis hybrid of fiction and philosophy.... The fusion of these two elements yields, as in a chemical compound, a product that differs from either taken separately" (469). For the tale part, the story is not required to be realistic (in the conventional sense of the word). The philosophy part, no systematic presentation or critical approach is expected. In fact, the philosophy presents an argument, where the literary devices of satire, allegory, irony, and even word play are employed. Also, the philosophical part means that the idea(s) take center stage while the usual concerns of character development, plot, and setting become subordinate. The combination of both of these two parts means that the writer can portray distortions of characters, situations, and settings to make a point, whether in a serious or trivial vein, about religion, politics, science, emotions, morals, and philosophy in ways that other types of literature cannot.[5]

Frederick Keener identifies the nature of the philosophical tale, especially when compared to the novel. Both literary forms emerged into prominence during the eighteenth century. They were rivals, with the novel winning out by the nineteenth century. He holds that these two forms should be viewed as complementary and not as opposites. Keener argues that the novel's realism is "a matter of form and content," while the philosophical tale's is "centrally and most importantly a matter of theme" (3–4). So each form can present a story in a way that the other cannot. It depends on what the author wants to convey to readers.

After Voltaire, the fate of the philosophical tale did not parallel that of the novel. It faded from the literary scene, but never completely, emerging every now and then, with Cixin Liu's trilogy providing a stellar example.

Chinese Literature

The relationship between Chinese philosophy and literature can be traced back to ancient times. Confucius (551–479 BCE) provides the starting point. For him, to find the proper ethics for life, one must look to the past and read the classical texts and study the actions of the ancient sages. In terms of literature during these early days, the attitude emerged that literature should only be valued and appreciated for the moral patterns it can reveal to the reader. Philosophical discourse and the formal essay became the only forms sanctioned as legitimate literature among society's elites. Because of this development, the Chinese did not distinguish philosophy from literature; literature was at the service of philosophy. Argument became the central concern. As a result, a story's accuracy and its reliability for factual accounts were now subordinate to the argument. This approach to literature became the general Chinese approach throughout the centuries. Even during the transition to modern times (in the late nineteenth century and twentieth century) this attitude persisted.[6] So, from the very beginning, Chinese philosophical literature shares important elements with those of Voltaire's philosophical tale.

Literary fiction was introduced during the T'ang era (618–907). Most modern scholars view these works as the "first consciously created fiction" in China (Nienhauser 593). They trace these stories to a genre they label *tales*, meaning that they were "transmissions of the strange" or "of the strange" (Nienhauser 579). Furthermore, scholars have traced the source of the tale to the biographical tradition in China. Paralleling the Western philosophical tale in this regard, these biographies did not require accuracy or realism when attempting to convey some sort of truth that the person in question represents. Later, vernacular stories and the novel emerged during the Sung (960–1279) and Yüan (1271–1368) dynasties.[7] These stories take up one of four themes: 1) usurpation and plotting, 2) love and intrigue, 3) superstition, and 4) brigandage and lawless characters. These stories were most popular in the mid-seventeenth century and continued to influence Chinese literature in later periods.

Twentieth-century Chinese literature can be viewed as being bracketed by two periods of modernization. The first (1897–1916) centers around writers encountering the European and American culture being imported. Translations play a most important role. In addition to the classics from the West, its popular literature also was translated to meet the almost insatiable demand of the new literate classes. All genres of Western fiction were sought after, including science fiction. In fact, the three most translated writers turn out to be A. Conan Doyle, H. Rider Haggard, and Jules Verne.[8] The native writers wrote Western-inspired genre fiction but still maintained the classical tradition of enlightening its readers. Instead of looking to the past, this time they focused on restoring the country's status as a great power. Towards the end of this period, however, they began to experiment with the latest literary developments from the West.[9]

The May Fourth Movement of 1919 caused many intellectuals to reject the West due to their disillusionment with the diplomatic outcome of World

War I (Japan received favorable settlements over former European spheres of influence) and their perception of the Western liberal democracies as being hypocritical. As a result, they split into roughly two groups: the Neo-Traditionalists (reviving Confucian thought) and Radicals (especially the birth of the Communist Party). Meanwhile, at the popular level, Chinese Western-influenced genres continued to flourish. The Second World War saw a severe reduction in literary output and the subsequent Communist government (1949-76) exercised strict control over what was written. After the death of Mao Zedong (1893-1976), the second period of modernization began. Literature opened up again to new ideas. Outside influences and even criticism of the Cultural Revolution of the mid-1960s were allowed. After a brief period of retrenchment during the 1980s, Chinese literature, both popular and elite, modernized and flourished and has been doing so for the last twenty-five years, culminating in the emergence of Cixin Liu.

Chinese Science Fiction

The development of Chinese science fiction parallels that of Chinese literature in general during the twentieth century—it is bracketed by two periods of modernization. During the first period, translations of Western works also played a pivotal role. Jules Verne's works and Edward Bellamy's *Looking Backward: 2000-1887* (1888) made big impressions. Chinese writers used science fiction as a vehicle to criticize society and offer solutions. Science fiction seemed to be especially appealing as writers were able to stretch their imaginations to a degree not possible with other types of fiction. As David Der-Wei Wang concludes, "by writing out the incredible and the impractical ... writers laid out the terms of China's modernization project, both as a new political agenda and as a new national myth" (453).

Science fiction experienced widespread publication among the literate classes until the advent of World War II. During Mao Zedong's rule the genre became subjugated to strict party control and was published only as an educational tool for the young, an expression of proper Marxist thought, or as an example of government-sponsored optimism. With the ascension of Deng Xiaoping, science fiction flourished again and, except for the reactionary period of 1983-89, continued to develop and expand. Wu Yan identifies three characteristics of Chinese science fiction emerging from the post-Mao era: 1) liberation from the old cultural, political, and institutional systems, 2) analysis of China's relationship to Western science and culture, and 3) the future of China and its culture. He also differentiates the Western genre from the Chinese one: "Whereas Western sf is focused on the opportunities and losses of technoscientific development, Chinese sf, although it examines similar ideas, is more focused on anxieties about cultural decline and the potential for revitalization" (Wu 5).

Cixin Liu has been grouped with writers Wang Jinkang and Han Song, with the three being referred to as the "three generals"; that is, they are considered as China's three most important writers of the contemporary era (Clements and Wu). To most readers these three have been the most successful in establishing modern adult fiction in science fiction, thus freeing their works from Chinese science fiction's roots as a didactic literature while still being concerned with political, cultural, and social issues (Clements and Wu). Others have designated Liu as "China's greatest living SF author" (Bai and Qin).

As Chinese literature of the early twentieth century in general served as a reflection of Chinese concerns about entering a modern world dominated by the West, today's writers in this genre face a world of rapid globalization in which their own country is a rising power, encountering both the benefits and threats of rapid change. As Xia Jia writes,

> After taking in a variety of settings, images, cultural codes, and narrative tropes through Western science fiction, Chinese science fiction writers have gradually constructed a cultural field and symbolic space possessing a certain degree of closure and self-discipline vis-à-vis mainstream literature and other popular literary genres. In this space, gradually maturing forms have absorbed various social experiences that cannot yet be fully captured by the symbolic order, and after a series of transformations, integrations, and re-organizations, resulted in new vocabularies and grammars. *It is in this sense that the Chinese science fiction of the era dating from the 1990s to the present can be read as a national allegory in the age of globalization.* (italics added)

With the above background in mind, the mixed literary heritage present in Liu's novels becomes apparent.

Analyzing Liu's Two Novels

Briefly, Liu's two novels tell the story of Earth's first contact with an alien civilization, the Trisolarans, who inhabit a planet in Earth's neighboring star system, the Alpha Centauri system, which is composed of three stars. This system, its orbital mechanics, and the devastating effects on the aliens' planet comprise the main focus of *The Three-Body Problem*. The aliens, having failed to solve their problems living in their three-body sun system, decide to take over Earth's more stable solar system instead. The Trisolarans send an invasion fleet, but the journey of four-light years will take four centuries. *The Dark Forest* relates how both the Earth and the Trisolarans act as they communicate and prepare to confront each other.

Early in *The Three-Body Problem* a genre familiar to Western readers appears: the hard-boiled detective story. This genre embodies the character of police detective Captain Shi Qiang, who is called upon to solve the mystery behind the occurrence of suicides among many prominent scientists. While pursuing leads in this case, Shi encounters the scientific world and its wondrous technology. When he finally uncovers the story behind the deaths, nothing short of Earth's Armageddon is discovered: Earth has contacted an alien race and the results are not friendly.

At this point, the American science fiction genre comes to the forefront. The usual concerns of advanced science arise: including relativity, quantum mechanics, space travel, virtual reality, artificial intelligence, cosmology, and advanced technology unknown to humans. Here the extrapolative nature of the American novel becomes obvious. Perhaps the most impressive of these descriptions is the aliens' development of the sophon (in Chinese, this name is a pun on the word for proton) (*Problem* 361). This device could sabotage Earth's cutting-edge research by disrupting particle accelerator experiments and, eventually, would place all of humanity under constant surveillance. Applying the latest ideas on subatomic particles, engineering at both micro and macro scales, and the existence of dimensions beyond the conventional three (four, if one counts time), the novel describes the Trisolarans' construction of the sophon. These devices would even be able to communicate instantaneously between star systems, despite the four-plus light year distance and limit of light's speed (much like Le Guin's ansible).[10]

In addition to technological extrapolations, the novels present social extrapolations. *The Three-Body Problem* describes a heavily populated urbanized world in which the major political powers live in an uneasy coexistence. *The Dark Forest* reveals a future world two hundred years in the future in which the Earth has suffered a tremendous fifty-year ecological upheaval, called the Great Ravine, that reduced Earth's population from 8.5 to 3.5 billion. Humanity decides to manufacture space defenses at all costs, ignores environmental concerns, and causes the Great Ravine. Humanity recovers, reclaiming its lost standard of living through constructive technological application and political and social enlightenment (recapitulating past revolutions).

This renaissance proves fruitless when the aliens send a mysterious vehicle, three and a half meters long, in the shape of a teardrop and made of an absolutely smooth surface that proved to be impenetrable. In a brief period of time, this small craft annihilates almost the entire Earth space fleet (whose ships were three to four times the size of the largest of aircraft carriers) by merely ramming through the ships. Sophons limit the Earth's technoscientific advancement. This deadly mysterious craft represents the next stage of development forbidden to humanity. The novel gives no detailed descriptions of this craft as it did of the sophons, outside of its opacity to human probing, as if to tell the reader that here is where extrapolation ends and fear of the unknown begins.

Despite all the similarities with Western genres, there are also elements of traditional Chinese fiction, including the four above mentioned genre-like themes from the Yüan dynasty. For the theme of usurpation and plotting, the acts of the four Wallfacers in *The Dark Forest*, Manuel Rey Diaz, Bill Hines, Luo Ji, and Frederick Tyler, and their antagonists, the Wallbreakers, come to mind as the former group attempts to fool the Trisolarans through subterfuge while the latter group attempts to thwart them. The ultimate acts of usurpation occur in *The Three-Body Problem* when the scientist, Ye Wenjie, betrays Earth by informing the Trisolarans of humanity's existence, and the activist, Mike Evans, funds the group Earth-Trisolaris Organization that supports human surrender to the aliens. For the theme of love and intrigue, the most significant relationship occurs in *The Dark Forest*, where Luo and his wife, Zhuang Yan, are given whatever they want due to Luo's status as a Wallfacer. While the two settle down and raise a family, everyone else wonders what Luo's plan is for fooling the aliens. For the theme of superstition, two examples emerge in *The Dark Forest*. The first focuses on the admiration of the Wallfacers turned into a cult, as many viewed them as humanity's saviors. The second occurs when Luo supposedly casts a spell at a distant star system. Though this act actually helped humanity's chances of survival immensely, what looked like a wasteful superstitious act at the outset turned out to be the ultimate in secret planning. For brigandage and lawlessness, one could turn to the reactions of many people on Earth who, having given up hope for humanity's future, decide to act out all their desires regardless of the consequences, including resorting to rioting, looting, and public orgies.

Philosophical Aspects

The various characteristics of the philosophical tale can be found quite readily in these two novels. Perhaps the most prevalent is the portrayal of major characters in simplistic terms to argue a point. The Trisolarans and humans are described as being opposites. The Trisolarans' exaggerated austere character and culture result from their having to survive the dreadful environmental conditions in the Alpha Centauri system. This society turns out to be efficient in a totalitarian manner, to the point of terminating all lives deemed no longer useful. Calmness and numbness of one's spiritual core—i.e., no emotions—become the basis for a successful civilization. All effort must be dedicated to survival, so there is no time for literature, art, or pursuit of beauty. When a dissident Trisolaran, the one who warned Ye Wenjie not to respond to the Trisolarans' message, argues with the Trisolaran leader that there should be more to life than developing the most efficient way to survive, the leader responds that those societies who did possess freedom, emotion, and culture turned out to be "the weakest and the most short-lived" and that maybe after conquering Earth "we can also create such a life for ourselves" (*Problem* 354). The dissident doubts it.

Humans, on the other hand, are not unified, disciplined, or efficient. They engage in self-destructive actions to the point of causing a global ecological disaster (the Great Ravine) that wipes out over half of the population. When the threat of the Trisolarans are revealed, factions emerge to halt human defense preparations. These outcomes of human emotions and freedom only reconfirms the Trisolarans' leader's observations.

The novels describe two other major differences. This time they end up giving humanity a chance to overcome a Trisolaran invasion. The first, discussed in *The Three-Body Problem*, involves the rate of progress for both races. The Trisolarans, as one might surmise, are methodical and advance at a slow and steady pace. Humans, meanwhile, progress at a faster pace. Though the Earth may be behind the Trisolarans, humans possess the capacity to surpass them. Hence the Trisolarans' development of the sophons to negate that advantage. Whether this human advantage is due to their nature is not made clear. However, human beings' ability to lie and deceive becomes the second major difference, revealed in *The Dark Forest*, for which the Trisolarans do not have a proper antidote. The Trisolarans live in a totally transparent society where one's mind is open to all. Humans, on the other hand, can think one thing and do another. Unlike the Trisolarans, the human mind is not for all to see. This advantage supplies humanity its last hope to defeat the enemy. Liu demonstrates this point through Luo Ji's act of casting a spell to a distant star system. While the other three Wallfacers act in ways that most understood, Luo—an underachiever all his life—seemed to use his privileged status just to satisfy his desires and nothing else. But he turns out to be the one who saves the Earth from invasion because of this action.

In addition to simplifying societies, Liu simplifies his characters to make a point. This simplification becomes especially apparent in *The Three-Body*

Problem in the sections dealing with the virtual reality computer game that was constructed by the Trisolarans for the humans to help solve the three-body problem in physics. During its early usage, famous figures from China's ancient past are displayed, including well-known ancient kings Wen of Zhou (ruled 1099–1050 BCE, founder of Zhou Dynasty) and Zhou of Shang (ruled 1075–1046 BCE, notorious tyrant), and the famed philosophers Confucius and Mozi, founder of the Mohist school. This scenario takes place in the Warring States Period (475–221 BCE). Here Liu introduces a satiric element not present elsewhere in the novels. Note the anachronistic nature of this game, following the spirit of philosophical tales where accuracy lies in what the characters represent and not in chronological exactitude. Both philosophers flounder in their attempts to solve the three-body problem. Confucius and his concept of *li*, i.e., proper behavior toward relationships within the community, are made fun of when the virtual version tried to solve this problem with his concept. He feels that the universe should follow the *li* and when it does not and the sun vanishes, Confucius ends up "frozen into a column of ice. And there he remains" (*Problem* 141). Mozi's attempt, despite his more empirical approach, fares no better. So inept was the classical Chinese way of doing things that it takes figures from the West's past to advance the game.

In a subsequent scenario, the figures of Aristotle (384–322 BCE), Leonardo da Vinci (1452–1519), Copernicus (1473–1543), Galileo (1564–1642), and Pope Gregory (no identifying numeral is given, but it could be Gregory XIII [1502–85], who commissioned the Gregorian calendar) appear. These figures also receive satirical treatment: Pope Gregory issues the order to "burn him," Galileo criticizes Mozi's ideas, Aristotle, paralleling the role of Confucius, pronounces the illogic of others' speculations and even holds a zippo lighter to ignite a fire to burn a game player at the stake, and even the charred corpse of Giordano Bruno makes an appearance. The game announces that a higher level has been attained with Copernicus's heliocentric discovery. Later sessions of the game bring up such figures as Newton (1642–1727), Leibniz (1646–1716), Einstein (1879–1955), and von Neumann (1902–55).

The Philosophical Shift

While aspects of the philosophical tale are shared in both Western and Chinese literatures, the philosophical essay as literature is more distinctly Chinese. In *The Dark Forest*, Liu actually presents a philosophy of existence for a time where science has advanced the understanding of the universe immensely, but still not completely. At the beginning of the novel Ye Wenjie urges Luo Ji, since he has background in both astronomy and sociology, to combine the two and establish a theoretical foundation for what she called a "cosmic sociology" (*Dark Forest* 12). What follows in this dialogue comes closest to a formal essay.

Ye produces a philosophy that comes with two axioms that are accompanied by two concepts. The axioms are:

> First Axiom: "Survival is the primary need of civilization."
> Second Axiom: "Civilization continuously grows and expands, but the total matter of the universe remains constant." (*Dark Forest* 13)

The two accompanying concepts are:

> First Concept: "chains of suspicion"
> Second Concept: "the technological explosion"

The two axioms are self-explanatory. The first concept deals with how civilizations should act when encountering another. One does not really know what the other is really like, whether friendly or threatening, hence the chains of suspicion are established. The second concept refers to the ability to develop technology at a faster pace. A younger civilization, as in the case of Earth, might be able to improve its technology faster than an older one (Trisolarans). There will always be uneven levels of development, thus threatening any balance that may exist between two civilizations.

Luo concludes in a much more dramatic fashion towards the novel's end,

> The universe is a dark forest. Every civilization is an armed hunter stalking through the trees like a ghost, gently pushing aside branches that block the path and trying to tread without sound.... The hunter has to be careful, because everywhere in the forest are stealthy hunters like him. If he finds other life ... there's only one thing he can do: open fire and eliminate them. In this forest, hell is other people. An eternal threat that any life that exposes its own existence will be swiftly wiped out. (*Dark Forest* 484)

The title of the second novel is now explained. This bleak picture of existence enables Luo to convince the Trisolarans to halt their surveillance and invasion of Earth. When Luo asks them if they too realize that the universe is a dark forest, they responded, "Yes. We knew about it long ago. What's strange is that you only realized it so late" (*Dark Forest* 505). The ideas expressed here do reflect Liu's actual views. In his postscript to the American edition of *The Three-Body Problem*, he states clearly that humanity must learn to live together in trust and understanding while maintaining a vigilant attitude towards any other possible intelligent life (*Problem* 395).

The novel does end on a hopeful note. Luo is conversing with the Trisolaran who originally warned Ye Wenjie not to answer the Trisolarans' first message. They briefly discuss the role of the emotion love and its possibility that it can change the nature of existence. They both hope so, as Luo concludes, "I have a dream that one day brilliant sunlight will illuminate the dark forest" (*Dark Forest* 512).

From this brief analysis one can appreciate elements of both Western and Chinese literary developments. Even if the third novel, as Liu says, turns out to be primarily an American science fiction genre-like novel, the first two novels remain otherwise. Liu may have taken many literary paths to tell his story, but his story still tells of a single journey, that of humanity's future—a future filled with both promise and threats, but one in which China must take its place in a world that is rapidly becoming a global village. In this new global society, perhaps this long story contained in three novels can be a harbinger of global expressions to come, filled with particular traditions, yet focused on the single destiny facing humanity.

Notes

1. For more information see my *The Anticipation Novelists of 1950s French Science Fiction: Stepchildren of Voltaire* (2011).

2. Liu is known in the West with his name inverted, Cixin Liu, as opposed to Liu Cixin, as is the convention in China. To avoid confusion, all Chinese names except Cixin Liu in both the text and footnotes of this article will be presented using the Chinese convention. However, if the person possesses a Western first name, then he or she will be listed in the conventional Western style.

3. Gary Westfahl's *Hugo Gernsback and the Century of Science Fiction* (2007).

4. For more information, see Brian W. Aldiss's *Trillion Year Spree: The History of Science Fiction* (1986) or John Clute and Peter Nicholls's *The Encyclopedia of Science Fiction* (1993).

5. See David Coward's *History of French Literature from Chanson de Geste to Cinema* (2002).

6. See Michael Puett's "Philosophy and Literature in Early China" (2001).

7. See Yenna Wu's "Vernacular Stories" in *The Columbia History of Chinese Literature* (2001).

8. See David Der-Wei Wang's "Chinese Literature from 1841 to 1937" in *The Cambridge History of Chinese Literature, Volume II: From 1375* (2014).

9. See Milena Doleželová-Velingerová's "Fiction from the end of the Empire to the Beginning of the Republic (1897–1916)" in *The Columbia History of Chinese Literature* (2001).

10. See Le Guin's *The Dispossessed* (1974).

Works Cited

Aldiss, Brian W. *Trillion Year Spree: The History of Science Fiction*. New York: Antheneum, 1986. Print.
Bai, Jenny and Cecilia Qin. "Science Fiction in China—2008." Tor Books. *World SF*, 8 April 2015. Web. 31 Oct. 2015.
Bellamy, Edward. *Looking Backward: 2000–1887*. 1888. New York: Oxford UP, 2009. Print.
Clements, Jonathan and Wu Dingbo. "China." *Encyclopedia of Science Fiction*. Eds. John Clute and Peter Nicholls. 20 May 2015. Web. 23 Oct. 2015.
Clute, John and Peter Nicholls, eds. *The Encyclopedia of Science Fiction*. 2nd ed. New York: Saint Martin's, 1993. Print.
Coward, David. *History of French Literature from Chanson de Geste to Cinema*. Oxford: Blackwell, 2002. Print.
Doleželová-Velingerová, Milena. "Fiction from the end of the Empire to the Beginning of the Republic (1897–1916)." *The Columbia History of Chinese Literature*. Ed. Victor H. Mair. New York: Columbia UP, 2001. 697–731. Print.
Gernsback, Hugo. "A New Sort of Magazine." *Amazing Stories* 1.1 (April 1926): 3.
Keener, Frederick M. *The Chain of Becoming, The Philosophical Tale, The Novel, and a Neglected Realism of the Enlightenment: Swift, Montesquieu, Voltaire, Johnson, and Austen*. New York: Columbia UP, 1983. Print.
Le Guin, Ursula K. *The Dispossessed*. New York: Harper & Row, 1974. Print.
———. *The Word for World is Forest*. 1972. New York: Putnam, 1976. Print.
Liu, Cixin. *The Dark Forest*. Trans. Joel Martinsen. New York: Tor, 2015. Print.
———. *Death's End*. Trans. Ken Liu. New York: Tor, 2016.
———. *The Three-Body Problem*. Trans. Ken Liu. New York: Tor, 2014. Print.
———. "The Worst of All Possible Universes and the Best of All Possible Earths: *Three Body* and Chinese Science Fiction." Trans. Ken Liu. Tor Books. *World SF*, 7 May 2014. Web. 5 Nov. 2015.
Lyau, Bradford. *The Anticipation Novelists of 1950s French Science Fiction: Stepchildren of Voltaire*. Jefferson: McFarland, 2011. Print.
Nienhauser, William H., Jr. "T'ang Tales." *The Columbia History of Chinese Literature*. Ed. Victor H. Mair. New York: Columbia UP, 2001. 579–94. Print.
Puett, Michael. "Philosophy and Literature in Early China." *The Columbia History of Chinese Literature*. Ed. Victor H. Mair. New York: Columbia UP, 2001. 70–85. Print.
Robinson, Kim S. *Blue Mars*. New York: Bantam Spectra, 1996. Print.
———. *Green Mars*. New York: Bantam Spectra, 1994. Print.
———. *Red Mars*. New York: Bantam Spectra, 1993. Print.

Vartanian, Aram. "On Cultivating One's Garden." *A New History of French Literature*. Ed. Denis Hollier. Cambridge: Harvard UP, 1989. 465- 71. Print.

Voltaire. *Candide, or Optimism*. 1759. Trans. Lowell Bair. New York: Bantam, 1981.

Wang, David Der-Wei. "Chinese Literature from 1841 to 1937." *The Cambridge History of Chinese Literature, Volume II: From 1375*. Eds. Kang-I Chang and Stephen Own. Cambridge: Cambridge UP, 2014. 413–564. Print.

Wells, H. G. *The War of the Worlds*. 1898. New York: Signet Classics, 2007. Print.

Westfahl, Gary. *Hugo Gernsback and the Century of Science Fiction*. Jefferson: McFarland, 2007. Print.

Wu Yan. "'Great Wall Planet': Introducing Chinese Science Fiction." Trans. Wang Pengfei and Ryan Nichols. *Science Fiction Studies* 40.1 (2013): 1–14. Print.

Wu, Yenna. "Vernacular Stories." *The Columbia History of Chinese Literature*. Ed. Victor H. Mair. New York: Columbia UP, 2001. 595–610. Print.

Xia Jia. "What Makes Chinese Fiction Chinese?" Trans. Ken Liu. Tor Books. *World SF*, 22 July 2014. Web. 31 Oct. 2015.

CROSSING THE THRESHOLD OF B-MOR

Instrumental Commodification and the Model Minority in Chang-rae Lee's *On Such a Full Sea*

■ ■ ■

JESHUA ENRIQUEZ

When the *Wall Street Journal* reported on a string of suicides at Foxconn, the leading Chinese manufacturer of consumer electronic components supplying Apple and multiple other American companies, public attention brought scrutiny to systems of overseas manufacturing that make affordable, high-end electronics like the iPhone viable. Where previous outrages over the American outsourcing of labor were centered on tangible human rights violations like child workers and unsafe conditions, this tragedy was peculiarly different. The corporation's responses, including suicide-prevention nets and Buddhist prayer services, redefined some of the system's dangers as social, psychological, and even spiritual. As American corporations sought to increase production efficiency and reduce costs by outsourcing the means of production to Asia, cases like the Foxconn suicides signaled that American corporations were also outsourcing dehumanization, mechanization, and commodification to optimize commercial gain.

Chang-rae Lee's novel *On Such a Full Sea* (2014) presents a particularly globalized and market-driven dystopian vision that carries this process to its logical conclusions. Within its future, racial commodification and mechanized social controls are leveraged to achieve corporate production goals but are ultimately subverted by the internal potential of the oppressed community to imagine more. This examination of that vision will analyze three key elements responsible for that dynamic arc.

Firstly, the conceptualization and commodification of the Asian American subject for a deliberate purpose looms over the narrative as an implicit and unspoken but wholly defining facet of the future society's operation. In the aftermath of a national collapse, American civilization in *On Such a Full Sea* arises in purposefully stratified sub-societies. Lacking a centralized government, communities organize within three general categories: Charters, Facilities, and Open Counties. Where the Open Counties are unregulated, unsanctioned by any official authority, and unable to rise above the condition of daily survival, Charters and Facilities coordinate in a symbiotic interrelation. At the top are the affluent Charter cities, coveted enclaves whose population is generally White and born into the community, possessing access to the highest standard of living and the most desirable commodities. The Charter cities' lavish food, healthcare, and technology contrast with the poverty of the devastated landscape outside their gates. In order to meet the citizens' demand for high-quality, meticulously-sourced goods, Charters require exceedingly efficient supply chains.

In order to maximize production, the wealthy Charters sponsor a community of Chinese immigrants and their descendants, manipulating its development and behavior for the dominant group's own benefit. Retitled B-Mor in what is both an abbreviation and a suppressed subconscious mandate, a gated colony for the immigrants is constructed on the site of Baltimore's ruins. One of many Facilities, B-Mor's production specialty runs towards fish and produce, which are micromanaged in tightly-controlled environments to ensure the Charters' specifications are met. Similarly, the inhabitants themselves are raised under a regime of highly-ordered control and observation. This purposeful cultivation illustrates a twofold system of exploitation. The Chinese inhabitants are conceptualized as a homogeneous array of mechanized laborers as well as a "model minority": a population that is commended for traits beneficial to the governing White group, and is expected to docilely provide service without requiring equal status. As Claire Jean Kim has explained in the modern-day U.S. context, this type of purposeful exploitation relies on the "simultaneous valorization and ostracism" of Asian Americans in order to preserve the dominant group's control and privilege (129). Within the novel, the dominant class creates a system of control predicated on just this valorization and ostracism in order to fulfill its production requirements.

As a second key element, the immigrant community responds to its subjugation and purpose by conceiving of itself as a collective, united and safe but lacking in agency and imagination. The inhabitants' suppressed personhood and desires result in the creation of a communal legend that embodies their longing for freer subjectivity and agency. This tale centers on Fan, a sixteen-year-old B-Mor resident assigned to care for the community's prime export as a diver in the Facility fish tanks. When the governing body inexplicably abducts her boyfriend Reg, the previously unremarkable Fan enigmatically poisons the fish in her assigned tank and then escapes in search of her lost love. Within the Facility, Fan's escape signifies the last action of which B-Mor inhabitants have any direct knowledge. As social discontent begins to rise, however, the communal narrators create a mythic tale around Fan's exploits outside the gates, expressing their own metaphorical aspirations to be more and get out of B-Mor. Characterized by a shared first-person narrative voice and the collaborative creation of faraway adventures, this mythopoeic storytelling will ultimately engender social and psychological empowerment for the community. That latent potential can only actualize, however, at a time when the social framework of control has been weakened.

That sociological structure, deployed to maintain obedience and offset the mental and spiritual discontent of the exploited community, makes up the third key element of this analysis. In our present-day context, cautionary tales like the 2010 Foxconn suicides illustrate the psychological dangers of human commodification, but the *On Such a Full Sea* portrays a future corporate entity that applies deliberate skill to offset these dangers as a matter of standard procedure. B-Mor's "Directorate," the governing body that hands down dictums and oversees daily practices, monitors the population's mood and modifies food, recreation, and commodities the same way the divers who oversee the fish tanks do for their stock. The Directorate exercises biopolitical power to tie the daily lives B-Mor residents with the process of production itself, applying business management routines and controls to the business of living. Simultaneously, the Directorate fosters community traits it finds useful, such as family dedication and work ethic, by rewarding those characteristics with protection and resources in a typical manifestation of model minority ideation. As a result of these psychological influences promoting complacency and interdependence, social groupthink takes hold among the inhabitants and prevents rebellious actions. When market forces disrupt the control system, however, the resulting cultural insurgence decreases the elements of groupthink and allows the population to cross psychological thresholds into action. This experience foments an essential change, planting seeds of dissension and agency in the oppressed community's self-conceptualization.

The Commodification of the Asian American Subject

B-Mor's oppression and lack of agency stem from its purposeful founding and maintenance as a means of production. For those at the top of the food chain, so to speak, the community serves as a manufacturing system to be administered and leveraged. Much like a modern consumer expects mass-produced, high-end goods that can only be manufactured through the conveniences of overseas labor, the Charter citizens demand artisanal quality items from an efficiently planned and maintained, out-of-sight apparatus. The governmental structure, having implemented the system of Facilities, provides a supply to meet market demand without even having to navigate international trade or expansion. They import the economic advantages of globalization, embodied in the migrant Chinese community, who become instrumentalized in various ways. By conveniently farming out labor to a community that is near, while that community's members are segregated and denied civic power, the corporate Charters enjoy both the low cost of outsourced labor and the convenience of local immigrant labor. The Charter community has effectively purchased a Chinese society as a living tool, an organism of livestock-like production, breeding and cultivating it to provide for the Charter's needs.

The B-Mor population, not surprisingly, identifies closely with its primary product of tank-grown fish. Like those export specimens, the imported B-Mor inhabitants were brought in for a pragmatic benefit to an external community; they are bred in captivity to maintain a sustainable population; they are monitored and maintained at very specific parameters of food, scheduling, and behavior; and they are kept in a tightly enclosed space that constitutes both protection and imprisonment. The residents' predetermined function and identification with the fish is so internalized that when the Directorate implements modifications to B-Mor's product, the residents relate that "Charter biologists and engineers revised our feed and tank formulas" (Lee 115). The human narrators describe the change not as one to the fish's formulas, but to "our" formulas.

Examining the history of B-Mor's origin reveals just how fundamentally the community's pragmatic usefulness to the Charters is responsible for its existence, an entire society founded on the model minority ideal. For example, the oldest B-Mor inhabitants remember "pockets of residents" on the city outskirts who were "descendants of nineteenth-century African slaves and twentieth-century laborers from Central America and even bands of twenty-first-century urban nostalgics," pockets that "inexorably declined and finally disappeared" (21–22). These communities did not have "the unique advantage of being husbanded by one of the federated companies," receiving none of the guidance, resource allocation, or official sanction that fostered a flourishing B-Mor. B-Mor's residents understand in retrospect that corporate managers supported the Chinese colony while the government allowed the colonies of Black, Latino, and corporate-unaffiliated inhabitants to flounder from neglect; they undermined those communities by withholding resources, education, and opportunities. The attitude towards the immigrated Asian community was custodial, obliging, and supportive in order to harness benefits for social and economic gain, but settlements of other races were perceived as a nuisance or a threat. Baltimore's population, which in present day is predominantly Black, is purposefully replaced with a population amenable to the Directorate's aims, and even small pockets of the original residents are undercut.

This background illustrates how the "racial triangulation" relationships posited by Claire Jean Kim were active in B-Mor's founding and continue to define its culture. Within a system of racial triangulation, the dominant White group valorizes the subordinate group of Asian Americans over the subordinate group of Blacks "in order to dominate both groups" (Kim 107). The ruling tier portrays Black and Latino communities as lazy and inferior while praising behavior in the Asian American group that is cooperative and advantageous to that tier. The dominant group benefits from "emphasizing internal sources of success or failure" via these portrayals since these "myths decisively shift attention away from structural determinants of group outcomes, including institutionalized White dominance" (121). Furthermore, racial valorization of desirable characteristics is used to seed subjugation in B-Mor's internal cultural mores and psychological makeup. The "cultural values of diligence, family solidarity, respect for education, and self-sufficiency" (Kim 118) feature prominently in B-Mor's stories of its own founding and early years, making up a model minority myth that was likely cultivated by the sponsor corporation.

This does not mean the Asian American community is elevated to equality for its praiseworthy traits, however. Instead, the dominant group employs "civic ostracism" to exclude them from "the body politic and civic membership" (Kim 107). Accordingly, the B-Mor population is sustained and rewarded as long as its values and behavior benefit the dominant group, but it is also characterized as "immutably foreign and unassimilable" (107), kept separate and without political agency. The conception of B-Mor inhabitants as a model minority is responsible for its initial survival, but it also justifies the marginalization of B-Mor as a foreign settlement separate from Charter identity and power. Sociopolitical planning based on the model minority myth is thus carried to extreme, but logical, conclusions in Lee's future depiction: the effective breeding, upkeep, and suppression of a servile, usable group—one that recognizes itself as "husbanded."

The Communal Story and Collective Protagonist

The way B-Mor inhabitants react to their existence as elements of a commodified, instrumentalized system sets the stage for the social conflict to come. Finding value in the stability and familiarity of their collective society, they refer to themselves and each other as "B-Mors," identifying each individual as a synecdochic part of the community whole. B-Mor ties are so close and their time together so constant that residents gain "ingrained knowledge of one another" and acknowledge the "insoluble bond of blood" (Lee 100), fostering an extremist manifestation of collectivist psychology. In fact, this collective self-conception is so extreme that it defines the single most important technical element of the novel: the first-person plural narrative voice.

The narrators of the novel have no individual identity, representing through lack of specificity the collective experience of the B-Mor population as a whole, though clues do provide the narrators with some context. For example, the narrators reveal, they are descended "from two of the first generations of growers" (Lee 8). The narrators are also placed within a particular generation: one that remembers elder family members since lost to history and bemoans "younger B-Mors" who overlook the importance of their own community's history (18). This link to the original founding ties the narrators to the roots of B-Mor society, awarding them the cachet to speak on the customs and traditions that have defined it.

Inevitably, the narrators' knowledge of B-Mor history and culture bring awareness of the commodification and control illustrated in the previous section. The B-Mors recognize their mental and emotional states are being managed, and their psyches enclosed. They bemoan the realization that "the reach of our thoughts has a near ceiling" because it means their "imagination might not be limitless" (Lee 127). Their imagination has been restricted by their particular experience, something they worry has made them "too fearful or comfortable, too cautious or reluctant," even though they publicly deny this is the case. These fears and the desire to go beyond them drive the creation of a surrogate in Fan, and the creation of a collective story through which B-Mors can escape the ceiling of their environment.

Although Fan seemingly features as the primary protagonist, she is inescapably a figure of mythic projection, one whom the plural narrators admit they have infused with mythopoeic lore. The same way that "sayings are employed for a purpose, reflecting what we want of them and the larger world, as well as the very time of that wanting" (Lee 278), the details of Fan's story are "apt to change" (243) according to the society's needs. Each teller of the Fan tale intends to remain true not to the literal Fan, nor even to the idea of Fan, but rather to the previous teller. "You want nothing more than to be an echo of the previous speaker," explain the narrators (243). The telling of the story is communal, social, a responsibility to the group. Nevertheless, a moment arises for each teller "that compels a freelancing, perhaps even rebellious, urge" (243). In this rebellious urge the Fan story is most loyal to the interiority of the B-Mor residents because in the rebellion of individually imagining an adventure, an escape, each resident reaches beyond the safety and complacency of intricately regulated B-Mor society.

In the segments that focus on Fan's adventures, the narrative distances itself from the first-person voice and maintains a more traditional third-person perspective. Unlike the usual second-person plural voice who speaks communally and authoritatively about the familiar and known, the storytelling voice here reaches beyond the community, into explorations of the unknown. Even though it comes from within B-Mors, the Fan story makes fathomable something new and different from their present selves. The storytelling exercise, and its accompanying uprisings in vandalism and protest, might be disorganized and ultimately ineffectual in and of themselves, but they evidence the development of new possibilities.

The Racial Framework of Social Control

In order for these possibilities to have any chance at fruition, however, the strictly-ordered structures of control that have so effectively suppressed B-Mor agency must somehow be loosened or worn, to make room for action. An analysis of the sociological strategies that make up this restrictive framework will clarify how such conditions for action could be created and what eventual gains could be won through that action. Since the Charter and Facility system brings twentieth century corporate strategies to planning advanced social organizations, it should come as no surprise that twentieth century business psychology can elucidate the structure. When psychologist Irving Janis methodically outlined the dangers of "groupthink" in the early 1970s, he emphasized the fittingness of the word's similarity to the terminology of the conformist, authoritarian-government-ruled dystopia in George Orwell's

1984 (1949). Within his own book, about twenty years after the term's coining in business magazine *Fortune*, Janis described the negative repercussions of groupthink for a business enterprise.

The deterioration of independent thinking, questioning, and judgment caused by groupthink proves catastrophic when flaws in major high-risk decisions go unchecked, he explained. Group behavior, which "can bring out the worst as well as the best in man" can lead to "instances of mindless conformity and collective misjudgment of serious risks" (*Victims* 3). This misjudgment of risks is usually typified not by overestimation of danger but rather "collective complacency" that prevents action (3). A "group cohesiveness" and "solidarity" can arise based on "positive valuation of the group and [the members'] motivation to continue to belong to it" (4–5), crippling judgment and agency. Within B-Mor, with its focus on "stability" as paramount production "day by night by day" and its reliance on the "bonds of blood" (Lee 8), group cohesiveness motivates the population to accept its restricted situation, underestimating the risks of consistently submitting to the Directorate and propagating its social mores. These traits conducive for groupthink, including "strong family values" and "respect for authority," are part of what characterize the model minority stereotype (Kim 121), and the Directorate nurtures their propagation to achieve its ends of commodification and control.

In fact, while Janis's descriptions are cautionary, the Directorate approaches B-Mor with the deliberate goal of cultivating groupthink. The ruling class uses the conventions Janis warns against to its advantage, suppressing autonomy and agency in favor of a conformist disposition that ensured pliability to authority. According to Gregory Claeys's examination of utopia and dystopia, this type of groupthink can be seen as a utopian characteristic: "Episodic modifications of behavior, which either intentionally or accidentally increase sociability . . . represent what we may term *utopic* moments and/or spaces" (151). Claeys further notes that "These events or places share a heightened sense of communal belonging or identity, and the merging of the ego in the collective. . . . These heightened emotional moments exhibit the tribal or group aspects of our nature, or the psychology of conformity" (151). The ruling society succeeds in implementing this particular utopian characteristic in B-Mor, manipulating group behavior by micromanaging routines and rewarding acquiescence. To some degree, they achieve the goal of fostering a population "sweet, docile, and eager to follow White directives," as Kim describes what the dominant group would consider a "suitable model for other minorities" (122).

How, then, if the elements of groupthink have been so deeply ingrained, and the fine-tuned system of control which held B-Mor in thrall has been so expertly deployed, do the rebellions that make up the conflict in the novel take place? One answer lies in the very market relationships upon which the Charters have predicated B-Mor society. The Directorate has created a system in service to the commercial market, yoking humans as mere mechanisms to meet demand. Inevitably, the unpredictability of market forces eventually bring a period of unexpected disorder, disrupting the interwoven economic and social spheres of B-Mor. In the wake of this type of cultural anxiety, complacency gives way to that symptom of public discord most dangerous to authoritarian powers: questioning.

Specifically, when unexpected events lead to a sharp decline in the demand for B-Mor fish, the economic effects spill over into the social world, opening the way for independent thought and action. As routines and processes that fostered docile harmony break down, the established Groupthink does as well. Janis describes elements that might lead to a reduction in groupthink, including "setting up a group norm" that prioritizes "critical appraisal" (*Victims* 178). B-Mor's general disharmony during its time of socioeconomic stress allows just this criticism to manifest, in the form of public graffiti, online discussions, and personal nonconformance. Janis also prescribes avoiding "insulation" in order to weaken groupthink, "involving more than one group," whenever possible (*Victims* 180). The involvement of multiple groups in B-Mor political life occurs when the population splinters into multiple ideological positions during the crisis, some actively supporting rebellion and defacing public structures while others promote a more conservative course of action. Finally, Janis writes, "the more amiability and esprit de corps among the members of an in-group of policy-makers, the greater is the danger that independent critical thinking will be replaced by groupthink" (*Victims* 198). In the escalating conflict, everyday B-Mor residents become "policy-makers" deciding how to react to the Directorate, and their opposing, debating, questioning voices replace groupthink with critical thinking.

The effects of this change make themselves apparent quickly. Only "a few weeks after Fan left B-Mor" (Lee 107), a seemingly spontaneous burst of commotion surrounds the prized fish of the community park ponds. What begins as a single child littering, a meaningless and minor infraction that "should have been the end of it" becomes a spreading wave of disorder. After an anonymous "someone else" reacts by throwing items as well, "provoking another thrashing about the pond," there quickly followed additional action from more and more individuals (107–8). The narrators find it remarkable "how quickly the few tossed tidbits here and there turned into a full-scale onslaught," a "frenzy" and a "fray" that itself ends in minutes but then motivates "a rash" of similar incidents "at most of the other parks in B-Mor," which also "ar[i]se spontaneously" and "bloom[] with startling speed and fury" (109). Considering the B-Mor residents have been commodified and conditioned to resemble the docile fish, it is emotionally and symbolically suitable to their outrage that the fish ponds serve as the site of their disobedience. In the B-Mors' newfound ability to critically appraise their own behavior, the fish ponds serve as scathing reminder of their own subjugation and they contaminate the space with their defiance—the same way Fan poisoned her fish tank before escaping.

The sudden spread of rebellious flare-ups in this mutiny resembles an epidemiological outbreak, as if the will to personal agency was a public contagion in the social sphere, infecting the ordered system at particular sites and disseminating outwards. In relation to these outbursts, we can turn again to the work of social theorists. For instance, author Malcolm Gladwell invokes Stanford sociologist Mark Granovetter's research into the spread of "destructive violence that involves a great number of otherwise normal people who would not usually be disposed to violence" (Gladwell). Where earlier arguments examined individuals in violent situations as isolated "rational actors" who "saw what was at stake and recalculated their estimations of the costs and benefits," Granovetter instead saw group violence as "a social process, in which people did things in reaction to and in combination with those around them" (Gladwell). Granovetter presents an "elegant theoretical model" predicated on the hypothesis that "social processes are driven by our *thresholds*—which he defines as the number of people who need to be doing some activity before we agree to join them" (Gladwell; italics in original). According to this theory, those who have a low threshold are willing to commit a transgressive act even if they are the first to do so and those with a higher threshold are thus emboldened to act. As the number of people involved increases, those with higher and higher thresholds are also instigated and the successively larger group motivates ever more agents in an expanding snowball effect. We can apply this model to B-Mor, as the decline of regulatory groupthink allows initial thresholds to be crossed, enabling a swell of deregulated behavior from a culture acting in its own interests rather than its subjugators' interests for the first time.

Eventually, though, the agitating elements reverse. The market conditions stabilize in time and the Directorate appeases the B-Mor population with commodities and leisure. At this point, those with the highest thresholds fall beneath the necessary threshold to rebel. This results in less rebelling agents overall, which bring additional groups beneath their own thresholds and back to normative behavior in a cycle of reverse thresholds. As more residents revert to ordinary conduct, the elements conducive for groupthink such as amiability and insularity return and the society as a whole reclaims its usual complacent routines of existence.

Fan's Legend

In spite of a return to the status quo, however, a significant meaningful change takes hold within the population. This change is effected in the performative action of the Fan story's creation but catalyzes repercussions that extend far beyond it. As the communally produced conception of a world outside their walls, the Fan story engenders knowledge that internally alters the nature of B-Mor society. As they create her, Fan brings to the B-Mor residents a way to actively identify, acknowledge, and critique the limits imposed on them, which is work they had been reluctant to undertake before. They recognize in their storytelling that B-Mor is a place of exacting order and gates, of structures which surround and encapsulate and are made all the more safe and restrictive by the residents' willing belief in a "ceiling" to their own imagination (Lee 127). An individual instantiation of that collective imagination, Fan mediates through her travels between walls and dreams, complacency and agency, instrumentality and independence, as the story B-Mor tells itself about itself.

More than simply bemoaning limits, the Fan story also expresses a latent desire to go beyond them. However much they are "tethered to the universe" of their familiar commodified role, there is now also admission that B-Mors' dreams are sometimes "wild" and reach above their enclosure (Lee 127). Faced with walls, Fan "made a leap, which was a startling thing in itself" (127). Her leap startles B-Mors not only through the adventurous nature of her escape but through her willingness to leave the secure and the familiar at all. In Alexander Nazaryan's words, "a dystopian novel is predicated on precisely such a rejection of the hive's psychic warmth, on a renegade willing to shatter collective delusions." Fan's story, based on rejecting B-Mor's complacent safety and instrumentalized submission, confronts the inhabitants with their own desires and possibilities. B-Mor discovers in itself Fan's "conviction of imagination" (Lee 7) and begins to privilege this imagination of the possible over the delusions the dominant Charters have deployed to define them.

The expression of this imagination itself exceeds the imposed limits of the community, in fact, and manifests B-Mor agency. The corporate and political powers founded B-Mor as a tool of production and expend a great amount of effort planning and maintaining its efficient operations through social engineering. The Charters and Directorate expected that their methods of social behavior control would prevent spiritual and psychological upheavals born from human commodification—the kind of upheavals exemplified in our present-day context by the Foxconn suicides. Eventually, however, conditions allowed for the community's questioning, contemplation, and self-definition and the B-Mor residents took advantage of this opportunity, fomenting internal change. B-Mor's resistance to the psychological limitations of the Facilities, and resistance to the narrow range of subjectivity offered by the model minority cultivation, broke through.

B-Mor's inhabitants have changed fundamentally through their experience of free thought and rebellion, even if that experience was short-lived. Where the actual Fan literally crosses the threshold into the Open Counties, the Fan that B-Mor imagines provides the people a vehicle to cross the threshold of their own psychological and spiritual subjugation. The narrative voice in its first person plural is a psychic terrain that cannot be harnessed, and Fan as its collective instantiation is a subject who cannot be captured or confined. Culturally empowered to let Fan go, B-Mor's citizens say to her within their mythic narrative's conclusion, "We'll find a way. You need not come back for us" (Lee 407). They go on with their lives, without immediately apparent solutions or great revolutions, but they carry new awareness of their desires, their barriers, and their possibilities. The alteration their period of social noncompliance created is larger, more powerful, more dangerous than the minor ripples of the superficial social rebellions that externally characterized it; the internal difference is a sea change. They stand within the B-Mor gates, but with a disassembled ceiling to their imagination.

Works Cited

Claeys, Gregory. "News From Somewhere: Enhanced Sociability and the Composite Definition of Utopia and Dystopia." *History* 98.330 (2013): 145–73. Print.

Dean, Jason and Ting-I Tsai. "Suicides Spark Inquiries." *The Wall Street Journal* 27 May 2010. Web. 20 Mar. 2016.

Gladwell, Malcolm. "Thresholds Of Violence." *New Yorker* 91.32 (2015). Academic Search Complete. Web. 10 Dec. 2015.

Janis, Irving. "Groupthink." *Psychology Today* Nov 1971: 43–46. Print.

———. *Victims of Groupthink*. Boston: Houghton Mifflin, 1972. Print.

Kim, Claire Jean. "The Racial Triangulation of Asian Americans." *Politics & Society* 27.1 (1999): 105–38. Print.

Lee, Chang-rae. *On Such a Full Sea*. New York: Riverhead, 2014. Print.

Nazaryan, Alexander. "Choose Your Dystopia." *Newsweek Global*. Newsweek.com, 22 Jan. 2014. Web. 20 Mar. 2016.

Orwell, George. *1984*. New York: Signet, 1977. Print.

Whyte, William H. "Groupthink." *Fortune* Mar 1952: 114–17. Print.

PART THREE

Dis-Orienting Planets

BENDING CULTURE
Racebending.com's Protests against Media Whitewashing

■ ■ ■

ROBIN ANNE REID

This essay considers the question of the extent to which the gap between the categories of cultural, or fan activism, and political activism may be changing, especially with regard to younger people's participation in online activist sites.[1] The distinction between "cultural activism" and "political activism" comes from sociology, where current scholarship is beginning to question the usefulness of the separate categorization in the context of internet activism (Earl and Kimport). I focus primarily on one internet community, Racebending.com, which originated in a protest against the casting of white actors in a live-action adaptation of a popular anime in 2008. The community began with a purpose that is common in fan groups, to affect the quality of the adaptation, but it has remained active after the failure of the original protest and well after the release of the film, shifting from the fan focus on a single film to engaging in politically and theoretically informed ways with the systemic problems of racial stereotyping and discrimination in employment in the United States media in general.

    I argue that the group's online activities since the release of the film show how fan activism overlaps with political activism and how both are connected to current academic scholarship in critical race and intersectional studies, thus complicating the binary between "cultural" and "political" activism. This essay will discuss the origins of the Racebending community, group actions since the release of the film that was the focus of the original protest, and the anti-racist fandom context in which the community exists, an activist context which has tended to be ignored by scholars of fan, or cultural, activism, who tend to assume participation by unmarked subjects (that is, primarily white and male).

The Origin of Racebending: Aang Ain't White

On December 11, 2008, the "Aang Ain't White" LiveJournal community was created to coordinate a letter-writing campaign to the Kennedy/Marshall production company. The campaign was to protest casting white actors to play the main characters in M. Night Shyamalan's live-action adaptation of *The Last Airbender* ("Saving the World with Postage"). The original *Avatar: The Last Airbender*, a children's animated series, aired on Nickelodeon from 2005 to 2008 and was celebrated by fans for its differences from mainstream media productions; the show incorporated religious, historical, cultural, and material elements from Pacific Rim and indigenous cultures. As detailed in the community's list of materials documenting studio blunders that led to the protest, one 2007 casting call requested "Caucasian or any other ethnicities" ("The Last Airbender Primer"). Other cultural blunders occurred in later calls ranging from asking Korean applicants to wear kimonos ("F. A. Q.") to limiting roles for Asian actors to minor and supporting characters ("The Last Airbender Primer"). The Fire Nation characters (a genocidal group who destroy the hero's tribe) were all played by actors of color while the heroes were played by white actors.

The goal of Aang Ain't White's campaign was a fairly simple one that fits easily into the standard definition of cultural or fan activism: fans working collectively to influence the production elements of the film. In the post titled "Saving the World with Postage," the group appeals to fans directly: "We all want this movie to be good—let's do what we can to help that happen!" However, the specific action these fans were asking of the producers—casting Asian American or Asian actors instead of white actors to play the lead roles in a major film—situated the group from the start in a political context, moving outside the world of the text, to oppose racist hiring practices (Lopez).

The film was released in 2010. While the goal of the letter-writing campaign—casting Asian or Asian American actors in the primary roles—was not met, the fans' concerns about whitewashing were covered in a number of media articles and reviews ("Media Archive"). Don Aucoin's article in the *Boston Globe* is an example of the extent to which the media covered the controversy in relation to the film, incorporating quotes from the president and founder of the Media Action Network for Asian Americans (MANAA) and from Michael Le, a Racebending.com spokesman. The film received a number of negative reviews, as well as winning five Golden Raspberry Awards or "Razzies," including Worst Director and Worst Picture ("Sequels"). While the film was considered a failure by fans and film critics, it earned more than $319 million worldwide ("The Last Airbender"). Debate between fans and the director continues to the present.

After the Film

After the release of the film, the Racebending group continued, broadening their focus to consider other film and media projects and working through a much increased social media presence across multiple platforms. Six years later, the original LiveJournal community is no longer active.[2] Instead, a website, Racebending.com, is the central space for creating and organizing the group's efforts, complemented by a Facebook group and Tumblr and Twitter accounts. The content posted differs across platforms, although links to the Racebending Blog entries often appear in the others. For the purpose of this essay, I focus on content created for the blog.

The Racebending website is well designed with clear links to different types of information and is updated regularly. Tagging of individual entries with clearly reocgnizable language allows for easy searching of the content. Interested readers can easily find information about the group's activities, educational resources, and information on how to get involved in the various campaigns, and they can read an active blog with content created by the group's staff and guest contributors. The link to "Learn More" takes readers to a page with links to information concerning the definition of terms, resources on the history of discrimination, and the blog as well as a section titled "Current Diversity Highlights." The "Diversity Highlights" link, at the time this essay was written, led to eight pages of additional links (ten per page) featuring content that includes "book reviews, TV reviews, movie reviews, and articles spotlighting rising stars in the entertainment industry" ("Learn More"). The header image picture on the site's home page is an animated one that moves through a sequence of images, each image linking to a blog entry.

The group continues to track developments in the original fandom, including the creation of comic books and a new show in the Avatar series, *The Legend of Korra*, but is also running other campaigns and engaging in a range of online and offline activities. Active campaigns include the adaptation of *Akira*, a Japanese manga and anime; *All You Need is Kill*, a Japanese science fiction novel; the film adaptation of *The Hunger Games*; and *Runaways*—all campaigns focusing on casting decisions ("Our Campaigns"). The campaigns are distinguished from ongoing commentary on other media projects as being those projects where the group has "taken formal advocacy steps" ("Our Campaigns"). They are described briefly on a dedicated page, with links to longer articles about each project with additional links to articles posted in the blog. Several of the identified projects are still in production, and the group reports mixed success with different studios.

But as well as running formal campaigns against whitewashing, the group has expanded their offline activities to include presentations on their work at fan conventions (including San Diego Comic Con and Chicago Comic & Entertainment Expo) and at community and university events, often coordinating with the Media Action Network for Asian Americans and the Organization of Chinese Americans ("About Us"). Additionally, Racebending staff present at academic and professional conferences such as the Convergence Culture Consortium conference at MIT. Regular entries appear in the Racebending.com blog documenting these activities, and discussing the cultural politics of race and representation. The blog articles are where I see academic discourse appearing, specifically historically and theoretically informed commentary on race and representation and intersectional issues. While a number of the blog articles are more typical of fan discourse, the political focus of the group informs both the fan and the academic articles.

One type of article appearing regularly on the blog is interviews, a common feature on fan sites. The range of interview subjects is broad, including novelists, actors, graphic novel and comics writers or artists, and musicians. The interviews range from bringing together larger groups of actors and creators at a ComicCon panel (Marissa Lee, "Super Asian America!") to individual creators, including white allies as well as Asian Americans. And while the major focus is on the experiences of Asian Americans, media racism in portrayals of African Americans and other ethnic minority groups is also featured as well as information on anti-racist strategies. An interview with Keegan Michael-Key, Jordan Peele and their director Peter Atencion on the topic of "talking race with humour" (Mike Lee) at the 2014 ComicCon is a featured article, and another featured article deals with the implications of the success of the television show, *Sleepy Hollow*, highlighting praise by fans for the show's handling of diversity, as well as describing how a Black Twitter campaign resulted in a published correction from the *New York Times* after calling the African American female protagonist played by Nicole Beharie a "sidekick." The article quotes an interview with the executive producer, Heather Kadin, about the choice to "[invert] the trope where characters of color are killed off first in horror" (Marissa Lee, "Sleepy").

I argue that another category of blog entry, often tagged as "History and Concepts," moves beyond typical fan discourse into the fan genre of *meta*, i.e. non-fiction essays that analyze some aspect of the central text of the fandom or fandom activities. Matt Hills defines this genre of fan writing as "fan scholarship," defining fan scholars as fans who use the tools of academic scholarship to create scholarship for an audience of fans. "Scholarship" covers a wide range of topics and methods, including explication and close reading of texts, but the Racebending.com material is drawing on a specific sub-set of academic scholarship that is related to anti-racist movements and intersectional theories circulated in academic disciplines. These entries can be historical, documenting the histories of racism in Hollywood films and popular media in general, or can critique contemporary casting and production issues, whether with regard to the current campaigns the group is running or to other media projects. An example of the historical essay, "A look back at Racebending and the Academy Awards," analyzes historical patterns in casting and nominations affecting people of color during the past eighty-six years, covering different types of racebending in films that won the Academy Awards. This article focuses primarily on the problem of white actors using makeup to play characters who are people of color (Hitchcock).

Marissa Lee provides an example of the critique of contemporary projects with "DreamWorks Will Whitewash 'Ghost in the Shell' Remake" (2015). This article criticizes the casting of Scarlett Johansson to play the female protagonist, Motoko Kusanagi, who is a Japanese cyborg. But Lee contextualizes the casting in the history of recent difficulties with movies casting white actors, specifically *The Lone Ranger* (2013) starring Johnny Depp and *Edge of Tomorrow* (2014) starring Tom Cruise. Lee summarizes published scholarship and data that contradict the popular belief that white actors are necessary for popular success: the material she cites includes an article from *The Journal of Behavioral Studies in Business*, multiple studies by universities, including the Harvard Business School, and statistics from the Motion Picture Association of America. Then she provides additional and original research on ethnicity and casting of "first-billed actors" in all Dreamwidth films from 1997 to the time of posting.[3]

A recent article by Jenn Fang, "Hollywood's 'Strange' Erasure of Asian Characters," is an example of an intersectional approach. Looking at the response to Marvel's casting of Tilda Swinton to play the character of "The Ancient One," an elderly Tibetan who is the mentor for Dr. Strange, Fang notes media praise by feminists for the genderbending of the character and the lack of criticism for the whitewashing. Fang criticizes the extent to which this character is an example of Orientalism in superhero comics while noting that the other option in these works is compete erasure: "Yes, the Ancient One is horribly Orientalist: yet, historic racism's solution can neither be faithful recreation of those offensive stereotypes nor the total erasure of people of colour" ("Hollywood's"). Identifying as a feminist of color and specifically disclaiming any fan enjoyment or knowledge of the comic that is being adapted, Fang's intersectional analysis notes the difficulty of asking for acceptance of "the erasure of that which would represent our race order to justify a representation of our gender," noting that it would have been possible to cast an Asian or Asian American woman to play a genderbent Ancient One ("Hollywood's").

Fang's essay was originally posted at her blog, *Reappropriate*, and ends with a Twitter hashtag: "#AStrangeWhitewashing." This essay, as well as Lee's essay on *Ghost in the Shell*, were multiply linked to from other sites, on a variety of platforms, including blogs, Facebook, Twitter, and Tumblr, as well as a fandom newsletter ("Metanews") and Disqus, a third-party blog comment hosting network.[4] The Twitter hashtag leads to a number of Asian American political and activist blogs, as well as posts by other bloggers of color. The blogs that link to Racebending.com's content also contain content that would meet the definition of political rather than cultural activism, including entries on the efforts in various states to change and expand the ways in which data on "Asian American and Pacific Islander" (AAPI) communities is collected and reported on, specifically moving from aggregating the different cultural groups to disaggregated data (Fang; Angry Asian Man).

Racebending.com's focus has clearly moved not only beyond discussion of the adaptation of one film but also beyond the original focus on casting Asian and Asian American actors to consider national, ethnic, and racial representations in American media more broadly. While they still focus on letter-writing campaigns, mobilize fans of the works to call for better casting, and meet with studio executives, their work also includes posting theoretically and politically informed articles that are designed to educate readers on the issues. The theoretical perspectives include language and approaches that are used in critical race and intersectional theory. The posts on the blog and on the other platforms discuss a wide range of ongoing media productions involving whitewashing casting and racial representation, not only through articles written by the staff but by providing links to work done by other popular media critics.[5] Reflecting the changes in the community, the mission statement was revised from the original one posted on LiveJournal. The original statement consisted of one line of text supplemented by an image from the original show with added text. The one line is: "Coming together to call shenanigans on orientalist casting!" The image features the two main characters with "Not White" and arrows next to them, and a caption which reads: "Dear Hollywood: your racism is showing. Plz get that checked out" ("Profile").

The new statement not only has a broader focus than casting choices in one film, but also deletes informal fan diction (such as "shenanigans" and "Plz") for more formal and activist language: "grassroots . . . media consumers":

> Racebending.com is an international grassroots organization of media consumers who support entertainment equality. We advocate for underrepresented groups in entertainment media. Since our formation in 2009, we have been dedicated to furthering equal opportunities in Hollywood and beyond.

Reception and Context for Anti-Racist Fan Activism

Despite the media and internet attention given Racebending.com during the past six years and despite the extent to which their concerns overlap with current scholarship in a number of academic disciplines, only one academic article has been written on the group. In "Fan Activists and the Politics of Race in *The Last Airbender*" (2011), Lori Kido Lopez uses ethnographic and text-based approaches to explore how the major founders and participants "transition[ed] from everyday fans to political activists," a transition "facilitated through the language and culture of fandom itself" (432). Working with evidence gathered from interviews with the leaders as well as analyzing the texts produced from January 2009 to June 2011, Lopez provides an excellent introduction to the origins and development of the community and a strong argument for how the group's use of fan discursive practices identifies the group as participating in a type of activism that differs from typical fan demands relating only to the world of the texts. Lopez argues convincingly that Racebending's growth and development proves that fan activism can incorporate political activities, including creating alliances with existing non-profit groups outside fandom, and "seeking to expand their knowledge of political discourse and the real-world implications of their fandom" (432). Lopez raises concerns about four issues: how sustainable the group will be; the importance of their difficulties translating online activities into offline protests; the conflict between fans as consumers and fans as activists; and the concerns of some fans about the extent to which the original series was an example of "white Orientalism" (436).

Examining the activities of the group during the past four years, I would judge that Racebending.com has not only sustained but expanded its online activities, proving its sustainability. After the early failures to muster offline numbers for protests at studios that Lopez notes, the group seems to have shifted to focusing on offline educational and consciousness-raising activities at fan and academic events to complement their attempts at on-going communication with media producers. These activities, in conjunction with the types of articles created for the blog, are what I argue add another type of identity category and discourse to the "consumer" and "activist" categories Lopez and other scholars consider: academics or educators. The question of authenticity in representation is a complex one, and beyond the scope of this article: as scholars in cultural studies note, the concept of "authenticity" in cultural texts is often connected to historically racist and atemporal concepts of marginalized cultures. Anthony Sze-Fai Shiu analyzes *Duke Nuke'em 3D* (1996) and *Shadow Warrior* (1997) in the historical context of yellowface and black minstrelsy to discuss the ongoing complexities of egalitarian movements (including scholarship on social constructions of identity) attempting to dismantle racial hierarchies by reinscribing an essentialized concept of "race." Shiu grounds his work in an analysis of "concepts of race, culture, and authenticity, especially in light of recent critical work carried out in Whiteness Studies and Asian American studies" (110). Fang's essay on the casting of Tilda Swinton as The Ancient One includes an analysis of the Orientalism of the character, and of portrayals of the few Asian characters in superhero comics generally, as well as noting the problems of erasure of even Orientalist characters. The issue deserves further analysis.

Lopez's essay focuses on the work done by Racebending.com but does not discuss the larger fan activist context for the community, a context which supports her general argument about the ways in which fan communities can draw on fandom discourses to engage in political activism. The group formed at a time when discussions of race and representation in science fiction and fantasy were increasing in online media fandom communities: the Racebending campaign overlaps Racefail 2009, a three-month online debate (January–March 2009) about racisms in popular culture and media representation ("Racefail"; Reid; Wong). Aang Ain't White was one of a number of independent sites created by fans engaged in activist and collective efforts to critique racist aspects of popular culture during this period, efforts that continue to the present and that include antisexist activism as well.[6]

Racebending's alliance with non-profit groups concerned with race and representation, especially with regard to Asian Americans, occurred early. In the post of January 30, 2009, besides discussing plans for a protest at the Philadelphia casting call, the group announced the chance to buy items (or the images to make the items) for the protest at cost. The post noted that the group did not want to make any profits on the items and encouraged donations to an Asian American theater group, the East West Players ("So Many Ways to Speak Out"). The East West Players is a non-profit theatrical organization that began in 1965 in order to create increased opportunities for Asian Pacific and Islander artists; a number of voice actors for the original *Last Airbender* series were associated with the organization ("So Many Ways to Speak Out"). The post of February 21, 2009, linked to an open letter protesting the *Airbender* casting from the MANAA, a non-profit group formed in 1992 to "address the negative stereotypes long perpetuated by the media which detrimentally affects all Asian Americans, hurting not only their self-image, but how non-Asians treat them" ("History of MANAA").

Given the growth in anti-racist activities in online fandom communities, the lack of attention paid by fan studies scholars to the efforts of Racebending and other groups is beginning to be apparent. The last two decades have seen a growth in scholarship on fan activities and growing attention paid to the engagement and activities of fans as reflecting more than passive consumption. Henry Jenkins originated the concept of science fiction and fantasy fans as active participants in regard to media they consume, emphasizing the participatory nature of fan culture and the spread of participatory culture via the internet to convergence culture. Participatory culture is one of the elements of convergence culture, which Jenkins defines as a type of thinking that "is reshaping American popular culture and in particular, the ways it is impacting the relationship between media audiences, producers, and content" (*Convergence* 12).

Jenkins has long argued that fans' interactions with both the products and the producers of media are a vital part of contemporary culture deserving of scholarly attention because of how fans have moved "from the invisible margins of popular culture and into the center of current thinking about media production and consumption" (12). In *Convergence Culture* (2006), Jenkins notes that the fans he studies are the "relatively elite" early adopters, those who are "disproportionately white, male, middle class, and college educated," whose economic important and cultural status make their views important to the corporate producers of products (23). In a 2008 interview published in *Transformative Works and Culture*, Jenkins makes a direct call for scholarship focusing on "inequality and exclusion" in fan studies (TWC Editor).

Despite his calls for more attention being paid to diversity, the growing scholarship drawing on Jenkin's concepts of participatory fandom has not begun to significantly engage with the activities of fans such as the Racebending group. Scholarship on race and fans tends to be more focused on sports and music, or in fandoms where race is a visible element of the source text

(Sperb). A recently anthology, *Fan CULTure: Essays on Participatory Fandom in the 21st Century* (2013), edited by Kristin M. Barton and Jonathan Malcolm Lampley, strongly builds on Jenkins' work, specifically the concept of participatory fandoms. One of the three sections of the anthology focuses on fans' interactions with the producers concerning the extent to which fan activities and direct interactions influence the productions in the following franchises: *Chuck*, Disneyland, LEGO, *Lost*, *Firefly*, and *Supernatural*. The other two sections cover fan creations and fans' use of social media.

These essays, and the anthology as a whole, provide strong and useful analyses of a range of participatory fan activities in different fandoms, all with a strong awareness of how the Internet and other contemporary technologies and corporate marketing strategies are driving aspects of fans' participatory culture. However, in a typical fashion, the anthology fails to discuss fan collective and political activities relating to race and representation, mentioning race twice in the entire anthology. The first occurs in Meyrav Koren-Kuik's "Designing the Tangible: Disneyland, Fandom, and Spatial Inversion," where in the larger discussion of Walt Disney's marketing strategies there is a brief mention that awareness of fan demographics of consumers for the Disney princesses have resulted in the creation of princesses of color in a few films and their associated merchandise.[7] The only other mention of race in the anthology occurs in Malcolm Lampley's "Afterword" where he notes that one of the changes in fandom is that the participants are no longer primarily white and male. None of the fandom activities covered in the anthology focus on fan demands relating to representations of race or on the issues of whitewashing for an adaptation of an original work. Instead, the essays focus on fans that want new content rather than changes in an existing text and emphasize fans as consumers who are considered important because of marketing strategies. Perhaps because of the lack of attention paid to race, the outcomes and interactions covered tend to have positive results compared to Racebending.com's protest.

Scholarship that does incorporate critical race approaches to fan studies tends to be produced primarily by women. The online peer-reviewed journal, *Transformative Works and Cultures* (*TWC*) edited by Kristina Busse and Karen Hellekson, tends to be the primary journal publishing fan scholarship that covers anti-racist fan activities as well as other types of fan productions, creations, and activities.[8] In fact, *TWC* featured a group of essays on "Race and Ethnicity in Fandom" in a double-theme issue in 2011 (Gatson and Reid). A recent print anthology, *Fan Girls and the Media: Creating Characters, Consuming Culture* (2015), edited by Adrienne Trier-Bieniek, stands out not only for its coverage of fandom activities in multiple types of fandom, including but not limited to science fiction such as comedy, video games, and reality television, but also for a number of essays in which race and gender are the focus of analysis.

While fans as a general group may have become more visible to producers and to academics tracking the reception of media texts, this visibility seems primarily limited to white fans, albeit no longer exclusively to white male fans. The collective, participatory, and activist activities of fans such as the creators and producers of Racebending.com and other online fans who have been actively engaged in anti-racist activities goes relatively undiscussed. These fans work to change the area of "cultural practices" but the cultural practices they focus on are directly related to historical and contemporary racist ideologies which, increasingly, are being protested by a wide variety of groups in both online and offline venues and which are being critically analyzed by academics in a variety of social science and humanities disciplines, showing the extent to which the previously perceived boundaries between cultural productions and the economic and political realities of life are blurring.[9] Clearly, the Racebending fans are actively trying to shape American popular culture and the media and have been maintaining their efforts for over six years, including presenting at academic conferences. The extent to which their work, and other anti-racist activism by fans, continues to be overlooked by fan studies scholars is a growing problem that should no longer be ignored.

Acknowledgments

Early work on this essay was supported by a faculty development leave granted by Texas A&M University-Commerce during the spring semester of 2014.

Notes

1. Philippa Collin argues that young people's political identities are changing, citing additional scholarship done in Britain, showing a greater interest in organizing around online communities created by interest groups and young people rather than government sites (536).

2. The last entry in the LiveJournal, dated April 26, 2009, and titled "Some Good News," contains a link to Racebending.com. The Racebending.com blog covers ways to follow their postings via an RSS feed for syndication, as well as stressing the importance of "liking" the Facebook group and following them on Tumblr and Twitter.

3. Lee, one of the co-founders of Racebending.com, is the author of the article, but she credits Jonelle D., Sade A. and Michael Le for their help in creating it.

4. A basic Google search using the title of Lee's and Fang's articles found over 8000 mentions of the *Ghost in the Shell* article (published in January 2015), including an online petition, and over 18,000 mentions of the Dr. Strange article (published in June 2015). The numbers include multiple mentions of the title on a web site but serve to show the extent to which material on Racebending.com circulates across a wide variety of platforms, allowing discussion in multiple spaces.

5. The links to content published online occur primarily in the Facebook, Twitter, and Tumblr sites. For example, an August post in the Facebook Racebending community linked to an article reporting on a project by the USC Annenberg Media Diversity & Social Change Initiative that shows the inequalities and discrimination in the most popular films in recent years that relate to gender, race, and sexual orientation.

6. Two recent examples of organized resistance toward changing demographics of fandom since the Racefail 2009 debates are Gamergate and the slate-voting against perceived affirmative action in the Hugo awards. Both controversies have been covered by mainstream media as well as fan and entertainment media; for an overview of Gamergate, see Erik Kain's article in Forbes.com. For an overview of the Hugo Awards controversy, see Kameron Hurley's article in *The Atlantic*.

7. The recent announcement by Disney about casting a young Native Hawaiian woman, Auli'i Cravalho, to play the role of Moana, described as a Hawaiian princess, reflects ongoing efforts by Disney (Cutler).

8. I am a member of the *Transformative Works and Cultures*' Editorial Board.

9. Jill Lane, in "ImpersoNation: Toward a Theory of Black-, Red-, and Yellowface in the Americas" (2008), analyzes the extent to which "impersoNation" as a cultural practice is a key component of national discourses.

Works Cited

"About." East West Players. n.d. Web. 1 June 2015.
"About Us." *Racebending.com*. n.d. Web. 1 June 2015.
Angry Asian Man. "New Report Examines Asian American & NHPIS in the West." *Angry Asian Man*. 10 Oct. 2015. Web. 13 October 2015.
Arthur, L., and S. P. Tasha. Views from inside the Net: How Websites Affect Young Adults' Political Interest. *The Journal of Politics* 67.4 (2005): 1122–42. Print.
Aucoin, Don. "'Airbender' Reopens Race Debate." *Boston.com*. 4 July 2010. Web. 1 June 2015.
Avatar: The Last Airbender. Nickelodeon. 2005–8. Television.
Barton, Kristin M. and Jonathan M. Lampley, eds. *Fan CULTure: Essays on Participatory Fandom in the 21st Century*. Jefferson: McFarland, 2013. Print.
Chuck. NBC. 2007–12. Television.
Collin, Philippa. "The internet, youth participation policies, and the development of young people's political identities in Australia." *Journal of Youth Studies* 11.5 (2008): 527–42. Print.
Conway, John. "Notes on Slacktavism." *The Huffington Post Blog*. 25 March 2012. Web. 10 July 2015.

"Current Diversity Highlights." *Racebending.com*. n.d. Web. 10 July 2015.
Cutler, Jacqueline. "New Disney Princess, Moana, Getting Warm Reception." *New York Daily News*. 7 Oct. 2015. Web. 10 Oct. 2015.
"Demographics of Racebending.com Supporters." *Racebending.com*. 30 April 2010. Web. 31 May 2015.
Duke Nuke'em 3D. GT Interactive Software. 1996. Videogame.
Earl, Jennifer, and Katrina Kimport. "Movement Societies and Digital Protest: Fan Activism and Other Nonpolitical Protest Online." *Sociological Theory* 27.3 (2009): 220–42. Print.
Edge of Tomorrow. Dir. Doug Liman. Warner Brothers, 2014. Film.
Fang, Jenn. "CA Gov. Jerry Brown Vetoes #AAPI Data Disaggregation Bill." *Reappropriate*. 8 Oct. 2015. Web. 13 Oct. 2015.
———. "Hollywood's 'Strange' Erasure of Asian Characters." *Racebending.com*. 2 June 2015. Web. 13 Oct. 2015.
"F. A. Q." *Racebending.com*. n.d. Web. 1 June 2015.
Firefly. Fox. 2002. Television.
Gatson, Sarah N. and Robin Anne Reid. *Transformative Works and Cultures* 8 (2011). Web.
"History of MANAA." Media Action Network for Asian Americans. n.d. Web. 1 June 2015.
Hitchcock, Robin. "A Look back at Racebending and the Academy Awards." *Racebending.com*. 18 Feb. 2014. Web. 10 July 2015.
Hills, Matt. *Fan Cultures*. London: Routledge, 2002. Print.
Hurley, Kameron. "Hijacking the Hugo Awards Won't Stifle Diversity in Science Fiction." *The Atlantic*. 9 April 2015. Web. 10 June 2015.
Jenkins, Henry. *Fans, Bloggers, and Gamers: Exploring Participatory Culture*. New York: NYUP, 2006. Print.
———. *Convergence Culture: Where Old and New Media Collide*. New York: NYUP, 2006. Print.
Kain, Erik. "GamerGate: A Closer Look at the Controversy Sweeping Video Games." *Forbes*. 4 Sept. 2014. Web. 10 June 2015.
Koren-Kuik, Meyrav. "Desiring the Tangible: Disneyland, Fandom and Spatial Immersion." *Fan CULTure: Essays on Participatory Fandom in the 21st Century*. Eds. Kristin M. Barton and Jonathan M. Lampley. Jefferson: McFarland, 2013. 146–58. Print.
Lampley, Jonathan Malcolm. "Afterword: The Past and Future of Fandom Studies." *Fan CULTure: Essays on Participatory Fandom in the 21st Century*. Eds. Kristin M. Barton and Jonathan M. Lampley. Jefferson: McFarland, 2013. 191–96. Print.
Lane, Jill. "ImpersoNation: Toward a Theory of Black-, Red-, and Yellowface in the Americas." *PMLA* 123.5 (2008): 1728–31. Print.
The Last Airbender. Dir. M. Night Shyamalan. Paramount Pictures, 2010. Film.
"The Last Airbender." *Box Office Mojo*. n.d. Web. 1 July 2015.
"The Last Airbender Primer." *Racebending.com*. 21 Oct. 2009. Web. 1 June 2015.
Lee, Mike. "Key and Peele on Tackling Race with Humor." *Racebending.com*. 31 July 2014. Web. 10 July 2015.
Lee, Marissa. "Avatar: The Last Airbender—The Search Ties Up a Loose End and Raises an Interesting Question." *Racebending.com*. 31 Oct. 2013. Web. 15 July 2015.

———. "DreamWorks Will Whitewash 'Ghost in the Shell' Remake." *Racebending.com*. 13 Jan. 2015. Web. 15 July 2015.

———. "Media Takes Note of 'The Hunger Games' Casting." *Racebending.com*. 4 March 2011. Web. 15 July 2015.

———. "Sleepy Hollow Sparks Fan Discussions on Diversity in the Media." *Racebending.com*. 25 Sep. 2014. Web. 15 July 2015.

———. "Super Asian America! at San Diego ComicCon 2015." *Racebending.com*. July 2015. Web. 13 Oct. 2015.

The Lone Ranger. Dir. Gore Verbinski. Walt Disney Pictures, 2013. Film.

Lopez, Lori Kido. "Fan Activists and the Politics of Race in *The Last Airbender*." *International Journal of Cultural Studies* 15.5 (2011): 431–45. Print.

Lost. ABC. 2004–10. Television.

Media Archive. *Racebending.com*. n.d. Web. 1 June 2015.

"Our Campaigns." *Racebending.com*. n.d. Web. 1 Oct. 2015.

"Profile." Aang Ain't White. n.d. Web. 1 June 2015.

Racebending. "There has been no change 'in the portrayal of apparent race/ethnicity' from the previous seven years." Facebook. 6 Aug. 2015. Web. 13 Oct. 2015.

"Racefail." Fanlore. n.d. Web. 1 June 2015.

Reid, Robin Anne. "'The Wild Unicorn Herd Check-In': The Politics of Race in Science Fiction Fandom." *Black and Brown Planets: The Politics of Race in Science Fiction*. Ed. Isiah Lavender III. Jackson: UP of Mississippi, 2014. 225–40. Print.

Romano, Aja. "M. Night Shyamalan Says 'The Last Airbender' Flopped Because Adults Didn't Get It." *The Daily Dot*. 31 May 2015. Web. 1 June 2015.

"Saving the World with Postage." *LiveJournal*. 11 Dec. 2008. Web. 1 June 2015.

"Sequels, Remakes, and 3-D Rip-Offs Dominate 2010 RAZZIE Award 'Winners.'" The Razzie Awards. n.d. Web. 1 June 2015.

Shadow Warrior. GT Interactive Software. 1997. Videogame.

Shefrin, Elana. "Lord of the Rings, Star Wars, and Participatory Fandom: Mapping New Congruencies between the Internet and Media Entertainment Culture." *Critical Studies in Media Communication* 21.3 (2004): 261–81. Print

Shiu, Anthony Sze-Fai. "What Yellowface Hides: Video Games, Whiteness, and the American Racial Order." *The Journal of Popular Culture* 39.1 (2006): 109–25. Print.

Sleepy Hollow. Fox. 2013–16. Television.

Smith, Stacy L., Marc Choueiti, Katherine Pieper, Traci Gillig, Carmen Lee, Dylan DeLuca. "Inequality in 700 Popular Films: Examining Portrayals of Gender, Race, & LGBT Status from 2007–2014." USC Annenberg's Media, Diversity, & Social Change Initiative. n.d. Web. 10 Oct. 2015.

"So Many Ways to Speak Out." Aang Ain't White. 20 Jan. 2009. Web. 10 June 2015.

"Some Good News and a Few Reminders." Aang Ain't White. 21 Feb. 2009. Web. 1 June 2009.

Sperb, Jason. *Disney's Most Notorious Film: Race, Convergence, and the Hidden Histories of Song of the South*. Austin: U of Texas P, 2012. Print.

Supernatural. The WB/The CW. 2005–16. Television.

Trier-Bieniek, Adrienne. *Fan Girls and the Media: Creating Characters, Consuming Culture.* New York: Rowman & Littlefield, 2015.

TWC Editor. Interview with Henry Jenkins. *Transformative Works and Cultures* 1 (2008). Web. 5 Sept. 2015.

Wong, Rydra. "Racefail '09." Dreamwidth. 2 Feb. 2002. Web. 1 June 2015.

THE MAKO MORI FAN CLUB

■ ■ ■

CAIT COKER

When I was a kid, whenever I'd feel small or lonely, I'd look up at the stars, wondered if there was life up there. Turns out I was looking in the wrong direction. When alien life entered our world it was from the deep beneath the Pacific Ocean, a fissure between two tectonic plates. A portal between the dimensions, a breach.... The world came together, pooling its resources, throwing aside old rivalries for the sake of the greater good. To fight monsters we created monsters of our own.
—**Raleigh Becket's** opening narration in *Pacific Rim*

Pacific Rim (2013), arguably one of the most subversive action films in American history, which may seem surprising considering its description, can easily be condensed into "people in giant mech suits beat up giant monsters to save the world." And yet, both of these things are true: from its use of the female gaze to its emphases on diversity and internationalism in an action genre that typically promotes the rugged individualism of the white male hero, *Pacific Rim* takes the visual and storytelling language of contemporary science fiction (SF) film and turns it on its head. Within days of its release, gif sets, fan art, and short fanfictions appeared across Tumblr, LiveJournal, Archive of Our Own, and Deviant Art celebrating the film. These active readings turned a minor blockbuster into a cult classic among a small but active body of fans.[1]

Fan works are generally discussed for how they demonstrate points of resistance to dominant cultural works, but they are seldom examined as sources of viable criticism.[2] Fan communities come together not only through the love they share for their favorite text, but through the ways they choose to read that text. This notion becomes most apparent in "ship wars," when various factions champion the romantic pairing of their choice. *Pacific Rim* contains no canonical romance, though fans can and do read romantic and sexual interest into the various characters. Above all else, *Pacific Rim* fans celebrate what they see as the positive gender and communal politics of the film, especially as illustrated through the interpersonal relationships depicted in the film. Fan writing and fan art are only just beginning to be discussed as representations of serious analysis[3], but the commentaries and discussions of *Pacific Rim* take such close readings for granted. Attentive fans deconstructed scenes to locate elements that indicate various character traits and world views outside of the visual literacies that del Toro promulgates. To this end, I examine the major motifs of *Pacific Rim* fandom online and consider its relationship with a film that seemingly "failed" in the American market but exploded internationally. Likewise, I consider how the depictions of close, but not necessarily romantic, relationships are celebrated in both the film and in fandom as illustrating a cooperative ideal that is generally not seen in popular, mainstream media.

Making Monsters to Fight Monsters: The World of *Pacific Rim*

Pacific Rim juxtaposes time, place and language, simultaneously presenting a world familiar and alien. The first words the viewer sees are definitions—for *kaiju*, a Japanese word meaning "giant beast," and for *jaeger*, a German word meaning "hunter"—followed by an introduction describing "K-day," when the first kaijus attacked on August 13, 2013—a setting exactly a month after the film itself debuted on July 12, 2013. The location of the eponymous earthly "Pacific rim" functions as a through-point to another dimension; humanity encounters alien life in the seas rather than in the stars. Finally, the use of the Pacific as an Eastern locus which is so often viewed in Western art, literature, and politics as a place to be colonized becomes the point of resistance to the colonial forces of alien powers.

Historically, the Pacific as depicted in Western science fiction functions as the setting for various scientific experiments (H.G. Wells's *The Island of Doctor Moreau* [1896]) or utopias (Samuel Butler's *Erewhon* [1872] or Austin Tappan Wright's *Islandia* [1942]). At the same time, Japanese SF and anime demonstrate a cultural preoccupation with invasion and the monstrous, perhaps best demonstrated by *Godzilla* (1954) or *Neon Genesis Evangelion* (1995–96). As Joseph Milicia writes,

For some writers, Pacific isolation allows for unhindered experiments, whether scientific or social, often with tranquil beaches in contrast to savage or sophisticated interiors. For others, the appeal is almost purely that of the unknown—hence those lost worlds and strange cultures and creatures. (735)

In contrast, the "lost world" of *Pacific Rim* embodies the pre-attack world of the early twenty-first century, when humans only feared one another, and the "strange cultures" include that of the jaeger pilots with their telepathic connections to one another and of the kaiju-worshipping death cults that are only glimpsed on the streets of Hong Kong.

The solemn, documentary-style exposition of Raleigh Becket's (Charlie Hunnam) account combines snippets of real-world news footage of world leaders with fictional, CGI monsters and devastation. This form of remix, in which US President Barack Obama can be spliced with other talking heads and mechas[4] the size of buildings, provides a grounding effect to the viewer. We know this juxtaposition is not real, but it could be. Throughout the movie's remainder, news programs in the background quickly undercut the typical trope of "governments join to fight a greater foe." For example, a politician explains that much of the population has been moved inland for safety even as a reporter counters, "That's the rich and powerful—what about us?" Elements of utopia (inter-government cooperation) and dystopia (wages are paid in ration booklets) combine to reveal a near future not much different from today, albeit with real monsters. This intellectual disjunction, gestured at only briefly in the film, became a speculative goldmine for fans who wanted to unpack what these sequences represented within the context of this world. Tumblr user dontneedyourheroact asked these questions:

> can you imagine how much the Jaeger Program meant to the poor and weak of the world?
> like it is explicitly stated that the rich and powerful lived way inland, safer from the kaiju than those along the Pacific coastlines of the world. Can you imagine the interiors of various countries gentrifying, forcing lower-income families further and further from safety? Can you imagine having to tell your kids that you can't afford your suddenly hyper-expensive home in, say, Idaho, and your best chance of being able to get an affordable house is on the coast of Oregon, where any day an enormous monster could pop up to say 'hi fuck all of you'?
> can you imagine how beloved the jaeger pilots are by the people on the coast?

As Raleigh Becket explains, the jaeger pilots were considered rock stars, and a montage shows pilots on TV shows and in ticker tape parades. We might consider how the jaeger pilots are treated in this world versus those of our real-world "heroes," such as military veterans who subsist on food stamps and without healthcare, or the various types of emergency personnel who usually fall on the appallingly low end of wage labor. This valorization of government-funded, communal service for the public good is at odds with the current trend of films in which superheroes are highly individualistic and usually in conflict with the public state.[5]

Another news sequence later in the film shows jaeger pilots being interviewed after a kaiju attack, along with clips of rioting after the news has been released that the jaeger program is being shut down in favor of a "wall of life." Fan discussions turned to analyzing the forms that economics and gentrification would take in a world in which wealthy populations retreated to continental interiors and the world's poor were sent to the literal margins of the coastlines. hamburgerjack comments,

> I keep wondering what the actual endgame of the world leaders was ... if they didn't think the Kaiju would ever strike farther inland if left to run rampant, or if they thought the walls and the target-rich environment on the other side of them would always slow them down enough to be brought down with conventional weaponry, but at the end of the day I think it's perfectly realistic to believe they had no endgame.
>
> What's the endgame on denying climate change? What's the endgame on vulture capitalism destroying the consumer class that makes capitalism possible? What's the endgame on propping up this quarter's profits by stripmining the future? Strategies that literally have no future in them still win out.

These pieces of meta-commentary drive at one of the root causes of American audience backlash against the film: the generational gap between baby boomers and millennials. And it is the millennials, as characters, who appear as the heroes of *Pacific Rim*.[6]

Screenplay author Travis Beacham created his own Tumblr account to answer questions about the world of *Pacific Rim*, including confirming ages of characters and dates of events, as well as adding enough additional background on the film's world, both canonical and extracanonical, so as to almost create a shared universe.[7] We learn that the "old guard" of the film, Stacker Pentecost (Idris Elba) and Herc Hansen (Max Martini), were born in the early 1980s and that the younger characters who make up most of the cast were born in the late 1990s and early 2000s. Fans noted that in this future characters could be military and have tattoos and dyed hair because skills necessary to collaborative survival trump appearance. Tumblr user starseedjenny posted, a couple days ago i saw someone raise the question of why Pacific Rim only seems to be resonating with millennials, and i didn't know the answer, but i've been thinking about it a lot and suddenly i understand

it's because it's a movie about young people who are smart and capable but nonetheless handed a broken and nightmarish dying world, which is hurting everybody but especially them because they're the ones who have to live their whole lives in it ...

and everyone knows there's no chance that things will get better. they *know* that everything is going to be terrible for the rest of time

and these young people *take* that world and the pathetic bottom of the barrel that's been left for them and they spit and rebel in the faces of all of that, screaming that they won't let it take them down after all

it's a story about young people, together, exercising hope and power when they are afforded none and the stakes are so high (bolding and italics in original)

Conversations such as these approach depths not typically associated with the action genre; it is worth noting that these analyses only appear in fan writing and not in any of the reviews that appeared in traditional media, nor have they yet appeared in academic publications on Guillermo del Toro's work. To date, the only "professional" analysis of *Pacific Rim* appears in Keith McDonald's and Roger Clark's *Guillermo del Toro: Film as Alchemic Art* (2014), a chapter largely concerned with chronicling the film's production rather than with textual criticism.[8] While I hope more academic work will be forthcoming, we must still ask ourselves: Why was mainstream response to the film so different than fan response?

Globalism, "Problems" of Response, and the Limitations of Language

After the film's release, American reviewers provided a muted critical response. The satire site Honest Trailers articulated what appears to be a common conception, that the film was "The most awesome dumb movie ever made or the dumbest awesome movie ever made" (Screen Junkies). The film was consistently criticized for the simplicity of its plot. Indeed, the plot is simple, and perhaps given the recent fashion for overly elaborate twists and turns, as in both *Iron Man 3* (2013) and *Star Trek Into Darkness* (2013), it makes sense for a straightforward story to be read as "too easy." Feminist geek site *The Mary Sue* (*TMS*) published one of the few positive reviews, declaring that *Pacific Rim* was a saving the world movie where the ability that put humanity over the top was not our ability to survive at any cost, our intelligence, our breeding power, or our common cold virus, but rather our ability to form strong interpersonal relationships of all kinds: friend to friend, parent to child, lover to lover, and sibling to sibling (to sibling, even). (The Mary Sue Staff)

The *TMS* review echoed the sentiments of many fans, declaring the characters' relationships and community as being the source of both fascination and valorization.

Other media outlets seemed to see only the colorful explosions. Scott Mendelson wrote a column for *Forbes* arguing that *Pacific Rim*'s "overseas success represents ... an example of a most interesting and arguably increasing anomaly: films that disappointed, if not out-and-out bombed, in America only to do so well overseas that they were relatively profitable anyway." Anthony Lane, in contrast, offered a blistering review of the film which tied into its locus:

> The clue to "Pacific Rim" is in the title. It represents not just an important location for the plot (the Kaiju have their eye on Hong Kong) but a courteous nod to the market where films such as this are intended—or designed—to thrive. Overseas sales account for an ever-swelling percentage of Hollywood's box office, and it's naïve to assume that forthcoming products will not reflect that cultural spread. That is why, in this instance, the stars are a mélange of British, Asian, Russian, and Australian, some speaking with American accents, some not. What's more, even as the story hops between Alaska, San Francisco, Sydney, Vladivostok, and the Far East, you begin to realize that it could be happening anywhere, or nowhere. Small wonder that it ends up beneath the waves. (80)

The globalism of the film that Mendelson posits as its saving grace and Lane as its weakness imparts its fans and writers a strong thesis: it is only through sharing language (which is used interchangeably by all characters) and resources that humanity can survive in the film and, probably, real life as well.

This concept of a literal "meeting of minds" outside of language demonstrates the most important aspect of fighting and surviving in *Pacific Rim*. The telepathic neural drift shared by jaeger pilots encompasses empathy, compassion, equality, and most of all, trust as the key elements of human interaction. Most often, drift compatibility proves strongest between those with familial ties (brothers, father and son, married couples), but it is also revealed between the feuding scientists who might not share nationalities or temperaments, but who do share goals.[9] Among the jaeger pilots, even the arrogant hotshots still sacrifice themselves for humanity. Using his own Tumblr, Travis Beacham offered,

> Consider the example of the Hansens—shooting flares in a giant monster's face in a desperate effort to give ten million people *who don't even speak their language* an extra minute or two to get to safety. The future of mankind, I think, hangs on people of different backgrounds deciding to care about one another. ("Consider"; italics added)

The element regarding language provides the key to understanding the intellectual substance of the film and fans' response to it. Verbal language often acts as a limiter to understanding and comprehension; we might speak of the "universal language" of emotions such as love, but the concrete language of speech often hinders understanding of one another. This notion perhaps best epitomizes the Honest Trailers description of Mako Mori (Rinko Kikuchi) as "a girl so bad at speaking English sometimes she just gives up mid-sentence" (Screen Junkies). What some viewers found amusing or inexplicable was, to others, a pointed commentary. In another scene, Mako speaks her last words to her adopted father in Japanese, which go untranslated on screen. The audience knows it has to be some variation of "I love you," but the choice to leave this deliberate language gap plays directly into the motifs of global communication and shared experience.

Finally, the very notion of "drift compatibility" among pilots illustrates these motifs. Testing for drift compatibility utilizes martial arts; Raleigh explains that the exercise "is a dialogue, not a fight," which is explicated more fully in the *Pacific Rim* novelization:

> First: the more a fighting pair could anticipate and counter each other's moves, the more likely they were to be able to anticipate each other's thoughts. Second: If you could kick someone's ass easily in a fight, how could you take that person seriously as an equal when you had to share your inner-most thoughts with them and trust them with your life? (Irvine 115–16)

This element represents the key to understanding not only the jaeger pilots as characters but also the gender politics of the film. We see two sets of male-female pilots, Raleigh Becket and Mako Mori, and Aleksis (Heather Doerkson) and Sasha Kaidanovsky (Robert Maillet). Though the Kaidanovskys' have little time dedicated to them in the film, it must be noted that they share the same first name; Aleksis and Sasha are the masculine and feminine versions of "Alexander" in Russian, which is further twisted by reversing the actors' genders assigned to the roles. Director Guillermo del Toro also told the actors playing the Kaidanovskys' that he wanted them to choose their relationship, whether they were siblings or a married couple, and to keep their choice a secret from both himself and the rest of the cast. It was only after the film came out and the characters developed a fan following that the actors revealed through Twitter that they had chosen to act as a married couple. Thus, the audience can see how much of our gendered relationships in real life are in many ways both elusive and indeed performative. Unlocking performances within the source narrative and trying to locate who the "real" character is beyond a handful of lines and images, remains the goal of both close readings and fan readings.

The Mako Mori Test: Problems of Representation

Raleigh Becket and Mako Mori's relationship signifies a key point in the ways this film subverts typical action tropes. Earlier I mentioned that Raleigh features as the classic rugged individualist hero who is quickly rewritten. As Mako explains, his American action hero trait of disobeying orders is what makes him "dangerous" and "not the right man" for the job of saving the world. But by conforming to international command, taking orders as assigned, and working in a cooperative group, Raleigh Becket succeeds by film's end. In fact, his primary role for much of the film as an emotional nurturer is traditionally assigned to a woman's part. When Mako verbally knocks him down a peg during the compatibility trials, he does not react as if his masculinity has been threatened; instead, his expression reveals awe with something like the beginnings of delight. Clearly elated after their fight sequence, which ends in a draw, Raleigh declares that he wants Mako as his co-pilot and no one else. While the typical tropes would have Raleigh spending the bulk of the middle acts grappling with grief and emerging from his shell, instead he heals off-screen and becomes an active advocate for Mako's heroic journey. At this point, we come to understand that in many ways, Mako is the main hero of this film, and Raleigh is the narrator telling of *her* journey.

Indeed, Mako's story clearly adheres to the Campbellian monomyth[10]: Mako *refuses the call to adventure* when Raleigh declares her his partner, reaches *atonement* with the father when Stacker Pentecost answers his promise for her to become a jaeger pilot and avenge her family. She *crosses the threshold* when she enters the jaeger, and then *enters the belly of the whale* when she goes out of telepathic alignment and "down the rabbit hole" during her near-catastrophic first Drift. She *reaches apotheosis* when she is freed from the Drift by Raleigh, *undergoes three trials* when she is denied the pilot rank, relives the horror of the "rabbit hole" and her family's deaths, and is rebuked for failing the Drift. She *receives the ultimate boon* when she goes into battle the first time and achieves *magical flight* through the miraculous safe fall from space; in the final battle she provides the fighting tactics with the sword arm (representative of her family) and when it is lost and she is losing oxygen, she is *rescued from without* by Raleigh when he jettisons her safety pod. She is the *master of two worlds* for having safely shepherded Raleigh to both the Shatterdome and to the Breach, and in the end she has the *freedom to live* in the new world. While Raleigh's story echoes and encapsulates Mako's through the narrative, he does not undergo any trials (he is returned to pilot status immediately), he attains neither atonement nor an ultimate boon, and he largely acts as the support for Mako, as does Stacker Pentecost. Pentecost's final words to Mako are ones of reassurance as well as a command to succeed, "You can finish this," even as he clarifies their imminent self-sacrifice to his co-pilot, "We can clear a path for the lady." Of the two-person team, the leaders consider Mako in command.

The narrative further destabilizes the male characters by using the camera as a point-of-view stand-in for Mako. Whereas most action films cater to the male gaze and unabashedly objectify women's bodies, *Pacific Rim* features a pseudo-voyeuristic sequence in which *Mako* admires Raleigh's partially unclothed body. After she has escorted him to his quarters in the Shatterdome, Raleigh starts to change clothes with Mako right there and his door open. Mako hurriedly leaves and goes to her own quarters but continues to stare until he notices, at which point she closes her door but then continues to look through the peep-hole until Raleigh finally closes his own door. Popular culture generally tends to shame women for sexual desire, but the usage of the camera in this sequence makes Mako the audience's stand-in. Further, if we continue to consider the monomyth, Raleigh acts as a temptation to Mako, while Raleigh himself has no temptation—and is thus located outside of the position of hero and closer to that of as guide or shaman. This moment best illustrates the monomyth when Mako is lost in the Drift and relives the day her family died; relegated to being a passive viewer, Raleigh sees what she sees.

Finally, narratives in which women are heroes have at least one element where they must prove themselves to the male heroes and win their approval. Here, Raleigh gives approval when she accepts the hero within herself, first at the candidate trials and later in donning the pilot suit. In an interview with *The Vine*, Director Guillermo del Toro explains why he wanted to develop Mako as an unconventional heroine:

When you say, normally, 'There is a young, Japanese girl pilot,' you imagine a super-sexy, skimpy clad girl that has her t-shirt wet every five minutes, and is, you know, I wanted very much to have a character that [was] on equal terms with Raleigh; that they didn't have to have a love story, but instead have love and respect as colleagues. It was important for her to be strong, and be strong from a feminine core; I didn't want her to be the girl that turns into [either] a sex object or a guy, which is the normal thing in action movies. ("Guillermo")

Online conversations erupted regarding women in film and cultural expectations. As disturbing as it is to realize, Mako represents one of the very few Asian women in post-World War II American filmmaking who is *not* a prostitute, is *not* evil, and is *not* dead by the end.[11] The men around her also conform to her culture and not vice versa: both Raleigh and her adoptive father and mentor Stacker Pentecost address her in her native language. Japanese-American fans were vocal in expounding the cultural resonances of a bilingual heroine who is not shamed for using imperfect English or dropping back into Japanese and calling her mentor "sensei." Several moments in the film feature untranslated Asian languages, as when the Wei triplets discuss Raleigh in Chinese, or when Mako tells her mentor she loves him with Japanese inflections of great respect. To be non-American is not to be exoticized, but only to be non-American, no more and no less. Culture, like gender, denotes part of a character, but not the defining point of that character. In the narrative as given, it would have been easy to "other" Mako through her language, or to make her status as a jaeger pilot "special" in a way that Raleigh's is not. Instead, Mako's status as hero was only reinforced, and this, to some, created a disconnection to the film.

Reflections on Mako as the true protagonist of the film led to a clash when considering that, despite the film's feminist elements, it nonetheless does not pass the Bechdel Test. The Bechdel Test famously queries films by whether there are two women characters who talk with one another about something other than a man; a staggering number of films routinely fail this very simple test, including *Pacific Rim*. *The Daily Dot* picked up on the discussion and published an article on the topic, describing how Tumblr user chaila developed an analog to the Bechdel Test as the Mako Mori Test, in which a film passes "if the movie has: a) at least one female character; b) who gets her own narrative arc; c) that is not about supporting a man's story" (chaila). In turn, Aja Romano concluded that

> extremely sexist movies can pass Bechdel while still contributing to a harmful message about women. On the other hand, if only one woman at a time can be

allowed her own mature, nuanced narrative in a film, then the Mako Mori Test might ultimately enable the status quo rather than critique the widespread "man's world" pattern of filmmaking

This debate brought to the fore the problems of diversity that have been brewing in film and in science fiction fandom for the past decade. While the film world seemingly goes out of its way to dodge the issue, numerous eruptions online and in print reiterate the contentious divide within science fiction fandom. That the "Mako Mori Fan Club" seemingly illustrates both the strengths and weaknesses of this debate makes *Pacific Rim* an emphatic example of this moment's *Zeitgeist*. From Racefail 2009 to the 2015 Hugogate, emphatic conservative resistance to people of color, women, and queer voices has escalated in increasingly public and vicious ways, reflecting continuing cultural schisms. Representation matters in popular culture, and that our current preoccupations with problems of gender, race, and age are both enacted on screen through the film itself and in our response to it speaks to how very much it does matter.

Coda

Prior to *Pacific Rim*'s cinematic release, Legendary Pictures released a graphic novel prequel by Beacham entitled *Pacific Rim: Tales from Year Zero* (2013)—a mosaic narrative, linear only in terms of the unnamed journalist who hears some of the stories told through interviews she conducts for a puff piece entitled "Why We Fight." Half a lifetime of writing such propaganda pieces leaves the journalist cynical and exhausted. Only in hearing the stories of people from the Shatterdome, which includes not just the jaeger pilots but also the support staff, does she understand that everyone has a story to tell and a battle to fight. Notably, Mako appears in this comic in only a few panels in flashback scenes, while the full stories shown belong to Choi, Pentecost, the Becket brothers, and several new characters who do not appear in the film at all. While Mako is not omnipresent, her appearances emphasize her place in the narrative; she is *there* while others come and go. She cannot be erased.

Notes

1. Fandom, broadly considered, is a community. Most often (especially with genre media) it is a community of women exchanging fiction and art online, in a nebulous space both public and private. While some fan archives are locked to members only, much more is available more or less freely through social media platforms like Livejournal or Tumblr. All of the texts cited in this essay are (currently) available to the browsing public online.
2. Leading proponents of this form of reading include Camille Bacon-Smith and Henry Jenkins, who view fan culture and fan readings as their own form of participatory culture.
3. For further discussion, please see my essay "The Angry!Textual!Poacher! is Angry! Fan Works as Political Statements" in *Fan Culture Theory/Practice* (2012).
4. "Mecha" focuses on robots and machines controlled by people. Popular examples include anime such as *Gundam* (1979) as well as American interpretations, such as the Mobile Infantry battle suits in Robert Heinlein's *Starship Troopers* (1959).
5. Notably, the Marvel Cinematic Universe expressly examines American ambivalence about superheroes and the state in films including *Iron Man 2* (2010), *Captain America: The Winter Soldier* (2014), and *The Avengers* (2012) and *The Avengers: Age of Ultron* (2015) as well as the forthcoming *Captain America: Civil War* (2016); the use and misuse of "enhanced" individuals and technology recurs as a theme.
6. *Pacific Rim* demonstrates the millenial generation taking charge, unlike in *The Hunger Games* (2012) or *The Maze Runner* (2014) series, both of which take place in a nebulous future younger than the millenials by at least 200 years, if not more. That is to say, the young protagonists do not represent millenials alone but young people of every generation.
7. A detailed timeline can also be found online at the Pacific Rim Wiki, but key dates include August 10–15, 2013, "K-Day," or the date of the first kaiju attack; February 29, 2020, when Raleigh Becket leaves the Pan Pacific Defense Corps; and January 12, 2025, the "Triple Event" and the closing of the Breach ("Timeline").
8. See chapter 7, "From Development Hell to the Pacific Depths: *The Strain* and *Pacific Rim*."
9. While I do not have the space to discuss this topic further, keep in mind that the character of Hermann Gottlieb (Burn Gorman), a prim German scientist at odds with the outgoing American scientist Newt Gieszler (Charlie Day), was also celebrated in fandom for being portrayed with a physical handicap that did not lead to his death or to his turning evil. This movement might seem like a very small thing, but in the ablest discourse of science fiction and fantasy, this is not the case.
10. Joseph Campbell introduced the basic monomyth concept in *The Hero with a Thousand Faces* (1949), where a hero goes through seventeen stages on a journey of transformation.
11. While Puccini's classic opera *Madame Butterfly* (1904) personifies this stereotype, recent examples from popular American film include *Memoirs of a Geisha* (2005), based on the American novel of the same name about the life of a fictional courtesan; the American remake of *47 Ronin* (2013), which includes a literalized "dragon lady;" and *Wolverine* (2013), in which the titular superhero saves his love interest from a suicide attempt as well as her murderous husband, to whom she was "sold" as part of a business deal.

Works Cited

47 Ronin. Dir. Carl Rinsch. H2F Entertainment, 2013. Film.
Bacon-Smith, Camille. *Enterprising Women: Television Fandom and the Creation of Popular Myth*. Philadelphia: U of Pennsylvania P, 1992. Print.
———. *Science Fiction Culture*. Philadelphia: U of Pennsylvania P, 2000. Print.
Beacham, Travis. *Pacific Rim: Tales from Year Zero*. Legendary Comics, 2013.
———. "Consider the example of the Hansens." *travisbeacham.tumblr.com*. Tumblr, 7 Aug. 2013. Web. 28 Oct. 2015.
Butler, Samuel. *Erewhon, or, Over the Range*. Baltimore: Penguin, 1935. Print.
Campbell, Joseph. *The Hero with a Thousand Faces*. Princeton: Princeton UP, 1949. Print.
Captain America: The First Avenger. Dir. Joe Johnston. Marvel Studios, 2011. Film.
Captain America: The Winter Soldier. Dirs. Joe Russo and Anthony Russo. Marvel Studios, 2014. Film.
Captain America: Civil War. Dirs. Joe Russo and Anthony Russo. Marvel Studios, 2016. Film.
chaila. "I was thinking more about why . . ." *chaila.tumblr.com*. Tumblr, 15 Aug. 2013. Web. 20 March 2015.
Clembastow. "Guillermo del Toro on Pacific Rim and why 'making a movie is like sex.'" *The Vine*. 20 July 2013. Web. 20 March 2015.
Coker, Catherine. "The Angry!Textual!Poacher! is Angry! Fan Works as Political Statements." *Fan Culture Theory/Practice*. Eds. Katherine Larsen and Lynn Zubernis. Newcastle upon Tyne: Cambridge Scholars, 2012. 81–96. Print.
dontneedyourheroact. "Can you imagine how much the jaeger program meant . ." *dontneedyourheroact.tumblr.com*. Tumblr, 30 July 2013. Web. 20 March 2015.
Godzilla. Dir. Ishirō Honda. Toho, 1954. Film.
Golden, Arthur. *Memoirs of a Geisha*. New York: Knopf, 1997. Print.
Guardians of the Galaxy. Dr. James Gunn. Marvel Studios, 2014. Film.
"Guillermo del Toro on Pacific Rim and why "making a movie is like sex."" *The Vine*. 12 July 2013. Web. 28 Oct. 2015.
Gundam. Created by Yoshiyuki Tomino. Sunrise, 1979. Television.
hamburgerjack. "alexandraerin-hamburgerjack." *glempy.tumblr.com*. Tumblr, n.d. Web. 28 Oct. 2015.
Heinlein, Robert. *Starship Troopers*. New York: Putnam, 1959. Print.
The Hunger Games. Dir. Gary Ross. Lionsgate Studios, 2012. Film.
Iron Man. Dir. Jon Favreau. Marvel Studios, 2008. Film.
Iron Man 2. Dir. Jon Favreau. Marvel Studios, 2010. Film.
Iron Man 3. Dir. Shane Black. Marvel Studios, 2013. Film.
Irvine, Alex. *Pacific Rim, The Official Movie Novelization*. London: Titan, 2013. Print.
Jenkins, Henry. *Textual Poachers: Television Fans and Participatory Culture*. New York: Routledge, 1992. Print.
Lane, Anthony. "Grim Tidings." *The New Yorker* 22 July 2013: 80–81. Print.
Marvel's The Avengers. Dir. Joss Whedon. Marvel Studios, 2012. Film.
Marvel's The Avengers: Age of Ultron. Dir. Joss Whedon. Marvel Studios, 2015. Film.

The Mary Sue Staff. "The Mary Sue's 2013 Summer Movie Wrap-Up." *The Mary Sue*. 3 Sept. 2013. Web. 28 Oct. 2015.
The Maze Runner. Dir. Wes Ball. Twentieth Century Fox, 2014. Film.
McDonald, Keith and Roger Clark. *Guillermo del Toro: Film as Alchemic Art*. New York: Bloomsbury Academic, 2014. Print.
Memoirs of a Geisha. Dir. Rob Marshall. Columbia Pictures, 2005. Film.
Mendelson, Scott. "'Pacific Rim' And More Domestic "Flops" That Became Global Hits." *Forbes.com*. 2 Sept. 2013. Date accessed: 28 Oct. 2015.
Milicia, Joseph. "South Pacific." *The Greenwood Encyclopedia of Science Fiction and Fantasy: Themes, Works, and Wonders*. Ed. Gary Westfahl. Westport: Greenwood, 2005. 733–35. Print.
Neon Genesis Evangelion. Dir. Hideaki Anno. TXN (TV Tokyo). 1995-96. 26 episodes. Television.
Pacific Rim. Dir. Guillermo del Toro. Legendary Pictures, 2013. Film.
Puccini, Giacomo. *Madama Butterfly*. 1903. Opera.
Romano, Aja. "The Mako Mori Test: 'Pacific Rim' inspires a Bechdel alternative." *The Daily Dot.*, 18 Aug. 2013. Web. 28 Oct. 2015.
Screen Junkies. "Honest Trailers—*Pacific Rim*." YouTube. 22 Oct. 2013. Web. 28 Oct. 2015.
Star Trek Into Darkness. Dir. J. J. Abrams. Paramount Pictures, 2013. Film.
starseedjenny. "A couple days ago I saw someone raise the question . . ." *starseedjenny.tumblr.com*. Tumblr, 26 July 2013. Web. 20 March 2015.
Thor. Dir. Kenneth Branagh. Marvel Studios, 2011. Film.
Thor 2: The Dark World. Dir. Alan Taylor. Marvel Studios, 2013. Film.
"Timeline." *pacificrim.wikia.com*. n.d. Web. 28 Oct. 2015.
Wells, H.G. *The Island of Doctor Moreau*. London: William Heinemann, 1896. Print.
The Wolverine. Dir. James Mangold. Twentieth Century Fox, 2013. Film.
Wright, Austin Tappan. *Islandia*. New York: Farrar & Rinehart, 1942. Print.

INDIA, GEOPOLITICS, AND FUTURE WARS

■ ■ ■

SUPARNO BANERJEE

Genre, Origins, and Patterns

The beginning of the twenty-first century has seen a rise in futuristic narratives focusing on India by Western as well as Indian authors, such as Humphrey Hawksley's *Dragon Fire* (2000), Ruchir Joshi's *The Last Jet-Engine Laugh* (2001), Ian McDonald's *River of Gods* (2004), Anil Menon's *The Beast with Nine Billion Feet* (2009), Manjula Padmanabhan's *Escape* (2008), and numerous short stories by Vandana Singh. The extrapolative nature of these works allows them a speculative freedom in imagining India's role in the future geopolitics and social mores of South Asia. Many of these stories, however, foreground the precarious power-balance of the region, and express the anxieties of an armed conflict among its volatile neighbors—India, Pakistan, and China. These narratives depict either war among nations, or armed conflicts within India; if they do not present war directly, these futuristic tales show dystopian scenarios resulting from or treading towards such wars. Examples of the first kind can be seen in *Chimera* (2013) by Vivek Ahuja, Hawksley's *Dragon Fire*, and Joshi's *The Last Jet-Engine Laugh*, while the examples of the second kind are Kylas Chunder Dutt's "A Journal of Forty-Eight Hours of the Year 1945" (1835), Shoshee Chunder Dutt's "The Republic of Orissa: A Page from the Annals of the Twentieth Century" (1845), and McDonald's *River of Gods*. Texts such as Priya Sarukkai Chabria's *Generation 14* (2008), Rimi B. Chatterjee's *Signal Red* (2004), and Padmanabhan's *Escape* are some prominent examples of the third type. For the purpose of this essay, however, I will focus only on the first two types—the narratives that directly imagine conflicts set at a future date—and explore the development of this subgenre in the context of India's shifting geopolitical significance. I claim that while the future-war narrative in India initially started as an anti-colonial initiative, the emergence of India as a military and economic power stimulates the present day stories of future conflicts.

Scholars often identify such consolidation of military and economic powers as causes prompting the emergence of future-war narratives in various parts of the world. For instance, in *Voices Prophesying War: 1763–1984* (1966), I. F. Clarke argues that the massive industrial growth fueling and demanding colonial expansions resulted in speculations about future geopolitical roles and conflicts among the European nations. In *Colonialism and the Rise of Science Fiction* (2008), John Rieder makes a similar assertion for the emergence of science fiction (SF), of which future-war stories can be considered a subgenre. Although Clarke identifies C. Oman's *The Reign of George VI, 1900–1925* (1763) as the earliest identifiably future-war novel in Europe, he argues that only with the publication of Sir George Tomkyns Chesney's *Battle of Dorking* in 1871, this subgenre came into its own: "Before the *Battle of Dorking* no author of an imaginary war of the future ever suggested that the deliberate use of new weapons could have a decisive effect on the outcome of a battle" (2). In his introduction to *Future Wars* (2012), David Seed supports Clarke's assertion about the flourishing of this new subgenre since the late nineteenth century. Seed, however, emphasizes the importance of *The Reign of George VI* in setting the tone of speculation regarding a nation's response to future threats from imperial competitors and its primarily political extrapolative nature. Two emerging trends can be identified from Clarke's and Seed's assertions: one highlights the technoscientific nature of futuristic narratives, making such texts apparently close to hard SF; the other primarily aligns itself with political speculations (with scant regard to technoscience), and thus is close to social SF. In both cases, though, futurity itself is the most potent estranging device complimenting the logically developed outcome of current sociopolitical and technoscientific trends engendering the "novum" of war and destruction. This formal characteristic, according to Darko Suvin, is also the core tendency of SF.[1]

However, the case of India, both as an originator and a setting of future-war narratives, differs considerably from the European scenario discussed above. The earliest future-war narratives, K. C. Dutt's "A Journal of Forty-Eight Hours of the Year 1945" ("Journal" henceforth) and S. C. Dutt's "The Republic of Orissa: A Page from the Annals of the Twentieth Century"

("Orissa" henceforth), were published towards the middle of the nineteenth century and were not driven by any industrial revolution or imperial ambition. Rather, both these texts emerged out of completely opposite impulses: preventing the British colonizers from exploiting local human resources and reclaiming political agency from the oppressors. In other words, both these texts were written out of anti-industrial and anti-imperialistic volitions. Thus, both "Journal" and "Orissa" depict future battles against the British in an effort to free the country from European invaders. While the future date of "Journal" (set in 1945) is prophetically close to the actual date of Indian independence in 1947, the warfare and technology depicted is no different from the author's current day. In a way it can be considered a prophesy for the first war of Indian independence (also known as the Sepoy Mutiny) in 1857, which was started by Indian soldiers in the British army but, like in the story, was guided by Indian feudal elites and finally failed in the face of a superior British army.[2] According to Arvind Krishna Mehrotra, "Orissa," too, describes a future (1916) battle of independence in the state of Orissa where the doubly oppressed tribes, not the urban educated middle class, start the revolution (94). The story unfolds against the backdrop of a fictitious Slavery Act passed by the British in 1916 and ends with the slow decline of British Empire in India (94).

Neither of these stories, though, addresses any future military or technological developments. The future dates are used mostly as a safeguard against British persecution of the dissenting authors and also as a sort of millennial vision. Given the lack of industrial development in India in the nineteenth century, this inattention to technological matters is very normal.[3] Nevertheless, both texts strongly speculate about political reactions of the Indian population to the oppressive British rule. As mentioned above, the revolution of 1857 happened just over twenty years from the publication of "Journal," while the Santhal Rebellion of 1855, which saw the uprising of the twice-oppressed Santhal tribe in the eastern part of India (not far from Orissa), was only ten years down the line from the publication of "Orissa."[4] Thus, the speculations in these works had more immediate resonances than the authors realized, or they deliberately masked such realization by assigning far future dates. As such, it is justifiable to identify these works with soft or social SF, where the temporal estrangement helps create a radically new social order.

The present-day novels, however, bear closer resemblances to their Western counterparts. The speculations in these texts are about relatively near futures. McDonald's India is the farthest removed at forty-three years in the future (2047), while Joshi (published 2001) goes as far forward as 2030. Most other texts, such as Hawksley's future history series or Ahuja's *Chimera*, either do not mention a specific date or are set very close to their time of writing. These recent works that appear more than one and one-half centuries after K. C. Dutt's and S. C. Dutt's stories, speculate about larger scale military conflicts involving India at a time when the nation has been established as one of the strongest economic, political, technological, and military powers of the world.[5] However, the India that we find in these works is mostly assertive, rather than aggressive and having imperial ambitions. The war that these works speculate about almost always begins as a result of external aggression. Such extrapolative writing is significant because of the political and military volatility of the region over the last sixty years—the hotly contested borders between Pakistan, India, and China, the regular terrorist attacks on civilians, and the internal security threats posed by separatist and political violence. Such simmering elements keep the ground fertile for large scale armed conflicts in this part of the continent and also highlight the crumbling of the utopian impulses of postcolonial Asia. In addition to these skirmishes, the nuclear arming of China, India, and Pakistan over the last sixty years, and increasing international assertion of Chinese and Indian economic, political, and military aspirations, have drawn attention of both Indian and Western authors in speculating about this region's future and its implications for the global arena.

In "Through a Mirror Darkly," Richard J. Norton classifies future-war narratives into three groups according to their agendas of speculation: "Cassandrans," "Prometheans," and "Seers" (125). According to this scheme, the Cassandrans "call attention to dangers and conditions that if not addressed will harm or even destroy the state," while the Prometheans hold a positive triumphant attitude (125). The Seers are mostly neutral, extrapolating from current technological and political observations without any professed agenda. Norton hints that all three types of authors have one thing in common: the primacy of the predictive impulse over the thought experimentation or satirical qualities of SF in general. While Norton's scheme serves as a useful tool for understanding the socio-cultural grounds of the future-war genre, such schemes should be employed cautiously, not only because the categories often bleed into each other, but also because narratives of future war are not necessarily predictive; they can very well be exhortative, dystopian, or satirical.[6] This is true for Norton's primary field of study—Western texts—but even more so for the texts under consideration in this essay.

While "Journal" can be considered a Cassandran work, its aim is actually more exhortative; similarly, "Orissa" can be seen both as Promethean and exhortative. The purpose of both these texts was to rally people against the British, rather than speculating about war scenarios a hundred years later.

Similarly, *Laugh* is a Cassandran work predicting a bleak, violence-ridden India, but is also definitely a dystopian work satirizing Indian jingoism and worldwide corruption of power. McDonald's India is even harder to classify. It is at once dystopian or satirical and optimistic—battles pervade the broken nation, yet people find ways to prosper through new technologies. Hawksley's and Ahuja's texts are simpler in nature. Both authors fully concentrate on the development of war scenarios and the international politics behind them. While Hawksley's *Third World War* (2003) is definitely Cassandran, spelling doom for human civilization, *Dragon Fire* is more of a Seer text, speculating about the future of a nuclear-armed Asia without any strong cautionary or triumphalist agenda. *Chimera*, on the other hand, seems like a Promethean text in the sense that Indian military reaches a stalemate with its war against China, due primarily to India's technological and strategic innovativeness.

The quality that all these disparate texts share, regardless of agenda, is an anxiety of an uncertain future—a failure of the apparent utopian ideals of a postcolonial and postwar Asia proclaimed at Bandung (Indonesia) in 1955, where the newly independent nations of Asia and Africa met to promote a common goal of modernization and development unencumbered by foreign interference (Ampiah; Herrera). Rather, these future-war narratives present a post-Cold War and often a terrorism-age scenario where not only have the nations discarded their apparent nonaligned position of the mid-twentieth century, and outgrown Cold War allegiances, they have exposed the age-old rifts that the anti-Western sentiments of the Bandung Conference masked. Ampiah rightly claims that the events leading up to Bandung already pointed to existing problems. With reference to the Colombo Conference of 1954, Ampiah asserts that "the meeting in Colombo exposed the rifts within the group: India and Pakistan disagreed over Kashmir and US economic assistance; India and Indonesia were ideologically divorced from Ceylon and Pakistan, and Burma hovered between the two entities" (8). Bandung also saw the end of Sino-Indian friendship (due to perceived geopolitical prestige issues) and the forging of a China-Pakistan alliance (Sharma 18–19). However, the anti-Western sentiment that elicited responses of suspicion and discomfort from Britain and the U.S. and often backing from the Soviet Union lays the foundation for the later political developments of the region and underlies the speculations in many of these future-war narratives.

Specifically for our India-centered study, these speculations show an interesting shift in the nation's geopolitical position over the last sixty years. From a professed nonaligned position in the 1950s and early '60s, India, with its socialist economic policies, slowly drifted towards the Soviet camp, although still eschewing Communism and maintaining an essentially neutralist position. In addition to three major wars (in 1947, 1965, and 1971) with Pakistan, several other factors contributed to this shift: the U.S. backing of Pakistan since 1954, the formation of the Pakistan-China alliance in the 1960s, the war with China (1962), and finally the American support for Pakistani genocide in Bangladesh (then East Pakistan) in 1971 firmly placed India in the Soviet camp between 1971 and 1990 (Chari; Wishon). Although liberalization of the economy in the 1990s attracted Western support, its nuclear program (the last testing was in 1998) and refusal to sign the Nuclear Non-Proliferation Treaty (NPT) at American insistence, India still maintained a somewhat antagonistic relationship with the West (and the U.S. in particular) into the early 2000s. However, since the 2001 terrorist attacks on American soil and the beginning of the War on Terror, India and the West, specifically the U.S., have drawn closer, pulled by similar economic and political concerns. Yet, Russia still remains India's biggest geopolitical partner and arms supplier, even after the recent diversification of India's defense spending (Kamalakaran).[7]

This shifting geopolitical posture of India is evident in all the texts speculating about future wars; all these works also highlight the disillusionment of a postcolonial nation discarding its utopian ideals of noninterference and nonalignment and getting involved in regional power struggles, slowly but invariably leading towards extensive armed conflicts. For the rest of the essay, I will examine *Dragon Fire* and *Laugh* in detail to illustrate the different patterns that such contemporary future-war narratives create.

India and the Bomb: *Dragon Fire*

British writer Humphrey Hawksley's *Dragon Fire* (2000) displays anxiety of the Western world over their diminishing clout in Asia. Written by a long time BBC Asia correspondent, this novel projects a near future conflict among China, India, and Pakistan in 2007. The approach of the book is journalistic and fact-based, an extrapolation of the political relationships among the nations from the author's extensive political knowledge of the region. The conflict in the book begins from long standing disputes between India and Pakistan regarding Kashmir, and India and China regarding Tibet and Arunachal Pradesh. Pakistan and India have already gone to war three times over Kashmir (in 1947, 1965, and 1999) and once over Bangladesh (in 1971). Pakistan-sponsored cross-border terrorism has been the thorn in both countries' attempts at peace. On the eastern front, in addition to the war of 1962, Tibet remains a perennial issue of disagreement between India and China, the former granting refuge to the Tibetan spiritual leader, the Dalai Lama, and the latter considering him a separatist. Furthermore, the northeastern Indian state of Arunachal Pradesh is also claimed by China as part of its territory, and the northeastern part of Kashmir (known as Aksai Chin) has been occupied by China since 1962, though it is claimed by India.

Dragon Fire depicts a scenario where China and Pakistan attack India to cement territorial control over the eastern and western fronts. The three pronged war begins with disputes over a cross-border strike by Tibetan commandos using Indian arms, while Pakistan sponsored terrorists strike in Kashmir. After initial encounters, Pakistan uses a nuclear device, and (nonnuclear) Indian retaliation completely destroys Pakistani military capabilities. On the other front, after early gains, China starts losing ground, and the international community, led by Britain and America, starts providing logistical support to India. Russia warns the Western nations of preemptive strikes, in case of any Western attack on China, which restrains their participation in the conflict. At this point China goes nuclear and destroys major Indian cities. India responds in kind, but China's larger military capabilities ultimately prove superior. In the aftermath of the war, China gains more international influence.

Dragon Fire presents extensive discussion of world and Asian politics, military technology, and strategies. In fact, to attest to the authenticity of the information, and by inference the logicality of the extrapolations, Hawksley even provides a "Select Bibliography and Papers" at the end of the book (363). This listing shows the solid research conducted by the author regarding the history, geography, and politics of South and East Asia. In addition, this journalistic stance suggests a neutral predictive approach rather than an outright political agenda. Nothing in the novel radically differs from the author's temporal reality—neither is the military technology drastically advanced, nor is the political situation any different (Pakistan and China are under dictatorial rules, while India functions as a democracy). The only major estrangement here (other than the seven-year projection) is the possibility of a nuclear holocaust. However, presentation of this nuclear destruction is a real "novum" in the South Asian context, a region primarily concerned with conventional warfare and bearing no direct legacy of the Cold War anxieties. This "novum" combined with Hawksley's careful political projections puts *Dragon Fire* primarily in the soft SF camp, rather than with hard SF or mimetic fiction, in spite of its realistic style and prominent display of military hardware.

Such close proximity to reality also indicates the shifting Western perspectives on India. In *Dragon Fire* as well as in *The Third World War* Hawksley presents India as the beacon of democracy in the developing world, an example to be followed by other underdeveloped nations. He focuses on India's strong presence in twenty-first century global politics and economy, indicating the country's development from a postcolonial nation negotiating internal problems to a nation able to assert itself at the international level. The novel further indicates India's strengthening political ties with the West. Hawksley also gives an evolving perception of India's nuclear program. India's 1998 nuclear tests were deemed disruptive of regional stability by the West, leading to the imposition of economic embargoes. However, since then, the international community has recognized India as a responsible nuclear nation, culminating in the Indo-U.S. and Indo-French nuclear treaties in 2008. These recent events clearly reflect the change of old geopolitical power relations.

Hawksley prophetically predicts such movements in international politics several years in advance. In fact, the predictive quality of the book can be further attested if we consider the terrorist strike on Mumbai in November 2008, which almost sent India and Pakistan to war (only one year off the mark). Indian Defense Minister George Fernandes probably pays the biggest tribute to Hawksley's vision. Gaurav Sawant quotes Fernandes in *The Indian Express*: "What lessons others draw from the scenario etched by Hawksley is their business. But the Indian people would do well to take the blinkers off their eyes and have a full-eyed look at both friends and foes. I commend this book to every Indian" (Sawant). Recent diplomatic tension with China over border disputes, the Chinese military's border incursions, China's Kashmir policy and Dalai Lama's visit to Arunachal Pradesh, further underscore the basis of Hawksley's prediction.[8]

Despite his close predictive ability, Hawksley misses the developments in Islamic terrorism in the West. Consequently, he could not imagine something like the 2001 attack on the World Trade Center, and in its aftermath, the U.S. and British military deployment in Afghanistan and the Middle East. Such presences change the whole equation of military activity in the region. Nevertheless, he rightly predicts the even closer alliance between India and the West in war against terrorism, and the designation of Pakistan as a failed state harboring terrorists and bleeding internally to balance itself between its Western benefactors and its Islamic radicals. However, Hawksley quickly incorporates these developments in his next novel, *The Third World War* (2003), to show a clear divide between "rogue states" (Pakistan and North Korea) and the "civilized world" (the U.S. and its allies with India playing a prominent role).

Conversely, Hawksley's well-researched book has its own problems when it comes to the depiction of the actual nations. His fact-based writing ends up only presenting broad political scenarios with no understanding of the social dynamics within the countries. Almost all characters in the book correspond to stereotypes—the emotionless hawkish Chinese, overreaching fanatical

Pakistanis, and confused but ethical Indians. Such depictions are highly simplistic at the least and out and out Orientalist at the worst. Suffering from crippling corruption and simmering communal and political tension, India is far from being a model democracy or society. The same can be said about the negative portrayal of China and Pakistan in their stereotypical roles. The Chinese Foreign Minister (from Hong Kong), Jamie Song, comes the closest to being a developed character with individual characteristics. The rest are all cardboard figures pushing the action of the novel. In addition, Hawksley's political stance is all too predictable. He presents the U.S. and Britain as future allies of India, while Russia restricts their involvement as a Cold War retribution. The undermining of Russia's role and omission of any mention of France, India's second largest military supplier and long-term strategic ally, indicates the assumed Anglo-American hegemony in Asian affairs. This projected rapprochement between India and the West presents a reality drastically different from the past: the U.S. navy sent warships into the Bay of Bengal to intimidate India during the 1971 India-Pakistan war, which was foiled by the Soviet navy's countering of the U.S. fleet.[9]

An important implication of such a representation of the Indo-American and Indo-British relationships is that although *Dragon Fire* acknowledges India as a technologically advanced modern nation, it is also a product of Western ideologies. India, the largest (stable) democracy in the world, reflects Western ideals, whereas China and Pakistan, both historically mostly militaristic or totalitarian governments, do not. One is connected to Communism, and the other to Islamic extremism; neither of these ideologies suit the West. This view can be summed up in *Dragon Fire* with the American President's comment on the dead Indian Prime Minister regarding Indian nuclear strikes in China: "Hari Dixit refused to go for the civilian targets, didn't he?" (357). This comment clearly endorses the democratic and humane values of India. However, this view is also the accepted perception of democracy in the West, and India as a democracy must fit in with it.

A Dystopian World-System: *The Last Jet-Engine Laugh*

In contrast to this, *Laugh*, written by Indian author, filmmaker, and columnist Ruchir Joshi, presents a much more complicated social, historical, and political scenario that frames the future war. Tracking the life of Paresh Bhatt, an aging photographer, this book presents dystopian, overcrowded, toxic, corporation-dominated (most of the corporations are Japanese), and lawless urban landscapes ruled by violent gangs rather than any functioning government. Located primarily in India, the disjunctive postmodern narrative of *Laugh* continuously jumps forward and backward in time: the early twentieth century colonial era, Indira Gandhi's emergency rule of the 1970s, and the dystopian year 2030. *Laugh* places the tendency of violence within Indian history and tradition, rather than ascribing it solely to Western colonialism or menacing external forces, and presents a very different perspective on geopolitical alliances from *Dragon Fire*. The U.S., rather than being an ally of India, is seen in its more familiar role, fueling Pakistani and Saudi ambitions out of its own agendas. But like *Dragon Fire*, *Laugh* also highlights the volatile military situation of the area and underlines the regional wars as both a cause and an effect of the dystopian scenario. Hence, like Hawksley's book, *Laugh* also displays a substantial predictive and resonating purpose. In addition, the technological innovations that determine the course and nature of the narrative also introduce more hard SF elements, despite *Laugh*'s primary focus on sociopolitical criticism.[10]

Joshi's novel mentions an enforced nuclear disarmament of both India and Pakistan as a result of reciprocal nuclear strikes. Although without any real-world referent, mention of a terrorist nuclear attack on Bombay (Mumbai) is an oblique allusion to the 1993 Bombay Stock Exchange bombing, the origins of which can be traced back to Pakistan. The future war in 2030 also has its resonances in the past; the novel itself recounts India-Pakistan wars of 1947, 1965, and 1971. Published in 2001, the novel comes at the heels of a fourth conflict in 1999. *Laugh* also highlights India's uneasy relationship with China in predicting a three-way conflict between India, China, and Pakistan in 2007 (precisely the same year as the war in Hawksley's book, and a year before a real-world Pakistani-backed massive terror attack in Mumbai in 2008). The book connects these past wars with the future ones through Paresh's memories, creating a much larger pattern of India's changing geopolitical role in Asia.

The political speculations in *Laugh* also seem to be a lot more skeptical than in *Dragon Fire*. Unlike Hawksley's grandstanding for American and British policies, Joshi puts the West on a murky moral ground through its self-serving power politics and subservience to global capitalism. In the story, the Saudi-Pakistani alliance is technologically supported by the U.S., which also destroys an Indian space station during the war; and although not spelled out in the book, grouping Saudi Arabia with Pakistan while mentioning their attempt to capture newly explored oil fields in Gujarat surely refers to well-known American oil interests in the Middle East. Furthermore, the mention of constant terrorist threats in Europe and systematic racial profiling resulting from Western meddling in the Middle East and North Africa undercuts any moral high ground claimed by the West. The same is true of the role played by Japanese corporations, the other capitalist power in the book.

On a related note, *Laugh* highlights the use of technology that trails and aids the expansion of global capitalism. Although Hawksley mentions military technology and strategy at length, he does not meditate upon their origin or sociohistorical implications. Joshi, however, demonstrates the power of technology not only in war but also in every-day life. And as a true instrument of global capitalism, this technology is borderless. It belongs as much to the neo-colonial West and the Japanese companies as it does to the Indian state. *Laugh* still refuses to condemn these ever-intruding technological presences. Rather, they are shown as an integral and inevitable result of modern industrial civilization, which slowly but surely leads towards battle for resources and territorial supremacy on an unprecedented scale.

At a different level, *Laugh* indicts India's internal disharmonies for the future conflicts. Joshi leaves unmistakable hints of volatile communal tensions with repeated yet oblique references to riots, Islamic terrorism, and Hindu fundamentalism. In doing so, Joshi links the tradition of violence and nationalism to uncorroborated anecdotes about Indian nationalist leader Subhas Chandra Bose, who led an armed rebellion against the British in 1944 and disappeared mysteriously at the end of World War II.[11] Bose's ideology, which in many respects was dictatorial and informed by militant Hindu nationalism, provides a mythical subtext that continuously informs all other violence depicted in this book. Joshi further buttresses the association of violence and nationalism through references to Durga (the demon-slaying warrior goddess), whom the militant nationalists, including Bose, worshiped. Not surprisingly, in *Laugh* Durga images are painted on the fighter-jets of the all-female squadron raiding Pakistan, the "modern day demon." Even the use of women for the purpose of war contributes to this association. Their bodies are almost fused to the bodies of the multi-armed machines, creating cyborg entities. All these connections ultimately assert the tradition of violence and domination that underlies Indian nationalism and Indian society in general. Thus, in *Laugh*, future-wars are not presented as sudden catastrophes instigated by outside forces, but as continuations of historical strife in the region over centuries, in which international politics is as much culpable as sociocultural disharmonies inside the nations.

Conclusion

These two different treatments found in *Dragon Fire* and *Laugh* are symptomatic of recent speculations regarding Asian geopolitics in SF. Although Hawksley's Western narrative is expectedly stereotypical and simplistic in its treatment of sociocultural complexities of the region or foregrounding of Western roles, it is still a Seer text in the sense that it does not try promoting any specific Western agenda. A similarly naïve treatment can be witnessed in *Chimera* by Ahuja, an expatriate Indian, who, in providing India a moral victory in its war against China, provides only scenarios of military encounter and a catalogue of advanced weaponry without any realistic consideration of the recent political developments either inside or outside the country. Yet, texts such as *Laugh* (Indian) or *River of Gods* (which is British and only concerned with conflicts within India) scrutinize the battles from multiple angles to the extent that they sometimes pay less attention to the actual war and military strategies. Regardless of their approach, all these works identify India as a major geopolitical force in South Asia.

Although none of these texts directly show India as an aggressor with an imperial aspiration, all of them underscore the nation's desire and ability to sustain the role of a regional power that can thus place itself against other nations with similar ambitions. Apparently, this is a different type of development than the one seen in "Journal" and "Orissa." Yet, a closer consideration would suggest that the instances of self-assertion in contemporary fiction are not too dissimilar from the rebelliousness of the nineteenth-century texts. Although anti-industrial and anti-imperial in theme, "Journal" and "Orissa" are actually about assertion and protection of political rights of the Indian people against a foreign invader. Similarly, although driven by technological development and large-scale military goals, most of the later texts are about assertion and protection of the nation against foreign aggressors.

In a way, this state of affairs suggests that Asia, and specifically the Indian Subcontinent, will remain a fertile ground for violence until the ideological and geopolitical circus playing for centuries somehow grinds to a halt. The awareness that no simple solution can cure the ills of a postcolonial Asia is probably the most important need for the future. If these books are any indication, the utopian discourses of democracy, self-rule, and liberation wear thin in the future of the region; instead, the under-sides of such utopian ideals are more likely to hold sway, engendered from and leading towards war in its many incarnations.

Notes

1. In *Metamorphoses of Science Fiction*, Suvin defines SF as an "interaction of estrangement and cognition" with an "imaginative framework alternative to the author's empirical environment" engendering a "novum," or something new and radically different from the author's reality (7).

2. See Vincent Smith's and Thomas George Percival Spear's *The Oxford History of India* (1967) for more information on the Mutiny.

3. Smith mentions that although modern transportation such as steamship and railways were introduced since the 1830s and '40s, any actual industry was absent from India. Indian industries were rather actively under-developed to promote monopoly of the East India Company's machine-made goods from England (641–44).

4. See Kathleen Gough's "Indian Peasant Uprisings" (1974) for a discussion on the various peasant rebellions including the Santhal insurrection of 1855–56.

5. According to *Global Fire Power*, India currently ranks fourth in military capabilities ("Countries"). *CNN Money* ranks India as the seventh largest economy in the world in 2015 (Bergmann).

6. Probably the best example of such satirical work is Stanley Kubrick's *Dr. Strangelove Or: How I Learned to Stop Worrying and Love the Bomb* (1964).

7. For a detailed discussion of India's military history in the context of South Asia's shifting geopolitical relationships, see Daniel Marston and Chandar S. Sundaram's *A Military History of India and South Asia: From the East India Company to the Nuclear Era* (2007).

8. Matters have not been helped by China's veiled media policy. Recently a supposedly "non-state approved" website has published a blueprint of India's dismemberment into smaller countries to further Chinese geopolitical advantage. Although the Chinese government has vehemently distanced itself from the anonymous post, it has raised quite a furor in India. However, Ananth Krishnan writes in the opinion column of *The Hindu* that this uproar might be a result of India's monolithic perception of China.

9. See Michael Walter's "The U.S. Naval Demonstration in the Bay of Bengal during the 1971 India-Pakistan War."

10. For a fuller treatment of these themes see my chapter "Dystopia and the Postcolonial Nation" in Raja, Willis, and Nandi's *The Postnational Fantasy* (2011).

11. See Marston and Sundaram.

Works Cited

Ahuja, Vivek. *Chimera*. CreateSpace Independent Publishing Platform, 2013. E-book.
Ampiah, Kweku. *The Political and Moral Imperatives of the Bandung Conference of 1955: The Reactions of the US, UK and Japan*. Folkestone: Global Oriental, 2007. E-book.
Banerjee, Suparno. "Dystopia and the Postcolonial Nation." *The Postnational Fantasy*. Eds. Masood Raja, Jason Willis, and Swaralipi Nandi. Jefferson: McFarland, 2011. 125–37. Print.
Bergmann, Andrew. "World's Largest Economies." CNN Money, 2015. Web. 8 June 2015.
Chari, P. R. "Indo-Soviet Military Cooperation: A Review." *Asian Survey* 19.3 (1979): 230–244. Print.
Clarke, I. F. *Voices Prophesying War, 1763–1984*. New York: Oxford UP, 1966. Print.
"Countries Ranked by Military Strength." *Global Fire Power*. 1 April 2015. Web. 8 June 2015.
Dr. Strangelove Or: How I Learned to Stop Worrying and Love the Bomb. Dir. Stanley Kubrick. Criterion Collection, 1992. DVD.

Dutt, Kylas Chunder. "A Journal of Forty-Eight Hours of the Year 1945." 1835. *Wasafiri* 21.3 (2006): 15–20. Print.

Dutt, Shoshee Chunder. "The Republic of Orissa: A Page from the Annals of the Twentieth Century." 1845. *Bengaliana: A Dish of Rice and Curry, and Other Indigestible Ingredients*. Calcutta: Thacker, Spink, 1880. Web.

Gough, Kathleen. "Indian Peasant Uprisings." *Economic and Political Weekly* 9.32/34 (1974): 1391–412. Print.

Hawksley, Humphrey. *Dragon Fire*. London: Macmillan, 2000. Print.

———. *The Third World War: A Future History*. London: Macmillan, 2003. Print.

Herrera, Rémy. "Fifty Years after the Bandung Conference: Towards a Revival of the Solidarity between the Peoples of the South? Interview with Samir Amin." *Inter-Asia Cultural Studies* 6.4 (2005): 546–56. Print.

Joshi, Ruchir. *The Last Jet-Engine Laugh*. New Delhi: HarperCollins, 2001. Print.

Kamalakaran, Ajay. "41 Years after the Indo-Soviet Friendship Treaty." *Russia & India Report*, 9 Aug. 2012. Web. 1 June 2015.

Krishnan, Ananth. "Does Beijing Really Want to "Break up" India?" *The Hindu* 16 Aug. 2009. Print.

Marston, Daniel and Chandar S. Sundaram. *A Military History of India and South Asia: From the East India Company to the Nuclear Era*. Westport Praeger, 2007. Print.

McDonald, Ian. *River of Gods*. New York: PYR, 2007. Print.

Mehrotra, Arvind Krishna. *A History of Indian Literature in English*. New York: Columbia UP, 2003. Print.

Norton, Richard J. "Through a Mirror Darkly: The Face of Future War, 1871–2005." *Naval War College Review* 62.1 (2009): 123–40. Print.

Rieder, John. *Colonialism and the Emergence of Science Fiction*. Middletown: Wesleyan UP, 2008. Print.

Sawant, Gaurav C. "George Gives Rave Review to Novel Painting China as Villain No 1." *Indian Express*. 24 Aug. 2000. Print.

Seed, David. *Future Wars: The Anticipations and the Fears*. Liverpool: Liverpool UP, 2012. E-book.

Sharma, Shri Ram. *India-China 1947–1971: Friendship Goes with Power Part-1*. New Delhi: Discovery, 1999. Print.

Smith, Vincent Arthur, and Thomas George Percival Spear. *The Oxford History of India*, 3rd ed. Oxford: Clarendon, 1967. Print.

Suvin, Darko. *Metamorphoses of Science Fiction: On the Poetics and History of a Literary Genre*. New Haven: Yale University Press, 1979. Print.

Walter, Michael. "The U.S. Naval Demonstration in the Bay of Bengal During the 1971 India-Pakistan War." *World Affairs* 141.4 (1979): 293–306. Print.

Wishon, Jeremiah. "Soviet Globalization: Indo-Soviet Public Diplomacy and Cold War Cultural Spheres." *Global Studies Journal* 5.2 (2013): 103–14. Print.

ENTANGLEMENT AND DIS-ENTANGLEMENT IN VANDANA SINGH'S SHORT FICTION

■ ■ ■

GRAHAM J. MURPHY

"A paradigm shift in our attitude toward other species is a prerequisite for change."
—**Vandana Singh**, "The Creatures We Don't See"

The global climate crisis has emerged as a dominant issue in today's sociopolitical debates as humanity's direct impact upon the globe and the concomitant changes that are being recorded all over the planet—including rising global temperatures; increased sea levels; warming oceans; shrinking ice sheets, declining arctic sea ice, and glacial retreat; ocean acidification; and long-term drought—threaten the long-term sustainability of life on Earth. At the same time the natural environment is undergoing such tectonic stresses, nonhuman animal life is experiencing similar pressures as an alarming number of life forms could be extinct by the end of the twenty-first century, if not sooner. Climate scientists, environmental activists, and (some) political leaders have the same message: the unmistakable evidence of the climate crisis and dwindling species diversity necessitates a realignment of priorities. The "old paradigm of the world as a machine," as Kim Stanley Robinson puts it, must be replaced by "a more accurate and sophisticated paradigm of the world as a vast organism, complexly interpenetrative in ways not previous imagined" (10). For Robinson, the environment is "our extended body, and we can no more live without it than we could live without our kidneys or our bones" (10). This understanding of the environment as an organism is similar to what famed American biologist and naturalist Edward O. Wilson has been calling *biophilia*, which is the recognition of emotional affiliation between human beings and other forms of life that form a larger pattern of complex patterns of behavior that govern all life on Earth. Biophilia is therefore "relevant to our thinking about nature, about the landscape, the arts, and mythopoeia, and it invites us to take a new look at environmental ethics" (Wilson 32). Both Robinson and Wilson speak to the complex biological connections that govern the natural world and the animals (nonhuman and human alike) that populate it, connections that must be fostered and protected lest diverse species, including our own, continue to pay the price for a human arrogance manifest in destructive resource extraction, dirty energy sources, excessive waste and trash, toxic pollutants belched into the atmosphere, and overpopulation.

As a relatively new voice to the field, science fiction (SF) author Vandana Singh has garnered increasing critical and popular attention on the strength of such stories as "The Woman Who Thought She Was a Planet" (2003), "Delhi" (2004), "Infinities" (2008), and "Ambiguity Machines: An Examination" (2015), as well as the novellas "Of Love and Other Monsters" (2007) and "Distances" (2008), to name only a few titles. Born and raised in New Delhi, she has parlayed her doctorate in theoretical particle physics into a teaching position at Framingham State University in the United States, but it is India, a culturally and linguistically pluralized country, that taught her "we live in an interdependent web of life, that every living creature plays a role, that we are only one of a bewildering number of species living on the planet" ("Creatures").[1] For this reason, Singh credits Wilson's biophilia as an influence upon her, remarking in an interview with Jai Arjun Singh that this affinity for nature "might actually be deeply ingrained inside us" except for the fact that "modern urban culture denies this connection to other living beings." As a result, "people lose a sense of connection to nature and fill that emptiness with dead things, and wonder why they are unhappy" ("Biophilia"). Singh's short fiction therefore often features characters undergoing a series of hardships before realizing or experiencing the innate connections that bind us not only to one another but also to our living biosphere. For example, cosmic trees guide Birha to profound philosophical questions about humanity ("Ruminations"); river deltas show to Gargi the multiversal nature of the universe ("With Fate"); infinite spider webs reveal themselves to the mathematician Abdul Karim after he has stepped into infinite space to realize "what he is seeing and feeling is part of vast pattern. . . . In the scaffolding, the skeletal structure of the multiverse is beautifully apparent" ("Infinities" 79); the wondrous power of the *Kathasāritsāgara*, an eleventh-century Sanskirt compilation of Indian folk tales and legends (loosely translated into English as the "ocean/stream of stories") assembled by the largely mysterious scholar-poet Somadevabhatta leads the space traveler Isha to also question the very nature of reality and her own existence ("Somadeva"); or, the complicated dance of the apian collective in "Delhi" leads Aseem to understand that "whatever you do affects the world in some small way. Sometimes the effect remains small, sometimes it grows and grows like a pipal tree" (36).

Singh's fictions are marked by a generally hopeful trend or narrative trajectory, which makes "Are You Sannata 3159?" (2010) a particularly striking story because any hopeful vision of the biosphere is sacrificed in favor of a bleak world of environmental decay and economic destitution. The story portrays an ecological dystopia dominated by horrifying images of consumption and discordance that offer a vision of the devastating long-term effects of rejecting biophilia in favor of an anti-biophilia that continues to treat the world as a machine by prioritizing economic profit, exploitation of resources, and cheap labor. As an anti-biophilia, "Are You Sannata 3159?" advances a deeply critical account of the exploitation of natural resources and labor in the so-called Third World (and elsewhere on our planet) where our commitment to capitalism seems at times intractable and ecologically disruptive.

From "Entanglement" to Dis-Entanglement

Biophilia is synonymous in Singh's fictions with entanglement, a term which marries quantum physics and biophilia.[2] The clearest example of entanglement is in the short story of the same name. "Entanglement" (2014) follows five characters who live worlds apart but are indivisibly entangled. Irene, a biogeochemist, explores the use of methanotrophs to reduce methane emissions on the Arctic floor. A reserved and isolated woman, she represses her Inuit identity and past history, preferring the Anglicized name "Irene" in place of her Inuit name "Enuusiq." The surrounding ice and cold Arctic waters, however, remind her of venturing out into the waters off Baffin Island with her grandfather and she turns to embrace her past after a diving error nearly kills her. A beluga whale miraculously saves Irene/Enuusiq by lifting her to the surface, upon which she realizes the "world she loved was woven into being every moment through complex, dynamic webs of interaction" (362).

Half a world away in Brazil, Fernanda has returned to the drought-stricken city of Manaus to lend her energies to reversing catastrophic climate change. She works for a green roof initiative that encourages residents to transform their rooftops with "native plants, chosen for their high rates of evapotranspiration, mimicking the radiative properties of the rain forest canopies" (366). While in Manaus, Fernanda watches a television report of a tornado in India, and Bhola's story provides a firsthand account of living through that tornado. As a low-caste Harijan, Bhola works menial jobs for the Rajput village of Songaon. Although Bhola is an orphan and raised by Bojhu kaku, he is schooled by "the professor," a man Bhola considers his grandfather, his dadaji. The professor rejects caste politics and takes to teaching Bhola, at least until the tornado destroys half of Songaon. Although the professor dies in the carnage, Bhola is able to save the children of a particularly powerful man, Ranbir Singh, but at the cost of breaking caste rules on propriety and social conduct. In spite of the great personal risk, Bhola's actions foretell a future where caste divisions are anachronistic and he vows to continue his dadaji's work by speaking for the children who are inheriting the world that is being left for them.

As a Texan senior citizen, Dorothy Cartwright works for the children and grandchildren of future generations. She has spent her life subsuming her identity in favor of her role as a housewife, but as a widow she now gradually finds her voice and gets involved in an anti-fracking protest. She is inspired by the children and grandchildren who need to be saved from the follies of older generations and the corporate greed that is destroying the planet. As one lone woman, Dorothy doubts whether she can truly make a difference until an injury at a protest site sends her to the hospital. This triggers larger anti-fracking protests and increased media attention. In an interview, she tells two journalists that her husband

> used to tell me how impractical it was to worry about the environment. Practical people run the economy, make sure things work. That attitude, combined with greed, has ruined the earth to a degree that threatens our grandchildren. I'm only a housewife, but I know that we need good, fresh air to breathe, and trees to grow, and we need the wild things around us ... That's why I believe we need to protect what the good Lord gave us, this blessed Earth, else how can we live? And what's more practical than that? (387)

Although Dorothy never meets Yuan, the protagonist of the final vignette, he comes to similar conclusions. Yuan, terminally ill, spends what remains of his life searching for a mysterious city he has seen in visions, a search that leads him to the hidden recesses of the Himalayas. He finds a monk who reveals the place Yuan is looking for was first a monastery and then a university, a place built "for those who sought to understand the world in a new way, and to bring about its resurrection" (389). Inspired by his teacher and mentor Dr. Amina Ismail, Yuan has come to understand the "world is an interconnected web of relationships—between human and human, and human and beast and plant, and all that's living and nonliving" (391). Bitterly disappointed, Yuan consequently learns from the monk all that remains of the mystical city are remnants and rubble. Unbeknownst to Yuan, the monk merely awaits one final avalanche to claim his life, but Yuan not only saves him from this fate but is also saved in the process: Yuan is no longer dying and the monk has helped him to see his vision was perhaps "a vision of the future ... After all, your teacher was real. If she mentioned this place to you, then that must mean others are dreaming the same dream" (394).

Aside from the narrative overlaps, the characters are all entangled. On a technological level, they are individually wearing an orange wristlet, a prototype Yuan has created whose software genie searches "the Internet for people who have similar values of certain parameters ... and it gauges security and safety as well. When you most need it, based on your emotional profile at the time, the software will link you at random to someone in your circle" (392). Although the prototype has its glitches, it does work and these characters have connected with one another, no matter how fleeting the connection. Irene, for example, links with Dorothy when she hears a voice speaking "with such clarity and concern, and there was such an emphasis on *be careful*—and weren't there kitchen sounds in the background, a pan banging in the sink, so incongruously ordinary and familiar?" (357). More profound are the entanglements with the natural environment, such as the beluga whale who saves Irene from drowning or the green roof initiative that inspires Fernanda (and others) to foster symbiotic relationships with urban and natural worlds, to name two examples.

The complex patterns in "Entanglement" exemplify the point that "we live in an interdependent web of life, that every living creature plays a role, that we are only one of a bewildering number of species living on the planet" ("Creatures"). This message is largely lost to the citizens living in Patal, the urban sprawl that is the setting for "Are You Sannata 3159?" As the "greatest of the undercities," this concrete jungle is made of huts and "wall-holes and swing-shacks suspended from the cables between the great concrete feet of the towers" (275–76). Patal is an eponymous city: known alternately as Patala or Pâtâla, Patal is the netherworld or underworld or lowest level in Hindu cosmology (Williams); thus, Jhingur, the protagonist of the story, is wholly accurate when he calls Patal "the hell that was his home" ("Are You" 279). Law and order are absent, replaced instead by a cycle of violence between two 'demon-king' street gangs, Johnny Walker IV and Ghatokacha. The vast

Undercity is also awash in ecological devastation: "The canyons were so deep between the sides of the great towers, with the first tier highways rising four to ten stories overhead, that sunlight couldn't reach all the way down. The sun was a dream" (275–76). Finally, Patal's crippling economic dislocation mirrors the socioeconomic cleavages that are increasingly defining the burgeoning cities and emergent economies in today's global metropolises. For example, overshadowing Patal is the socioeconomic privilege of Upside where Citizens live in a world of gleaming buildings and tall spires. Citizens line their apartments and office buildings with windows that double as video screens to obscure Downside festering beneath them. The only time Citizens deign to look Downside is through televisual fantasies: cameras "that dived down from the height above" subject the Undercity to a state of constant surveillance purely for entertainment purposes. The Net shows are the closest citizens come to Patal: "[T]hey know a little from the Net shows, like Reality Deep Down. But Patal is not what they want to see when they look out their windows" (279). Even Citizens who go outside are spared the view of the Undercity: they might be able to see through the windows of their "sleekers" as they speed along the Upside highways, the highways from which Patal is suspended, but road bridges such as the Narak fly-over conveniently offer Citizens an express route past the urban poverty and decay. The Narak fly-over, named for the Sanskrit word for "underworld," literally provides Citizens the ability to fly over this hellish underworld. In fact, a young woman from Upside shocks Jhingur when she leans out the window of a tall skyscraper and waves to him. Jhingur feels compelled to use a flashlight to try and communicate with her. He and Window-girl establish some distantly rudimentary connection when she returns his signals, prompting a three-day on-off-on exchange of incomprehensible messages of flashing light, at least until she disappears from the window. Jhingur experiences profound pain at this lost connection, and all that remains is to return to his dreary existence and the nighttime dreams of Window-girl as "a star against the darkness, falling toward him" (282). "Are You Sannata 3159?" therefore emerges as the anti-"Entanglement," a story predicated on dis-entanglement whose anti-biophilia comes into sharp relief upon the introduction to Patal of a slaughterhouse.

Dis-Entanglement and the Slaughterhouse

The arrival of a slaughterhouse is a turning point for Patal's Downsiders. On the one hand, it is ostensibly a symbol of hope as it "rose from the dust and filth of Patal like a shining metal dream" (276). As an upshot, the slaughterhouse provides a modicum of economic stability for Downsiders and gives them something of which they can be proud. For example, Jhingur watches his newly-uniformed mother and sister walk into the slaughterhouse to start their new jobs and is struck by their noble appearance: "His sister gave him a wave of pure happiness, and to him it seemed that the two of them, so strangely confident in their shiny blue uniforms, had become almost like Upside people, not quite real" (276). While the arrival of the slaughterhouse is heralded as the only salvation available to those literally hanging onto the underside of socio-economic privilege, it actually reinforces abject marginalization and socio-economic cleavages. Amy J. Fitzgerald explains that institutional slaughterhouses emerged in the nineteenth century and quickly became "characterized by extreme poverty, crowded conditions, delinquency, and environmental pollution" (60); at the same time, surrounding slums began "experiencing higher levels of violent crime in particular than other communities" accompanied by "housing shortages" and "increased demand for social assistance" (65). Tellingly, Patal inverts the historical record for dramatic effect: the squalid living conditions and socioeconomic disparities initially drew the slaughterhouse to Patal but the pattern of exploitation becomes cyclical and continues uninterrupted, even worsening as Jhingur learns more and more about what really takes place inside the slaughterhouse.

Exploitation takes place on both sides of the conveyor belt and the treatment of animals—human and nonhuman alike—proves to be the conceptual engine driving "Are You Sannata 3159?" Singh has previously lamented that humans are afflicted with a willing blind spot when it comes to our treatment of nonhuman animals. This blind spot allows us to "go about blindly and stupidly destroying the ecosystems on which we depend.... The tragedy is that as we tear apart the web of life, we destroy the basis of our own existence" ("Creatures"). This 'willing blind spot' compares favorably to what Nancy Williams calls an affected ignorance wherein a "choice is made not to investigate whether a practice one is involved in is immoral" (qtd. in Fitzgerald 59). The affected ignorance in the story is apparent when the slaughterhouse workers must consume a mysterious protein shake before each shift as a condition of employment. On one occasion, Jhingur's sister comes home traumatized after her shift. She accidentally spilled her drink earlier that morning, so she had to work her shift without the hallucinogen. Traumatized, she describes how animals are being loaded onto the conveyor belts while they are still alive and "when they hit them or shock them, the animals scream. All this time I couldn't see some of the animals were alive when I cut into them. I didn't know! The animals behind can see what is happening to the ones in front, and they can't move, because they are injured, and they just cry. Or they look at you, with those eyes" (285–86).[3] Her horror transforms into blissful acceptance, however, when her supervisor shows up to the house with a replacement shake. "I was just babbling nonsense," she tells Jhingur after drinking the mysterious concoction. "How silly of you to believe me!" (286). All returns to normal, except Jhingur's suspicions intensify and he looks upon the slaughterhouse with renewed skepticism and dismay. After all, Jhingur has been wary of the slaughterhouse since it opened its doors to its new workforce; for example, he "didn't think that people who work at a slaughterhouse should be cheerful or happy. He thought they should be grim and heroic and not talk so much, and flinch when they saw the animals being led to the guillotine" (283). Although he cannot pinpoint his objections, Jhingur has remained attuned to the dis-entanglement embodied by the slaughterhouse.

Although Jhingur rejects any offers of employment at the slaughterhouse, preferring to keep his dead-end job working for Langra, his guptman boss (i.e., junkshop or pawnshop owner), he still consumes the meat that now regularly finds its way into his diet, even if at times the meat is "tough and stringy instead of succulent" (283). As a rare luxury in Patal, meat signals power and luxury, however fleeting the effects. For example, when the street gangs are engaging in a revelry celebrating their fragile truce, the centerpiece of their shared feast is "a great hunk of meat, roasted to perfection" (281). At some point in the festivities, individual gang members throw portions of the meat to the surrounding crowd to brag about their purportedly elevated status. Jhingur snags a piece and quickly consumes it, "chewing as slowly as he dared.... The juices ran down his chin; he licked his lips. The taste! Oh, so this was Citizen meat! ... He almost wept when, after three bites, it was gone" (281). "Are You Sannata 3159?" therefore highlights an inherent contradiction: there is a "growing unease regarding the slaughter of animals for human consumption" but, at the same time, "the number of animals being slaughtered is increasing dramatically and their quality of life, if not death, have arguably been diminishing" (Fitzgerald 66). Sherryl Vint makes comparable observations about our general refusal "to confront the material foundations of our civilization and the exploitation upon which it is based," a refusal that "also enables the continuation of capitalist exploitation of both animals and other humans" (34). The slaughterhouse, therefore, represents an edifice of dis-entanglement honoring capitalist exploitation of human and nonhuman animals alike. It has created and perpetuated an "unprecedented break with nature" by distancing "people from the animals they consume, the act of killing, and the natural environment in which animals were raised" (Fitzgerald 66) while simultaneously valorizing meat consumption by making it a staple in most diets.

Jhingur's concern for how the nonhuman animals are being treated in the slaughterhouse arises from a naïve fantasy of 'hero worship' fostered by cheap virtual reality sessions he accesses during downtime at Langra's shop. In his favorite virtual reality fantasy, Jhingur is on grassland where a human tribe partakes in a sacrificial bison hunt. While the chief waits for a young bull to sacrifice itself for the needs of the tribe, an older bull willingly offers itself instead. As the fantasy concludes, "the humans honored his memory at every meal. They remembered, the vid said, that life is short and precious, and sacrifice is worthy of honor, and animals are our kin" ("Are You" 284–85). Although this simulation is digital, Jhingur is inspired by the affinity between human and nonhuman animals: "the story always made Jhingur weep, and he wondered if it had ever been true. He wanted to eat the meat of such an animal, to become like him, to sacrifice himself for his tribe" (285). Jhingur determines to infiltrate the slaughterhouse to secretly record the factory's horrific inner workings in what he believes is an exposé of animal abuse and deplorable worker conditions that will be perfectly suited to popular Net-based programming; thus, he joins the slaughterhouse workforce and captures illicit video of what takes place inside the factory, including the "terror of the animals, the relaxed composure of the workers, his mother's voice singing his favorite songs over the screaming" (289). "Are You Sannata 3159?" brutally depicts terrified animals and alienated workers as nothing more than sacrificial victims to a brutal logic of economic profit, a deplorable (but all-too-familiar) situation predicated upon inhuman(e) treatment of animals and the euphoria-inducing protein shake that lulls the workers into compliance.

An earlier conversation he had with Langra about the stringy meat his family has been eating lately also motivates Jhingur's exposé: "Yes, some of the meat is tough," Langra explains to Jhingur, "because they send the old people to the slaughterhouse, you know! Have you seen your grandmother today?" (283). As Jhingur starts to pay closer attention to his neighbourhood, he realizes "some other old people went away from the neighborhood, but they sent postcards from the old age facility, and they all seemed content. Then the neighbors' aunt went away ... and the postcards she sent sounded like they were written by someone else" (287). Jhingur shockingly realizes the succulent meat he voraciously consumed at the street gangs' truce celebration was truly *Citizen meat*. He now understands the truth behind "his dreams about [Window-girl] flying toward him, crossing that gulf in a great arc. She had fallen to her death, to be scavenged by the rat-folk and turned into a tribute for the demon-kings. He had eaten of her flesh without knowing" (292). More than simply a focus on inhumane actions in and by the slaughterhouse, Jhingur's exposé also demonstrates the consequences of dis-entanglement, culminating in a most horrifying analogy: capitalism cannibalizes and processes all aspects of biophilia in a comparable fashion to the slaughterhouse processing its animal victims, human and nonhuman alike, to the point where Downsiders are indiscriminately eating their own kin and those living Upside are literally surviving on human labor.

In spite of his heroic plans, Jhingur's pursuit of the truth proves fatal. Langra, his now-former boss, has mysteriously (and improbably) been elevated to the level of Citizen, but Jhingur cannot accurately remember Langra's digital address: is it Sannata 3154? or Sannata 3159? Hedging his bets, he sends his exposé to both addresses. His hopes turn futile when the slaughterhouse manager shows up at his home. The manager claims he had been alerted by Langra about the contents of the pirate video file and has offered to talk it over with Jhingur back at the slaughterhouse. Unfortunately, the naïve Jhingur ends up on the conveyor belt. After being drugged and shocked into submission, he is thrown onto the bloodied conveyor and undergoes processing; namely, he is hacked apart and turned into meat. In what is perhaps the most horrific scene, Jhingur's mother whistles the same lullabies she used to sing to Jhingur when he was a child while "she hack[s] off his hand. . She tosse[s] the hand expertly into a bin, without missing a beat, then aim[s] a blow at the animal behind him, as the conveyor belt move[s] him forward" (291). Jhingur aimlessly hopes Sannata 3159 will swoop down to save him, but much like his cricket namesake ('jhingur' is Hindi for 'cricket'), he can only chirp helplessly. His cries for salvation are met only by a sannata, the Hindi word for soundlessness or 'dead silence.' [4] Although he narrowly misses his sister's killing blow, this respite only leaves him alive long enough to meet his fate at the blades of the guillotine. At the same time, Jhingur learns firsthand the follies of believing virtual reality simulations are comparable to real-world conditions: his sacrifice is nothing like the old bison of his simulated dream-vid, and when his "flesh was packed neatly in plastic and sent away to the Citizens, or to his own people, those who ate him would not know him or honor him, as they would not know or honor the other animals" (293). In spite of Jhingur's gruesome ending, his final moments of life mark an authentic affinity towards those animals whose fate he shares. Jhingur forms a real, albeit short-lived, connection with a bull that is ahead of him on the line. Both victims look upon one another and in that moment both terror-stricken animals are calmed: "Jhingur maneuvered his good arm, gritting his teeth against the pain, reaching out so that his hand rested on the back of the beast, who shuddered once, then looked at him again, in silence and pain, and Jhingur once more felt the link between them, a jolt of love and understanding" (292–93). Jhingur has a brief epiphany in that animals are "fellow travelers on the great journey, who sang love songs to their mates, and knew joy and suffering and sacrifice" (292). Jhingur has achieved true entanglement, if only at the very end of his life.

In the end, Singh's anti-biophilia story shows how dis-entanglement threatens to process all animals—nonhuman and human alike—according to the logics of (economic) consumption, whether on the conveyor belt itself or in horribly dehumanizing working conditions. Dis-entanglement is not reserved to slaughterhouses: as the epigraph makes clear, Singh believes the ability to "see other living things as entities in themselves rather than in terms of their usefulness or threat to humankind, requires a giant paradigm shift" ("Creatures"). Singh encourages a profoundly different relationship with our surrounding ecosystem and its myriad inhabitants: "Imagine now that instead of being obsessed solely with our lives and bank balances, instead of trying to keep up with the neighbors or comparing the largeness of our houses and the number of vacations spent abroad, we were, instead, aware of the greater world, open to its wonders, appreciative of our belonging to it" ("Biophilia"). In questioning the path we are on today, "Are You Sannata 3159?" does not argue for widespread vegetarianism or veganism and the abandonment of meat consumption; instead, the story displays an expansive understanding of the affiliations that bind human and nonhuman animals. These affiliations form sinews of kinship that can allow us to reorient our paradigm away from a seemingly rampant 'affected ignorance' that is exemplified by the ubiquity of ever-expanding urban sprawls, the ongoing polluting of our biosphere, and the unethical and inhumane exploitation and cruel sacrifice of *all* animals, human and nonhuman alike, in the interests of economic gains. Singh then leaves it to readers to entangle ourselves accordingly.

Notes

1. Cultural touchstones rooted in Singh's formative years growing up in India common appear in her fiction. In "An Alien Nation" (2012), Suparno Banerjee writes that Singh's fictions are "deeply steeped in Indian culture and philosophy and [she] uses this cultural milieu as her source of inspiration as well as her object of examination" (285).

2. Entanglement, a term in quantum theory, refers to the interaction of particle properties that have intersected at some point in time and remain connected at future times regardless of the separation of space ("Quantum").

3. *New York Times* reporter Charlie LeDuff offers a remarkably similar description of the kill floor of a slaughterhouse in his article "At a Slaughterhouse, Some Things Never Die" (2003). See also Yuval Noah Harai's "Industrial Farming is one of the worst crimes in history" (2015).

4. My thanks to Vandana Singh for providing me the translation of "sannata" within the context of the story.

Works Cited

Bannerjee, Suparno. "An Alien Nation: Postcoloniality and the Alienated Subject in Vandana Singh's Science Fiction." *Extrapolation* 53.3 (2012): 283–306. Print.

Fitzgerald, Amy J. "A Social History of the Slaughterhouse: From Inception to Contemporary Implications." *Human Ecology Review* 17.1 (2010): 58–69. Print.

Harai, Yuval Noah. "Industrial Farming is one of the worst crimes in history." Science and Nature. *The Guardian.* 25 Sept. 2015. Web. 29 Sept. 2015.

LeDuff, Charlie. "At a Slaughterhouse, Some Things Never Die." *Zoontologies: The Question of the Animal.* Ed. Cary Wolfe. Minneapolis: U of Minnesota P, 2003. 183–97. Print.

"Quantum Entanglement." *A Dictionary of Physics.* 6th Edition. New York: Oxford UP, 2009. Web. *Oxford Reference.* 2009. Seneca Library. 24 September 2015.

Robinson, Kim Stanley. Introduction. *Future Primitive: The New Ecotopias.* Ed. Kim Stanley Robinson. New York: Tor, 1994. Print. 9–11. Print.

Singh, Vandana. "Are You Sannata 3159?" *Postscripts 22/23: The Company He Keeps.* Ed. Peter Crowther and Nick Gevers. East Yorkshire: PS Publishing, 2010. 275–93. Print.

———. "Biophilia, Intolerance, Future Ramayanas: Vandana Singh Q & A." Interview by Jai Arjun Singh. *Jabberwock.* 09 January 2009. Web. 28 April 2014.

———. "The Creatures We Don't See: Thoughts on the Animal Other." *Ecstatic Days.* Ed. Jeff Vandermeer. 10 October 2008. Web. 20 July 2014.

———. "Delhi." *The Woman Who Thought She Was a Planet and Other Stories.* New Delhi: Zubaan, 2008. 19–38. Print.

———. "Entanglement." *Hieroglyph: Stories and Visions for a Better Future.* Ed. Ed Finn and Kathryn Cramer. New York: William Morrow, 2014. 352–97. Print.

———. "Infinities." *The Woman Who Thought She Was a Planet and Other Stories.* New Delhi: Zubaan, 2008. 55–88. Print.

———. "Ruminations in an Alien Tongue." *The Year's Best Science Fiction: Thirtieth Annual Collection.* Ed. Gardner Dozois. New York: St. Martin's Griffin. 501–513. Print.

———. "Somadeva: A Sky River Sutra." *Year's Best SF 16.* Ed. David G. Hartwell and Kathryn Cramer. New York: HarperCollins, 2011. 99–114. Print.

———. "With Fate Conspire." *Solaris Rising 2.* Ed. Ian Whates. Oxford: Solaris, 2013. 409–39. Print.

Vint, Sherryl. *Animal Alterity: Science Fiction and the Question of the Animal.* Liverpool: Liverpool UP, 2010. Print.

Williams, George M. *Handbook of Hindu Mythology.* Santa Barbara: ABC+Clio, 2003. Print.

Wilson, Edward O. "Biophilia and the Conservation Ethic." *The Biophilia Hypothesis.* Eds. Stephen R. Kellert and Edward O. Wilson. Washington, DC: Island, 1993. 31–41. Print.

INTERSUBJECTIVITY AND CULTURAL EXCHANGE IN KIJ JOHNSON'S NOVELS OF JAPAN

■ ■ ■

JOAN GORDON

Kij Johnson's innovative use of storytelling forms enhances her exploration of human and other animal subjectivities. In two of her novels, *The Fox Woman* (2000) and *Fudoki* (2003), she uses traditional Japanese autobiographical literary forms to bridge gaps not only between an assumed Western contemporary audience and the medieval Japanese setting of her novels, but also between humans and other animals. These Japanese forms, using the careful eye of the observer and internal examinations of individual subjects, engage what I call the amborg gaze, collapsing the division between subject and object in relations between humans and other animals and, perhaps, between humans of different cultures.

The amborg gaze, as I have discussed it elsewhere, is a way of seeing that allows us not only to gaze *upon* the other but to imagine gazing *through* the eyes of the other, to imagine what it might be like to *be* the other.[1] Thus, the gaze is not something proprietary that denies the perceptions of the other or establishes a power relationship. Instead, it forms a feedback loop, in which gazes are exchanged and communication takes place in a dynamic inter-personal, inter-species relationship. Both parties are subjects, while imagination, cautious empathy, and careful observation, each of the other, builds a meaningful if incomplete understanding between individuals. The amborg gaze is complex and interactive, a hybrid form with a hybrid name meant to invoke ambiguity, ambition, and ambivalence; organisms, organizing, organicism; the cyborgs of science fiction and of Donna Haraway.[2] For Johnson, Japanese autobiographical forms offer a fresh way to represent the hybrid intersubjectivity of the amborg in speculative fiction.

Johnson planned to write a trilogy of novels taking place in Heian Japan (794–1192 CE) and employing animal viewpoints, although at present she says she is "so far away from the Japan books chronologically and emotionally that I can't even put myself back in that place" (Johnson, "Paying" 36). The two extant novels share not only an era and a general locale but experimentation with Japanese autobiographical forms, and, of course, human-animal transformation. Both use research not only about the historical period but about animal ethology to write stories that avoid exoticizing the other, be it an other era, other culture, or other species. By employing multiple viewpoints and multiple autobiographical forms, along with thorough research and fantastic premises, they create feedback loops, complex and dynamic visions in which no single viewpoint is privileged or authoritative, an amborg gaze that goes some way toward addressing the problem of exploring the other to oneself without the sort of cultural appropriation that results in speaking for or over the other.

The Fox Woman incorporates Japanese folk tales about fox fire and the fox wife, Japanese diaries, and works on fox behavior to build a story of a love triangle among a husband, a wife, and a fox. Each viewpoint is represented by a different alternating diary: the fox Kitsune's relatively straightforward diary, the husband Kaya No Yoshifuji's notebook, and the wife Shikujo's pillow book. *Fudoki* braids the story of a cat transformed into a warrior woman with the written memoir of a dying aristocratic woman looking back on her past, using the historical introduction of the first cats to Japan, and the traditional autobiographical forms called the fudoki and the monogatari, popular in the Heian period. *The Fox Woman* seems to take place near the beginning of the Heian period, while *Fudoki*, according to the author's note, takes place around the end of that period.[3]

The Diaries of *The Fox Woman*

In the first novel, as in the traditional folk tale, a fox falls in love with a man, transforms herself into a woman, and takes him as her lover. He lives with her in an illusory world of elegance until the spell is broken and he emerges filthy and emaciated into the real world and reunites with his wife. Johnson imagines the diaries of the three participants that explore their subjectivities:

as true subjects who observe and think and matter, and as subjective observers reflecting their individual viewpoints. Earl Miner, in his classic article on Japanese diary literature, or *nikki bungaku*, describes the range in such diaries from factual records, which he calls "natural diaries," to more artistic expressions using more fictional, stylistic, and poetic elements, which he calls "art diaries." All nikki bungaku are expected to have "a normative role for poetry and an awareness of time" (46). Of the three diaries represented in *The Fox Woman*, Kitsune's is the closest to a natural diary, and Shikujo's is the most self-consciously created art diary, with Kaya No Yoshifuji's lying somewhere in between.

Johnson says of her own diaries:

> I am intimately familiar with the ways I alternate between lying to myself and unpacking painful truths on the page, the strange private exhibitionism of baring my soul secretly—yet there's that frisson that somehow, some way, it might be seen by someone. I love the energy that comes from the seamless movement from the quotidian recounting of events and sensations to profound analysis of the self and others. ("Paying" 34)

She acknowledges the fictional elements of even the most "natural" diary, with its "lying to myself," consciousness of possible audience, and moments of "profound analysis." Kitsune's diary is personal in the way Johnson describes. To Johnson, while "her behaviors and tastes are foxlike, ... her mind is basically human—if uncomplicated" ("Paying" 35). Kitsune initiates her diary because she sees human beings writing them and believes that this process of self-examination (and self-delusion) is part of what makes them human, but she herself is not used to such self-conscious behavior. Kitsune talks about her attraction to the man, her bewilderment about poetry, and the pleasures and desires of a young fox. Johnson says that "animals are not necessarily simpler than we are, but I think their relationships are less cluttered with concealment than ours" ("Paying" 35). Kitsune's diary moves from the "uncomplicated" to "concealment" as she spends more and more time with the human man. She is finally even able to construct a poem. Her amborg gaze changes her in ways her diary reflects: Kitsune says in her diary, "The unaware self: humans strove for this, pursued it doggedly. Why should I not embrace it?" (Johnson, *Fox* 311). But the more time she spends with the human being, the more she loses that "unaware" self. Writing the diary leads to her final wise epiphany: that "We make our own worlds" (380). Because of the dynamic relationship she has shared with Kaya No Yoshifuji, she is no longer purely a fox any more than she has become a human being (380). The amborg gaze lets her imagine and participate in his world while he has done the same in hers. Yoshifuji's and Shikujo's diaries reveal that they too become more intermediate beings as a result of these exchanges, transformed by novel's end.

Yoshifuji's diary, labeled a notebook in the novel, describes in the present tense the events of his experience, along with his analysis of them. Like the men's diaries of Heian Japan, it emphasizes events over art, although it shares with most Japanese diary literature a stress on "love rather than marriage, death rather than mortal battles, the family rather than public life" (Miner 38). Nevertheless, it would be categorized as a "recording diary" (jiroku nikki), "relatively faithful to the immediate events they set forth," rather than as a "narrative diary" (tsukuri nikki) which Miner describes rather delightfully as floating "with considerable freedom above" the ties of fact (42). It is close in form to Kitsune's natural diary but, because he is a man with the cultural experiences of his time and place, it is less "unaware" than hers.

His first realization is that his wife is as much a subject as he: "I sometimes forget that she is a real person, not some pretty artifact in my life.... We meet each other's eyes and remember: *There is a soul on the other side of those eyes*" (Johnson, *Fox* 42; italics in original). Having come to realize the otherness of his wife to his man's world, and to imagine the subject beneath the artifice, he is better prepared to realize Kitsune's subjectivity in spite of her "significant otherness" (Haraway, *Companion* 3). On discovering the foxes' lair, he writes,

> I have always been the center of things in my life: *my* wife, *my* servants, *my* world. But there are other worlds, completely alien to me, and here, caught between *my* floor and the earth, in air clogged with another presence, I am not even irrelevant: I am *other*. (Johnson, *Fox* 62–63; italics in original)

He recognizes that the foxes' world is not his, that his world is constructed by his culture and by the act of writing in his diary as well, since the realization comes in the writing. Indeed, he sees his world as more artificial, less real, than the foxes.' He looks at an antique lamp "formed to look like grass bent in the wind" and concludes, "We look at this instead of the true grass, and this is art. The foxes lie in real grass.... There is no illusion at all in their lives. No art, no artifice" (96). But he is attracted to the world of the foxes: "The foxes are filled with life, immortality of a sort, and this draws me to them" (87). The more he enters into the foxes' world and acknowledges their reality, the more he is transformed. But no matter how much he pursues the "unaware self" of their world, he finally must return to his human family. Like Kitsune, he too has an epiphany made possible by the amborg gaze. In acknowledging the subjectivity of the alien other by imagining how she sees the world, he realizes that he must nevertheless face his own world, that his ability to enter into hers is illusory: "The least I can do is stop running from myself" (374). He cannot become unaware so the amborg gaze heightens his self-awareness and his awareness of others.

As carefully as Johnson constructs Kitsune's alien nature by consulting (and acknowledging) works of fox behavior by Michael Fox, Rebecca Grambo, and others, Shikujo, Yoshifuji's wife, seems in many ways the most alien of the novel's characters. The sensuous and exquisitely constructed world of artifice she describes in her pillow book is very far from our own. Given its name, we understand that Shikujo models her diary on the form of the famous *Pillow Book* of Sei Shōnagon, which Miner distinguishes from a diary, calling it a "*zuihitsu*" or "pensée" (44). Shikujo's writing, then, is less tied to fact than Kitsune's or Yoshifuji's and, like Shōnagon's, contains "loosely connected personal essays and fragmented ideas," poetry and impressions about courtly life and the changing seasons, meant to reflect the sensibilities of a refined but conventional woman ("Zuihitsu"). At least at first. One of the most touching and impressive developments in Johnson's use of the pillow book form is the ways in which its fictive author gradually breaks from convention and uses it less and less as concealment and more and more as revelation.

Here is how Shikujo begins:

> One wrote this on first seeing the home she left all those years ago:
> *Is the garden lost*
> *or merely hidden by the years' thick grasses?*
> And this question only delays the next: which would one prefer? This should be a
> simple enough question to answer: I am sure that civilization must always be preferable
> to barbarity. (Johnson, *Fox* 26; italics in original)

The entry uses "one," distancing its writer from her self; moves to a poem, making clear that this is an art diary; and then proclaims that "civilization" trumps its equally loaded opposite term, "barbarity." The entries that follow express "fear ... of the wildness, so far from the security of the city. Anything might happen out here" (32). Shikujo establishes herself insistently as a culturally constructed creature, completely bounded by the strictures of her class and gender, through what she says and through the vehicle of her pillow book.

But her pillow book, with its artistic freedom, gradually leads her to shed the concealment that its artifice had first allowed. In one of her last entries, Shikujo confronts her lover from long ago, another fox, a fox man, Kitsune's grandfather, and he tells her, "'I am sorry to leave just when your life is getting interesting. But I am glad I saw you awaken from your dream'" (361). What is that dream? The very restrictions and conventions of court life that she describes so gracefully at the novel's outset, the denial of her animal nature that she too had once explored. Johnson evokes a beautiful amborg gaze as Shikujo and the fox man part for the last time:

> The fox watched us [Shikuro and her son], and I spoke a poem to the fox. And we
> > knelt in the snow ... and bowed to him.
> > > The fox bowed his head in return and left....
> > > *Love and memory and thought and dream—*
> > > > *My favorite poems have never been written in words.* (362; italics in original)

Shikujo acknowledges both memory and dream in this amborg exchange between subjects who are alien to one another but linked by love and thought in an art diary form that, less strictly tethered to fact, attempts to express what has "never been written in words." The exchange of gazes becomes the poem.

The novel ends with each of the three characters transformed into an intermediate being, an amborg. Kitsune comes upon the pure white foxes (also called Kitsune) of the Shinto goddess Inari, who ask her if she is fox or human. Kitsune's answer: "'Both. Neither. I am myself'" (366). This is how it is for all three. They are neither wild nor tame, civilized nor barbaric, human nor nonhuman. Each has looked into the eyes of another species, and has imagined gazing through those other eyes. They have all been transformed by the experience into more hybrid forms. They have become amborgs. "Some humans learn joy and some foxes grow souls," Kitsune concludes, and although she never really masters the human artifice of poetry she sees that "our lives become the poems we were born to tell" (380).

The Memoirs of *Fudoki*

The second novel, published three years later, is short on poetry; neither the narrator nor the cat whose tale she tells has any time for poems. Further, Princess Harueme's memoir is much more metafictional than the diaries of *The Fox Woman*, and all the transformations of *Fudoki* occur within the frame of the princess's notebooks. Each chapter of the novel is titled with the description of the notebook in which it is inscribed ("The Michinoka-paper

Notebook" [124], "The *Mashi*-hemp Notebook" [224], and so on); the novel's conceit is that she is writing a memoir of her own life imbricated with the tale of a cat transformed into a woman. Since the memoir differs from a daily diary, since it draws attention to its artifice through metafiction, and since it uses more distanced forms of Japanese autobiographical writing, the monogatari and the fudoki, the second novel is less interior and intimate, yet it also invites and employs the amborg gaze, if in quite a different way.

Harueme has lived the restricted life of an aristocratic woman, without adventure or travel, bound by rule and custom. As she is dying she looks back on that life and how she struggled to follow her own interests and passions, using the conceit of the tale of a cat who represents the freedom Harueme could never have. Of course, freedom is a relative thing and the chapters often draw parallels between Harueme and the cat she imagines. While we know that the cat's tale is the narrator's invention, we fall into it as we do into any vividly told story so that it too becomes "real," as real as the narrator's story, just as *The Fox Woman* seems real on the page even though we understand that it is a construction of the author. The framing of *Fudoki* reflects back upon *The Fox Woman* to suggest that it too is a tale within a tale.

Fudoki emphasizes the fictionality of the cat's story, but it also stresses the nonhuman nature of the cat as it imagines the gaze from the other side. Johnson says that while she doesn't "feel much as though Kitsune in *The Fox Woman* is an especially other point of view," the cat "in *Fudoki* is closer to being a cat than Kitsune is to being a fox; but then, we're not inside her head, we're inside her *creator's* head, and it's easier to maintain strangeness from outside" ("Paying" 35; italics in original). Where *The Fox Woman* establishes an amborg gaze by entering into the minds of the three characters, *Fudoki* acknowledges the otherness of both subjects, human and cat, by maintaining a distance between them and from them, and by using less intimate autobiographical forms than the first novel.

Fudoki employs the Japanese autobiographical forms of the monogatari and the fudoki. The first is a precursor of the novel: Miner differentiates between the *jiroku monogatari* or recording tale, "dealing ... with actual historical events," and the *tsukuri monogatari*, or narrative tale, "borrowing from history and real social custom but dedicated to a fully developed fiction" (42). Harueme's memoir alternates between these two types: her own story is meant to be a recording tale and the cat's story a narrative one. Kij Johnson borrows them, and the fudoki, to make her fantasy novel. Harueme's recording tale is ordered by association. Each chapter or notebook combines description of the present moment with recollections of the past and inspires stories of the cat. The frame of Harueme's recording tale deals with the "actual historical events" of her fictional life. In terms of Johnson's research, Harueme herself "shares some characteristics with Shirakawa's real sisters," siblings of the historical Emperor Shirakawa who lived from 1053 to 1129 (*Fudoki* 315). Johnson shapes these events and characteristics into an art diary, even though it contains no poetry, that is rooted in the facts of the fictional character's life and in Johnson's research.

Almost every chapter demonstrates this tension between fact and fiction, recording and narrative monogatari. In chapter five, "The *Kihada*-dyed Notebook," for example, Harueme recalls an event in her childhood, when she caught a little mouse and asked her gardener about it. He tells her that "maybe the lesson they learn is grace in the face of unavoidable tragedy." Harueme thinks about his statement: "This made sense to me: *monogatari* tales are full of women (and sometimes men) dying gracefully. But—'What's graceful about mice? They don't write poems before they die.' . . . my nurse had been reading to me from Genji's tale" (87; italics in original). Here we see the princess, even as a child, considering the difference between fiction and fact (Genji's tale and her mouse). The elderly, dying princess draws the differences as well, describing "those irritatingly stupid women in *monogatari* tales" succumbing gracefully to death "with their elegant little death-poems, their lovely corpses floating on willow-clogged waters" (87; italics in original). Harueme doesn't want to write that kind of monogatari: instead, she writes a recording monogatari that avoids poetry and pretty fictions, to help her understand her struggles and the struggles of little mice as well. This more distanced record allows her to imagine how mice and princesses both see the world.

Nevertheless, Harueme writes a narrative monogatari as well, the story of the cat she invents and folds into her own story. Why? "Perhaps the only reason I tell the tale of the tortoiseshell cat is that, even after decades of living with cats, I still understand them not at all" (89). Here we see the tension again. Only the factuality of a recording diary can lead her to understand herself and the mice she observes, but only the fiction of a narrative diary can allow her entry into the alien minds of other creatures. "The *Kihada*-dyed Notebook" incorporates a part of the narrative monogatari in which the tortoiseshell cat, now transformed into a woman, meets a human woman with whom she forms a friendship. Harueme describes the nature of the friendship:

> The cat-woman expressed no affection and had little in common with Nakara, and yet they were friends. Nakara had her own concerns, so perhaps she saw the tortoise-shell woman's grief and her strangeness, and pitied them, and her. And Nakara had certain experience with the creatures

who could take human form [like Shikujo in the earlier novel, she has had a fox lover], and so it is possible that she saw a cat's nature in her companion, and so understood not to expect what she might from a woman. (90)

This friendship acknowledges the impossibility of understanding the other completely but makes the attempt anyway, accepting the profound differences but seeking affinities as well. It is a reserved friendship, to be sure, as the form of the story is reserved in comparison to the diaries and pillow books of *The Fox Woman*. But in the distancing and reserve the gaze is returned. And at this point the cat/woman receives part of her name, Hime, or princess, because "Princesses may say what they like" and "we all have things to say" (97). Princess Harueme expresses herself through this monogatari about a cat, but the cat herself does not find them very interesting because "there is no fighting.... No wonders, no strangeness. Not like the *fudoki* of my people" (99).

The historical fudoki "included descriptions of natural features and population centers, local resources and products, [and] bits of folklore and history" (315), and were thus not personal documents at all but reports back to the center of government by its representatives of what they saw in the field, attempts to accurately describe the other to the imperial court.[4] Johnson defines the fudoki in her "Author's Note": "*Fudoki*, which may be translated as 'records of wind and earth,' were eighth-century documents collecting information about individual provinces for the imperial court.... I adopted the word as the closest parallel to my cats' shared world" (315). The tortoiseshell cat, who becomes Hime, and then Kagaya-hime or Princess Glory, talks about her fudoki, described in the novel as "the chronicle of the females who have claimed a place, a river of cats that starts with the first to come to that place, and ends with oneself—when one grows experienced enough to have a tale to tell" (18). The cat loses her whole family in a fire at the beginning of the Princess's monogatari and so she feels she has lost her fudoki and therefore her identity. For the cat, the entire series of adventures in the narrative monogatari is the long search to find a place so she can find an identity and a story: a fudoki. The story she lives is full of fighting, wonders, and strangeness, but only at the end of her story, when she transforms herself into a cat once again, and talks to the ghost of another of her friends, the old warrior Takase, does she understand that "You are a one-cat *fudoki*" (303; italics in original). Having traveled all the way to the north, "This new land will belong to her, a part of a new *fudoki* that begins with her" (311; italics in original).

The cat's realization comes just before the closing chapter or notebook of the novel. There the human princess wonders, "Why might she [the cat] not have questions for me, just as I have questions for her?" (314). Just as the cat finds her identity in a story that extends beyond herself, so Princess Harueme finds a reality beyond her own limited experiences through her narrative monogatari: "She [the cat] saw things I did not expect, and felt things I did not mean her to" because Harueme imagines viewpoints beyond her own, and imagines seeing through the eyes of the other (314). From the beginning of her project, Harueme acknowledges the impossibility of imagining with complete accuracy the gaze of the other. "What does she see? And when I look at her, what do I see? Cats. Who can tell?" (19). She imagines it all the same, just as Johnson imagined the fox's viewpoint in the earlier novel, through a kind of anthropomorphism: "I guess what she might have seen or felt. . . . I imagine; I dream" (25). Such an act is a deployment of an amborg gaze, never a guarantee of understanding but always an attempt to find connections. A lucana is always present in imagining the other: "I try to write of the common people, but, really what do I know?" "Is it better," Harueme asks, "to write and think only of what I have myself experienced," when "much of my life bored me senseless" (65)? To write of other people requires a leap similar to that of anthropomorphism, with the attendant and inevitable failures, but with the attendant connections and illuminations as well. And so Princess Harueme uses her memoir not only to look back on the life she will soon leave, but to imagine other lives as well: "all my life I longed to see a place where the eye was drawn, not by delicate nuances . . . but by utter newness, a blow to the mind" (66). She describes the goal of all speculative fiction. Like the princess, Johnson has chosen to write of a time, a place, humans, and cats that are impossible to imagine accurately, but which will allow her, and us, "to see a place [of] utter newness."

Conclusion

All fiction takes a leap into the mind of another. Speculative fiction takes a greater leap: "history looks a lot like fantasy. Fabulous people doing things that we don't understand, in a culture we're not familiar with? That's the heart of fantasy" (Johnson, "Kij" 9). With Kagaya-hime's wonders and strangeness and Harueme's utter newness and blow to the mind, speculative fiction has the freedom to imagine others whom we cannot really know, but carefully provides enough rigor to avoid forcing those others into either exoticism or our own mundanity.

Whenever one writes about alien worlds, whether those of other cultures or those of other species, one risks some level of cultural appropriation, or in the words of the 1992 Resolution of the Writers' Union of Canada, "the taking—from a culture that is not one's own—of intellectual property, cultural expressions or artifacts, history and ways of knowledge" (qtd. in Rao and Ziff 1). Parul Sehgal, in a *New York Times Magazine* essay, says that it is "a word now associated with the white Western world's co-opting of minority cultures" (13). Philosopher Kei Hotoda adds that "no matter the techniques used or the quantity and quality of research, there will be some cultural appropriation," or at least something that is "not entirely authentic," so one must be constantly mindful of the possibility of false representation. She also points out that "a white perspective of a nonwhite culture/people is an important feature to note."

Fiction must somehow imagine beyond the author's world without falsely representing the world of the other, so that a careful observer can speak about, if not for, another. If only an authentic voice could speak about the historical Holocaust—e.g. a survivor, a Jew, in Yiddish—the event itself would be silenced. If we insist that only a survivor tell of the Holocaust, or a Japanese person of Japanese history, or a fox about its life, the Holocaust, Japanese history, and foxes will disappear from our imaginations. To ignore what we cannot know from experience is not the solution to the problem of appropriation. Pakistani novelist Kamila Shamsie calls for "more, not less, imaginative engagement with her country.... The moment you say a male American writer can't write about a female Pakistani, you are saying, Don't tell those stories.... Leave her and her nation to its Otherness. Write them out of history" (qtd. in Sehgal 15).

Johnson writes of Japan for readers of English, of Asian people as a white person, and of other animals for human beings. She is careful not to exoticize her subjects as utterly strange or trivialize them as more of the same. Rigorously researched historical narratives enable her to avoid trivializing or exoticizing the complexity of another view of the world, and it may be that casting one's narrative into the remote past, as Johnson's stories do, avoids some of the difficulty of power inequity. The tension in speculative fiction, and in historical fiction, between "strangeness" and "utter newness," or in Darko Suvin's term, "estrangement,"[5] on the one hand, and the familiarization that careful research provides forms something of a safeguard against cultural appropriation. Johnson's use of ethological research in her portrayal of the foxes and cats of her novels works similarly, even as she takes the leap into the fantastic by representing animal transformations and entering into other animals' minds.

The feedback loop formed by an amborg gaze that imagines both sides of a cultural exchange also enables these novels to engage with other beings in other worlds rather than simply appropriating their lives. Rather than appropriation of one by another, or transmission from one to another, there emerges instead the kind of interactive movement that changes all parties. It is necessarily incomplete and speculative, never truly "authentic," but it is neither dismissive nor without respect, and becomes possible not only through the intimacy of passion and the personal diary, as in *The Fox Woman*, but also through the distance of careful observation and autobiographical narrative modes, as in *Fudoki*. The hybridity of the amborg gaze allows both affinity and difference in fiction that honors the intersubjectivity of respectful cultural exchange.

Notes

1. See my "Animal Viewpoints in the Contact Zone of Adam Hines's *Duncan the Wonder Dog*," "Gazing Across the Abyss: The Amborg Gaze in Sheri S. Tepper's *Six Moon Dance*," and "Talking (with/for) Dogs: Science Fiction Breaks a Species Barrier," the last of which discusses a short story by Johnson, for further discussion of the amborg.

2. For more information see Haraway's foundational essay "A Cyborg Manifesto: Science, Technology, and Socialist-Feminism in the Late Twentieth Century" (1985).

3. The timing is actually rather more complicated than this. The memoir of the second novel is written, according to the note, in 1129 CE, while the cat's fudoki follows the style of "eighth-century documents" (Johnson, *Fudoki* 315). *The Fox Woman* takes place 180 years earlier than the memoir of *Fudoki* (Johnson, "Kij" 9), so in 949 CE. References to fox women and men in *Fudoki* connect with the fox men and women in *The Fox Woman*. As Johnson explains, "Characters in the second book [*Fudoki*] turn up in a much later timeframe than the first book, 180 years later. Time is folding because it is magic. Why not?" ("Kij" 9). The cat's tale in *Fudoki* is meant to take place in the time when "The emperor Ichijjo brought the first cats from Korea—my [the Princess's] great-grandfather, though this was long before I was born" (17). His reign was from 986 to 1011 CE, just after the time of *The Fox Woman*.

4. For an extended definition that confirms Johnson's, see Shūhei.

5. See Suvin's groundbreaking *Metamorphoses of Science Fiction: On the Poetics and History of a Literary Genre* (1979).

Works Cited

Gordon, Joan. "Animal Viewpoints in the Contact Zone of Adam Hines's *Duncan the Wonder Dog.*" *Humanimalia* 5.1 (2014). Web. 5 Oct. 2015.

———. "Gazing Across the Abyss: The Amborg Gaze in Sheri S. Tepper's *Six Moon Dance.*" *Science Fiction Studies* 35.2 (2008): 189–206. Print.

———. "Talking (with/for) Dogs: Science Fiction Breaks a Species Barrier." *Science Fiction Studies* 37.3 (2010): 456–65. Print.

Haraway, Donna J. *The Companion Species Manifesto: Dogs, People, and Significant Otherness.* Chicago: Prickly Paradigm, 2003. Print.

———. "A Cyborg Manifesto: Science, Technology, and Socialist-Feminism in the Late Twentieth Century." 1985. *Simians, Cyborgs, and Women: The Reinvention of Nature.* New York: Routledge, 1991. 149–81. Print.

Hotoda, Kei. Email to author. 28 Aug. 2015.

Johnson, Kij. *The Fox Woman.* New York: Tor, 2000. Print.

———. *Fudoki.* New York. Tor, 2003. Print.

———. "Kij Johnson: Inversions." Interview. *Locus* 69.4 (2012): 8+. Print.

———. "'Paying Attention to Otherness': An Interview with Kij Johnson." By Joan Gordon. *Paradoxa* 26 (2014): 31–41. Print.

Miner, Earl. "The Traditions and Forms of the Japanese Poetic Diary." *Pacific Coast Philology* 3 (Apr. 1968): 38–48. Print.

Rao, Pratima V. and Bruce Ziff. "Introduction to Cultural Appropriation: A Framework for Analysis." *Borrowed Power: Essays on Cultural Appropriation.* Eds. Pratima V. Rao and Bruce Ziff. New Brunswick: Rutgers UP, 1997. 1–27. Print.

Sehgal, Parul. "Takeover." *New York Times Magazine* 14 Oct. 2015: 13–15. Print.

Shūhei, Aoki. "Fudoki." *Encyclopedia of Shinto.* 2007. Web. 23 Aug. 2015.

Suvin, Darko. *Metamorphoses of Science Fiction: On the Poetics and History of a Literary Genre.* New Haven: Yale UP, 1979. Print.

"Zuihitsu." *Wikipedia.* 16 Jun. 2015. Web. 26 Aug. 2015.

CONTRIBUTORS

Suparno Banerjee is an assistant professor of English at Texas State University, San Marcos, specializing in and postcolonial studies. His scholarship has been published in such journals as *Journal of the Fantastic in the Arts, Extrapolation, Science Fiction Studies, South Asian Popular Culture, Journal of Commonwealth and Postcolonial Studies,* and *Visva-Bharati Quarterly*. He also contributed to the two recent books on postcolonial SF, *The Postnational Fantasy* (2011) and *Science Fiction, Imperialism, and the Third World: Essays in Literature and Film* (2010).

Cait Coker is an associate editor for *Foundation: The International Review of Science Fiction*. Her research focuses on the depictions of women and sexuality in SF and fantasy, and the history of women in nontraditional publishing. Her reviews and essays have appeared in *The Journal of Fan Studies, The Journal of Transformative Works and Cultures, The Future Fire,* and *The SFRA Review*. Her next projects include "a literary history of fandom" and, ideally, finishing her doctorate.

Jeshua Enriquez is a Ph.D. student in English at the University of California, Riverside, with a specialization in SF and technoculture studies. He holds an M.A. in Literature from Northwestern University. His research interests include twentieth century and contemporary SF, modernity and postmodernity, and the American novel.

Joan Gordon is a long-serving co-editor for *Science Fiction Studies* and *Humanimalia* and publishes widely on the intersection of science fiction and animal studies. She has been a Fulbright distinguished chair in American Studies at Marie Curie Skłodowska University and received the Science Fiction Research Association's Pilgrim Award for lifetime achievement in SF scholarship (2014).

Contributors

Veronica Hollinger is emerita professor of Cultural Studies at Trent University in Ontario, Canada. She is the co-editor of five scholarly collections, the most recent of which is *Parabolas of Science Fiction* (2013), and a co-editor of *The Wesleyan Anthology of Science Fiction* (2010). She is a long-time co-editor of *Science Fiction Studies* and the author of many essays on feminist, queer, and cyberpunk SF, on postmodernism and posthumanism, and on developments in SF theory and criticism. She is a past recipient of the Science Fiction Research Association's Pioneer Award for best critical essay (1990).

Malisa Kurtz recently finished a Ph.D. in the Interdisciplinary Humanities program at Brock University. She has published articles in *Journal of the Fantastic in the Arts*, *Paradoxa*, and *Science Fiction Studies* on postcolonial science fiction. Her dissertation focuses on the intersections of postcolonialism, globalization, and technoculture in twentieth and twenty-first century SF.

Isiah Lavender III is an associate professor of English at Louisiana State University, where he researches and teaches courses in African American literature and science fiction. In addition to his book *Race in American Science Fiction* (2011) and edited collection *Black and Brown Planets: The Politics of Race in Science Fiction* (2014), his publications on science fiction include essays and reviews in journals such as *Extrapolation*, *Journal of the Fantastic in the Arts*, and *Science Fiction Studies*.

Stephanie Li is the Susan D. Gubar Chair in Literature at Indiana University. She is the author of four books including *Playing in the White: Black Writers, White Subjects* (2015), *Signifying without Specifying: Racial Discourse in the Age of Obama* (2011), and *Something Akin to Freedom: The Choice of Bondage in Narratives by African American Women* (2010).

Bradford Lyau, a life-long reader and fan of SF and former educator (at several universities in California and Europe), now oversees a start-up company and is also a political activist and consultant. Holding a Ph.D. in history from the University of Chicago, he continues to publish scholarship on science fiction. He is also the author of *The Anticipation Novelists of 1950s French Science Fiction: Stepchildren of Voltaire* (2011).

Uppinder Mehan is Dean of the College of Arts and Sciences and Associate Professor of English at Fort Valley State University. He is editor, with Jeffrey DiLeo, of *Capital at the Brink* (2014) and *Terror, Theory and the Humanities* (2012) and with Nalo Hopkinson of *So Long Been Dreaming: Postcolonial*

Science Fiction and Fantasy (2004), and his essays have appeared in *Comparative Literature, Intertexts, Paragraph,* and *Foundation: The International Review of Science Fiction.*

Graham J. Murphy is a professor in the School of English and Liberal Studies (Faculty of Business) at Seneca College in Toronto, Canada. He is the co-editor of *Beyond Cyberpunk: New Critical Perspectives* (2010), co-author of *Ursula K. Le Guin: A Critical Companion* (2006), and his articles appear in *Science Fiction Studies, Extrapolation,* and *Foundation,* among other places. His current research interests include insect ontologies in SF, Indigenous Futurisms, and critical interrogations into cyberpunk.

Baryon Tensor Posadas is an assistant professor in the Department of Asian Languages and Literatures at the University of Minnesota, Twin Cities. He is currently at work on two book projects: the first on the doppelganger motif in Japanese film and literature, and the second on SF, empire, and Japan. His critical work has previously appeared in such journals as *Japan Forum, positions: asia critique,* and *Science Fiction Film and Television.*

Amy J. Ransom is a professor of French at Central Michigan University. She is the author of some two dozen articles on SF, horror, and the fantastic in Quebec's popular literature and film, as well as the books *Science Fiction from Québec: A Postcolonial Study* (2009) and *Hockey PQ: Canada's Game in Quebec's Popular Culture* (2014). She is a past recipient of the Science Fiction Research Association's Pioneer Award for best critical essay (2007).

Robin Anne Reid is a professor in the Department of Literature and Languages at Texas A&M University–Commerce. Her teaching areas are creative writing, critical theory, and marginalized literatures. Her research interests include feminist and critical race approaches to SF and fantasy as well as fan studies and stylistics. She edited the first encyclopedia on *Women in Science Fiction and Fantasy* (2008), and has published on fan anti-racist activism.

Haerin (Helen) Shin is an assistant professor of English, Cinema and Media Arts, and Asian Studies at Vanderbilt University. Her focus fields are Asian American literature, SF, visual and digital media, and critical theories that investigate the interrelationship between technology and ontology. Shin is currently working on a book about how the emergence of telepresence technology has been reshaping our understanding of being and reality.

Stephen Hong Sohn is an assistant professor of English at the University of California, Riverside. Sohn edited a special issue of *MELUS* (Winter 2008) on the topic of "Alien/Asian" and an issue of *Modern Fiction Studies* on the topic of "Theorizing Asian American Fiction" (2010). Sohn is the author of *Racial Asymmetries: Asian American Fictional Worlds* (2014).

Takayuki Tatsumi is a professor of American Literature at Keio University (Tokyo). His major works include: *Cyberpunk America* (1988); *Full Metal Apache: Transactions between Cyberpunk Japan and Avant-Pop America* (2006); and, with Christopher Bolton and Istvan Csicsery-Ronay, *Robot Ghosts, Wired Dreams: Japanese Science Fiction from Origins to Anime* (2007). He won the twenty-first Japan SF Grand Prize with his edited anthology *Japanese SF Controversies: 1957–1997* (2000). He is a past recipient of the Science Fiction Research Association's Pioneer Award for best critical essay (1994) and the International Association of the Fantastic in the Arts Distinguished Scholarship Award (2010).

Timothy J. Yamamura is a faculty member in the English department at Northern Arizona University, where he teaches classes on postcolonial, transnational, and world literature. A San Francisco native, Tim recently completed his PhD in Literature at UC Santa Cruz. Tim's scholarly work has appeared in the *Asian Theatre Journal*, the *U.S.-Japan Women's Journal*, and the *Pacific Reader*.

INDEX

Achebe, Chinua, 44, 54n1
Africa, 45–46, 54, 76, 86, 222
African Americans, 33, 46, 105, 110–11, 116n5, 130n3, 139, 142n2, 192
Afro-futurism, 5
Ahdieh, Renée, 57
Ahuja, Vivek, *Chimera*, 218, 220, 222, 229
Aldiss, Brian, 15, 30, 31, 33, 35, 40n3; "Another Little Boy," 6, 30–36, 39n2
Alien/Asian, 7, 91, 96, 100, 135
aliens, 4, 7, 15–18, 21, 35, 44–45, 48–49, 73, 89, 92, 99–100, 108–9, 134–35, 137, 145, 154, 160, 167–68, 204–5, 247–49, 251, 253
alternate history, 19, 20, 30, 33
alternate reality, 57
Amazing Stories, 161–62
amborg gaze, 9, 244–50, 253–55
AngloAmericans, 6, 14–16, 19, 35, 75, 148, 226
anime, 3, 34, 46, 189, 191, 205, 215n4
anti-biophilia, 234, 237, 242
antiracists, 189, 192, 193, 195, 197–99
Asian Americans, 8, 38, 102, 105, 107, 112–13, 119, 128–29, 135, 142, 176, 178–79, 190, 192, 194, 196–97
Asianness, 137, 140, 142n2
assimilation, 84, 156
atomic bombing, 6, 26, 30–32, 34, 37. *See also* Hiroshima; Nagasaki; nuclear war

Avatar: The Last Airbender, 190. See also *Last Airbender, The*; Shyamalan, M. Night
avatars, 50, 147–50, 152–53, 155–56

Baldwin, James, 110
Baudrillard, Jean, 103, 133, 137. *See also* hyperrealism; simulacra
Bechdel Test, 213
Bellamy, Edward, *Looking Backward: 2000–1887*, 165
Benjamin, Walter, 96
Bhabha, Homi, 96
Bierce, Ambrose, 29
Billings, Harold, 73, 74
biophilia, 9, 233–34, 241–42. *See also* anti-biophilia
biopower, 61, 65–66
biotechnologies, 7, 117, 120, 127, 129n1
black humor, 6, 26–30, 33, 39
black minstrelsy, 196
Blade Runner, 4, 104, 135
Blake, Kendare, 57
Bohr Maker, The, 7, 117–20, 124–26, 128–29. *See also* Nagata, Linda
Brahmins, 51, 91
Butler, Samuel, *Erewhon*, 205

Campbell, John W., Jr., 161–62
Capitalism, 4, 22, 23n1, 104, 124, 207, 227–28, 234, 241

Chang, HaJoon, 47
Chang, Ted, 135
Chatterjee, Rimi, 49, 52–54; *Signal Red*, 6, 43, 52, 218
Chicano/a futurism, 5
China, 5, 6, 7, 20–21, 23–24n3, 32, 56, 59, 73, 77–79, 81–83, 86, 102, 104, 116n2, 129n2, 161, 164–66, 170, 172, 218, 221–27, 229, 230n2
China doll, 132
Chinese science fiction, 5, 13–16, 18–22, 161, 165, 166
Chua, Amy, 102, 116n3
Chun Wendy Hui Kyong, 125–28, 152–53
Claeys, Gregory, 182
Clarke, Arthur C., 30; *Childhood's End*, 35; *The Last Theorem*, 34–35; *Rendezvous with Rama*, 45
Clarke, I. F., 87n1, 219
cloning, 52, 118, 122–23, 131–32, 138–39, 146
Cloud Atlas, 7, 131–33, 138, 140–42n2
cognitive estrangement, 8, 146, 154. *See also* Suvin, Darko
Cold War, 26–27, 31, 157, 222, 224, 226
Coleman, Beth, 117–19, 125, 127–29
colonialism, 3, 58, 61, 94, 122–23, 139, 145, 227
communism, 222, 226
comparative racialization, 3–4, 9
Csicsery-Ronay, Istvan, Jr., 13, 22, 156
Cuban Missile Crisis, 30. *See also* Cold War
cyborgs, 4, 33, 46, 103, 144, 149, 193, 228, 245
cyberpunk, 7, 24n5, 46–47, 50, 144, 146–48, 150–51, 153, 155–56
cyberspace, 148, 151–53

Dalai Lama, 224–25
degeneration, 53, 77, 83
dehumanization, 81, 96, 128, 175
del Toro, Guillermo, 8, 205, 208, 211, 212. *See also Pacific Rim*
Demilitarized zone (DMZ), 59–60
Derrida, Jacques, 36

disasters, 26–28, 30, 40n3, 169
dis-entanglements, 237, 239–40, 242
Dr. Fu Manchu, 75. *See also* Rohmer, Sax
Dr. Strangelove Or: How I Learned to Stop Worrying and Love the Bomb, 30, 40n3, 230n6
Dutt, Kylas Chunder (K. C.), 221; "Journal," 218–21, 229
Dutt, Shoshee Chunder (S. C.), 221; "Orissa," 218–21, 229
dystopias, 4, 8, 13, 18, 44, 52, 54n2, 102, 104, 105, 119, 132, 139, 146, 175, 181–82, 185, 206, 218, 221–22, 226–27, 234

East and West, 5, 15, 74, 92–94, 96, 98, 100, 135
East Asia, 59, 141, 142n6, 224
Eastward gaze, 135–36, 141
Edelman, Lee, 155
Edge of Tomorrow, 193
Edison, Thomas Alva, 27
ethnicity, 3, 29, 39, 57, 118, 137, 141, 193
exoticism, 7, 54, 118, 135, 152, 154, 253
extrapolation, 42–43, 52, 74, 155, 160, 162, 167–68, 223–24

Facebook, 103, 191, 194, 199n2, 200n5
Fan, Christopher T., 135
fan activism, 8, 189–90, 195
Fan CULTure, 198
Fan Girls and the Media, 198, 199
fandoms, 5, 8–9, 189, 191, 193–98, 200n6, 205, 214, 215n1, 215n9
Fang, Jenn, 193–94, 196, 200n4
fantasy, 22, 27, 57, 60, 75–76, 85, 105, 107, 110, 114–15, 141, 196–97, 215n9, 240, 250, 253
Far East, 7, 46, 74, 89–100, 209
Faris, Wendy, 53
Faulkner, William, 36
Fenkl, Heinz Insu, *Cathay*, 56
Fitzgerald, Amy J., 238, 239
Foucault, Michel, 68n8
Foundation, 21

Index

Frye, Northrop, 44, 54n2
Fu, Bien, 33
Full Metal Apache, 36, 148. *See also* Tatsumi, Takayuki
future-war, 9, 74, 79, 90, 219, 221–23, 228

gender, 8, 39, 60, 63–64, 66–67, 99, 133, 137, 140, 144, 146, 148–51, 153, 155–56, 194, 199, 200n5, 205, 210–11, 213–14, 248
genocide, 75, 77–79, 83, 223
genomics, 7, 117–25, 128
Gernsback, Hugo, 39n1, 91, 161–62
Ghost in the Shell, 193–94, 200n4
Gibson, William, 22, 24n5, 146, 151–52; *Neuromancer*, 46, 135, 144, 151
Gladwell, Malcolm, 184
Global South, 123
globalism, 208, 209
globalization, 6, 9, 14, 16, 21–23, 91, 100, 135, 166, 178
Godzilla, 205
Gomel, Elana, 20–22
Grant, Madison, 102
groupthink, 177, 181–84
Guardian, The, 21, 22

Haraway, Donna, 149, 245, 247, 255n2
Harootunian, Harold, and Masao Miyoshi, 157
Hashimoto, Yorimitsu, 75
Hawksley, Humphrey, 220; *Dragon Fire*, 9, 218, 222–28
Hayakawa's SF Magazine, 32
Hearn, Lafcadio, 90, 92
hegemony, 19, 119–20, 226
Heinlein, Robert A., 32–33; *Starship Troopers*, 33–34, 39n2, 215n4
Hinduism, 45, 48, 50–51, 53, 228, 236
Hiroshima, 6, 26, 30–32, 34–39. *See also* atomic bomb; Nagasaki; nuclear war
Holocaust, 254
Hong, Cathy Park, 56, 58, 68n2
Hong, Christine, 59, 60

Hotoda, Kei, 254
Huggan, Graham, 42–43
Hurricane Katrina, 6, 26–27
hybridity, 83–84, 255
hyperrealism, 131, 133–34, 137, 138, 140, 141. *See also* Baudrillard, Jean

Ichikawa, Tarahiko, 149
identity tourism, 7, 146, 150
imperialism, 93, 104, 155
India, 4–6, 5–7, 9, 32, 42–54, 142n6, 218–30, 234, 242n2
Indian subcontinent, 4, 5, 142n6, 229
Indianness, 43–45, 49
Indigenous futurism, 5
Iraq War, 36
Iron Man 3, 208

Jackson, Shelly, *Half Life*, 38, 39
Jameson, Fredric, 22–23, 103–5, 156
Janis, Irving, 181–83
Japan, 4–5, 28, 31, 34–37, 39n2, 46, 59, 61, 73–74, 77–79, 81, 83, 85, 89–93, 96–98, 136, 137–40, 144–45, 147–49, 151–55, 157–58, 165, 245, 247, 254
Japanese doll, 147, 152, 155
Japanese science fiction, 7, 32–34, 36, 146, 154, 156, 191, 205
Jenkins, Henry, 197, 198, 215n2
Jews, 26, 33, 113
Jia, Xia, 166
Jingjing, Xuyang, 19
Jinkang, Wang, 14, 166
Johnson, Kij, 244–55; *The Fox Woman*, 9, 244–50, 252, 255; *Fudoki*, 9, 244–45, 249–55
Joshi, Ruchir, 220; *The Last Jet-Engine Laugh*, 9, 218, 222–23, 226–29

kaiju, 205–7, 209, 215n7
Kang, Lydia, 57
Kang, Minsoo, *Of Tales and Enigmas*, 58, 60
Kilgore, De Witt Douglas, 78, 87n6

Kim, Claire Jean, 176, 179, 182
Knickerbocker, Conrad, 29
Komatsu, Sakyo, 30; *Nippon Chinbotsu (Japan Sinks)*, 36, 37
Korea, 5, 6, 33, 57–61, 63, 67–68n9, 91, 139–42n10, 255n3. See also North Korea; South Korea
Korean American SF, 6, 56–61, 65, 67
Kubrick, Stanley, 30, 40n3, 230n6
kungmin, 63, 65–67

labor, 52, 65, 66, 99, 122–24, 127–28, 138, 149, 175, 178, 207, 234, 241
Lacks, Henrietta, 123
Lai, Larissa, 117, 118, 120, 123, 127; *Salt Fish Girl*, 7, 117–20, 122–29
Last Airbender, The, 8, 190–91, 195, 197
Last Jet-Engine Laugh, The, 9, 218, 222–23, 226–29. See also Joshi, Ruchir
Latinos, 110, 112, 179
Le Guin, Ursula K., 160, 167, 173n10
Lee, Bruce, *Enter the Dragon*, 3
Lee, Chang-rae, 8, 56, 115n1, 175–85. See also *On Such a Full Sea*
Lee, Jin-kyung, 65
Lee, Marissa, 192–93
Lee, Rachel, 123–24, 130n4
Lee, Yoon Ha, 58–62; "Wine," 6, 58, 60–67
Lippit, Akira Mizuta, 34–35
Liu, Cixin, 8, 13–18, 21, 23, 160–73; *Dark Forest*, 23n2, 160, 167–72; *Death's End*, 23n2, 160; *The Three-Body Problem*, 160–61, 166–72; Three Body trilogy, 8, 14, 160, 161, 163
Livejournal, 190–91, 194, 199n2, 204, 215n1
Locus: The Magazine of the Science Fiction and Fantasy Field, 14–15
London, Jack, "The Unparalleled Invasion," 75, 104
Lone Ranger, The, 193
Lopez, Lori Kido, 190, 195–96
lost worlds, 154, 206

Lowell, Percival, 7, 89–101; *Chosön*, 91–93, 95, 98; *Mars*, 97–99; *Noto*, 91; *Occult Japan*, 91–92, 96, 99; *The Souls of the Far East*, 90, 92

magical realism, 29, 53–54
Mako Mori Test, 211, 213–14
Marchetti, Gina, 73
Mars, 7, 30–31, 37, 45, 89–91, 96–100, 161
Marwah, Anuradha, 49, 51, 54; *Idol Love*, 6, 43, 51–52
Masaki, Gorō, 146–56, 158n1; *Evil Eyes*, 146–47; *Venus City*, 8, 135, 146–53, 155–57
May Fourth Movement, 19–20, 164–65
Mayer, Ruth, 74, 87n3
Mbembe, Achille, 68n8
McDonald, Ian, 54, 220, 222; *Cyberabad Days*, 6, 43, 49–50; *River of Gods*, 6, 43, 49–51, 218
McHale, Brian, 37, 153
McHugh, Maureen, 102
mechas, 206, 215n4
Mehrotra, Arvind Krishna, 220
MELUS, 135
Menon, Anil, *The Beast with Nine Billion Feet*, 218
métissage, 74, 83, 85
Middle East, 46, 142n2, 225, 227
Milicia, Joseph, 205–6
militarism, 61, 63, 65, 67
militarized technogeometries, 6, 58–61, 64–67
Milner, Andrew, 14–15, 19, 23
Miner, Earl, 246–48, 250
mirroring, 78, 84, 91–100, 145, 221, 237
miscegenation, 86. See also racial mixing
Mitchell, David, 133, 142n3. See also *Cloud Atlas*
model minorities, 8, 129, 132, 175–79, 182, 186
modernity, 7, 47–48, 79, 89, 92, 95–96, 99, 100, 135, 139, 145
monogatari, 245, 250–53

Moon, Seungsook, 59, 68n10
monsters, 6, 38, 51, 204–6, 210
Morley, David, and Kevin Robins, 4, 104, 119, 121, 131, 144, 149. *See also* techno-Orientalism
Myers, E. C., 57

Na, Tari Young-jung, 63
Nagasaki, 6, 30–32, 34–36, 38–39. *See also* atomic bombing; Hiroshima; nuclear war
Nagata, Linda, 47, 117–18, 122, 125, 128; *The Bohr Maker*, 7, 117–20, 124–26, 128–29
Nakamura, Lisa, 135, 150–51
Nanda, Meera, 48, 51, 53
nanotechnology, 106, 118, 120, 125–26
nationalism, 6, 33–34, 48, 228
Native Americans, 26, 33
Neo Seoul, 131–32, 138–39, 141–42n2. *See also Cloud Atlas*
Neon Genesis Evangelion, 205
nikki bungaku, 246
9/11, 35–36
Niu, Greta A., 4, 47, 104, 118, 122, 135, 144
nonhumans, 9, 118, 121, 124–25, 127, 232–33, 238–42, 249–50
North Korea, 6, 35, 59–60, 225. *See also* Korea; South Korea
Norton, Richard J., 221
novum, 219, 224, 229n1. *See also* Suvin, Darko
nuclear war, 36. *See also* atomic bombing; Hiroshima; Nagaski

Oh, Ellen, 57–58
Okada, John, *No-No Boy*, 38
On Such a Full Sea, 8, 56, 115n1, 175–85
Orient, 5, 10, 54, 92–94, 100, 131, 133–35, 138, 142n6, 144, 152–53
Orientalism, 5, 7, 42, 46–47, 49, 54, 56, 73, 76, 82, 84, 86, 89, 91–94, 95–96, 98, 100, 110, 122, 128, 131–32, 134–35, 138, 140–41, 144, 146, 149, 151, 152, 157, 193, 195–96, 226
Orwell, George, *1984*, 181–82

otherness, 19, 43, 133, 137, 141, 149, 153, 247, 250, 254

Pacific Rim (film), 8, 204–10, 212–15n6, 215n8
Padmanabhan, Manjula, 54; *Escape*, 6, 43, 51–52, 218
Pakistan, 32, 218, 221–28
Park, Linda Sue, 57
Park, Suey, 131, 142n1
passing, 37, 86, 148, 150–51, 155
patriotism, 20, 33–34, 65–66
people of color, 5, 7, 117, 121–24, 129, 193, 214
philosophical tale, 160–64, 168, 170
Poe, Edgar Allan, 27, 29, 38, 161–62
Pohl, Frederik, *The Last Theorem*, 34, 35
political activism, 8, 189, 196
Posadas, Baryon T., 135, 144–59
postcolonialism, 5, 9, 47–48, 54, 118, 221–23, 225, 229
post-humans, 39, 105, 116n4, 119, 129, 155
postmodernism, 22, 29, 48, 105, 151, 227
post-racialism, 7, 120, 123, 125, 133, 136, 140–42n2, 150, 153
poverty, 16, 43, 52, 118, 122, 176, 237–38
Pynchon, Thomas: *The Crying of Lot 49*, 29; *Gravity's Rainbow*, 30; *Inherent Vice*, 27

queers, 60, 64, 68n9, 135

race, 3, 5–8, 10, 29, 35, 39, 73–75, 77–85, 100, 117–20, 122–29, 133, 137, 140–51, 160, 167, 169, 179, 189, 192, 194, 196–200n5, 214
Racebending.com, 8, 189–96, 198–200n4
Racefail 2009, 196, 200n6, 214
racial mixing, 77–78, 83–85. *See also* miscegenation
racial others, 6, 42, 73, 77–78, 81, 93, 108; ethnic other, 28, 153
racial tensions, 75, 147
racialization, 96, 117–20, 123–24, 129
racism, 4–7, 26–28, 34, 38, 73, 77, 81–82, 86, 117, 119, 123, 124, 127, 190, 192–96, 199
Reardon, Jenny, 119–20, 126

religion, 18, 20, 45, 50, 54, 107, 163
Renditions, 14, 16
Rieder, John, 90, 124, 145, 154, 219
Robinson, Kim Stanley, 160, 232–33
robots, 34, 40n3, 49, 119, 128, 136–37, 215n4
Robotskin, 7, 133, 136–38, 140
Rohmer, Sax, 75
Russia, 32, 223–24, 226
Russo-Japanese War, 26–27, 74–76, 154

Said, Edward W., 10, 54, 89, 92–93, 131, 134, 142n6, 144. *See also* Orientalism
Sakai, Naoki, 155
Salinger, J. D., 29–30; *The Catcher in the Rye*, 30
Schiaparelli, Giovanni, 97
Scholes, Robert, 29
Schulz, Max, 29
Science Fiction from China, 14
Science Fiction Studies, 5, 9, 13–15, 19, 23n1
science-fictionality, 22, 146, 157
Scott, Ridley, 4, 104, 135
Second World War. *See* World War II
Seed, David, 87n1, 219
Sehgal, Parul, 254
Sepoy Mutiny, 220
sexuality, 18, 20, 39, 130n4, 137
Shibano, Takumi, 33
Shih, Shu-Mei, 4. *See also* comparative racialization
Shiel, M. P., 6–7, 73–86; *The Dragon*, 6, 73, 75–76; *The Yellow Danger*, 4, 6, 73, 75–76, 78–80, 82, 84, 87n4; *The Yellow Peril*, 6, 73–76, 78, 80–81, 85–86; *The Yellow Wave*, 6, 73–77, 80, 82, 84, 86, 87n4
Shiu, Anthony Sze-Fai, 196
Shteyngart, Gary, 7, 102–5, 109. *See also* *Super Sad True Love Story*
Shyamalan, M. Night, 8, 190. *See also* *Avatar: The Last Airbender*; *Last Airbender, The*
simulacra, 7, 103, 110, 134, 136, 138
Singh, Vandana, 218, 232–43; "Ambiguity Machines," 233; "Are you Sannata 3159?," 9, 234, 236–42; "Delhi," 233–34; "Entanglement," 9, 234–36; "Infinities," 233; "The Woman Who Thought She Was a Planet," 233
Sino-Japanese War, 27–28, 76–77
slavery, 28, 33, 74, 78, 85, 94, 131, 132, 139, 178, 220
Sleepy Hollow, 192
Sohn, Stephen Hong, 6, 56–70, 78, 87n6, 89, 96, 100n1, 116n6, 135, 144, 154
Song, Hong, 13, 16, 18, 19, 22, 24n4, 166
Song, Mingwei, 14, 17, 19
South Asia, 218, 229, 230n7
South Korea, 6, 59–60, 65, 68n10. *See also* Korea; North Korea
Star Trek Into Darkness, 208
Stephenson, Neal, 46–47
stereotypes, 5, 7, 38, 46, 49, 50–51, 82–83, 103, 122, 129, 131–33, 144, 149, 182, 194, 197, 215n11, 225
Sterling, Bruce, 46
Stoddard, Lothrop, 102
subhumans, 52, 74, 121–22, 124, 138, 141–42n10
Super Sad True Love Story, 7, 102–16
Suvin, Darko, 154, 219, 229n1, 254, 255n5. *See also* cognitive estrangement; novum
Svenvold, Mark, 27

Tatsumi, Takayuki, 6, 26–41, 90, 148, 158n2. *See also Full Metal Apache*
techno-Orientalism, 4, 5, 7, 47, 56, 68n1, 91, 92, 94, 96, 98, 100, 103–6, 110, 114–15, 117–19, 120, 121, 124–25, 128, 129n1, 132, 133–37, 138, 140–42, 144–48, 151, 153–57, 158
technoscape, 52
technoscience, 15–16, 19–20, 22, 119, 166, 168, 219
terrorism, 28, 30, 35–36, 76, 112, 147, 221, 223–25, 227, 228
Tesla, Nikola, 27–28, 39n1
third world, 46, 52, 113, 123, 234

Index

Three-Body Problem, The, 160–61, 166–72. See also Liu, Cixin
Tidhar, Lavie, 20–21
tiger mom, 102, 116n3
Tiptree, James, Jr., 39
"Tondemobon," 26–27
Toyota, Aritsune: "Another Prince of Wales," 32, 33; *Pax Mongolica*, 33
Transformative Works and Cultures, 197–98
transgender people, 60, 64, 68n9, 135
translations, 13–14, 19, 21, 23, 97, 158n1, 160, 164–65, 243n4
trans/queer people, 60–67
Tsutsui, Yasutaka: "Everyone Other Than Japan Sinks," 36–37; "Vietnam Travel Bureau," 37
Tuchman, Barbara, 27
Tumblr, 191, 194, 199n2, 200n5, 204, 206–7, 210, 213, 215n1
Twain, Mark, 38; *Adventures of Huckleberry Finn*, 28; "The Fable of the Yellow Terror," 28; "Flies and Russians," 28; "The War-Prayer," 29
Twitter, 191–92, 194, 199n2, 200n5, 204, 206–7, 210, 213, 215n1

Ueno, Toshiya, 119, 129n2, 135, 144–45
utopias, 9, 13, 20, 22, 85, 93, 96, 100, 138, 150–51, 157, 182, 205–6, 221–23, 229

Venus City, 8, 135, 146–53, 155–57. See also Masaki, Gorō
Verne, Jules, 19, 162, 164–65
Vietnam, 27, 37, 65
Vietnam War, 37
Vint, Sherryl, 239
virtual reality, 147, 167, 170, 240, 241
virtual world, 147, 149–53, 155–56
Voltaire, 160–64
Vonnegut, Kurt, 28, 29, 29n3, 30, 40n3

Walter, Damien, 21, 22
Wang, David Der-Wei, 165, 172n8

War on Terror, 223
Weldes, Jutta, 22
Wells, H. G., 19, 162; *The Island of Dr. Moreau*, 205; *The War of the Worlds*, 90, 99, 160
Wenguang, Zheng, 20
West, 4, 5, 15, 18, 21, 44, 46, 47–48, 52, 54, 73–74, 76, 79, 84, 86, 91–92, 94, 96, 98, 100, 119, 134–35, 141, 149, 151–52, 161, 164, 166, 170, 170n2, 223, 225–28
white races, 3 75, 77–79, 81, 83, 85–86
white superiority, 79, 84
white supremacy, 6, 32–33, 37, 73–74, 78, 86
whiteness, 79, 89, 110, 113, 142n4, 196
whitewashing, 8, 189–90, 192–94, 198
Wilson, Edward O., 233. See also biophilia
"Wine," 6, 58, 60–67. See also Lee, Yoon Ha
Womack, Jack, 27
World War I, 164–65
World War II, 30, 31, 165, 213, 228
World War III, 30, 60
Worth, Aaron, 79
Wright, Austin Tappen, *Islandia*, 205

Xiaoping, Deng, 20, 165
Xun, Lu, 16, 18, 21–23

Yamamoto, Hiroshi, "Another Little Girl," 34, 39n3
Yamashita, Karen Tei, 38
Yan, Wu, 13, 15–16, 20–21, 165–66
Yano, Tetsu, 32–34
Yasusada Araki hoax, 37
Yellow Peril, 5–7, 27–28, 73–79, 81, 84–87nn2–3, 90, 104, 135, 144, 154
Yellow Peril, The, 6, 73–76, 78, 80–81, 85–86
yellow races, 75, 78–79, 81, 84
yellowface, 132, 140, 142n2, 142n4, 196

Zelazny, Roger, 44–46; *Lord of Light*, 44–45
Zepp, Josh, 131
Zevin, Gabrielle, 57, 68n3